THE I TATTI
RENAISSANCE LIBRARY

James Hankins, General Editor

BEMBO

HISTORY OF VENICE

VOLUME 2

ITRL 32

PIETRO BEMBO

✦ ✦ ✦

HISTORY OF VENICE

VOLUME 2 ✦ BOOKS V–VIII

EDITED AND TRANSLATED BY

ROBERT W. ULERY, JR.

THE I TATTI RENAISSANCE LIBRARY

HARVARD UNIVERSITY PRESS

CAMBRIDGE, MASSACHUSETTS

LONDON, ENGLAND

2008

Series design by Dean Bornstein

Library of Congress Cataloging-in-Publication Data

Bembo, Pietro, 1470–1547.
[Historiae Venetae libri XII. English & Latin]
History of Venice / Pietro Bembo ; edited and translated by Robert W. Ulery, Jr.
p.   cm. — (The I Tatti Renaissance library ; 28)
English and Latin.
Includes bibliographical references and index.
ISBN 978–0–674–02283–6 (vol. 1)
ISBN 978–0–674–02284–3 (vol. 2)
1. Venice (Italy) — History — 697–1508.   I. Ulery, Robert W.   II. Title.
DG677.A2B413 2007
945′.3103 — dc22   2007009602

Contents

ॐ§?§

Map   x

Book V (1499–1501)   2

· CONTENTS ·

· The Republic of Venice, ca. 1500. ·

Dotted line indicates borders of the Republic and its possessions.

Moldavia

Wallachia

Black

Sea

O T T O M A N

ulcigno

● Durazzo

Constantinople

●●Scutari

Sea of Marmara

●Thessaloniki

E M P I R E

Aegean

rfu

*Gulf of
Arta*

Sea

OTTOMAN EMPIRE

Lefkada

Lepanto
✕

Euboea

*Cyprus
to Venice*

phalonia

●Athens

to Genoa

0   100 miles

Zante

Methoni ●●Coron

●Monemvasia
Cape Malea

Rhodes

*to Knights
of St. John*

Sea of Crete

S E A

Crete
to Venice

HISTORY OF VENICE

LIBER QUINTUS

1 Dum haec in Gallia citeriore geruntur, ad Baiasetis novos motus, qui exercitum et classem magno studio comparabat, Antonio Grimano praefecto classis declarato, uti profectionem maturaret patres iusserunt. Is antequam conscenderet, propterea quod ab civibus, tot superiorum defessis continentium bellorum muneribus, lente ac morose tributa exigebantur, libras auri octoginta in remigum stipendia reipublicae mutuo dedit. Alteras octoginta secum se laturum est pollicitus, quibus Corcyrae reliquisque in locis ad classem constituendam uteretur. Constat illis diebus in Apulia corvos vulturesque tanta ex aere vi tantisque agminibus inter se conflixisse, ut carri duodecim eorum cadaveribus explerentur. Corcyrenses cum viderent in magnis parandae classis difficultatibus propter temporis angustias rempublicam versari, quod Baiasetis classis vela iam facere dicebatur, polliciti sunt, si eis frumentum et tormenta subministrentur, sese gripos sexaginta suis hominibus suaque pecunia ornaturos, quibus Antonius eo bello uti posset. Quod quidem Corcyrensium auxilium opportune oblatum senatus libentissime accipiens nummum aureum in singulos eorum qui conscenderent ad ea quae petierant Corcyrenses etiam addidit.

2 Iamque ab Iadertinorum magistratu litterae ad senatum datae certiores patres fecerunt Turcas equites ad duo milia incursiones in eorum fines fecisse magnumque agrestium hominum numerum abegisse, neque postea discessisse sed ibidem consedisse. Quae res omnem dubitationem expulit, quo esset classe rex irrupturus, cum in fines reipublicae terrestres copias induxisset. Nam eum nonnulli Rhodiis bellum esse illaturum etiam nunc arbitrabantur. Lecti

BOOK V

While all this was going on in Lombardy, Antonio Grimani was 1
declared captain-general of the fleet to deal with fresh manoeuvres 1499
on the part of Bayazid, who was making great efforts to get an
army and fleet ready. The senators ordered Grimani to set out
with all haste, but before he took ship, he loaned the Republic 80
gold pounds to pay the rowers, since taxes were being but slowly
and grudgingly wrung from a citizenry worn out by the burdens of
the endless succession of earlier wars. He undertook to take another 80 pounds with him, to be used on putting the fleet together
at Corfu and elsewhere. It is reported that there was at that time a
great fight between crows and vultures in the skies over Apulia;
such was the violence of the clash, and so great the flocks of birds,
that their carcasses filled twelve carts. The people of Corfu saw
that the Republic was having great difficulty in getting the fleet
ready owing to the shortage of time (Bayazid's fleet was said to be
already under sail), and so they promised to fit out 60 *grippi* with
their own men and money for Grimani to use in the war, so long
as they were supplied with food and artillery. This timely offer of
aid from the people of Corfu was readily accepted by the Senate,
which gave each man who took ship a gold florin[1] in addition to
what the Corfiotes had requested.

At this point the magistrates[2] of Zara sent the senators a letter 2
to inform them that some 2,000 Turkish cavalry had invaded their
territory. They drove out a great number of the countryfolk but
did not subsequently withdraw, taking up camp there. This removed all doubt as to where the sultan's fleet would invade, since
he had marched his land forces into the Republic's territory — up
to that point there were some who believed that he was going to
make war on Rhodes. Two proveditors were accordingly chosen,

itaque legati duo, Franciscus Ciconia, qui in Aetolia et Achaia reipublicae oppidis praeesset, Andreas Lauredanus, qui Corcyrae. Tum Andreas Zancanius item legatus cum praesidio in Carnos missus, cum patres eo etiam ab latere Turcas impetum facturos comperissent. Latum etiam ut biremes complures ornarentur, quae maris Hadriani praesidio essent contra biremes Turcarum, quas Eloi fluminis hostio Aulonem deductas senatus intellexerat; eisque biremibus Augustinus Maripetrus praefectus datus cum trireme una, quam ipse conscenderet.

3   Ob eas res atque bellum, quod quidem fore omnium quae civitas cum Turcis umquam gessisset maximum et formidolosissimum videbatur, aucta per senatum urbis vectigalia sunt parte ex tertia, vini panis carnis portoriis tantummodo exceptis, atque uti magistratus omnes urbani provincialesque mediam stipendiorum partem unius anni reipublicae remitterent, lex lata; cautum tamen ne quadragintaviralia iudicia ea lege tenerentur. Lecti etiam viri, qui censum civibus omnibus pro cuiusque opibus decernerent, ea condicione, ut is quem decrevissent reipublicae a quoque cive census donaretur, si auri semunciam non excederet; supra id mutuo erogaretur; neque tamen auri libras tres ullius civis census posset excedere.

4   Simul, quod illis ipsis diebus terrestres etiam equitatus et peditatus copias ex Gallorum regis foedere senatus contra Ludovicum cogere atque in Galliam mittere tenebatur, pecuniaque erat uno tempore in classem atque in exercitum separatim subministranda, lex est lata ut, quae civitates sub reipublicae imperio in continenti essent, iis litterae darentur: vellent pro suo in rempublicam studio, tam difficili eius tempore, subsidii nomine pecuniam publice ad urbem mittere, sua cuique civitati dicta et constituta summa: Patavinis auri libris centum, Vicentinis octoginta, Veronensibus totidem, Brixianis centum viginti, Bergomatibus quinquaginta quinque, Taurisanis quinquaginta, Cremensibus viginti, ceterisque

Francesco[3] Cicogna to take charge of the Republic's towns in
Aetolia[4] and the Morea, and Andrea Loredan, who was to govern
Corfu. At that time Andrea Zancani was also sent with a garrison
into Friuli as proveditor, since the senators had learned that the
Turks would attack on that front too. It was also decided to fit out
a number of small galleys to protect the Adriatic against the Turkish ships which, the Senate had learned, had been brought from
the mouth of the Bojana river to Avlona. Agostino Malipiero was
appointed captain of the small galleys, with a large galley for his
own use.

These measures taken for a war which seemed set to be the   3
greatest and most fearful of all that the city had engaged in with
the Turks led the Senate to increase taxes on the citizens by a
third, excepting only the tariffs on wine, bread, and meat, and a
law was passed requiring all urban and provincial magistrates to
return to the Republic half of a year's salary, though the Courts of
Forty were exempted from the provisions of the law. Men were
also chosen to levy an assessment based on the wealth of each individual citizen. The assessment thus determined would be freely
given to the Republic by every citizen so long as it did not exceed
half an ounce of gold; anything above that amount would be paid
over as a loan, though no citizen's assessment was to exceed three
gold pounds.

By its treaty with the king of France, the Senate was also   4
obliged at that very time to collect ground forces of cavalry and infantry against Ludovico and to send them to Lombardy, and so
funds had to be separately laid out on a fleet and an army at the
same time. A law was therefore passed to have letters sent to the
subject cities of the *terraferma* to say that for love of the Republic
in her hour of great need, they should send funds to Venice from
the public purse by way of subsidy, with a fixed sum apportioned
to each city: for Padua 100 gold pounds, Vicenza 80, and the same
for Verona, Brescia 120, Bergamo 55, Treviso 50, Crema 20, and

item infra haec; quae quidem civitates ut in rebus tam urgentibus libentes atque alacriter suam quaeque partem in aerarium contulerunt; Alexander etiam pontifex maximus omnium proventuum quibus sacerdotes in imperio reipublicae fruerentur partem plus tertiam in id bellum senatui concessit, cardinalium sacerdotiis exceptis.

5 Iis administratis rebus, aestatis parte iam praeterita, Baiasetis classis navium omnis generis circiter ducentarum septuaginta, quo in numero erant triremes septuaginta, biremes quadraginta, naves duae onerariae immani magnitudine, freto egressa Euboeamque insulam praetervecta ad reipublicae in Achaiae litora se convertit; et exercitus maximis instructus copiis, cui praeerat rex ipse, terrestri itinere eodem proficiscitur, cum rex, antequam Thessalonica discederet, cives Venetos qui Byzantii commorabantur in vincula conici mandavisset; in quibus erat Andreas Grittus, de quo supra dictum est. Is, quod ad magistratum qui erat Naupacti, caritate patriae iuvenilem animum stimulante, litteras notis conscriptas omnibus de rebus deque regiis consiliis dederat, duriore condicione quam reliqui omnes in custodia fuit; parumque abfuit quin interficeretur. Antonius, magna diligentia, omnibus ex reipublicae maritimis municipiis atque insulis, classe celeriter coacta pulcherrimeque instructa, quae quidem erat triremium quadraginta sex, longarum navium, ex iis quae ad mercaturam proficiscuntur, decem septem, navium onerariarum numero ad quadraginta, biremium et reliquarum item quadraginta, Methone ex ancoris quid Turcae facerent circumspiciebat. Pauloque post e portu apud Acritam egressos appropinquare eos intelligens, ad Sphagiam insulam, quae contra Methonem est, vela cum omnibus navibus facit.

6 Venetias cum esset nuntiatum classem Thraciam ad ea reipublicae litora processisse, quibus in litoribus et portubus esset Veneta, neque esse dubium, quin sint congressurae, supplicatio est a senatu decreta; tum in sacrarum virginum et sacerdotum[1] collegia farinae triticeae sestaria trecenta dono data; atque auri librae

the rest likewise in smaller amounts. In this crisis each of the cities willingly and speedily paid their share into the treasury, and to help the war effort, Pope Alexander granted the Senate more than a third of the total income enjoyed by priests in the Republic's dominion, with the exception of cardinals' benefices.

With these arrangements in place, and part of the summer now 5 gone, Bayazid's fleet of about 270 ships of every kind—including 50 galleys, 40 small galleys, and 2 merchant ships of huge size— emerged from the strait, and sailing past the island of Euboea turned toward the Venetian settlements on the coast of the Morea. An army led by the sultan himself and furnished with a vast number of troops marched there by land, following his order, made before he left Thessalonica, to have the Venetian inhabitants of Constantinople thrown into prison, among them the Andrea Gritti who was mentioned above.[5] Under the impulse of youthful patriotism, Gritti had written in code to the governor at Lepanto on a wide range of matters, in particular about the sultan's plans, and he consequently suffered harsher conditions of imprisonment than all the rest, and came close to being killed. With great dispatch, Antonio Grimani rapidly collected a fleet from each of the Republic's maritime communities and islands and fitted it out very handsomely, amounting to 46 large galleys, 17 galleys of the mercantile sort, about 40 cargo vessels, and another 40 of small galleys and other boats. Standing at anchor at Methoni, he sought to find out what the Turks would do. Learning shortly afterwards that they had left port at Akritas and were drawing near, he made sail with all his ships for the island of Sapientza, which faces Methoni.

When news reached Venice that the Turkish fleet had reached 6 the shores of the Republic, where the Venetian fleet was stationed or in harbor, and it became apparent that they would clash, the Senate decreed devout processions;[6] a gift of 300 bushels of durum flour was then made to the houses of nuns and the religious, and five gold pounds were distributed around the city to

quinque remigibus, senectute aut valetudine affectis, qui aliquando stipendia in classibus reipublicae fecissent per urbem distributae. Antonius, constituto qua ex parte hostes quotque cum triremibus quisque legatorum aggrederetur, quemque locum praefecti navium onerariarum maiorumque longarum caperent, quot naves post reliquas, ut subsidio laborantibus essent, se continerent, media ipse in acie quattuor circum se triremes ducens provectusque paululum in mare, cum naves Thraciae non longe ab eo iter facerent possetque illas secundo vento aggredi, proelium tamen distulit. At Aloisius Marcellus, navium onerariarum praefectus, ut ei erat imperatum, paulisper se ad classem hostium convertit; qua re animadversa, illi statim alia insulae parte se in portum qui Longus appellatur receperunt. Constat autem illis diebus ita eos reipublicae classis nomen perhorruisse, ut multi se suis cum navibus litori applicuerint, quo facilius, si classes congrederentur, terra fugam caperent. Antonius Methonem rediit. Idque cum bis terque postea paucorum dierum spatio accidisset, ut et Turcae portu egressi, conspecta classe Veneta, in eundem portum redierint aut in proximum se intulerint, et Antonius, eductis navibus ut confligeret, visis hostibus, cum ei visum non fuisset congredi, eos redire aut progredi sine impedimento permiserit, Turcae audentiores facti, quod existimarent Antonium metu perculsum ea facere.

7　　Pridie Idus Sextiles se, ut iter facerent, explicabant. Erant autem non longe a Methone, litori quam mari aperto propiores. Antonius classe educta, quod superioribus fecerat diebus, ut, quemadmodum ab initio, communi legatorum et praefectorum omnium consilio, constituerat, in eos impetum faceret se comparabat. Atque eo ipso tempore Andreas Lauredanus Corcyrae magistratus

oarsmen afflicted by age or ill health who had at some time been employed in the Venetian fleets. Grimani laid down from what direction and with how many galleys each of the proveditors was to attack the enemy, the position to be taken up by the captains of the cargo vessels and the larger warships, and the number of ships that were to hold themselves in reserve to the rear of the rest, so as to assist those in difficulty. Himself in the middle of the line, he led out four galleys flanking him on either side, and advanced a little into open sea. Yet though the Turkish ships were sailing by not far from him and he was able to attack them with a following wind, he still put off joining battle with them.[7] But the captain of the cargo vessels, Luigi Marcello, briefly turned on the enemy fleet, as he had been ordered. When they saw this happening the Turks immediately retreated to the other side of the island, into the harbor known as Porto Longo: it is clear that the reputation of the Republic's fleet was at that time so terrifying to them that many of them had hugged the shore with their boats, so as to afford an easier escape by land if the fleets engaged in battle. Grimani returned to Methoni. In the course of a few days it subsequently happened that the Turks emerged from port, caught sight of the Venetian fleet, and returned to the same harbor or put in at a nearby one, while Grimani, having led out his ships for a fight, decided against[8] engaging the enemy once he caught sight of them, and permitted them to return or go on their way without hindrance. When this had happened two or three times, the Turks became more adventurous, thinking that Grimani was acting in this way out of fear.[9]

On 12 August they deployed themselves for sailing. They were   7
not far from Methoni, closer to the shore than to the open sea. As he had done on the previous days, Grimani led out his fleet and prepared to make an attack on them, just as he had planned from the beginning on the unanimous advice of the proveditors and captains. And it was at that very moment that Andrea Loredan,

advenit, gripos undecim et naves onerarias quattuor, in quibus erant milites plus mille, secum afferens. Is ad Antonium recta profectus, venisse se ad rempublicam auxilio iuvandam proponit. Petit ut quid se facere velit imperet. Erat in Andrea magnus animus, magna virtus, plurima belli et rerum maritimarum experientia. Itaque illo viso universa classis clarum laetitiae signum dedit, salutatusque est plausu vocibusque militaribus mirandum in modum. Id an aegre tulerit Antonius, venisse hominem qui, si quid recte sit administratum, favore vulgi atque benevolentia eius rei omnem sibi laudem praeripiat, explorati nihil habeo; multi quidem certe crediderunt et testatum reliquerunt. Sed illi navem onerariam, ex duabus magnis reipublicae navibus quas habebat, uti conscenderet eique imperaret permisit.

8   Andreas, cumba ad navem statim vectus, neque enim temporis exiguitas longiorem moram dabat, in eam sese intulit. Altera in navi magna reipublicae erat Albanus Armerius praefectus. Is, ubi est imperatum ut in hostes impetus fieret, quod sciebat de concilii sententia datum sibi negotium ab Antonio ut navem Thraciam alterutram ex duabus de quibus supra dictum est adoriretur, ad eam ex illis quae quidem erat vastior contendit; Lauredanus sua cum navi ad navem hostium alteram approperat. Sed ea, fuga comparata, in mare sinistrorsum se proripuit. Tum Lauredanus suam et ipse navem in maiorem hostium navem convertit. Quam cum essent ambo consecuti, iniectis manibus ferreis eam religant. Erant in nave Thracia milites mille, qui se comminus acriter fortiterque defendebant. Id dum fit, ignis in navem hostium iactus puppim succendit; qui exstingui cum non posset, neque nostris navibus explicandi se ab illa facultas daretur, vento latus naves Venetas comprehendit. Ita tres earum classium maximae instructissimaeque naves conflagraverunt.

the governor at Corfu, arrived, bringing with him eleven *grippi* and four cargo vessels, in which there were more than 1,000 infantry. He made straight for Grimani and explained that he had come to assist the Republic with reinforcements. He asked him to tell him what he wanted him to do. Loredan had great spirit, great courage, very wide experience of war and maritime affairs. And so the entire fleet was plainly overjoyed to see him, and he was given an extraordinary reception to the cheers and chants of the soldiers. Whether Grimani resented the arrival of a man who in virtue of the people's favor and goodwill might snatch from him all the credit for any successful outcome, I cannot say for sure, but certainly many believed it and left testimony to that effect. He allowed him to board a cargo vessel, however, one of the two large Venetian ships that he disposed of, and take command of it.

Loredan was at once conveyed to the ship in a launch — the 8
press of time allowing no further delay — and he put himself on board. In the second of the Republic's large ships was its captain Albano d'Armer. When the order came to attack the enemy, aware that he had been given the task by Grimani, with his council's approval, of attacking either of the two Turkish ships mentioned above, d'Armer made for the one that was larger, while Loredan's vessel hurried toward the other enemy ship. But that ship was primed for flight, and veering to the left it burst through into open sea. Then Loredan too turned his boat on the larger enemy ship, and when both Venetian captains reached it, they cast their grappling-hooks and held it fast. There were 1,000 infantry in the Turkish ship, and they defended themselves manfully in fierce hand-to-hand fighting. While this was going on, a firebrand was thrown onto the enemy ship and set fire to the stern. It could not be put out, and there was no opportunity for our boats to cut themselves free of the enemy vessel, and so, carried by the wind, the flames took hold of the Venetian ships. In this way the fleets' three largest and best-equipped ships were consumed by fire.

9   Sed fuit quidem eorum qui in navi Thracia erant longe casus atque sors melior, propterea quod Turcae reliqui, ubi suam comburi navem viderunt, biremes naviculasque aliquot eo celeriter miserunt. Eae biremes atque naviculae, qui se in mare proiecerant milites, quod necesse erat fieri, eis auxilio fuerunt omnesque sustulerunt. Nostri homines, quibus in tempore subsidium adesse non potuit, caesi ab iis qui suis venerant auxilio, omnes interierunt, praeter paucos ex utraque navi quos Thomas Duodus, qui in oneraria erat, suae navis scapha sublatos conservavit, praeterque Albanum, quem Turcae inter suos e mari captum sustulerunt. Processerat eodem impetu atque ardore animi, una cum Albano cumque Lauredano, navis alia oneraria non ita magna, ut naves Thracias adoriretur. Sed ea, pilis ferreis ab hostium navibus pugnae initio coniectis depressa, suis cum militibus interiit. Unus Vincentius Polanus triremem cui praeerat (erat autem ex iis quae ad mercaturam instituuntur) in classem Thraciam magno animo intulit. Is parvo temporis spatio, circumscriptus ab hostium longis navibus omnis generis compluribusque, cum se fortissime horas duas defendisset navesque hostium nonnullas tormentis perforavisset, ipsos audacter in eius saepe navem conscendentes interfecisset, aliquot ex suis amisisset, vulnerata parte plurima, coorto forte vento velisque factis, sese hostibus eripuit.

10   Ex reliquis reipublicae navibus nulla comminus congressa, pilis tantum e longinquo emissis, omnes in mare dexteram ad partem, classe hostium relicta, abierunt; ex quibus Aloisius Marcellus, in navem hostium onerariam incidens, iniecta manu ferrea eam secum abduxit longeque ab reliquis navibus captam atque direptam incendit. Ibi Antonius, animo turbatus ob eos eventus quos tristes conspexerat, nihil praeterea temptare ausus, se recepit. Classis Thracia eodem ipso in loco se continuit; Veneti ad Prodromum[2]

But the luck of those who were in the Turkish ship proved 9
much the better, for when they saw their ship in flames, the other
Turks quickly sent some small galleys and boats there. The galleys
and boats came to the assistance of those soldiers who had of necessity jumped into the sea and took them all on board. Help
could not reach our men in time,[10] and they were slain by those
who had come to help their own men. All of them perished, except for a few men from each ship that Tommaso Duodo picked
up with the skiff of his cargo vessel and saved, and except for
d'Armer, whom the Turks took on board as a captive as they
picked up their own men. Another merchantman of smaller size
had moved to attack the Turkish ships with the same drive and
determination, alongside d'Armer and Loredan. But that was
sunk by cannonballs shot from the enemy ships at the very beginning of the battle and perished with all its soldiers. Showing great
spirit, only Vincenzo Polani bore down on the Turkish fleet with
the galley he commanded (it was one of those built for trade). In a
short space of time he was encircled by great numbers of enemy
warships of all kinds. He defended himself with great valor for
two hours and sent some of the enemy ships to the bottom with
his artillery, killing the enemy themselves in their frequent bold incursions onto his ship. He had lost some of his men, the greater
part of them wounded, when a breeze blew up by chance, and
raising his sails he made his escape from the enemy.

None of the other Venetian ships having joined in close-quarter 10
combat, merely firing cannonballs from a distance, all of them
turned off to the right into open sea and left the enemy fleet behind. Luigi Marcello's ship falling upon an enemy merchantman,
he threw grappling-irons onto it and carried it off with him; having taken it captive far from the other ships, he plundered the boat
and set it on fire. At that point, distressed at the unhappy outcome he had witnessed and not daring to venture any further
moves, Grimani retreated. The Turkish fleet stayed exactly where

insulam iactis ancoris constiterunt, cum tamen naves onerariae
complures maioresque triremes prope omnes biduum fere, antequam eo convenirent, consumpsissent. Albanus postea Byzantium
productus, dum[3] ei rex vitam se concessurum dixisset, si Maumet-
tum, Turcarum deum, deinceps coleret, negans id umquam se facturum, in duas sectus partes magna constantique voluntate mortem obiit.

11   Petierat ab Aloisio Galliae rege, iam a primo Baiasetis apparatu,
Rhodiorum magistratus classem, qua se tueri posset, propterea
quod eam ad insulam atque oppidum suas esse copias suamque
classem Baiasetem illaturum multorum vocibus et nuntiis afferaba-
tur. Rex, ne sui regni initio parum diligens ad reipublicae Chris-
tianae partes muniendas atque tuendas videretur, classem navium
duarum et viginti in Gallia Provincia coactam ad Rhodios miserat.
Ea classis uti cum classe reipublicae se coniungeret, quod Rhodiis
navium nihil opus esset, senatus ab rege libentissimo impetraverat;
qui etiam omnes suas opes seque ipsum per litteras perque legatos
in id bellum reipublicae obtulisset. Itaque dum Antonius eo loci
est, nuntiatur ei classem Gallicam Zacynthi esse. Qua intellecta re,
ipse tota cum classe Zacynthum profectus cum illa se coniunxit,
ad quam quidem Rhodii et ipsi naves onerarias tres adiunxerant.
Classis interim Thracia inferius aliquanto ad eum locum qui Tor-
nesium appellatur se receperat. Antonius Gallique eam aggredi
communi consilio decreverunt. Itaque cum omnes, ut videbantur,
alacriter ad eam Zacyntho contendissent, animadversum est Turcas classem ad litus accommodavisse sic ut fere terram puppibus
tangeret; proras navium in mare convertisse. Ea re cognita, Antonius naviculas onerarias sex minus ad bellum idoneas, hominibus,
tormentis, ceterisque rebus ablatis, ulva sicca implendas curavit,

it was, while the Venetians dropped anchor and took up position at the island of Prodromos,[11] although a good many of the cargo vessels and nearly all the larger galleys took almost two days to assemble there.[12] D'Armer was later taken to Constantinople and told by the sultan that he would spare his life if he would in future worship Mohammed, the god of the Turks. But on d'Armer's saying that he would never do so, he was cut in two, meeting his death with great steadfastness and constancy.[13]

At the very outset of Bayazid's preparations for war, the governor of Rhodes had asked King Louis of France for a fleet to enable him to protect himself, since it was being widely reported that Bayazid was going to take his forces and fleet to attack the island and its town. In case he should appear insufficiently energetic in defending and protecting the lands of the Christian commonwealth at the outset of his reign, the king had sent to Rhodes a fleet of 22 ships that he had assembled in Provence. At the Senate's request, the king gladly agreed to have this fleet join that of the Republic, since the people of Rhodes had no need of ships, for he had already offered himself and all his resources to the Republic in the war. While he was there, Grimani got word that the French fleet was at Zante. On hearing this he himself set out for Zante with the entire fleet and joined forces with it, the Rhodians themselves having added to the fleet three cargo vessels. Meanwhile the Turkish fleet had retreated somewhat lower down the coast to the place called Tornese.[14] Grimani and the French decided to attack it by common agreement. And so when all of them had left Zante and made for the Turkish fleet with evident eagerness, it was noticed that the Turks had arranged the fleet along the shore so that the sterns were almost touching the shore, with the ships' prows turned toward the open sea. On learning of this, Grimani took six cargo vessels that were not fit for combat and took off their men, artillery, and the rest of the gear. He had them filled with dry rushes mixed with gunpowder, so that the ships

pulvere ad comprehendendum ignem idoneo interiecto, quas incensas classi Thraciae obiceret. Is dies ea in re consumitur. Postero die mane iis cum navibus triremes magnae sexdecim Antonii iussu ubi se in hostes promoverunt, illi statim classis partem contra eas miserunt; quibus visis Venetae triremes sese continent; Turcae progressi naviculas sex, eas quae remulco longarum navium processerant, ab iis relictas qui attraxerant, capiunt. Veneti ea re commoti in illos se concitant; atque usque ad classem insecuti, aliquot eorum navigia deprimunt triremesque tres et biremem unam cum hominibus capiunt.

12   Biduo autem post, cum omnino aggredi classem Thraciam Antonius Gallique statuissent atque ad eam tam proxime accessissent, ut tormentorum pilae in hostes mitterentur, nescio quo fato paululum commorati redierunt; id quod a Gallis damnatum fuit. Demum eo triduo hostibus vela facientibus, ut sinum qui proximus erat caperent, Antonius classem explicuit; eosque consecutus, cum aggredi suo vento posset, eodem iniquo fato, ut tunc quidem creditum fuit, se continuit; aliquot tamen naves longas hostium audacter progressas, quae paulo ulterius ex Venetis processerant naves, facto in eas impetu, ceperunt. Quod si reliquis eadem vis animo fuisset, hostes deleri facile potuissent. Omnibus enim illis diebus quibus parte aliqua proelium commissum est, cum plures naves Thracias militibus rebusque omnibus instructas Veneti ceperint, nulla tamen ex eorum navibus cum hominibus est capta. Quin etiam illud accidit. Extrema erat navis una oneraria Gallorum eo in reditu, ut saepe fit, multo reliquis tardior; itemque ex Venetis altera. In eas praefectus classis Thraciae magnam suarum navium partem convertit, ut plus triremes ac biremes triginta navem Gallicam circumsisterent, Venetam plus viginti; quae tamen

could be set on fire and sent up against the Turkish fleet. Carrying this out took up a day. The next morning, when at Grimani's command sixteen large galleys pushed forward against the enemy with these ships in tow, the Turks at once sent a part of their fleet against them, at the sight of which the Venetian galleys held back. The Turks captured the six small boats that the warships had pulled forward on tow-ropes, cast adrift by the ships that had been towing them. Alarmed at this turn of events, the Venetians roused themselves against them,[15] and pursuing them as far as the Turkish fleet, sank some of their vessels and captured one small and three large galleys, along with their crews.

Two days later Grimani and the French really did decide to at- 12 tack the Turkish fleet, and approached it close enough to fire their cannon at the enemy, but by some ill chance they stayed there only a short while before turning back,[16] a move criticised by the French. Finally, as the enemy took sail for three days to make the nearest bay, Grimani drew up his fleet in battle order and gave pursuit, but just when he could have attacked with a following wind, by the same unlucky destiny (as was actually believed at the time), he held himself back. But some of the enemy warships that had made bold to come forward were attacked and captured by the Venetian ships that had got a little further ahead — and if the others had had the same spirit, the enemy could easily have been destroyed. For although the Venetians took many Turkish ships with their complement of soldiers and entire contents throughout that time, wherever and whenever there was fighting, yet none of their own ships was captured with its men. In fact quite the opposite occurred. The last boat in the retreat was a cargo vessel of the French, which, as often happens, was much slower than the rest, and another boat of the Venetians was similarly placed. The captain of the Turkish fleet turned the bulk of his ships on them, so that more than 30 large and small galleys surrounded the French ship, more than 20 the Venetian. Yet though they suffered a fierce

duae cum acriter diuque oppugnarentur, praeter pilas tormentorum quas hostes eiaculaverant, sagittarum vi tanta in eas coniecta,
ut mali antennae plutei latera earum denique signorum modo sagittis constipatis fixa essent, complures hostium biremes et triremes depresserunt, ut reliquae, magno accepto detrimento, eas reli-
querint. Galli post haec, cum sibi nulla in re defuisse viderentur
cognoscerentque fortunam omnibus nostrorum conatibus adver-
sari, Antonio relicto abierunt. Hostium classis Naupactum se
contulit; eodemque antea rex cum magno exercitu erat profectus.
Is cum oppidum terra marique uno tempore cinxisset, nullo a nostris auxilio allato, oppidani coacti deditionem faciunt.

13   Haec ad urbem allata civium animos, qui longe alium rerum
exitum exspectabant, magno dolore adfecerunt. Cumque vulgo legati reliquique qui separatim aut navibus onerariis imperaverant
aut longis praefuerant hominum sermonibus carperentur, Antonius ante alios totius populi, quem ad modum imperatoribus qui
res minus feliciter temptaverint plerumque solet accidere, maledictis lacerabatur, quod is tantam tamque speratam atque a dis immortalibus oblatam ac plane traditam augendi imperii facultatem
suis e manibus dimisisse videretur; si eam hostium classem Antonius iusto proelio superavisset, prout eum facere potuisse existimabant, omnem Peloponnesum Graeciaeque oram Euboeamque insulam sub reipublicae imperium redigere illum nullo negotio
potuisse; nunc cum omnia secus quam speraverant evenisse intelligerent, ac Lauredani et Armerii interitus memoriae haereret infi-
xus, omnes magno odio in eum ferebantur acerbiusque accusabant.

14   His atque talibus causis patres moti legem in decemvirum collegio tulerunt, ut Antonio praefectus classis sublegeretur, qui statim

and sustained assault — besides the cannonballs fired at them by the enemy, their masts, sail-yards, breastworks,[17] and the very flanks of the boats were struck by such a hail of arrows that they bristled like targets with the missiles stuck in them — despite all this, the two of them sank a good many of the enemy galleys large and small, so that the rest, after suffering great losses, left them alone. The French, who felt that they had not been found wanting in any respect, and were coming to realise that Fortune was adverse to all our men's efforts,[18] thereupon abandoned Grimani and went away. The enemy fleet took itself off to Lepanto, where the sultan had arrived beforehand with a great army. The sultan had at a stroke encircled the town by land and sea, and with our men bringing them no assistance, the townspeople were forced to surrender.

This news greatly upset the citizens when it reached Venice, for 13 they had been expecting a very different outcome. The proveditors and others who had commanded the individual merchantmen or captained warships were widely criticised, but, as generally happens to commanders of failed enterprises, it was Grimani above all who had to suffer the savage abuse of the entire populace[19] for having, as it appeared, let slip such an opportunity — an opportunity of extending the empire that they had so longed for, and which heaven had offered and virtually delivered to them.[20] They said that if Grimani had beaten the enemy fleet in a fair fight, as they thought he could have done, he would have been able to bring the whole Peloponnese and the coast of Greece and the island of Euboea under the dominion of the Republic without difficulty. Realizing now that everything had turned out quite the opposite of what they had hoped for, and with the deaths of Loredan and d'Armer very much on their minds, everyone felt a great sense of revulsion for Grimani and subjected him to biting criticism.[21]

These and similar reasons induced the senators to pass a decree 14 in the Council of Ten choosing a captain of the fleet to take ship

conscenderet; ipsi imperium abrogaretur; et quoniam Thomas Zenus, qui magni animi magnaeque virtutis esse vir ab omni plane civitate existimabatur, fisco pecuniam debebat — fisci autem debitoribus antiqua lege magistratus mandari nullus poterat — uti Thomae Zeno ea lex fraudi ne esset, quo minus ei navium praefectura quaelibet attribui per senatum possit, in lege decemvirum est additum. Itaque et Malchioni Trivisano, qui legatus bello Gallico Cremonam illis diebus per deditionem ceperat, maioribus comitiis classis est imperium delatum, et a senatu praefectura longarum navium maiorum decem septem Zeno tradita, magna cum potestate. Lectique a principis collegio earum navium praefecti tredecim veterum praefectorum loco, qui omnes statim profecti sunt cum militibus triginta quilibet. Latum etiam de veteribus ut ob male gestam rempublicam ad urbem redirent custodiaeque traderentur. Datumque triumviris ex advocatis reipublicae negotium, ut eos in iudicia deducerent, quibus a iudiciis, qua meriti essent, poena condemnarentur; idemque postea de Antonio constitutum. Lectus etiam per senatum, qui Corcyrae magistratus esset, Lucas Quirinus, cum militibus mille oppidi praesidio. Is et Zenus sine mora sunt profecti. Pauloque post Malchio, Cremona a senatu accersitus, vexillo reipublicae accepto conscendit, cum ei libras auri ducentas quinquaginta, quibus in classem uteretur, patres ex aerario dedissent.

15   Zancanius, mense Quintili in Carnos profectus, ut ab hostium impetu, quos eo patres venturos intellexerant, reipublicae fines tueretur, ratione hominum qui ferre arma poterant earum regionum habita, quorum fuit numerus circiter centum viginti milium, Graecis equitibus et levis graviorisque armaturae Italis quamplurimis, peditibusque coactis, munitissimo in castello apud Sontium flumen, quod Gradiscae appellatur, paulo ante nostram aetatem publice exaedificatum, multos est dies commoratus, dum ad eum[4]

at once in place of Grimani, who was relieved of his command. Tommaso Zen was generally regarded by all the citizens as a man of great spirit and courage, but he owed money to the treasury and by an ancient law no office could be given to those indebted to the treasury. An additional clause was accordingly put in the decree of the Ten that the law would not be a bar to Zen's being assigned any captaincy of ships by the Senate. And so general command of the fleet was conferred by the Great Council on Melchiorre Trevisan, who as proveditor in the French war had recently taken the surrender of Cremona, and the captaincy of seventeen larger warships with wide-ranging powers was given to Zen by the Senate. Thirteen of the ships had new captains chosen by the Doge's Council in place of their old ones, and they all set out at once with thirty soldiers each. With regard to the former captains, it was further resolved that they should return to Venice and be put in custody for their mismanagement of the Republic's affairs. The three state attorneys[22] were given the task of bringing them to a trial in which they would be sentenced to the punishment they had deserved, and the same procedure was later laid down for dealing with Grimani. The Senate also chose Luca Quirini to be governor of Corfu, with 1,000 infantry to garrison the town. He and Zen set out without delay. And shortly thereafter Trevisan was summoned by the Senate from Cremona, given the standard of the Republic, and took ship after being given by the senators 250 gold pounds from public funds to be spent on the fleet.

Andrea Zancani went to Friuli in July to defend the Republic's 15 territory against the enemy attack which the Senate had learned was about to take place there. He made an estimate of the men of those parts who were fit to bear arms, numbering about 120,000, and after assembling the stradiots, a great many Italian cavalry, both light and heavy, and foot soldiers, he stayed many days in a very strong fortress on the river Isonzo called Gradisca, which had been built a little before our time at the Republic's expense, until

ex Gallico exercitu auxilia convenissent. Turcae interea equites septem milia, magno ac difficili itinere confecto per Iapidum et Liburnorum fines, Sontio traiecto, non longe a Gradiscis castris positis, se continuerunt, eo consilio ut, si Zancanius castello exiret, proelium committerent. Eorum dux ubi Zancanium extra munitiones non audere egredi animadvertit, duo milia equitum praedatum mittit; iubet quoquoversus incursiones faciant, celeriterque uti redeant monet.

16 Equites, planitiem nacti magnam atque apertam, agrestes homines inopinantes, quod se ab illis tutos, opposito reipublicae exercitu, fore credebant, capiunt, vi eos diripiunt, incendunt; qui se defendere parant, interficiunt; in quibus fuerunt agrestes ducenti, qui Vicetia missi, ut ad Zancanium contenderent, in eos ex itinere inciderunt. Ea re a proximis audita, usque eo fugere omnibus ex partibus contenderunt ut, cum duorum fluminum obiectu, Plavis Silisque, hostes impedirentur, quorum alterum nullo tempore vado transiri potest, alterum ita saepe augetur ut magnum etiam detrimentum vicinitatibus inferat, ad urbis tamen aestuaria plerique, nullo loco commorati, pervenerint; neque Taurisanorum modo, sed Patavinorum etiam magna multitudo timore se in oppida receperit. A Foroiuliensium magistratu autem Graeci equites Italique qui sagittis utebantur ex oppido emissi trecenti, ut, si qua possent, hostibus nocerent, partem nacti centum eorum occiderunt. Quod si Zancanius cum suis, quorum erat magnus numerus, in hostes impetum audacter fecisset, honestiorem res exitum habere potuisset. Sed is pedem porta egredi, adoriendi hostes causa, nemini omnino homini ex suo exercitu permisit. Turcae qui excurrerant praeda facta cum ad ducem redire vellent, atque ad Tillaventi fluminis ripas, quod ea nocte creverat, pervenissent, quo latum flu-

reinforcements from the French army could join him. In the meantime 7,000 Turkish cavalry, after making a long and difficult traversal of Istria, crossed the Isonzo and pitched camp, taking up position not far from Gradisca with the intention of engaging in battle if Zancani left the fortress. When their captain observed that Zancani did not dare to leave his fortifications, he sent 2,000 cavalry out for plunder, ordering them to make indiscriminate raids throughout the vicinity, but warning them to make a speedy return.

This cavalry reached a great open plain and took the 16 countryfolk unawares — with the Republic's army stationed facing the enemy, they had thought they were safe from them. They forcibly plundered them and burned their villages, killing those who were ready to defend themselves, among them 200 peasants sent from Vicenza to join Zancani as they encountered the Turks on their journey. But after hearing of the situation from people nearby, they made haste to escape on all sides, so much so that when the enemy was checked by the barrier of the two rivers Piave and Sile (one cannot be forded at any time, while the other is often so swollen that it actually causes great damage to the area), most of them managed to reach the lagoon of Venice without stopping en route. A great mass of people, not only of Treviso but of Padua too, retreated into their towns in panic. The governor of Udine having despatched 300 stradiots and Italian mounted archers out of the town to do the enemy harm wherever they could, they happened upon a detachment of them and killed a hundred. Yet if Zancani had made a bold attack on the enemy with his great numbers of soldiers, the matter might have had a more honorable outcome, but he absolutely forbade anyone from his army to set foot outside the gate with a view to assailing the enemy. Their pillaging accomplished, the Turks who had been on the raid wanted to return to their commander. When they arrived at the banks of the Tagliamento, which had risen during the night, they slew

men traicere facilius possent, superioris aetatis quos habebant captivos in ripa fluminis ad duo milia interfecerunt, reliquos traduxerunt, et praeda onusti una cum duce qua venerant abierunt.

17   Zancanius imperii male gesti accusatus, cum in senatu a magistratibus defenderetur iique legem tulissent, qua lege Zancanio imperium prorogabatur, Franciscus Bolanus, quadragintavirum rerum capitalium magister, legem tulit, ut is ad urbem e vestigio rediret carcerique se dederet; eamque legem senatus frequens, damnata altera, comprobavit. Qua ex re Bolanus, magnopere laudatus, paulo post, quo die cives sexaginta suffragiis comitialibus deliguntur, qui annum in senatu sint (usu autem semper fit ut omnes civitatis principes et natu maiores ad id muneris deligantur), ipse non unus modo ex eo numero fuit, quod tamen ipsum ei aetati atque ordini magnum et inusitatum videri poterat, sed pluribus etiam suffragiis, quam ceteri complures, eum magistratum est adeptus, quod prope incredibile ante illum diem fuisset: tantam eo tempore imperator, legati praefectique, ob ignaviae opinionem civitatis, in se invidiam excitaverant. Amorem autem et benevolentiam conciliaverat fortitudo. Nam et Antonius Lauredanus, Andreae Lauredani frater, et Aloisius Armerius, Albani frater Armerii, magistratum sale procurando omnibus suffragiis sunt adepti; quem omnino per sese dignitatis et civitatis gradum decennio post uterque posse assequi ne speravisset quidem. Et Iacobo Polano, Vincentii Polani, eius de quo sermonem habuimus, patri, magno consensu locus datus est inter sexaginta cives qui quotannis senatui adici solent. Itaque Zancanius, ad urbem rediens custodiaeque traditus a senatu, condemnatus est ut Patavii annos quattuor exularet; neque ei profuit, quod Antonii et reliquorum qui rempubli-

those prisoners of advanced age that they had with them, about 2,000, in order to cross the broad river more easily, and taking the rest across, left the way they had come alongside their captain, weighed down with plunder.

Zancani was accused of mismanagement of his command, but 17 was defended in the Senate by the magistrates, who passed a law extending his command. Francesco Bollani, however, Head of the Criminal Court of Forty, promulgated a decree that Zancani should return to the city at once and surrender himself to prison, and this law was approved by a crowded Senate, the other being cancelled. Bollani won high praise for this and a short while later, on the day when the 60 citizens were chosen to serve in the Senate for the year by elections in the Great Council — by long custom it always happens that all the leading and eldest citizens are chosen for this task — not only was he one of that number, which in view of his age and rank might in itself have appeared a great and rare distinction, but he also won office with more votes than a great many others, something that would have been well nigh incredible up to that day: such was the resentment at the time that the captain-general, the proveditors, and the officers had brought on themselves, thanks to the citizens' belief in their cowardice. Valor in battle, on the other hand, secured their affection and goodwill, for both Antonio Loredan, brother of Andrea, and Alvise d'Armer, brother of Albano, were unanimously elected to the Salt Office. Neither of them would have as much as dared to hope of attaining that level of civic distinction on their own even ten years later. And Giacomo Polani, the father of the Vincenzo Polani that I mentioned above,[23] was by widespread agreement given a place among the 60 citizens added each year to the Senate.[24] And so on Zancani's return to the city, he was taken into custody by the Senate and condemned to four years' exile at Padua. Nor did it help him that the friends and relations of Grimani and the others who were said to have mismanaged the Republic's business spoke up

cam male gessisse dicebantur necessarii et propinqui ei faverent, ut vel omnino absolveretur, vel levissime condemnaretur, quo patres huius exemplo iudicii placabiliores in sese fierent; quae eos opinio fefellit.

18   Naupacto Antonius amisso navibus longis maioribus et onerariis compluribus abeundi facultatem concessit. Ea res molestissima fuit patribus, qui, nuntio de Naupacti deditione accepto, per litteras Antonio mandaverant ne classem diminueret, visumque est multis id Antonium non satis bono consilio fecisse. Ipse deinde Cephallenem insulam aggressus, ubi nihil se proficere cognovit, Corcyram reliqua cum classe se recepit; ibi acceptis de senatus consulto imperioque abrogato litteris, classe, pecunia rationibusque publicis legatis traditis, ad urbem rediit; cui praesto fuit Dominicus filius, vir philosophiae studiis clarus, e cardinalium insuper collegio, Roma veniens, ut, si quid posset, apud civitatem sua pietate atque officio ordinisque amplissimi auctoritate patrem sublevaret. Neque multo post tamen, maioribus comitiis causa in vinculis dicta, quod senatus lenitatem triumviri, qui eum accusabant, veriti rem ad multitudinem et iudicium totius nobilitatis deduxerant, exilio in Illyrici maris insulas Apsorum et Crepsam damnatus exulatum abiit. Nicolaus Michaeles, unus ex triumviris, magno favore civitatis eius locum ad aedis Marciae procurationem suffectus tenuit.

19   His rebus civitate domi forisque occupata, quoniam Alexander a senatu atque ab rege Galliae impetraverat uti eorum voluntate aliquot in Flaminia oppida, quae Romani iuris essent, Caesari Borgiae, eius filio, obtinenda cederentur, Caesar sua cum manu, cumque iis quas ab rege altero cum duce Mediolani acceperat co-

for him[25] by saying that he should either be absolved altogether or given a very light sentence, hoping that in the light of such a judgment the senators would take a more lenient view of themselves; but they were disappointed of their hopes.

After the loss of Lepanto, Grimani gave the larger warships and   18
many of the merchantmen permission to depart. This was deeply unwelcome to the senators, who, on hearing news of the surrender of Lepanto, had written to Grimani telling him not to reduce the size of his fleet, and many people thought that this action on Grimani's part was ill advised. Grimani himself then attacked the island of Cephalonia, but when he saw that he was making no headway, he withdrew with the rest of the fleet to Corfu. He there received the letter about the Senate's decree and his removal from command of the fleet, and having given the proveditors the ships, money, and accounts, he returned to Venice. His son Domenico, a distinguished philosopher as well as a member of the college of cardinals, was there to meet him; he had come from Rome to support his father in whatever way he could out of filial piety and a sense of duty and with all the influence of his elevated rank with the citizens. Not long after that, however, his case was pled in the Great Council while he remained in prison[26] (the state attorneys who were prosecuting him feared that the Senate might show clemency, and so had sent the matter to be judged by the nobility at large), and being sentenced to banishment on the islands of Cherso and Ossero in the sea of Dalmatia,[27] he went off to live in exile. Niccolò Michiel, one of the attorneys, took his place as Procurator of St. Mark's to popular acclaim.

While the city was occupied with these matters at home and   19
abroad, Pope Alexander had prevailed upon the Senate and the king of France to give their assent to granting some towns in Romagna which were part of the Papal States to his son Cesare Borgia. With his own forces and some troops which he had had from the king at Milan along with a commander, Borgia now

piis, in Flaminiam est profectus. Erat is antea, ut superioribus libris dictum est, in cardinalium collegio; sed magistratu repudiato uxorem in Gallia duxerat. Ac primum quidem Forum Cornelii et Forum Livii oppida ipsa, castris ad muros positis tormentisque adductis, acri oppugnatione ad deditionem compulit. Arces vero eorum oppidorum, quod erant munitissimae, varios eventus habuerunt. Altera enim, complures dies obsessa, condicionibus acceptis Caesari anni exitu deditur; Foroliviensium arcem autem, in qua erat Caterina ipsa, diu ac magnis oppugnatam viribus, paulo post Caesar, muro tormentis deiecto, militibus irrumpentibus, multa cum suorum caede tandem cepit, Caterina captiva facta. Interea, ut suos et eorum fines senatus quos e Flaminia in fidem recepisset ab Alexandro atque ab Caesare, tantum exercitum habente, si quid aggredi et conari vellent, tueretur, tria militum milia, duo equitum Liviano duce Ravennam misit, quos per oppida distribueret. Simul legati duo, Franciscus Capellus, Christophorus Maurus, alter Ariminum, alter Faventiam profecti, qui eis oppidis reipublicae nomine praeessent.

20   Arce Foroliviensium capta, Caesar, cum Pisaurum vellet patribus permittentibus exercitum adducere, propter novos Mediolani motus destitit. Nam patres, cum ad urbem Ioannes, princeps Pisaurensium, de Caesaris in se voluntate certior factus, venisset oppidumque vellet reipublicae tradere, modo ipsi aliquid in reipublicae finibus oppiduli aut castelli senatus daret, quo se alere et sustinere posset, consulto senatu responderunt nolle se ei praesidio esse qui reipublicae obesse voluisset. Id autem propterea patres commemoraverant quod Ludovici legatos, ad Turcarum regem

marched into Romagna. He had previously been a member of the college of cardinals, as was mentioned in earlier books,[28] but had resigned the office and taken a wife in France. After pitching camp and bringing his artillery up to the walls, his first act was to force the surrender of the towns of Imola and Forlì by a fierce attack. But things fared differently with the citadels of the towns, since they were very well fortified. That of Imola was besieged for many days, but at length accepted terms and surrendered to Borgia at the end of the year;[29] on the other hand, the citadel of Forlì, where Caterina Sforza herself was,[30] had been under attack by a strong force for a long time when Borgia shortly afterwards knocked down the walls with his artillery, and with his soldiers bursting in, finally took it with many casualties on his own side, Caterina being taken captive. Meanwhile, in order to defend their own territory and that of the Romagnoli that they had taken under their protection from any aggressive move on the part of Alexander and Cesare Borgia, who had such a powerful army, the Senate sent 3,000 infantry and 2,000 cavalry to Ravenna under the leadership of Bartolomeo d'Alviano for him to distribute among the towns. At the same time two proveditors set out, Francesco Capello and Cristoforo Moro, one to Rimini, the other to Faenza, to govern those towns in the Republic's name.

After taking the citadel of Forlì, Borgia wanted with the Senate's permission to lead his army against Pesaro, but owing to new developments at Milan, he stayed where he was. When Giovanni Sforza, the lord of Pesaro, learned of Borgia's intentions toward him, he went to Venice with the hope of handing over the town to the Republic, provided that the Senate granted him some small town or fortress within its borders from which he could make a living and support himself. But after consultation with the Senate, the Signoria replied that they were not willing to protect a man who had been ready to oppose the Republic. Now the Signoria brought this up because they had earlier found out that Sforza

20

contra rempublicam missos, Ioannem hospitio accepisse, navibus, rebus omnibus iuvisse, regisque item ad Ludovicum legatum nave Pisauri egressum domi suae habuisse clamque ad illum misisse, tum ipsum singulis de rebus quae in urbe agerentur litteras ad regem dedisse antea cognoverant.

21   Sed Mediolani motus fuerant eiusmodi. Ludovicus, copiis non maximis in Raetis comparatis, eorum factione quos Galli irritaverant quique res novas moliebantur magnopere adiutus, in fines se regni contulerat, insequente anno inito. Eius adventu Triultius duxque regius ex duobus alter, vehementer permoti atque perturbati, quod civitatis defectionem timebant, copias regias quae cum Caesare aberant revocaverunt atque ad se celeriter reverti iusserunt. Itaque Caesar, multo maiore sui exercitus parte ablata, de Pisauro expugnando cogitationem in aliud tempus omisit Romamque se contulit. Ludovico ad recuperanda quae amiserat cum exercitu revertente, senatus decrevit ut milites equitesque reipublicae omnes in agrum Cremonensem e vestigio contenderent; ut Helvetiorum militum tria milia celeriter accerserentur; legatique ad bellum Petrus Marcellus, Christophorus Maurus lecti. Ipse interea Ludovicus, Como per suos sine vi atque celeriter recepto — Galli enim qui in eo erant, veriti ne ab oppidanis atque ab hostibus intercluderentur, municipio relicto discesserant — Ascanium fratrem cum parte copiarum Mediolanum praemisit; quo appropinquante, cives armis captis Triultium et Gallos eiecerunt eique portas aperuerunt; biduoque post ipse, cum reliquo exercitu adveniens, in urbem est receptus.

22   His intellectis rebus, decemviri legem tulerunt, uti civis probata virtute Cremonam mitteretur, qui arci oppidi praeesset; missusque

had welcomed the ambassadors of Ludovico il Moro when they were sent to the Turkish sultan against the Republic; he had given them ships and all manner of other assistance, and had also entertained the sultan's ambassador to Ludovico in his house when he disembarked at Pesaro, and had sent him to Ludovico in secret; on top of that, he had written letters to the sultan giving details of everything that was discussed at Venice.

But to return to the developments at Milan: Ludovico had assembled a modest force in the Tyrol, and with the strong support of a group of those who had been angered by the French and who were aiming at their overthrow, he made his way into the territory of the duchy at the beginning of the next year. Trivulzio and the second of the two French commanders[31] were extremely worried and disturbed at his arrival, for fear that the citizens would go over to him, and they recalled the king's troops that had left with Borgia, ordering them to return with all haste. With the great majority of his army thus removed, Borgia put off to another occasion any thought of conquering Pesaro and took himself off to Rome. As Ludovico was returning with his army to recover what he had lost, the Senate gave orders for all the Republic's infantry and cavalry to make at once for the territory of Cremona and for 3,000 Swiss soldiers to be raised, Pietro Marcello and Cristoforo Moro being appointed proveditors for the war. Meanwhile Como was quickly retaken by Ludovico's men without a fight—the French who were inside had abandoned the town and left, fearing that they would trapped by the townspeople and the enemy—and he himself sent his brother Ascanio ahead to Milan with part of his troops. At Ascanio's approach, the citizens seized arms, drove out Trivulzio and the French, and opened the gates to him. Ludovico himself arrived two days later with the rest of the army and was welcomed into the city.

On learning of these events, the Ten passed a decree that a citizen of proven courage should be sent to Cremona to take com-

est, ipsorum suffragio lectus, Nicolaus Priolus decemviralis. Missi etiam alii quattuor egregii nominis, qui totidem oppidorum in Cremonae Abduaeque fluminis finibus arces custodirent. Mediolani Ludovicus paucos commoratus dies, dum a civibus humili subdolaque oratione pecuniam corrogaret, Ticinum proficiscitur; neque ullo in loco magnopere impeditus, Gallos, qui se cottidie in ulteriorem regni partem recipiebant, insequens, postremo Novariam, quam Triultius praesidiis firmaverat, aggreditur; et quod erat a muralibus tormentis imparatior, crebris assultibus premere oppidum insistit. Simul ad illum Sequani equites sexcenti, auxilio a Maximiliano missi, adveniunt. Iis ad summovendos hostes usus, et modo per insidias detrimento accepto, modo fusis hostibus illato, abductis demum a Triultio praesidiis, quod diffidere oppidanis coeperat, neque iam commeatus interclusis suppetebat, Novariam se dedentem recipit.

23   Interea exercitus reipublicae Cremonam Abduaeque ad ripas confestim profectus, Laudem Pompeii, quod iam oppidum Ludovici milites introduxerat, misso praesidio expulsisque militibus, regi retinuit. Placentiam nutantem per se atque labantem confirmavit. Triultius, reversis iis qui cum Caesare in Flaminiam ierant Gallis, simul ab rege missis ad eum equitibus ex Gallia Transalpina atque ab Helvetiis coacto exercitu, non longe ab Novaria contra Ludovicum castra posuit, itineribusque ne commeatus Ludovico supportari posset prope interceptis, paulo post commisso proelio illum in oppidum reppulit, posteroque die, cum se fugae dare decrevisset, omni cum exercitu oppido egressum, veste pabulatoria et strigoso in equo inter milites se celantem, permittentibus Helvetiis, perquisitum cepit. Ea re cognita, pars regni omnis quae

mand of the town's citadel. Niccolò Priuli, who was one of the
Ten, was chosen by their vote and sent there. Four other distinguished men were also despatched to take charge of the fortresses
of four more towns in the neighborhood of Cremona and the river
Adda. Ludovico stayed at Milan for a few days while he begged
the citizens for funds with talk that was both abject and insincere,
leaving then for Pavia. Encountering no great resistance anywhere,
he pursued the French, who were every day retreating further into
the duchy, and eventually attacked Novara, which Trivulzio had
fortified with garrisons. Being rather short of siege-artillery,
Ludovico proceeded to keep the town under pressure with frequent attacks. At the same time 600 Burgundian cavalry arrived,
sent by Maximilian to support him. These he used to drive off the
enemy, by turns suffering losses from their ambushes and inflicting
losses on them by putting them to flight. In the end Trivulzio
withdrew the garrisons because he had begun to distrust the
townspeople and supplies were no longer getting through to those
trapped inside, and Ludovico accepted the surrender of Novara.

Meanwhile the Republic's army had marched in haste to   23
Cremona and the banks of the Adda. They sent reinforcements to
Lodi, a town which had already let in Ludovico's soldiers, drove
them out, and took back the town for the king. They secured
Piacenza, which on its own was wavering and on the point of giving way. The Frenchmen who had gone into Romagna with Borgia
having returned, along with cavalry that the king had sent him
from France and an army raised from the Swiss, Trivulzio pitched
camp against Ludovico not far from Novara. A little later, with the
routes fairly blocked so as to cut off supplies to Ludovico, battle
was joined and Trivulzio drove him back into the town. On the
following day, when Ludovico had decided to take flight, he left
the town with his whole army, concealed among the infantry
dressed as a forager and riding a scrawny horse, but though the
Swiss let him through, Trivulzio hunted him down and took him

defecerat ad regem statim rediit. Ludovico capto, Ascanius principesque civitatis permulti, ex iis qui Ludovici rebus favebant, una Mediolano aufugerunt Padum flumen versus, ut se in tutum reciperent. Verum ab Soncino Benzonio, turmae equitum reipublicae praefecto, qui, id quod re evenit opinione existimans futurum, itinera observabat, in Cremonae finibus intercepti sunt; Ascanius etiam Venetias adductus in comitii turricula publice observatus est. Pauloque post, rege illum ab senatu petente, saeptus custodibus in Galliam transmisit; quo antea Ludovicus perductus custodiaeque traditus ea in custodia aliquot post annos est mortuus. Ea aestate, propterea quod Gaspar Severinas reliquique fratres, Roberti liberi, bellum contra rempublicam gesserant, senatus consulto Cittadella oppidum receptum, et bona eorum fisco sunt addicta.

24 Sed Naupacto amisso, ut docuimus, Aloisium Manentium, in decemvirum collegio scribam, senatus Byzantium ad regem misit questum quod, nulla lacessitus iniuria, pacem quam paulo ante cum Zancanio legato firmaverat, bello terra marique illato, violavisset, postulatumque ut mercatores Venetos, qui nihil deliquissent, quorum etiam adventu eius portoria facta essent meliora, quos belli initio in vincula coniecerat, liberaret; Naupactum, iniusto bello captum, reipublicae restitueret; demum, si id nollet, pacem renovaret. Id autem ea de causa sibi temptandum senatus decreverat, quod ab nonnullis qui plurimum apud regem poterant spes ei proponebatur, fore ut, si legatum mitteret, pax inter ipsos conciliaretur; tum quod gravissimum civitati fore intelligebat, si

captive. When this became known, all of the duchy that had defected returned to the king at once. After the capture of Ludovico, Ascanio Sforza and a good many of the leading citizens who had supported Ludovico took flight together from Milan and sought safety by heading for the Po. But they were intercepted in the Cremonese by Soncino Benzoni, captain of a Venetian cavalry squad, who was guarding the roads against that very eventuality. Ascanio was actually taken to Venice and placed in state custody in the little tower of the Great Council. Shortly after that, the king asked the Senate to deliver him up, and he crossed into France under heavy guard. Ludovico had already been taken there at an earlier stage and put in prison, where he died some years later. That summer, by decree of the Senate, the town of Cittadella was taken back from Gaspare da Sanseverino and his brothers, the sons of Roberto Sanseverino, because they had gone to war against the Republic, and their property was made over to the public treasury.

After the loss of Lepanto described above, the Senate sent the 24 secretary of the Council of Ten, Alvise Manenti, to the sultan in Constantinople to complain that though he had been provoked by no injury, he had violated the peace he had only recently signed with their ambassador Zancani by waging war against them on land and sea. He was also to request the release of Venetian merchants: though they had done no wrong and their presence had actually enhanced his toll revenues, the sultan had had them thrown into prison at the beginning of the war; and to ask further for the restitution to Venice of Lepanto, which had been taken in an unjust war; and if he refused that, Zancani was to seek a renewal of the peace agreement. The Senate had decided to try this course of action because some persons of great influence with the sultan had held out to them the hope that if they sent an ambassador, a peace between them could be achieved. In the second place, they realized that it would be very hard for the state to put to-

classis eo etiam anno esset comparanda, contritis per tot bella non urbanis modo opibus, sed etiam provincialibus, republica insuper nihil prospere contra illum moliente. Nam cum, Naupacto ab hostibus expugnato, Cephallenem insulam capere primo Antonius, ut antea dictum est, deinde Zenus, postremo etiam Malchio, classe adducta, diuturna oppugnatione temptavissent, labor tamen omnis omnium irritus et inanis fuit. Manentius anni initio profectus Byzantium ubi pervenit, nihil eorum quorum causa missus fuerat impetrare potuit; rex enim ita respondit: pacem Veneti si velint, Methonem, Coronem, Naupliam, quae haberent in Peloponneso oppida, sibi tradant aurique libras centum stipendii nomine singulis annis dependant; alia se condicione pacem cum republica non facturum; itaque infecta re discessit.

25   Sed Manentio ab urbe profecto, quod nuntii afferebantur in Epiri finibus magnum Turcarum equitum numerum cogi, senatus, veritus eam manum, superioris anni praeda impunitateque allectam, in Carnos finesque reipublicae esse venturam, Petrum Orium, Angelum Barotium legatos creavit, qui una cum Foroiuliensium magistratu earumque rerum peritis regiones inviserent et, quibus in locis atque itineribus operae pretium esset, munitiones instituendas curarent, quibus hostes repelli possent; Livianumque, cum equitibus quibus praeerat, et Gurlinum Ravennatem, qui priores ordines gerebat, cum militibus duobus milibus, legatis dedit. Petrus etiam Marcellus, alter ex duobus in Gallico exercitu legatis, iussus cum copiis in Carnos proficisci. Turcae tamen, propterea quod rex eorum ducem Byzantium evocaverat, se in Carnos non intulerunt. Aestate autem media, quod eadem rursus fama

gether a war fleet for yet another year, when their resources had been used up over the course of so many wars, not only in Venice itself but in the provinces as well, added to which the Republic had met with no success at all in its undertakings against the sultan. For after Lepanto was conquered by the enemy, first Grimani, as mentioned above, then Zen, and finally Melchiorre Trevisan too tried to take the island of Cephalonia, the last bringing up a fleet and attacking it at length, but all the efforts of every one of them were unavailing and ineffectual. Manenti set out at the beginning of the year, but when he arrived at Constantinople, he was unable to obtain any of the demands he had been sent to make. The response of the sultan was that if the Venetians wanted peace, they should cede to him Methoni, Coron, and Nauplia, towns they held in the Peloponnese, and pay him 100 gold pounds a year in tribute; he would not make peace with the Republic on any other terms; and so Manenti left without accomplishing his mission.

After Manenti had set out from Venice, the Senate was 25 brought reports that a large force of Turkish cavalry was being collected in Albania. Worried that this force might be lured by the booty they had had in the previous year and the lack of retribution for it, and invade Friuli and Venetian territory, they appointed Pietro Orio and Angelo Barozzi as proveditors to inspect the area in the company of the governor of Udine and experts in the matter. In those places and on those routes where it was worth the effort, they were to see to the setting up of fortifications to keep the enemy back. The Senate assigned to the proveditors Bartolomeo d'Alviano and the cavalry he commanded, and Gurlino of Ravenna, one of the front-rank captains, along with 2,000 infantry. Pietro Marcello, one of the two proveditors in the French army, was also ordered to proceed to Friuli with his troops. The Turks, however, did not invade Friuli because the sultan had recalled their commander to Constantinople. But in midsummer

crebrioribus nuntiis percrebuerat, parari hostium exercitum, qui sit in fines reipublicae impetum facturus, Nicolaus Ursinus cum magna copiarum parte cumque Ioanne Baptista Caratio, militum omnium reipublicae praefecto, senatu iubente in Carnos est profectus, omnesque eius regionis incolae se et sua in oppida et castellos contulerunt. Hostes, vel quod loca communita scirent esse, vel quod iis in bellum Peloponnesiacum, de quo dicturi sumus, uti rex voluerit, ab incursionibus in eam reipublicae partem se continuerunt.

26 Manentius tantum ad urbem redierat, cum patres, Corcyrae insulae veriti, propterea quod ea in potestatem hostium redacta, quae oppidum munitum et portus egregios haberet, omnis Adriani maris navigatio et in Ionium reliquaque maria exitus magnopere impediebantur, decemvirum lege Angelum Quirinum, Aloisium Decanalem cum militibus centum eo miserunt, qui duabus oppidi arcibus praeessent; quae quidem arces, quod promontoriolis item duobus oppido coniunctis sunt impositae spatiumque perangustum habent, multorum propugnatorum non indigent.

27 Nuntii deinde Aprili mense venerunt, classem Thraciam quae Naupacti ea hieme fuisset magno studio esse refectam aliamque in sinu Ambracio institutam classem deduci, ut se cum illa coniungeret; ipsum regem maximo cum exercitu brevi in Peloponnesum venturum, ut quae oppida in pacis condicionibus a Manentio petierat bello persequatur. Iis rebus cognitis, senatus decrevit uti naves longae decem, ex iis quae ad mercaturam instituuntur, onerariaeque magnae quattuor armarentur; decemque iis qui imperaret Iacobus Venerius datus, singulis autem navibus suus praefectus cuique; auctaque iis stipendia, quo libentius proficiscerentur. Missusque ad supplendam classem remigum opportunus numerus, quem ex continenti senatus conduxerat. Iussi etiam praefecti mili-

the same rumor again became widespread, with ever more frequent reports that an enemy army was being readied to attack Venetian territory, and so Niccolò Orsini with a large part of his forces and with Gian Battista Caracciolo, overall captain of the Venetian infantry, set out for Friuli by order of the Senate, all the inhabitants of the region taking themselves into their towns and castles. Either because they knew that those places were strongly defended, or because the sultan wanted to use them for the war in the Peloponnese of which we are about to speak, the enemy refrained from making raids into that part of the Republic's territory.

The senators had become anxious about Corfu: if it fell into enemy hands, with its fortified town and excellent harbors, it would prove a great hindrance to all navigation of the Adriatic and passage into the Ionian and other seas. Manenti had scarcely returned to the city when by decree of the Ten the senators sent Angelo Querini and Alvise da Canal with 100 infantry to take command of the town's two fortresses; being placed on two ridges that reached the town, with very little space between them, these fortresses do not need many men to defend them. 26

Then in April came the news that the Turkish fleet which had been at Lepanto that winter had been very thoroughly refitted, and that another fleet had been built in the Gulf of Arta and was being launched to join it; the sultan himself would soon come into the Peloponnese with a great army to attack the towns that he had sought from Manenti in the peace terms. Learning of this, the Senate decided that ten warships of a commercial sort and four large merchantmen should be fitted out for war. Giacomo Venier was assigned the command of the ten ships, each individual ship being given its own captain, and their pay was increased to increase their enthusiasm for the journey. The Senate hired a suitable number of oarsmen on the mainland and sent them to fill out the fleet's complement. Twenty officers with a good many men and 27

tum viginti, bona cum manu cumque iis rebus quae idoneae ad
munitiones faciendas essent, Methonem proficisci, pecunia insuper in classis stipendium missa. Senatus etiam consultum factum,
ut naves longae minores non paucae prioribus adderentur, biremesque complures confestim armarentur classique submitterentur.

28 Malchio et ipse, qui Corcyram venerat, navibus aliquot relictis
ad Cephallenae insulae non tam quidem oppugnationem, quam ut
in statione ibi essent, ne praesidium hostibus submitti posset, recentioribus de classe Thracia regioque exercitu nuntiis certior factus, uti e Creta milites et commeatus et tormenta Naupliam mitterentur, curam et diligentiam adhibuit. Et quod Naupliam primum
omnium venturum regem multi existimabant, pars ab illo praefectorum militum est eo transmissa; commeatum etiam omnis generis Methonem misit. Ipsi etiam oppidani, qui frumenta in agris pabulaque omnia circum oppidum corruperant, aedificia
combusserant, ne hostibus opportuna fierent, munitionem in
portu magni operis effecerunt aggeremque in mari excitaverunt,
quo ab aggere naves hostium arcerentur ne ad muros propius accederent; aditumque uni tantum navi reliquerunt, quo se tueri facilius possent, quam si cum multis uno tempore navibus eis esset
propugnandum.

29 Malchio deinde Zacynthum profectus classem eo convenire iussit navium longarum et onerariarum circiter septuaginta, in quibus
erant naves longae magnae sexdecim. Turcae interea suam classem
duobus locis comparatam apud insulam Leucadiam coegerant,
magna reipublicae populorum querela, quod Malchio quique
praeerant legati, ne id per hostes fieri posset, minus prohibuissent;
partem eius classis utramlibet, separatam ab altera parte atque semotam, superari ac deleri non maximo negotio potuisse; nunc eam
coniunctam atque plenam nihil non ausuram, ad exitumque per-

materials for making fortifications were also ordered to leave for Methoni, with additional funds sent to pay the fleet. There was also a Senate decree that an appreciable number of smaller warships should be joined to the existing ships, and that many small galleys should be fitted out for war with all speed and sent to the fleet.

Having left behind a number of ships at Cephalonia, not so 28 much with a view to attacking the island as to have them stationed there so that the enemy could not send in help, when Trevisan reached Corfu, he was given the latest intelligence on the Turkish fleet and the sultan's army, and he took great pains to have infantry and provisions and artillery sent to Nauplia from Crete. Many thought that the sultan would first of all go to Nauplia, and so some of the officers were despatched there by Trevisan, who also sent all kinds of provisions to Methoni. The people of Nauplia themselves destroyed all the grain and fodder in the fields around the town, and burned down buildings in case they should be useful to the enemy. They also carried out massive fortification works in the port and raised a breakwater in the sea from which enemy ships could be kept from coming any closer to the walls, and left space for only one ship to enter at a time, so that they might defend themselves more easily than if they had to fight off a number of ships at once.

Trevisan then set off for Zante and gave orders that the fleet, 29 comprising about 70 warships and merchantmen, among them 16 large warships, should gather there. The Turkish fleet had been raised in two places but they had in the meantime united them near the island of Lefkada, which led to much criticism by the Venetian subjects that Trevisan and the proveditors in charge had done too little to prevent their doing so. They said that either part of the fleet could have been beaten and destroyed with no great effort had it been on its own and not joined with the other, but as things stood now, with the fleet united and at full strength, there

ducturam. Adiungebatur ad eas querelas etiam hoc, quod Malchio laborare adversa valetudine coeperat. Sed rex, coacta classe navium omnis generis plus ducentarum viginti, cum exercitu in Naupliae fines est ingressus, missa equitum parte, qui ad oppidum accederent. Cum iis oppidani equites congressi mille quingenti proelium secundissimum fecerunt; itaque Nauplia relicta rex Methonem venit. Praemissi autem ab eo Turcae Pylon oppugnare sunt aggressi, quod quidem abest Methone milia passuum decem, loco edito impositum, portu adiecto. Ii, quod eo ipso tempore Contarenus legatus, cum navibus longis aliquot adveniens, auxilium propugnatoribus attulerat, repulsi, spe castelli capiendi amissa, abeuntes cum reliquo se exercitu coniunxerunt. Inter haec Malchio apud Cephallenem moritur; pauloque post legatorum et praefectorum omnium suffragio Hieronymus Contarenus legatus Malchioni pro imperatore sufficitur, quoad patres quem praeesse velint imperent.

30   Rex, Methonem omni cum exercitu acerrime oppugnans, magnam proöppidi murorum partem tormentis deiecerat. Milites qui priores ordines gerebant, a senatu missi, principesque municipii, veriti non posse se eam partem tueri, rebus omnibus et materia quae in eo erat ablata atque in oppidum abducta, proöppidum reliquerunt. Hostes ingressi maiore iam spe murum oppidi deicere, labore non intermisso, institerunt. Dum haec ad oppidum geruntur, Contarenus omni cum classe Zacyntho proficiscitur, ut, si qua posset, aut adferret oppidanis auxilium, aut classi hostium noceret; cuius classis naves onerariae Sphagiam insulam circumvehebantur; reliquae naves e Pyli portu se promovebant. Quas ubi Veneti e longinquo viderunt, eas aggredi magno animo decreverunt; itaque

was no venture it would not undertake and carry off.[32] Added to
this was the further complaint that Trevisan had begun to suffer
from ill health. The sultan, on the other hand, having raised a fleet
of more than 220 ships of every sort, invaded the territory of
Nauplia with his army after sending part of his cavalry against the
town. The Nauplian cavalry of 1,500 horse engaged with them and
fought a highly successful battle, and so the sultan abandoned
Nauplia and went to Methoni. He sent men on ahead and they
began to attack Navarino, which is ten miles from Methoni, situated on high ground next to a harbor. But at that very moment
the proveditor Contarini had arrived with some warships and
brought the defenders reinforcements, and so the Turks were
driven back, and having lost hope of taking the fortress, left and
rejoined the rest of the army. While all this was going on, Trevisan
died in Cephalonia, and a little later the proveditors and captains
all voted for the proveditor Girolamo Contarini to replace him as
acting captain-general, pending an order of the senators as to
whom they wished to take command.

The sultan launched a fierce attack on Methoni with his entire   30
army and knocked down much of the walls of the town's outskirts[33] with artillery fire. The front-line captains that the Senate
had sent and the town authorities feared that they would be unable to defend the district and withdrew from it, carrying off all
the property and timber in it and bringing it into town. Their
hopes raised, the enemy now entered the outskirts and began
knocking down the wall with unflagging vigor. While this was going on at the town, Contarini set out from Zante with his whole
fleet to see if he could either relieve the townspeople, if that were
possible, or do damage to the enemy fleet. The merchantmen of
the Turkish fleet were sailing around the island of Sapientza, their
other ships advancing out of the harbor of Navarino. When the
Venetians saw them in the distance, with great spirit they decided
to attack them. Dividing the fleet as a whole into three lines, they

tribus effectis ex omni classe cornibus, in hostes contenderunt; quorum in uno naves erant longae minores universae, in altero maiores continebantur; tertium cornu naves onerariae conficiebant. Atque hoc aperto mari, illud litori propius erat. Naves triremes magnae medium, satis idoneo inter utrasque spatio relicto, classis locum obtinebant. Hostes ubi contra se veniri animadvertunt, naves longas circiter centum in Venetos converterunt.

31   Venerius medio e cornu cui praeerat, signo pugnae dato, omnium primus impetum in hostes facit; trirememque contra se venientem unam ex prioribus aggreditur; ex eaque trireme magnus hostium numerus tormentis est interfectus; ex reliquis triremibus magnis sex et ipsae cladem non parvam classi Thraciae intulerunt compluresque triremes depresserunt; ex minoribus viginti proelium commiserunt; eoque res est deducta, ut Turcae, quemadmodum postea cognitum est, litori naves impingere fugamque capere cogitarent. Reliquae triremes congredi non sunt ausae. Obfuit autem plurimum etiam fortuna ipsa, quae multum in bellis potest, quod naves onerariae tranquillitate magna oborta se movere non potuerunt. Turcae utrumque conspicati, et naves onerarias vento silente detineri, et longarum magnam partem a pugna conserenda deterreri, animum sumpserunt; proelioque redintegrato atque ad noctem perducto, cum horas tres continenter pugnavissent, ex Venetis triremibus maioribus una depressa interiit; altera, interfectis quam plurimis, est capta, cum omnibus abeuntibus tamen sola totam noctem impetum hostium sustinuisset. Contarenus proimperator, navi sua perforata atque aqua eam degravante, in aliam se contulit; Zacynthumque, ut et illam et reliquas aliquid ex concursu passas incommodi reficeret, est profectus.

accordingly made for the enemy with all haste. The first was made up of all the smaller warships, the second of the larger ones, while the third line was composed of the merchantmen. This last was in the open sea, the first closer to shore, while the large galleys held the middle position in the fleet, leaving a decent interval between them and the other two. Noticing them coming on the attack against them, the enemy turned about 100 of their warships on the Venetians.

From the middle line which he commanded, Venier gave the 31 signal for battle and himself made the very first assault on the enemy, attacking one of the leading galleys that were driving against him. A great number of the enemy were killed in that galley by artillery fire. Six of the remaining large galleys also inflicted no small carnage on the Turkish fleet and sank many of their warships, and twenty of the smaller Venetian galleys joined battle. Matters reached such a pitch that (as it was later learned) the Turks considered dashing their ships against the shore and taking flight. The remaining Venetian galleys did not dare engage. But the greatest obstacle was Fortune herself, a potent force in war, because a great calm having arisen, the merchantmen were unable to sail. Observing these twin happenstances — the merchantmen held back by the wind dying away, and a large part of the warships frightened of joining battle — the Turks took heart. They rejoined the fray and carried on into the night, when after nonstop fighting for three hours, one of the larger Venetian galleys was sunk and foundered, while a second was captured with a great many casualties, having withstood the enemy onslaught all night on its own when the others had all departed. Deputising as captain-general, Contarini, with his ship holed and weighed down by water, took himself onto another boat, and set out for Zante to repair both his own ship and the others which had been damaged in the action.

32   Interea cum de Malchionis adversa valetudine senatui esset nuntiatum, patres e vestigio ut ei classi imperator sublegeretur decreverunt; qui si eum salvum offendisset, reipublicae nomine hortaretur ut ad urbem rediret. Idque eo deliberatius fecerunt, quod de Malchione cottidie quae non magnopere vellent audiebant. Itaque maioribus comitiis Benedictus Pisaurus magna cum potestate lectus, pecunia in stipendium largiter ei curata, die ab ea die tertia conscendit. Contarenus refectis navibus auxilium et commeatum Methonem mittere cum decrevisset, veritus ne oppidani, omni subsidio desperato, sese hostibus dederent, naves longas quinque omni ex classe delegit atque in iis quae opportuna essent imposuit. Ante tamen, optimum esse ratus oppidanos ea de re certiores facere, ut se ad frumentum atque arma reliquasque res celeriter ex navibus extrahendas compararent, hominem fortem atque audacem, cumba ei tradita, cum remigibus decem eo misit. Is per mediam hostium classem, omnibus inspectantibus, quod erat meridiei fere tempus, celeritate adhibita pervolans, mandata Contareni oppidanis pertulit; posteroque die, qui dies erat ante diem quintum Iduum Sextilis, Contarenus, nactus idoneam tempestatem, Methonem versus vela omnibus cum triremibus facit.

33   Hostes classe visa, id quod erat rati, ad oppidi se portum opposuerunt. Contarenus, praefectos cohortatus ut magno animo ad oppidum contenderent remque suorum civium opis et virtutis egentem sublevarent, eos ab se dimisit. Ex iis quattuor triremes, inter hostium naves elapsae, se ad oppidum magna difficultate contulerunt. Una, quod erat tardior, multis hostium navibus iter impedientibus, cum reliquarum celeritatem se imitare posse diffideret, ad Contarenum rediit. Oppidani, navibus auxiliariis conspectis, ut ea quae afferebantur celeriter in oppidum asportarent, laeti ad portum convolaverunt. Tantaque fuit eius rei cura, ut ii

When in the meantime Trevisan's poor health was reported to   32
the Senate, the senators immediately decided to appoint a captain-
general of the fleet to replace him. And if he found him alive and
well, he should urge him to return to Venice in the name of the
Republic: they did this with all the more determination for hearing daily reports about Trevisan that they did not much like.
Benedetto Pesaro was therefore chosen by the Great Council,
given wide-ranging powers and a generous sum of money for the
payroll, and took ship three days later. Having repaired his ships,
Contarini decided to send help and provisions to Methoni, for fear
that the townspeople would give up all hope of being relieved and
surrender to the enemy. He accordingly selected five warships
from the whole fleet and loaded them with useful supplies. First,
however, since he thought it best to inform the townspeople of the
matter so that they might be ready to quickly unload the grain and
weapons and so on from the ships, he sent a man of courage and
resource to Methoni, giving him a small boat with ten rowers. The
man took Contarini's instructions to the townspeople at great
speed, flying through the very middle of the enemy fleet in full
sight of everybody, it being around midday. And on the following
day, the 9th of August,[34] Contarini made sail with all his galleys
toward Methoni while the weather was good.

When the enemy saw the fleet, they sized up the situation and   33
took up position facing the harbor of the town. Urging his captains to make for the town with all alacrity and alleviate the plight
of their fellow citizens at a time when they needed their help and
courage, Contarini dismissed them. Four of the galleys slipped
through the enemy lines and with great difficulty reached the
town. One that was slower found the way blocked by a large number of enemy ships and returned to Contarini, since it was not
confident it could match the speed of the rest. When the townsfolk saw the ships coming to their rescue, they rushed to the harbor to carry off the supplies at once into the town. So eager were

etiam qui muros alia ex oppidi parte contra hostium exercitum servabant, cum festinari ab aliis viderent, eodem et ipsi accurrerent stationesque relinquerent sic ut murus defensoribus spoliaretur. Id ubi hostes ab exercitu conspexerunt, occasione rei bene gerendae non omissa, per ruinas murorum quas tormenta fecerant, scalis positis nixi, paucis defendentibus interfectis, se in oppidum intulerunt.

34   Oppidani praefectique et milites, praesidio et commeatu iam e navibus abducto, ea de re certiores facti, hostibus medio in oppido occurrerunt; atque ibi proelio acerrime commisso, cum diu fortiterque pugnavissent ac magnum eorum numerum occidissent, demum crescente hostium multitudine, plenis iam omnibus et obsessis viis, circumsaepti undique ac pressi, prope omnes interfecti sunt una cum praefectis navium, qui tunc venerant, duobus remigibusque permultis. Ex municipibus ii qui superfuerant omni ex parte oppidum incenderunt suaque omnia et suos comburere voluerunt; ita oppidum ardens ac semicombustum capitur, cum quidem Veneti multam in noctem se defendissent. Eo capto rex Pylon ducem suum misit. Is, ut fidem oppidanis faceret Methonem in regis potestatem venisse, magistratum reipublicae, qui Methone erat in vinculis adductum, eis ostendit cum civibus Venetis nonnullis. Quibus visis, ea condicione ut neque libertatem neque quicquam ex rebus suis amitterent, oppidum regi tradiderunt.

35   At classis Veneta cum Zacynthum reverteretur, magna coorta tempestate, cursum non tenuit; itaque navibus omnibus disiectis, nonnullae longinquas insulas Cretamque usque delatae, vel amissis gubernaculis vel malo infracto vel dissutis contignationibus, iactura facta aegreque se in tutum receperunt; triremis una impacta litori salvis hominibus interiit. Coronem post haec cum magna

48

they to do so that when they saw the rest rushing off, even those who were guarding the walls against the Turkish army on the other side of town ran there themselves, deserting their posts and leaving the walls bare of defenders. When the enemy army noticed this, they seized the opportunity thus presented and mounting on scaling-ladders and killing the few defenders, forced their way into the town through the breaks in the walls made by their artillery.

Once the reinforcements and supplies had been taken off the 34 ships, the townspeople, commanders and soldiers were apprised of the situation and hurried to face the enemy in the middle of the town. A fierce battle then ensued, but though they fought long and hard and slew a good many of them, the numbers of the enemy grew ever greater, filling and jamming all the streets, so that in the end, surrounded and hemmed in on all sides, nearly all of them were killed, including two ship captains who had made their way there and a great many oarsmen. The surviving townspeople set fires throughout the town, prepared to burn all their property and kinsfolk. And so the town was taken, in flames and half burned down, although the Venetians at least defended themselves late into the night. When the town was taken, the sultan sent his commander to Navarino. In order to convince the townspeople that Methoni had come into the sultan's power, the commander showed them the Republic's governor, who had been brought from Methoni in chains, along with some Venetian citizens. On seeing them, they surrendered the town to the sultan on condition that they would lose none of their property or their freedom.

As the Venetian fleet was returning to Zante, a great storm 35 arose and they were unable to hold to their course, and so, with the ships all scattered, some were carried all the way to Crete and the distant islands. Suffering damage from the loss of the rudder, a broken mast, or shattered timbers, they managed with some difficulty to reach safety. One galley was driven ashore and was lost, but its men were saved. After that, one of the Turkish command-

exercitus parte unus ex ducibus, ab rege missus, oppidanis proposuit sese, antequam oppidum obsidione cingeretur, regi dederent; fore ut bonis condicionibus uti possent; sin vim exspectarent, omnes ad unum interituros. Quibus intellectis rebus, Coronaei, casu Methonensium perterriti, spretis praefectorum imperiis, qui se ad propugnationem comparaverant, aequissimis condicionibus ducem intromiserunt.

36   Rex deinde, Naupliam eadem qua Coronem celeritate suo se imperio adiecturum existimans, exercitus partem in Naupliorum fines induxit; missoque ad oppidum cum suis equitibus Paulo Contareno, cive Veneto egregia virtute, Bernardi Contareni (eius qui bello Neapolitano Epirotarum equitum praefectus mortem obierat) fratre, qui Corone uxorem duxerat illisque in regionibus erat notissimus, quemque rex, ut ad id uteretur, Corone in deditionem recepta habere secum voluerat, iussit illum oppidanis suadere ut se regi dederent. Is medio in sermone, quem cum Naupliis, ad urbis muros atque portam vocatis, ingressus fuerat, equo incitato equitibus imprudentibus se subripuit; atque in oppidum, vallo saltu equi superato, est receptus. Oppidani primo, cum Pauli hortatu ac studio, tum per sese plane paratissimi, magno animo impetum hostium sustinuerunt egressique praeterea per occasiones proelia nonnulla secundiora fecerunt. Postea vero quam rex cum reliquo exercitu eo venit, portas clauserunt et munierunt; itaque inclusi magna se virtute atque constantia tuebantur. Interim ex classe Thracia, quam rex Naupacto, ut terrorem hostibus incuteret, Naupliam veterem convenire universam voluerat, naves tri-

ers was sent to Coron by the sultan with the majority of his army, and proposed that the townsfolk should surrender themselves to the sultan before the town was laid under siege. They would be able to get good terms, he said, but if they waited till it came to a fight, they would perish to a man. On this understanding, and terrified at the fall of Methoni, the people of Coron ignored the orders of their magistrates, who were prepared to put up a defense, and admitted the Turkish commander on very reasonable terms.

Thinking to add Nauplia to his realm with the same speed that 36 he had added Coron, the sultan then marched part of his army into Nauplian territory. A Venetian citizen of great courage, Paolo Contarini (the brother of the Bernardo Contarini who had met his death in the Neapolitan war as captain of the stradiots), had taken a wife at Coron and was extremely well known in the area. After taking the surrender of Coron, the sultan had decided to keep Contarini by him so he could make use of him for the following purpose: he sent him to Nauplia with a company of Turkish cavalry and instructions to persuade the townspeople to surrender to the sultan. Summoning the Nauplians to the walls and the city gate, Contarini had entered negotiations with them when he bolted his horse, got away from the unsuspecting cavalry, and jumping over the rampart on his horse was taken into the town. Ready for battle on their own account but also spurred on by Contarini's eager encouragement, the townspeople initially put up a spirited defense under the enemy onslaught, even venturing outside the walls when opportunity offered and carrying off some successful engagements. But after the sultan arrived with the rest of his army, they shut the gates and strengthened them, and under blockade in this way defended themselves with great courage and firmness of purpose. In the meantime, the sultan having arranged for his entire fleet to leave Lepanto and converge on Monemvasia in order to strike terror into the enemy, thirty ships from the fleet

ginta Aeginam ad insulam missae oppidum capiunt; relictisque regio nomine qui praeessent, Naupliam revertuntur.

37   Haec dum sic administrarentur, Benedictus Pisaurus, Corcyram deinde Zacynthum profectus, dies ibi aliquot, antequam classis, quae propter tempestatem aberraverat, eo conveniret, se continuit. Coacta classe navium longarum maiorum duodeviginti, minorum viginti quinque, onerariarum plus viginti, quam quidem paucorum dierum spatio magna cum diligentia, tum vero etiam severitate adhibita, remigibus, militibus rebusque omnibus ornatiorem melioremque reddiderat, ad hostium classem insequendam sese promovet, eo animo ut, si assequi posset, proelium committeret. Sed rex, de illius ad Zacynthum adventu certior factus, suae classis praefectis ut domum redirent Byzantiumque se reciperent imperavit. Posteroque die ipse, qui quidem non magnopere suis iam copiis confidebat, propterea quod neque parvam neque sane spernendam militum equitumque partem eorum qui Methonem obsedissent eo in bello expugnationeque amiserat, omni cum exercitu abiit.

38   Eodem tempore Pisaurus, Naupliam speculatoriis praemissis navibus, classem Thraciam et exercitum abiisse certior factus, Aeginam contendit, expositisque militibus Turcas qui praeerant interfecit, eorum duce capto, atque insulam reipublicae restituit; Mitylenen deinde triremibus levioribus accelerans, quo appulsos hostes intellexerat, ferro atque igni omnia demetens, praedam et quidem opulentam quam abegerat remigibus et militibus concessit; posteroque die Tenedum diripuit, incendit; classisque hostium fugientis atque in euripi[5] angustias iam ingressae reliquias assecutus, naves complures extremo in agmine cum hominibus cepit; fixisque utroque in litore non unis crucibus, captos Europae atque Asiae spectaculo reste suspendit, agros et vicos depopulatus, ut qui oras incolerent magnopere perterrerentur. Samothraciam ad

were despatched to the island of Aegina and took the town. Leaving men behind to govern it in the sultan's name, they returned to Monemvasia.

While all this was going on, Benedetto Pesaro had reached 37 Corfu and then Zante, but had to remain there for some days before the fleet arrived, having been driven off course by a storm. He collected a fleet of 18 great galleys, 25 light galleys, and more than 20 merchantmen, and in the space of a few days by dint of his great energy as well as severe discipline he had brought it up to a good fighting standard with sailors and soldiers and all the necessary equipment. He then advanced to attack the enemy fleet, with the intention of joining battle if he could catch up with them. But when the sultan learned of his arrival at Zante, he ordered the captains of his fleet to go home and withdraw to Constantinople. The next day, not being entirely confident of his own forces, since he had lost an appreciable part of his footsoldiers and horse besieging Methoni in that engagement, he himself left with all his army.

At the same time Pesaro had sent spy-ships on ahead to 38 Nauplia, and on learning that the Turkish fleet and army had left, he made haste for Aegina. Putting his infantry ashore there, he killed the Turks in charge of it, took their captain prisoner, and recovered the island for the Republic. He then hurried with his light galleys to Mytilene, where he had learned the enemy had landed, and laid waste with fire and sword all before him, giving the quite considerable booty he carried off to his sailors and soldiers. The next day he sacked and burned Tenedos. Catching the remnant of the enemy fleet in its flight when it had already entered the narrows of the strait,[35] he took a good many ships at the rear of the column along with their crews. After ravaging the fields and villages, he put up a number of crosses on either shore and had the captives hung so they could be seen from both Europe and Asia, to strike terror into the inhabitants of the coast. He thereupon

insulam post haec eadem celeritate adveniens, cum intellexisset oppidanos aegerrime Turcarum imperium perpeti, Aloisio Decanali, triremis praefecto, ad oppidum misso, eos libentissimos in deditionem recepit; petentibusque civem Venetum, qui praeesset, pollicitus est se missurum. Illi partem decimam suorum fructuum quotannis ei se daturos receperunt. Deinde Carysto direpta ad naves longas maiores onerariasque rediens, Naupliam se contulit; municipibusque et militibus collaudatis, stipendio quos oportuit recreavit et sua liberalitate sublevavit. Iis confectis rebus discedens, dum Corones litora praetervehitur, de Carolo Contareno, qui magistratus reipublicae Pylo praefuerat oppidumque situ et natura communitum hostibus nulla coactus vi obsidioneque tradiderat, in suae navis prora supplicium sumpsit.

39   Ibi cognoscit Hispaniae regum classem reipublicae auxilio missam Zacynthum venisse. Ii enim reges, Aloisii Galliae regis praedicatione permoti, qui regnum Neapolitanum bello aggredi statuisset, tum classe ab rege Thracio comparata, ne insulam Siciliam sine praesidio relinquerent, classem et ipsi confecerunt illoque miserunt, Consalvo Ferdinando praefecto, qui bello Neapolitano dux eorum fuerat. Eam classem ut reges auxilio reipublicae vellent esse, posteaquam suis iam finibus nihil timerent, senatus ab iis impetraverat, Alexandro adiuvante. Ea erat navium plus quinquaginta; quibus in navibus milites imposuerant numero ad septem milia.

40   Cognito Consalvi adventu, Pisaurus Zacynthum ad illum venit. Quem quidem reipublicae magnopere prodesse cupientem cum repperisset, rebus belli rationibusque omnibus una cum illo communicatis, ex ipsius et reliquorum Hispanarum navium praefectorum, quos Consalvus in concilium adhibuerat, et legatorum sen-

made with equal speed for the island of Samothrace, having learned that the townspeople were chafing under Turkish rule, and sending the galley captain Alvise da Canal to the town, received their willing surrender. When they asked for a Venetian citizen to govern them, he promised he would send one, to whom they undertook to give a tithe of their produce every year. Then, after sacking Carystos, he returned to his great galleys and merchantmen and made his way to Nauplia. With praise for the townspeople and the soldiery, he revived their spirits with pay or alleviated their hardships with his bounty, as the case required. After seeing to this business, Pesaro left, and as he sailed past the coast of Coron had Carlo Contarini executed on the prow of his own ship. Contarini had been the Venetian governor at Navarino, a town well defended by its natural setting, and though under no compulsion from force or siege, he had surrendered it to the enemy.

At that point Pesaro learned that a fleet of the Spanish sovereigns had been sent in aid of the Republic and had arrived at Zante. The sovereigns had been alarmed by public statements of King Louis of France, who had decided to make war on the Kingdom of Naples, and also by the Turkish sultan's putting together a fleet, so they themselves assembled a fleet so as not to leave the island of Sicily unprotected. This was sent there under the leadership of Gonzalo Fernández de Córdoba, who had been their captain in the Neapolitan war. With Pope Alexander's help, the Senate had prevailed upon the Spanish sovereigns to have this fleet assist the Republic once their fears for their own territory had passed. It comprised more than 50 ships, on which they had put about 7,000 soldiers.

When he learned of Gonzalo's arrival, Pesaro went to meet him at Zante. Finding him very eager to help the Republic, he shared with him his view of the war situation and his whole strategy. By agreement with Gonzalo himself and the other Spanish captains that he had advising him, and with the proveditors, he resolved to

39

40

tentia, statuit ad Methonem recuperandam una proficisci. Eam ad profectionem atque bellum quod res multae materiae indigebat, cum ad castella, quae parare instituerant, excitanda, tum ad navium scaphas contegendas, quibus in primis uti decreverant, dato omnibus qui aderant iureiurando, ne quis quid enuntiaret, concilio dimisso, Cephallenem ad insulam, quae silvis admodum abundabat, uterque suam classem adduxit. Illis prope diebus, cum ex Ioannis Crispi, de quo dictum est, qui Naxum insulam obtinebat, liberis is qui natu erat maior Mathei Lauredani filiam in matrimonium duxisset, senatui placuit ut magistratus reipublicae amplius eo non mitteretur, Naxiique Ioannis filio iam adulto restituerentur, dum is paterni regni formam ne vellet imitari, senatusque liberalitate ad iustitiam et temperantiam uteretur. Interim autem, dum ad Cephallenem materia caeditur, et turres reliquaque, quae sane plurima eius belli administratio requirebat, per fabros conficiuntur, ne reliqui milites tempus temere contererent, communi consilio statuerunt Cephallenes oppidum aggredi, turpe futurum existimantes, si ab insula re non temptata discessissent; posse Turcas gloriari duabus classibus tam paratis atque tantis animum ad id capiendum defuisse.

41   Iis constitutis rebus, navis una oneraria trium milium amphorarum, Genuae ab Aloisio rege Galliae auxilio reipublicae comparata, Cephallenem appellitur, ut Pisauro praesto esset. Ad eius navis praefectum, qui erat infirma valetudine, Pisaurus legatos misit salutatum actumque regi gratias, quod in rempublicam liberalis tam opportuno tempore fuisset. Praefectus exspectare sese navem alteram dixit, quae item Genuae instructa secum una solvisset tempestateque acta cursum non tenuisset; earum navium et militum mille quingentorum, qui in illis erant, trium mensium stipendia regem subministravisse; ea stipendia desinere ad diem duodecimum Kalendarum Decembris. Is autem dies, quo die illa dicebantur, erat ante diem sextum Iduum Novembrium. Eis si na-

set out with them to recover Methoni. The expedition and forthcoming campaign called for a good deal of timber, not only for
constructing the fortresses they intended to make, but also for
cladding the ships' skiffs, which they would mainly be using. After
an oath swearing them to secrecy was taken by all present, the
meeting broke up and each of them took his fleet to the island of
Cephalonia, which had trees in abundance. At about that time,
the eldest son of Giovanni Crispo (the former lord of Naxos that I
mentioned above)[36] having taken the daughter of Matteo Loredan
in marriage, the Senate decided that a Venetian governor would
no longer be sent there, and that the Naxians would be restored to
Giovanni's now adult son, provided that he would not rule them
in the manner of his father and would avail himself of the Senate's
generosity with justice and moderation. In the meantime, while
the timber was being cut at Cephalonia, and the towers and the
other things needed in quantity for the prosecution of the war
were being constructed by carpenters, it was decided by common
agreement to attack the town of Cephalonia, so as not to have the
rest of the soldiers waste their time pointlessly. They reckoned
that it would be shameful to leave the island without making the
attempt, for the Turks would be able to boast that two such large
and well-equipped fleets had lacked the spirit to take it.

With these arrangements in place, a cargo vessel of 3,000 bar-   41
rels, which had been got ready at Genoa by King Louis to assist
the Republic, put in at Cephalonia to be at Pesaro's disposal.
Pesaro sent envoys to welcome the ship's captain, who was in poor
health, and to render thanks to the king for his generosity to the
Republic at such a critical time. The captain said that he was
awaiting a second ship, which had also been fitted out at Genoa
and had set sail with him, but had been driven off course by a
storm; the king had provided three months' pay for the ships and
the 1,500 soldiers on them, which was due to run out on 20 November. Now this was said on 8 November. If they wished to use

vibus post eum diem uti vellent, ipsos stipendia praestare oportere. Ad ea Pisaurus respondi iussit se nisi de senatus auctoritate
nihil acturum litterasque de eo ad senatum daturum. Praefectus
ubi ei rei moram esse interpositam vidit, nactus idoneam tempestatem, vela fecit atque abiit. De navi altera post illa nihil est audi-
tum.

42   Pisaurus interea Consalvusque, tormentis muralibus eductis,
oppidi muros verberare complures dies institerunt. Nam quod erat
loco editiore, monti etiam pluribus a partibus praerupto oppidum
impositum, ea res magna cum difficultate administrabatur. Deinde
suo cuique legatorum et praefectorum navium attributo munere,
ut quam quisque oppidi partem signo dato aggrederetur irrumpe-
reque conaretur antea cognosceret, statuerunt experiri quantum in
hostibus ad propugnationem animi virtutisque inesset. Erant autem, quemadmodum a profugis intellectum est, milites oppidi
praesidio trecenti. Die oppugnationis dicta, eiusmodi tempestates
fuerunt ut res differri oportuerit. Demum pluviis remittentibus,
pilis ferreis frequentioribus eiaculatis, omnes se ad muros contulerunt; conscendereque scalis positis aggressi, hostibus saxis, sagittis,
omni missilium telorum genere acerrime se defendentibus, oppidum capere non potuerunt. Itaque nonnullis interfectis, vulneratis
compluribus, se in castra receperunt; quorum ex numero fuere
Hispani praefecti aliquot Venetique cives sex, et Gurlinus, vir
egregia explorataque virtute, quem Pisaurus Nauplia obsessa plurimum oppidanis profuisse et praeclara multa oppido tuendo insti-
tuisse effecisseque cognoverat et secum abductum militibus suis
omnibus tum praefecerat. Atque is, magno nostrorum omnium et
Consalvi dolore, qui ei largiter iam tribuebat, paucis post diebus

the ships after that date, he continued, they should provide the pay themselves. To this Pesaro told the envoys to reply that he would do nothing without the authority of the Senate and would send them a letter about it. When the captain saw that resolution of the matter involved delay, he made sail and departed on a favorable wind. Nothing was heard of the second ship after that.

Pesaro and Gonzalo, meanwhile, brought out their siege-artillery and set about pounding the walls of the town of Cephalonia for quite a few days; because the town was situated on high ground, actually on a mountain that fell sheer away in many places, this could only be done with great difficulty. After giving each of the proveditors and ship captains their individual assignments, so they should know in advance what part of the town they were to attack and try to storm it when the signal was given, they determined to find out how much spirit and fight there was in the enemy for defending the place — they had learned from fugitives that the town's garrison had 300 soldiers. On the day set for the attack, the storms were such that they were obliged to put the matter off. When the rains finally slackened off, after a barrage of a considerable quantity of iron cannonballs, they all made their way to the walls. They set out to climb the wall with scaling-ladders, but were unable to take the town, as the enemy put up a fierce defense with rocks, arrows, and all sorts of missiles. With some slain, and a good number wounded, they therefore retreated to the camp. Among them were some Spanish captains and six Venetian citizens, and Gurlino of Ravenna, a man of outstanding and proven valor. Knowing that he had been of the utmost assistance to the townspeople in the siege of Nauplia, and had organised and carried out many heroic deeds in the defense of the town, Pesaro had taken him along and put him in command of the entire infantry force. To the great distress of all our men and of Gonzalo, who had already formed a great respect for him, he died a few days later. After suffering this loss, the commanders told the

42

est mortuus. Eo accepto detrimento, duces vallum excitari usque eo, ut munitionem quam hostes intra oppidum deiecto muro fecerant superaret, suis militibus mandaverunt.

43   Dum haec ad Cephallenem geruntur, Pylos per insidias ad rempublicam rediit. Erat in Pisauri trireme miles signifer, Demetrius quidam Methonensis. Is amicum Epirotam item militem in Pyli praesidio cum haberet, ad eum bis terve amicitiae nomine ubi venit, hominem spe pollicitationibusque impulit, sibi ut socius magni facinoris vellet esse. Re constituta ad Pisaurum revertitur. Pisaurus ei milites quinquaginta ex omni classe deligendi potestatem facit; eos ei milites attribuit. Ille cum iis trireme impositus Pylon noctu proficiscitur, expositusque clam in Epirotae domum, oppidi muro vicinam, se atque milites occuluit, quoad die inlucescente portae oppidi aperirentur; apertis portis Demetrius cum suis in oppidum irrumpit et Turcas, qui oppidi erant praesidio, imparatos obtruncat circiter quinquaginta, paucis elapsis qui se muro deiecerunt. Ita oppidum recipitur. Ad id Pisaurus triremes duas cum militibus et Hieronymo Pisano legato, qui praeesset oppidumque communiret, Venetoque cive Sylvestro Trono, quem is magistratum ibi relinqueret, statim misit; nam quod erat portu egregio, reipublicae fore usui ad classes recipiendas et tuendas mirum in modum existimabatur. Eo capto equites centum quinquaginta cum uxoribus et liberis Corone se Pylon e vestigio contulerunt oppidumque munierunt.

44   Sed iam vallo ad Cephallenem excitato, uti de superiore loco nostri in oppidum introspicerent, duces oppugnare, quibus a partibus poterant, uno tempore sunt adorti, eo uterque animo eaque cura ut utrius plures essent eo in bello partes non facile dignosceres, Consalvusque civis esse Venetus et ipse videretur. Neque eius quidem milites ullo in munere a nostris se militibus relinqui susti-

soldiers to raise a rampart high enough to rise above the defenses which the enemy had made within the town after the wall was knocked down.

While this was going on at Cephalonia, Navarino was restored 43 to the Republic by a trick. There was a certain soldier in Pesaro's galley, a standard-bearer named Demetrio of Methoni. He had an Albanian friend, himself a soldier, in the garrison of Navarino. He approached him two or three times as a friend, and by holding out hopes and promises prevailed upon the man to agree to act with him in a great venture. With that settled, he returned to Pesaro. Pesaro gave him the choice of 50 soldiers from throughout the fleet, and assigned the men to him. Boarding a galley with them, Demetrio set off for Navarino at night, and when secretly put ashore, he hid himself and his soldiers in the Albanian's house near the town wall until the gates of the town should be opened at daybreak. Once the gates were open, Demetrio broke into the town with his men and taking them unawares slaughtered about 50 Turks of the garrison, save for a few that slipped away by jumping down from the walls. And so the town was recovered. Pesaro immediately sent there two galleys with infantry and Girolamo Pisani as proveditor to take command of them and secure the town, and a Venetian citizen, Silvestro Tron, to stay there as governor; since it had a fine port, it was thought that it would serve the Republic extremely well for harboring fleets and keeping them safe. Once it was taken, 150 cavalry, with wives and children, made their way at once from Coron to Navarino and fortified the town.

But with the rampart at Cephalonia now built up so that our 44 side could look down into the town from above, the commanders began a simultaneous attack from any point they could, both of them with such spirit and application that it was hard to tell which took the greater part in the fight — Gonzalo himself seemed to be a true Venetian. Nor did his soldiers allow themselves to be outstripped by ours in any task, being tough men and accustomed

nebant, homines duri parcoque victu assueti et cum audaci in primis virtute, tum maxime habiles qui oppidorum oppugnationibus adhiberentur. Ea in aggressione Marcus Orius, navium onerariarum praefectus, una cum Hispano homine impigro, quem ei Consalvus muneris socium dederat, militesque aliquot se in muro atque munitionibus primi omnium illatis signis ostenderunt. Ea re hostes perterriti cedere seque recipere in arcem oppidi cum vellent, irrumpentibus omni ex parte reliquis, caesi captique sunt, praeter paucos, qui se primo impetu in arcem intulerunt; qui tamen paulo post se Consalvo dediderunt, cum Venetorum iram, quos et ipsi saepius elusissent et rex eorum maximis incommodis affecisset, non iniuria pertimescerent.

45   Cephallene in reipublicae dicionem anni exitu redacta, oppido Aloisius Salomonius, arci Ioannes Venerius, toti insulae Franciscus Leo a Pisauro sunt praefecti dati in annos duos. Arx etiam ut multo communitior fieret institutum. Missaque Pylon navis oneraria magna, qua in navi Coronei qui cum familiis eo venerant Cephallenem adveherentur. Nam quod eam insulam propter bonitatem agrorum maxime esse feracem intelligebant, et illi qui libere Pylo exire atque agros colere hostibus Methonem obtinentibus non poterant, et multi praeterea homines, Turcas perosi, eo ad incolendum e continenti commigraverunt. Quam quidem ad rem portus perampli perque optimi facultas, quo nullus est eo toto mari fere praestantior, magnum adiumentum afferebat. Itaque parvo temporis spatio a magna est advenarum multitudine coli coepta, cum per biennium a classibus reipublicae vexata cultoribus infrequentior fuisset.

46   Illis diebus triremes duae, Naupliam a Pisauro missae, dum redeunt, biremes Thracias quattuor expugnaverunt, birememque

to meagre rations, and not only superlatively bold and courageous but also extremely useful in storming towns. In this attack the captain of the merchant fleet, Marco Orio, together with a lively Spaniard assigned by Gonzalo to partner him in the action, and a number of soldiers were the first to advance and show themselves on the walls and fortifications. Terrified at this turn of events, the enemy were ready to give way and retreat into the town's fortress when the others broke in on all sides, and they were all killed or captured, except for a few who had entered the citadel at the initial assault; those men, however, surrendered to Gonzalo a little while later, since they quite rightly feared the anger of the Venetians, whom they had often mocked and on whom their sultan had inflicted the greatest damage.

With Cephalonia brought back under the Republic's sway at the end of the year, Pesaro appointed Luigi Salamone governor of the town, Giovanni Venier of the fortress, Francesco Leone of the island as a whole, all for two years. It was further resolved that the fortress should be made much stronger. A large cargo vessel was sent to Navarino to transport to Cephalonia the people of Coron, who had gone there with their families. They were aware that the island was specially fertile thanks to the quality of its soil, and on account of that, those who had been unable to go out freely from Navarino to cultivate their fields while the enemy controlled Methoni, and many people besides who hated the Turks, migrated to Cephalonia from the mainland to live there. This process was greatly helped by Cephalonia's having the advantage of a very large and extremely good harbor, almost without equal in that whole stretch of sea. And so within a short time it began to be inhabited by a great mass of foreigners, after having become rather depopulated during two years of being harassed by the fleets of the Republic.

At about that time, two galleys sent to Lepanto by Pesaro captured four small Turkish galleys on their way back, and they recov-

45

1501

46

63

unam Venetam, quam illi ad Aeginam insulam ceperant, recupera-
verunt. Consalvus, qui suam classem in aqua menses complures
habuisset magnamque navium partem inutilem ad navigandum
brevi futuram videret — Methones autem recuperandae negotium
Pisaurus in aliud tempus distulisset, quod Turcae, Pylo amisso,
eam militibus apprime communierant diligentiusque tuebantur —
se reversurum vere ineunte pollicitus, ad classem reficiendam primis anni diebus in Siciliam rediit. Ante autem quam proficisceretur, vini Cretici amphorae quingentae, casei librae sexaginta milia
ei dono a Pisauro datae. Alia etiam ab urbe munera pretiosiora a
senatu mitti nuntiatum; quae ille, senatui gratias agens, se non cupere prae se tulit; suorum enim regum in rempublicam benevolentiae causa venisse; quibus satis omnibus pro muneribus esset
par atque mutua senatus in illos voluntas et benevolentia. Senatus
tamen, posteaquam de Consalvi abitu est ei nuntiatum, legem tulit, uti Consalvo civitas cum iure comitiorum daretur, civisque Venetus cum libris argenti fabrefacti ducentis sexaginta sex in Siciliam ad illum mitteretur, qui eum de republica optime meritum
diceret. Lectusque Gabriel Maurus, unus ex magistratibus qui res
maritimas in senatu procurant, paulo post est profectus.

47   Pisaurus cum sciret in sinu Ambracio naves longas complures,
quas hostes fabricari curavissent, esse iam deductas, navibus longis
aliquot onerariaque una Cephallenae praesidio relictis, decimo
Kalendas Februarias sua cum classe triremium leviorum quattuordecim, graviorum octo, navium onerariarum quattuor — reliquas
enim missas fecerat — ad insulam Leucadiam est profectus. Eius in
insulae portu, in quo nihil offendi poterat, ex omni triremium numero levioribus lectis octo, atque in illas ex reliquis navibus quos
visum est remigibus et militibus impositis, cum iis ad sinum
Ambracium provehitur, reliquis navibus in portu relictis. Is habet

ered a Venetian one which the Turks had taken at the island of
Aegina. Gonzalo had kept his fleet at sea for many months and
saw that a large part of his ships would soon be unseaworthy
(Pesaro indeed had postponed the task of retaking Methoni, because after the loss of Navarino the Turks had greatly reinforced
its garrison and had it under close guard), and so promising to return at the onset of spring, he returned to Sicily at the beginning
of the new year to refurbish his fleet. But before he set out, Pesaro
made him a present of 500 barrels of malmsey and 60,000 pounds
of cheese, with the announcement that other more valuable gifts
were being sent from Venice by the Senate. Gonzalo thanked the
Senate for the gifts, but maintained that he had no desire for
them: he had come on account of his sovereigns' goodwill toward
the Republic, and the Senate's matching and reciprocal sympathy
and goodwill toward them would suffice to take the place of any
reward. On receiving the news of Gonzalo's departure, the Senate
nevertheless passed a law granting him citizenship and noble status, and ordered that a Venetian citizen should be sent to him in
Sicily with 266 pounds of wrought silver and a declaration that he
had done the Republic a great service. Gabriel Moro was chosen,
one of the magistrates charged with the supervision of maritime
affairs in the Senate,[37] and he set out shortly thereafter.

Pesaro knew that a good many warships which the enemy had   47
arranged to build had already been launched in the Gulf of Arta.
Leaving behind some warships and a merchantman to protect
Cephalonia, he accordingly set out on 23 January for the island of
Lefkada with his fleet of fourteen light galleys, eight great galleys,
and four merchantmen — the rest he had let go. In the harbor of
the island, where he would encounter no obstacles, he picked eight
light galleys from the entire galley fleet, and put on board oarsmen
and soldiers from the other ships as he thought best. He then
sailed out with them into the Gulf of Arta, leaving the other ships
in harbor. The gulf has a very narrow entrance for the passage of

sinus aditum perangustum, qua naves commeant, ut lapide manu iacto fere traiciatur. Reliqua latitudo, vadis brevioribus impedita, navigia triremesque non recipit. In eius ore sinus turris est communita, ad arcendos si qui ingredi vi experiantur. Pisaurus citatis remigibus dum turrim praetervehitur, iactu[6] ab ea tormentorum tribus aut quattuor militibus interfectis, ad triremes Thracias numero undecim, rebus iam omnibus armamentisque instructas, processit.

48 Portus est in sinu Ambracio, in quem flumen, quod nunc appellatur Prevesa, influit. Eo in portu navalia ad tuendum locum idoneo sunt castello proxima; aditus vero ad portum eiusmodi, ut singulae tantum triremes ingredi possint. Iis in navalibus fabricatae naves Thraciae tum in portu stationem habebant. Eo ingressus Pisaurus, expositisque militibus, hostes castello egressos, quique naves adservabant, acerrime cum iis congressos fudit, incensisque aedificiis, praeda etiam rerum ad armandas naves comparatarum ingenti facta, triremes hostium novas omnes remulco e portu abduxit; duas veteres, quae semiplenae aqua ad litus erant deligatae, incendit, cum iis in rebus administrandis quadraginta ex suis, praeda cupidius allectos temereque procurrentes, amisisset. Abductas deinde lateri suarum navium adglutinans atque ad turrim conversas trahens, reliquis omnibus incolumibus, ad eos quos in portu Leucadiae reliquerat rediit, Corcyramque omnibus cum navibus ad supplendam classem ante diem Kalendarum Februarii venit. Ibi Hieronymo Contareno legato reperto, qui ex Leucadiae litoribus valetudinis (ut aiebat) causa, nullo Pisauri permissu, Corcyram discesserat, eum ignominia notavit, ut legatione praefecturisque omnibus annos duos careret.

49 Eodem tempore, uti qui pro republica mortem oppetiissent inornati ne relinquerentur, in senatu lex est lata, ut Gurlini Raven-

ships, so much so that it is hardly a stone's throw across. The remaining stretch is obstructed by shallows and does not admit sailing vessels and galleys. At the mouth of the gulf there is a fortified tower to keep out anyone trying to enter by force. Spurring on his oarsmen as he passed in front of the tower, three or four soldiers being killed by artillery fire from it, Pesaro headed for the Turkish galleys, eleven in number, and now well supplied with equipment and gunnery.

There is a harbor in the Gulf of Arta into which flows a river   48
now called the Prevesa. In the harbor are shipyards, next to a fortress designed to defend the place, but the approach to the harbor is such that only one galley at a time can enter. The Turkish ships constructed in the shipyards were anchored in the harbor at the time. Entering the harbor, Pesaro put his soldiers ashore. The enemy that had left the fortress and those that were guarding the ships engaged the infantry in a fierce fight, but Pesaro routed them, and after setting fire to the buildings, and taking besides a vast haul of material meant for arming the vessels, he pulled all the enemy's new ships out of the harbor on a tow-rope. Two old ships, which were tied to the shore half full of water, he burned, though in carrying out these actions he lost 40 of his men who had rushed forward recklessly in their greed for booty. Then he attached the ships he had carried off to the side of his own galleys and dragged them so that they faced the tower and protected the rest. He then returned to the men he had left in the harbor of Lefkada, and with all his ships went to Corfu to refit the fleet on 1 February. Finding there the providitor Girolamo Contarini, who for reasons of health (as he said) had left the shores of Lefkada for Corfu without his permission, Pesaro gave him a formal reprimand, barring him from the office of provveditor and any magistracy for two years.

At the same time, so that those who had met their death in the   49
service of the Republic should not go uncommemorated, the Sen-

natis, qui Cephallenae, Antonii Fabri, Pauli Epirotae, praefectorum militum, qui Methone interfecti fuerant, liberis, quoad vive-
rent, pensiones annuae curarentur; ipsorum praeterea filiabus sex
dos sesquilibra auri singulis constituta. Neque multo post Aloisii
Michaelis liberis, et Ioannis Maripetri fratribus, quos utrosque,
triremium praefectos auxilio Methonensium a proimperatore missos, ab hostibus interfectos dixeramus, arcis Mestrinae itemque
Patavinae ad Medoaci in oppidum influxum praefecturas, alteris
per annos quindecim, alteris quoad eorum maior natu viveret, et
uni virgini dotem civitas dono dedit. Reliquis triremium praefectis
qui Methone capti eodem impetu fuerant seque pecunia redeme-
rant, Alexandro Gotio Corcyrensi in ea insula magistratus, Nicolao Cucaro Hydruntino in sua urbe item magistratus et auri libra
unciaeque septem annuae, Iacobo Balbo Parensi auri itidem[7] libra
unciaeque. Item singulis omnium tributorum immunitas attributa,
praemia insuper in complures vivos qui se fortiter atque amanter
gesserant ex Pisauri litteris honorifice collata; dataque lectis ad id
magistratibus cura, ut Methonensium quibus quidem aut parentes
aut fratres aut liberi pro republica interfecti fuissent, qui Venetias
venissent, causas cognoscerent deque eis ad patres referrent, ut pro
cuiusque incommodis et iacturis a senatu sarcirentur aut omnino
sublevarentur. Latum praeterea de Naupliis ut eis bello confecto
immunitas per annos decem concederetur, domusque eorum, quas
ipsi dirui permisissent ut oppidum communitius fieret, reipublicae
pecunia restituerentur.

50   Iis rebus domi forisque administratis, Caesar, Alexandri filius,
cui paulo ante a republica, petente patre, cum iure comitiorum ci-

ate passed a law that annual pensions were to be paid to the sons of Gurlino of Ravenna, killed at Cephalonia, and those of the constables Antonio Fabbri and Paolo of Albania, killed at Methoni, for as long as they lived; further dowries of one and a half gold pounds each were laid down for their six daughters. Soon afterwards the state made a gift of the command of the fortresses of Mestre and Padua, where the Brenta enters the town, to the sons of Alvise Michiel and the brothers of Giovanni Malipiero, both of whom, as I mentioned,[38] were killed by the enemy when they were sent by the acting captain-general as ship captains in aid of Methoni, the former to have it for fifteen years, the latter for as long as the eldest lived; and a daughter was given a dowry. Awards were made to the other ship captains captured at Methoni in the same attack, who had arranged their own ransom: to Alessandro Gozio of Corfu a magistracy in that island; to Niccolò Cuccaro of Otranto likewise a magistracy of his city and an annual pension of a pound and seven ounces of gold, and the same amount to Giacomo Balbi of Paros. Also granted to each was freedom from all taxation, and additional honorific rewards were bestowed by Pesaro's letters on many still alive who had acted with valor and patriotism. Specially appointed magistrates were given the task of investigating the cases of citizens of Methoni who had come to Venice, whose parents or brothers or sons had been killed fighting for the Republic, and of reporting to the senators on them so that they might be compensated, or at least assisted, by the Senate in proportion to the difficulties and losses each had experienced. A further law was passed that at the conclusion of the war the people of Nauplia should be granted exemption from taxes for ten years, and that their homes, which they had themselves allowed to be destroyed to make the town more secure, should be restored at the Republic's expense.

Such was the state of things at home and abroad when Alexander's son Cesare Borgia, to whom citizenship and noble status had   50

69

vitas data fuerat, puellam ex Elisabetae Metaurensium reginae fa-
mulatu, ad Carratium, reipublicae militibus praefectum, cui erat
nuptui tradita, proficiscentem, medio inter Ariminum Raven-
namque itinere, missis Cesena suis equitibus, vi rapuit, comitatu
eius pulso, vulneratis compluribus. Eius ille oppidi paucis ante
mensibus regnum obtinuerat, Alexandro tradente, tum Pisauri
atque Arimini, republica aegre illa quidem quod ad Ariminum attinet ac paene subinvita, sed tamen, ut perpetuis Alexandri postulatis precibusque satisfieret, una cum Aloisio rege Galliae, qui suas
ei copias iterum dederat, annuente atque permittente. Ea erat
puella mirae pulchritudinis. Itaque amore incensus adolescens,
cum pretio aut precibus assequi sese posse nihil videret, sumptis a
novo regno animis, ad vim faciendam se convertit et virgine per
scelus est potitus.

51   Ea re ad patres celeriter delata, decemvirum decreto Aloisius
Manentius est ad Caesarem eo ipso die iussus contendere (is erat
Fori Cornelii) questum de iniuria tam insigni, quam respublica
pro suis in eum beneficiis nihil meruisset, puellamque repetitum.
Posteroque die Aloisii regis legatus, re a patribus graviter apud illum expostulantibus cognita, sua sponte ad Caesarem iisdem cum
mandatis est profectus, cum eam fraudem atque iniuriam etiam ad
suum regem, qui Caesarem, ut Flaminia potiretur, adiuvisset, exis-
timaret pertinere. Nihiloque secius litterae sunt ad Alexandrum a
senatu datae, magna cum querela. Sed neque Manentius neque regis legatus quidquam apud eum valuerunt; nedum litterae ad patrem missae proficerent. Pernegavit enim ille suo iussu id fecisse,
qui puellam rapuissent, neque se, qui essent, adhuc quidem com-
perisse; repertis autem raptoribus, cui quidem rei omnem esset di-

been granted a little earlier by the Republic at his father's request, forcibly abducted a girl of the household of Elisabetta Gonzaga, Duchess of Urbino, on the road midway between Rimini and Ravenna. The girl had been on her way to Caracciolo, an officer of the Venetian army to whom she was betrothed, when Borgia sent his cavalry from Cesena and put her retinue to flight, with many of them wounded. He had become lord of that town a few months earlier, Alexander handing it over to him, and also of Pesaro and Rimini, something to which the Republic reluctantly and somewhat against her will (at least as regards Rimini) nevertheless assented and suffered to happen in order to satisfy Alexander's incessant requests and pleas, as did King Louis of France, who had again given Borgia his troops. The girl was amazingly beautiful. And so the young man, inflamed by passion and realizing that neither money nor pleading would get him anywhere, took courage from his new position of power and resorted to the use of force, taking criminal possession of the maiden.

These events were soon reported to the senators: Alvise 51 Manenti was ordered by decree of the Ten to go to Borgia that very day (he was at Imola) to lodge a complaint about this extraordinary outrage, which the Republic's kindnesses toward him had so little deserved, and to ask for the girl's return. On the following day King Louis' ambassador, who had learned of the matter from the senators' forceful complaints to him, of his own accord set out to go to Borgia with the same mission, since he regarded the offense and injury as touching his king as well, Louis having given Borgia help in taking control of Romagna. The Senate sent Pope Alexander a letter along the same lines, with much remonstration. But neither Manenti nor the king's ambassador got anywhere with Borgia, nor did the letter sent to his father do any good. He flatly denied that those who had abducted the girl had done so on his orders, nor had he yet discovered who they were. But once the kidnappers were found, which he would exert himself to bring

ligentiam adhibiturus, se daturum operam ut et rex et senatus Venetus et omnes homines intelligerent quam aegre tulerit suis in finibus id fuisse facinus atque flagitium perpetratum; puellas sibi non deesse quas habere facile possit, ne hac, tanta cum reipublicae offensione atque invidia et suo cum probro, per vim atque fraudem potiri concupierit. Patres verba sibi dari intellegentes, cum mittendis nuntiis ac litteris multos dies consumpsissent, quod rebus belli ab ea cogitatione avocabantur, Carratium, qui ad eos questum venerat, consolati, eius vindictam sceleris in aliud tempus distulerunt.

52 Post haec autem reipublicae legati, qui ad Vladislaum Pannoniae regem anno superiore missi fuerant, ut illum ad bellum in Turcas incitarent, foedus cum rege aliquando tandem percusserunt. Quo ex foedere bellum regi Thracio inferre omnibus copiis Vladislaus iubebatur; res vero publica mille auri libras tribus pensionibus regi Pannoniae mittere quotannis tenebatur, quoad bellum esset confectum. Ei foederi feriendo Alexander et auctoritatem adhibuit suam, misso Roma legato e cardinalium collegio, et auri libras annuas quadringentas[8] regi Pannoniae per triennium pollicitus est se daturum. Domi vero inter haec, ne ad bellum pecunia deesset, lex est lata, uti qui fundos atque agros in continenti possiderent pro quoque soli culti iugero siliquas argenti septem in aerarium conferrent, semel quidem tantum, praeter Carnos, quorum se in fines Turcae superiori anno intulissent. Litteraeque ad civitates datae, quae eas hortarentur tam duris reipublicae temporibus ne deessent atque urbem laborantem sublevarent.

53 Pisaurus, classe Corcyrae remigibus reliquisque rebus instaurata, ad naves longas quas Turcae in Loi fluminis ripis aedificave-

about, he would make sure the king and the Venetian Senate and everyone else knew how distressed he was that that disgraceful deed had been perpetrated in his territory. There was no lack of girls that he could easily have, without lusting to possess this particular one through criminal violence, to his own shame and with such great outrage and indignation on the part of the Republic. The senators realized that they were being deceived, but after spending many days in sending messengers and letters, they were called away from further consideration of the matter by the war. They expressed sympathy with Caracciolo, who had come to put his grievances before them, and postponed punishment of the crime to another time.

After that, ambassadors of the Republic who had been sent the   52
previous year to King Ladislas of Hungary to urge him to go to war against the Turks finally struck a treaty with the king. By the terms of the treaty, Ladislas was required to make war on the sultan of Turkey with his entire army, while the Republic for its part was obligated to send the king of Hungary each year 1,000 gold pounds in three installments, until the war was concluded. Alexander too lent his weight to the signing of the treaty with the despatch of an envoy from the college of cardinals, and he promised to give the king 400 gold pounds a year for three years. Meanwhile on the home front, a law was passed to ensure that there were sufficient funds for the war: those who possessed estates and farms on the mainland were to make the treasury a one-off payment of seven grains of silver for each acre[39] of land under cultivation, an exception being made for the people of Friuli whose territory the Turks had invaded the year before. Letters were sent to the subject towns, urging them not to fail the Republic in such hard times and to support Venice in her hour of difficulty.

Once his fleet had been replenished at Corfu with oarsmen and   53
so on, Pesaro turned his attention to capturing and burning the warships that the Turks had built on the banks of the Bojana and

rant atque in flumen deduxerant capiendas aut incendendas animum adiecit. Itaque cum sciret eius fluminis ostium adiri magnis a navibus non posse, alveo diffundente sese magis quam demittente, nisi cum flumen ex imbribus crevisset, tametsi invecta hostium navigia satis alta aqua excipiebat, onerariarum et longarum navium scaphas complures integi iussit. Quibus in scaphis atque in biremibus duabus milites imposuit Marcumque Orium, navium onerariarum praefectum, qui se obtulerat, ei negotio praeposuit. Ipse Aulonam cum longis navibus est aggressus, ut hostes occupatos ea in propugnatione distineret ne suas peti naves existimarent. Porro Turcae, vel de ea re, ut saepe fit, certiores facti, vel ipsimet propter recentem in sinu Ambracio navium suarum iacturam idem in Loo flumine metuentes, eas naves longius ab ostio in flumen introduxerant passuum milia quattuordecim, atque una composuerant sic, ut proras secundum cursum fluminis conversas haberent, ipsae, quod remi nondum erant impositi, inter se coniunctae totum flumen caperent. Ripas autem Turcae tormentis communierant ad naves hostium repellendas.

54   Orius, audacissime superato flumine, cum navibus Thraciis appropinquavisset, eas magno militum praesidio fultas atque instructas est conspicatus; tum missis in eum ex utraque ripa frequentibus tormentorum pilis, ad illas propius accedere non potuit. Itaque omnem aditum frustra expertus, crescente hinc atque hinc hostium multitudine, scaphas retrahi imperat. Redeuntibus Turcae summis in ripis atque ipso prope in flumine occurrerunt naviculamque unam, truncis ramisque arborum, quos in flumen deiecerant, impeditam, oppresserunt. Ipse cum reliquis incolumibus ad ostium fluminis cum revertisset atque interim mare, quod

74

launched on the river.[40] He knew that the mouth of the river could not be approached by large vessels, since except when the river rose due to rain, the channel spread out rather than deepened, though the water was deep enough for the enemy vessels once they were in. Pesaro accordingly ordered the skiffs of the merchantmen vessels and galleys to be given coverings. He had soldiers board these skiffs and two small galleys, and put in charge of the mission the captain of the merchantmen Marco Orio, who had volunteered for the job. Pesaro himself attacked Avlona with the galleys, so that while the enemy were busy defending themselves, he might distract them from thinking their ships were being targeted. But the Turks in turn were either told of this plan, as often happens, or following their recent loss of ships in the Gulf of Arta were themselves fearful that the same might happen in the Bojana river, and they had in consequence taken their ships further upriver, fourteen miles from the mouth. They had disposed them in such a way that the prows were turned in the direction of the river's flow, and, the oars not yet having been fitted, the ships themselves were yoked together so as to take up the whole width of the river. The Turks had also fortified the banks with artillery to repel enemy ships.

Sailing up the river with great boldness, Orio approached the   54
Turkish vessels and saw that they had been armed and equipped with a large force of soldiers, and under a dense barrage of cannonballs from both banks, he was unable at that point to get any closer to them. And so having tried every approach without success, as the numbers of the enemy grew ever greater on both sides, he ordered the boats to retreat. As they returned they met opposition from the Turks on the edges of the banks, and practically in the river itself, and one small boat was sunk when its path was blocked by tree trunks and branches which they had thrown into the river. When Orio got back to the mouth of the river with the remaining boats safe and sound, the sea, which was full of shoals

vadosum late erat, magno coorto vento se excitavisset, erumpere ausi mediis in vadis naufragium fecerunt. Quorum pars interiit, atque in his Hieronymus Maurocenus propinquus meus, navis onerariae bellicae praefectus, magno animo magnaque virtute. Reliqui plerique in litus eiecti ab hostibus capti sunt, praeter naviculas pauculas, quae tempestate superata se Dyrrhachium contulerunt, quo iam venerat Pisaurus, eaque illum de re certiorem fecerunt. Marcus Orius et Vincentius Pascalicus, navis item bellicae praefectus, capti. Ac fuit, eorum qui interierunt et qui in manus hostium pervenerunt, numerus circiter trecenti.

55   Pisauro Dyrrhachio digresso, Georgii Castriotae Epirotae hortatu et Antonii Boni legati, sponte se Alexiani dediderunt. Est Alexium in Drino flumine, quod vado transiri non potest, insula triquetra, mare uno ab latere attingens, ab reliquis flumen, quod ipsa dirimit. Eorum quodque laterum tria milia passuum efficit; ipsa vallo circummunita. Quam ad insulam, capta ab rege Thracio Scodra, eorum locorum sese homines contulerunt atque incolere coeperunt. Ea Turcae ad mercaturam utebantur, magnumque frumenti numerum, quo montani late homines earum regionum alerentur, neque parvam salis copiam quotannis eo convehebant. Picis autem ceraeque ac mellis magnam vim, eodem ab interioribus Illyrici finibus atque ab Epiro importari solitam, coemebant. Iisque reipublicae usui futurus locus videbatur.

56   Eo tempore Alexander, triremes reipublicae viginti pecunia sua sacraque se armaturum pollicitus, quibus civitas bello Thracio uteretur, quindecim modo per suos ministros ut instruerentur diligentiam adhibuit; reliquas quinque senatui armandas remisit, cum

over a wide area, had in the meantime been whipped up by a strong wind. They ventured to break out but ran aground amid the shallows. A part of them perished, among them my relative Girolamo Morosini,[41] captain of a cargo warship and a man of great spirit and great courage. Many of the rest were captured by the enemy as they were cast up on the shore, with the exception of a very few small boats which survived the storm and made their way to Durazzo. Pesaro had already arrived there, and was informed of these events by the survivors. Marco Orio and Vincenzo Pasqualigo, another warship captain, were captured; those who perished or came into enemy hands numbered about 300.

After Pesaro left Durazzo, the people of Alessio surrendered of   55
their own accord at the urging of Giorgio Castriota of Albania and the proveditor Antonio Bon. Alessio is a triangular island in the river Drino,[42] which is not fordable, washed by the sea on one side, on the others by the river, which it splits in two. Each of the sides is three miles long; the island itself is surrounded by a rampart. After the capture of Scutari by the Turkish sultan, the people of those parts made their way to the island and began to live there. The Turks turned it to commercial advantage and shipped a large quantity of grain there each year, which was widely used to feed the mountain folk of those regions, and a considerable supply of salt. They would purchase there, on the other hand, great quantities of pitch and beeswax and honey, which was commonly imported to the island from the hinterland of Illyria and Albania. It was thought that these assets of the place would be useful to the Republic.

Alexander had promised the Republic he would equip twenty   56
galleys with his own money and that of the Church for the city to use in the Turkish war, but at this point he had exerted himself to have only fifteen fitted out by his agents. He left it to the Senate to get the other five ready, since he had allowed them to use for the

ei pecuniam sacram quam homines in imperio Veneto, ut, crimini-
bus et maleficiis obnoxii ob commissa post mortem apud inferos
poena liberarentur, ex Alexandri litteris persolverent, bello Thracio insumendam permisisset; quarum omnino viginti navium imperium legatus ab sese datus obtineret. Is fuit Iacobus Pisaurus,
episcopus Paphiorum, ex Veneta nobilitate; qui etiam maiori earum navium parti, quam Venetiis armandam curavit (nam reliquam in Flaminiae maritimis municipiis et[9] Anconae instruxerat),
praefectos cives sibi Venetos adlegit.

57   Pecuniae vero sacrae summam libuit mihi huic loco adscribere,
ut intelligi possit quanta quamque ardens eo tempore fuerit in hominum mentibus religionis existimatio et deorum immortalium ti-
mor. Porro in urbe auri librae ducentae nonaginta septem eo nomine sunt confectae, Patavii una et sexaginta, Vicetiae sexaginta
quattuor et semilibra, Veronae una et triginta, Brixiae quadraginta
octo, Bergomi fere quadraginta quattuor, Cremonae duodecim,
Cremae plus novem, Taurisi viginti quattuor, Feltriae duodecim et
semilibra, Cividali Carnico novem, Utini quadraginta duae. Atque
ut a claris urbibus ad tenuiora oppida descendamus, Fossa Clodia
libras auri paulo minus octo facile contulit; Portus, quem Grua-
rium appellant, fere undecim; Colonia, qui quidem vicus est in Vi-
cetinorum finibus, quattuor; itemque supra quam quis crederet
alia in continenti castella vicique; ut esset summa omnis auri librae
septies centies et nonies, eoque amplius.

58   Atque illo ipso tempore Caesar, Alexandri filius, diu pressam
armis atque acri obsidione Faventiam, a qua patres Alexandri precibus legatum suum revocaverant, certis condicionibus tandem
cepit; Hestorique puero ea lege se dedenti, uti salvus sospesque esset, fidem fregit, Romamque adductum atque in custodia complures menses adservatum necavit. Per eos etiam dies Patavii Baptista
Zenus, e cardinalium collegio, moritur, grandi pecunia argentique
fabrefacti magno pondere testamenti tabulis suae genti et propin-

Turkish war the Church funds which, in accordance with his bull, people guilty of crimes and misdemeanors in the Venetian dominions were paying to be free of post-mortem punishment in hell for their deeds. The overall command of the twenty ships was to be held by a proveditor furnished by the pope. This was Jacopo Pesaro, the bishop of Paphos and a Venetian nobleman, who also appointed Venetian citizens as captains for the larger part of the ships, which he had arranged to have armed at Venice (the rest he had had fitted out in the maritime communities of Romagna and at Ancona).

I wanted to record at this point the total of the Church funds 57 to convey just how great and ardent the regard for religion and fear of Almighty God were in the minds of men at that time. In Venice, then, 297 gold pounds were collected for the purpose, at Padua 61, at Vicenza 64 and a half, at Verona 31, at Brescia 48, at Bergamo almost 44, at Cremona 12, at Crema more than 9, at Treviso 24, at Feltre 12 and a half, at Cividale del Friuli 9, at Udine 42. And to pass from well-known cities to lesser towns, Chioggia easily brought in a little under 8 gold pounds; Portogruaro almost 11; Cologna (the village in the territory of Vicenza), 4; and likewise from the other castles and villages of the *terraferma* on an incredible scale, so that the grand total came to more than 709 gold pounds.

It was at that very time that Alexander's son, Cesare Borgia, fi- 58 nally took Faenza, on certain conditions. The senators had recalled their proveditor from there at Alexander's request, and Cesare Borgia had long been pressing the town hard with his army and a bitter siege. The boy Astorre Manfredi gave himself up on condition that he would remain safe and unharmed, but Borgia broke his word; after being taken to Rome and kept in custody for many months,[43] he was put to death by Borgia. At the same time,[44] Cardinal Battista Zen also died at Padua, leaving in his will a large amount of money and great mass of silver-work to his

quis et sacerdotum[10] collegiis et reipublicae relicto. Absconderat
is Roma veniens aliquot ante annos auri libras ducentas sexaginta
Anconae in aedis sacrae pariete. De eo Alexander a senatu certior
factus aurum abstulit. Zeno ad urbem delato, funus amplissimum
publice curatum. Laudavit Angelus Gabriel. Postea ei ex testa-
mento senatus in aedis Marciae porticu sepulcrum ex aere ponen-
dum locavit.

59   Interea in Achaia magnum incommodum publice est acceptum,
Pylo ab rege Thracio iterum capta. Is enim cum eo et terrestri itinere equitum milia complura, et mari triremes quattuordecim et
biremulas quinque (sic enim naves eas appellant, quae fere semitri-
remium loco sunt) Camali praefecto misisset, essentque in Pyli
portu triremes reipublicae tres sine ulla statione aut specula, eas
Camales improviso aggressus non magno negotio cepit. Aliquot ex
iis qui in eis erant, fuga in scaphis elapsi, ad triremes quinque
maiores reipublicae, quae cum mercibus Beryto illo ipso tempore
venerant erantque in ancoris portui vicinae, se contulerunt. Eae
quinque, eadem formidine usae, cum terrori esse hostibus potuissent, velis factis abierunt. Quarum conspecta fuga, qui Pylo praeerant sese hostibus dediderunt. Earum triremium praefectis eo minus ignoscendum fuit, quod paulo ante Cretae cum essent, a
Pisauro eis erat imperatum ut se Pyli exspectarent. Isque postero
die cum triremibus quindecim eo venit. Sed Camales, cum Pisauri
classem e longinquo venientem ii qui in specula erant positi con-
spexissent — id enim ne accideret verebatur, ut in Pisaurum, quem
brevi eo venturum a captivis intellexerat, imprudens incideret — e
vestigio triremes captas abducens litusque proximum legens, ei se
vitabundus eripuit.

60   Pisaurus deinde Corcyram adveniens, quod audierat naves longas Turcas e Loo flumine quae in eo erant brevi educturos, trire-

family, relatives, monasteries, and the Republic. When he had come from Rome some years earlier, he had hidden 260 gold pounds in the wall of a church at Ancona. Learning of this from the Senate, Alexander made off with the gold. When Zen had been brought to Venice, a lavish state funeral was arranged. Angelo Gabriel delivered the eulogy. In accordance with his will and testament, the Senate later put out a contract for the erection of a bronze tomb for him in the portico of St. Mark's Basilica.

In the Morea, meanwhile, the state suffered a great setback with the recapture of Navarino by the Turkish sultan.[45] He had sent there overland several thousand cavalry, and by sea fourteen galleys and five small galleys (that is what they call those ships which are fairly equivalent to half-galleys) under the command of Kemal. In the harbor of Navarino were three Venetian galleys without any guard or lookout, which Kemal attacked without warning and took with little difficulty. Some of their crew escaped by fleeing in skiffs and made their way to five great galleys of the Republic, which at that very moment had come with merchandise from Beirut and were at anchor near the harbor. Those five ships were gripped by a common fear, though they were in a position to instill terror into the enemy, and they made sail and departed. Seeing them flee, the commanders at Navarino surrendered to the enemy. This was all the more unforgivable on the part of the ship captains, in that when they had been at Crete shortly before, Pesaro had ordered them to wait for him at Navarino. The following day he arrived there with fifteen galleys. Kemal was afraid that he might inadvertently run across Pesaro, having learned from prisoners that he was soon to arrive there, and so when the Turks who had been put on guard duty caught distant sight of Pesaro's fleet approaching, he at once led the captured galleys away, and hugging the shore, took himself out of the way to avoid him.

Pesaro then went to Corfu because he had heard that the Turks would soon be bringing out of the Bojana the warships that were

59

60

mes aliquot misit, quae ostium fluminis adservarent. Ipse cum reliqua classe longarum navium viginti quinque in Achaiam revehitur atque in Corones finibus magnum hominum numerum cum uxoribus et liberis suis in navibus imposuit, quos Cephallenem ad incolendum traduceret. Paulo post, Aeginae cum esset intellexissetque Megarae et biremes fabricari et frumenti magnam copiam esse, Aloisium Lauredanum legatum cum navibus octo, si quid ex usu efficere posset, eo misit. Is, bireme una cum hominibus, altera vacua captis, expositis militibus et equitibus Nauplii adhibitis, proelio cum Megarensibus commisso, eos fudit atque arcem, quae a Thracibus defendebatur, magno impetu cepit; ac reste suspensis iis qui oppugnationi superfuerant quosque cum biremi ceperat, frumentoque omni abducto, oppidum incensum ac solo aequatum delevit, ne impedimento Naupliis esset, quominus eo ab latere quam vellent libere vagari eis liceret. Idem postea complures ad insulas, postremo ad Euboeam profectus, praedam et quidem opulentam abegit oppidaque aliquot et castella multa incendit; ac magnum propugnatorum numerum interfecit, ingenti undique omni illo in mari terrore hostibus atque formidine incussa.

61   Quo quidem tempore, captis ab se oppidis rex metuens, Coronem Methonem Pylon muris et propugnaculis reliquisque rebus ad hostem repellendum idoneis et militum praesidio apprime communivit. Nauplii autem equites, cum hostes ad illos lacessendos in eorum prope suburbia irrupissent, egressi eos fuderunt; ex quibus ducenti quinquaginta interfecti atque capti. Idem paulo post alii hostium equites Catarbeio duce aggressi, omnes a Naupliis capti sunt praeter ducem, qui cum duobus equitibus aufugit. Reverso Corcyram Pisauro, ut classem regis Galliae itemque regis Lusitaniae, de quibus proximo libro dicetur, exspectaret, magistra-

there, sending some galleys to guard the mouth of the river. He himself sailed back to the Morea with the rest of the fleet, 25 warships, and in the territory of Coron he put on board a large number of men with their wives and children, to take them to live in Cephalonia. Shortly thereafter, while he was at Aegina, he learned of small galleys being constructed at Megara and of a large supply of grain there, so he sent Alvise Loredan as proveditor with eight ships to see if he could accomplish anything useful there. Loredan captured one small galley with its crew and a second one without. Putting his soldiers ashore, and supported by the Nauplian cavalry, he engaged the people of Megara in battle and put them to rout, and in a great assault took the fortress, which was defended by Turks. He hung those who had survived the attack and the men he had captured with the small galley, carried off all the grain, set fire to the town and razed it to the ground, in case it should prove an obstacle to the people of Nauplia and not allow them to roam as freely as they wished on that side. He later went to a number of islands, to Euboea last of all, making off with some rich booty indeed, and set fire to some towns and many castles. He killed a large number of defenders, striking great terror and dread into the enemy on all sides throughout that whole stretch of sea.

At the same time, the sultan, fearing for the towns he had cap- 61 tured, greatly strengthened Coron, Methoni, and Navarino with walls and ramparts and everything else needed to repel the enemy, and with a garrison of infantry. The cavalry of Nauplia, when the enemy had almost broken into the outskirts intent on harassing them, came out and put them to flight; 250 of them were killed or taken prisoner.[46] A little later, other Turkish cavalry under the command of Catarbejo attempted the same thing and were all taken prisoner by the men of Nauplia, except for the captain, who fled with two cavalrymen. When Pesaro had returned to Corfu to await the fleets of the kings of France and Portugal (to be dis-

tus reipublicae qui Dyrrhachio praeerat morbo affectus, ut valetu-
dinem curaret, Olcinium se contulit caeli salubrioris gratia. Eam
occasionem nacti hostes, noctu Dyrrhachium furtim aggressi, scalis ad murum positis, se in oppidum intulerunt; interfectisque
paucis somno expergefactis, oppido sunt potiti. Sed ea aestate foris, Pylo atque Dyrrhachio amissis, nullo autem negotio quod magnopere ex usu esset confecto, domi Augustinus Barbadicus vita
functus est de mense Septembri, cum annos quindecim civitatis
principatum obtinuisset.

cussed in the next book), the Venetian governor of Durazzo, who was ill, went to Dulcigno to take advantage of the healthier climate.[47] The enemy seized the opportunity and made a surprise night attack on Durazzo, putting scaling-ladders against the walls and invading the town. Having killed a few men roused from their sleep, they took over the town. That summer, with the loss of Navarino and Durazzo, and no great achievements accomplished abroad, on the home front Agostino Barbarigo died in September after fifteen years as doge.

LIBER SEXTUS

1   Talibus iactatae incommodis civitati malum etiam inopinatum ab
longinquis gentibus et regionibus extitit. Petri enim Pascalici,
apud Emanuelem Lusitaniae regem legati, litteris patres certiores
facti sunt regem illum per Mauritaniae Getuliaeque oceanum
convehendis ex Arabia Indiaque mercibus itinera, suis temptata
saepe navibus, demum explorata compertaque habuisse, navesque
aliquot eo missas pipere et cinnamis eiusmodique rebus onustas
Olysipponem revertisse; itaque futurum ut, eius rei facultate Hispanis hominibus tradita, nostri in posterum cives parcius angus-
tiusque mercarentur, magnique illi proventus, qui urbem opulentam reddidissent toti paene terrarum orbi rebus Indicis tradendis,
civitatem deficerent. Eo nuntio patres accepto non parvam animi
aegritudinem contraxerunt, quam tamen compendiis aliorum populorum solabantur. Simul et illud cogitabant: amabile profecto
esse novas regiones alterumque prope acquiri orbem, gentesque
abditas atque sepositas celebrari. Ac postea quam hunc ad locum
meorum me commentariorum cursus perduxit, non alienum esse
arbitror, quod eius rei, omnium quas ulla aetas umquam ab hominibus effectas vidit maximae atque pulcherrimae, fuerit initium,
tum quae terrarum portio post id quaeve gentes et quibus moribus
sint repertae, quantum suscepti operis ratio permittet, breviter dicere.

2   Erat Columbus homo Ligur ingenio peracri, qui multas emen-
sus regiones, multum maris et oceani perlustraverat. Is, ut est hu-
manus animus novarum rerum appetens, Ferdinando et Isabellae,
Hispaniae regibus, proponit edocetque illud, quod omnis fere an-

BOOK VI

Shaken by these setbacks, the city suffered an unexpected misfor- 1
tune at the hands of distant peoples and lands. The senators were 1501
informed by letter of Piero Pasqualigo, ambassador at the court of
King Manuel of Portugal, that the king had at last discovered and
explored routes through the West African ocean[1] for the transport
of goods from Arabia and India, something his ships had repeat-
edly attempted. Some ships sent there, he wrote, had returned to
Lisbon loaded with pepper and cinnamon and the like; now that
the Iberians had got this ability, it was inevitable that our citizens
would have to conduct their trade on a smaller and more restricted
scale, and our city would lose those vast profits which had made
Venice wealthy by carrying Indian spices more or less throughout
the world. The receipt of this news caused the senators no little
distress of mind, though the gains accruing to other peoples
brought them some consolation. At the same time it provoked this
further reflection, that it was a really fine thing to acquire new
lands — almost another world — and to place on record peoples
who had been concealed and cut off from us. And now that the
course of my narrative has brought me to this point, I think it is
not out of place to give a brief account, as far as the plan of my
work allows, of how this all began, the greatest and most splendid
achievement that any age has seen accomplished by man, and then
of the areas of the earth and the nations and their customs that
were thereafter discovered.[2]

Columbus was a man from Liguria with a very sharp mind who 2
had travelled through many lands and ranged through much of the
sea and ocean. In line with the appetite of the human heart for
fresh discoveries, Columbus expounded and explained to the
Spanish sovereigns, Ferdinand and Isabella, that the almost uni-

tiquitas credidit—quinque esse caeli partes, quarum media caloribus, extremae duae frigoribus sic afficiantur, ut quae sub illis sint totidem terrae plagae incoli ab hominibus non possint, duae tantum inter eas sub eisdem positae caeli partibus possint—inanem esse antiquorum hominum fabulam, et nullis veris rationibus fultam et confirmatam descriptionem; improvidum prope necesse esse haberi Deum, si ita mundum sit fabricatus, ut longe maior terrarum pars propter nimiam intemperiem hominibus vacua nullum ex sese usum praebeat; globum esse terrae hunc eiusmodi, ut commeandi per omnes eius partes facultas hominibus ne desit. Cur sub media caeli conversione degi non possit, ubi diei calor cum noctis frigore, pari dimenso utriusque morae spatio, temperetur? praesertim cum tam cito sol in alterutram declinet partem, cumque sub iis caeli conversionibus, in quibus nostro vertici propior longinquam sol moram trahit, tamen degatur? Algentes sub septentrionalibus esse terras, sed eas hominibus non defici; sic sub australi terras esse frigidas vertice, esse animantium atque hominum genus; quem Oceanum scriptores appellarint, eum non esse inertis magnitudinis, sed insulis atque terris scatere, quas homines inhabitent; itaque vigere atque incoli universum globum qui ubique sit vitalis aurae particeps. Hac oratione apud reges habita, petit ut sibi liceat eorum opibus novas insulas, nova litora quaerere; spem se habere non defore inceptis fortunam, dicionemque ipsorum magnopere iri auctum, si rem susceperint, confirmat.

3   Ab regibus nova spe allectis sententia Columbi, quam quidem totum septennium reiecerant, ad extremum comprobata (quam tamen multo antea Posidonii philosophi, Panaetii discipuli, primum, deinde etiam Avicennae medici fuisse video, magni et praeclari viri), anno ab urbe condita millesimo septuagesimo primo tribus cum navibus Columbus ad insulas Fortunatas, de quibus superio-

versal belief of antiquity—that there are five regions of the sky, of which the middle is afflicted by such heat and the two extremes by such cold that the corresponding climatic zones of the earth beneath them are uninhabitable by mankind, and that only the two intermediate zones set under the corresponding parts of the sky are habitable—was a foolish fable of the ancients, and a description neither based on nor confirmed by any well-founded theory. It would almost be necessary to consider God improvident if he had so fashioned the world that by far the largest part of it was empty of men because of the extremes of climate and offered them nothing useful. The terrestrial globe was so made that men had the faculty of traveling through every part of it. Why should it not be possible, he continued, to live at the equator, where the heat of the day is tempered by the cold of the night, each having an equal duration, especially when the sun sets so quickly on either side of the equator, and when life is still possible in those latitudes where the sun is closer to our pole and lingers for a long time? The lands in the northern regions are chilly, but there is no lack of people; in the same way the lands under the southern pole are cold, but animals and people exist there. What writers have called the Ocean is not a vast emptiness, but is full of islands and places inhabited by men. Any part of the entire world that shares the breath of life is therefore thriving and inhabited. After delivering this speech before the sovereigns, Columbus asked for their support in seeking out new islands and new shores, declaring that he expected his endeavors would be crowned with success, and their dominion greatly increased, if they took on the enterprise.

In the end, after rejecting Columbus' idea for a full seven years, 3 the sovereigns conceived fresh hopes of it and gave it their approval (though I see it was much earlier the idea first of the philosopher Posidonius, the pupil of Panaetius, and then of the famous physician, the great Avicenna). In the year 1071 from the founda- 1492 tion of the city of Venice, Columbus set out in three ships for the

ribus libris sermonem habuimus, quas Canarias appellant, profectus, atque ab iis tres et triginta totos dies occidentem secutus solem, sex numero insulas reperit, quarum sunt duae ingentis magnitudinis; quibus in insulis lusciniae Novembri mense canerent, homines nudi, ingenio miti, lintribus ex uno ligno factis uterentur. Frumentum hi habent, quod *maicem* appellant, multo quam nos spica et culmo grandioribus, harundineisque foliis, et plurimo ac rotundo grano, quod spicae infixum membrana pro aristis vestitur, quam quidem maturescens reiciat. Animalium quadrupedum genera habent perpauca, ex his canes pusillos, qui muti etiam sint nec latrent; avium vero longe plurima, nostris tum grandiora, tum etiam minora, adeo ut aviculae inveniantur quae singulae suo cum nido vigesimam quartam unciae partem non exsuperent; psittacorum magnam copiam, forma et colore variam. Vellera sponte nascentia ex nemoribus atque montibus colligunt. Sed ea cum volunt candidiora melioraque fieri, ipsi purgant atque apud domos suas serunt. Aurum, quod in fluminum arenis legunt, habent; ferrum non habent. Itaque praeduris atque acutis lapidibus et ad lintres cavandos et ad reliquam materiam in usum domesticum formandam aurumque molliendum pro ferro utuntur. Sed aurum cultus tantummodo gratia molliunt, idque auribus et naribus perforatis pendulum gerunt; neque enim nummos noverunt neque stipis ullo genere utuntur. Harum duarum insularum unius cum rege amicitia foedereque inito, Columbus, duo de quadraginta ex suis apud illum relictis, qui mores et sermonem gentis addiscerent seque brevi rediturum exspectarent, decem ex insularibus secum ducens in Hispaniam rediit. Haec illorum itinerum origo institutaeque ad incognitas orbis terrarum oras navigationis initium hoc fuit.

4   Anno autem insequente, ut pollicitus fuerat, Columbus, cum navibus decem septem et militibus et fabris et commeatu omnis generis, missu regum eodem rediens, cum se ad laevam versus parumper flexisset, quamplures ad insulas est delatus; quarum par-

Fortunate Isles, the so-called Canaries, which I mentioned in previous books.[3] Heading from there into the setting sun for 33 days together, he discovered six islands, two of them very large indeed, where nightingales sing in November and naked men of a gentle nature use boats made of a single tree trunk. These people have a cereal which they call *maize*, with much bigger ears and stalks than ours, reedy foliage, and very numerous plump grains which are attached to the ear and covered with a sheath in place of beards, which it casts off as it matures. They have very few kinds of quadrupeds, among them tiny dogs which are actually mute and do not bark. But they do have a great many types of birds, both larger and smaller than ours, so that some little birds are found which together with their nests weigh no more than a 24th of an ounce each. There are parrots of various shapes and colors in great abundance. They collect fleeces which grow by themselves from the woods and hills, but when they want to make them whiter and finer, they clean them and plant them by their homes. They have gold, which they collect in the sands of the rivers; they do not have iron. In its place they use specially hard and sharp stones, both for hollowing out their boats and for shaping other wood for domestic use and working gold. But the gold they work only for ornament, wearing it suspended from their pierced ears and nostrils—they are indeed unacquainted with coinage, nor do they use any kind of money. Having entered into a treaty of friendship with the king of one of these two islands, Columbus left 38 of his men with him, to learn the customs and language of the tribe and await his early return, and taking ten of the islanders with him, he returned to Spain. Such was the genesis of those travels and the beginning of voyages to unknown parts of the world.

Sent by the Spanish sovereigns the following year, Columbus 4 returned as promised to the same place with ten ships, and soldiers and builders and provisions of all sorts. Veering a little to the south, he was carried to a great mass of islands, some of them in-

tem homines incolebant feri trucesque, qui puerorum et virorum carnibus quos aliis in insulis bello aut latrociniis cepissent vescebantur (a feminis abstinebant), *Canibales* appellati. Vicos hi habebant vicenis aut tricenis domibus singulos; domusque erant omnes ligneae ac rotunda forma, palmis et stipulis contectae certarumque arborum et arundinum foliis ad arcendos imbres. Aere utebantur adeo temperato, ut Decembri mense avium aliae nidos ponerent, aliae pullos educarent suos. Sed cum ad illam insulam a qua reditum anno superiore apparaverat Hispaniolamque ipsam appellaverat Columbus revertisset, propter soli bonitatem magnitudinemque insulae, oppidum opportuno loco condere ac terram colere coepit. Arbores frondibus nullo anni tempore spoliabantur, una aut altera exceptis, quarum Hispani praeter pinum palmamque nobis cognitam viderunt nullam.

5   Insulares duobus se e specubus terra proditos atque natos dicunt. Deos penates, quos appellant *Zemes*, colunt. Eos plebs habet communes, suum vero ex regibus quilibet, eorumque simulacra lana contexta in bellum profecturi capiti alligant iuvarique se ab iis maiorem in modum putant. Noctu vagari mortuos credunt posseque omnia humana membra sumere praeter umbilicum. Ab suis *Zemibus* eiusmodi responsa non multos ante annos accepisse illos constat: venturam eo indutam vestibus gentem quae regionem subigeret et ipsorum aboleret deos. Sed vicinae huic insulae hominibus, alterius ex duabus de quibus supra dictum est insulis, quam quidem et propter magnitudinem Hispani terram esse continentem crediderunt et hominum genere atque auri copia multum praestare ceteris intellexerunt et Cubam appellari didicerunt, serpentes nova totius corporis specie ac forma praediti, sesquipedis plerumque longitudine, qui ex terra et ex aqua vivunt, in lautioribus erant epulis. Verum enimvero et illi et qui proximas obtinebant insulas, quarum magnus erat numerus, plerique auream aeta-

habited by a wild and fierce people called *Cannibals*, who fed on the flesh of boys and men they had captured in war or raids on other islands (the women they left alone). These people lived in villages of 20 or 30 homes each, all circular and made of wood, covered with palms and straw and the leaves of certain trees and reeds, to keep out the rain. They enjoyed such a mild climate that some birds built their nests while others raised their young in the month of December. But on his return to the island from which he had left for Spain the year before, the one he had named Hispaniola, Columbus set about building a town at a suitable spot and putting the land under cultivation, in view of the fertility of the soil and the size of the island. With one or two exceptions, the trees kept their leaves throughout the year, but the Spaniards saw none that are known among us, save for the pine and the palm.

The islanders say that they were produced and born from two 5 caves in the earth. They worship household gods, which they call *zemi*. The ordinary people hold these in common, but each of the kings has his own, and they strap images of them made of wool to their heads when setting out to war, thinking they give them considerable help. They believe that the dead wander abroad by night and can assume the shape of the human body in all its parts except the navel. It is widely believed that their *zemi* gave them the following prophecy not many years ago: a people dressed in clothes would come there who would subjugate the region and abolish their gods. As to the second of the two islands mentioned above, owing to its size the Spaniards believed it was part of the mainland; they found it far surpassed the rest in the quality of its people and abundance of gold, and learned that it was called Cuba. Among the choicer dishes of the men of this neighboring island were serpents whose whole body was of a novel appearance and shape: they are generally a foot and a half long, and live on land and water. Yet in truth both those people and the inhabitants of the nearby islands (of which there were a great number) lived

tem agere; nullum agri modum noscere; non iudicia, non leges habere; non litteris, non mercatura uti; non in posterum sed in dies vivere.

6   Ac dum haec conquiruntur, Ioannes Lusitaniae rex per legatos apud Hispaniae reges queritur sua litora suasque regiones ab ipsis temptari; eas quas reperissent insulas ad se spectare, qui Hesperides habeat et cuius maiores Oceanum percurrere ante omnes alios sint ausi. Contra Hispaniae reges dicere, quae non fuerint ullo ab homine ante parta, omnibus hominibus patere; se nulli esse iniurios, si ab ceteris ignorata labore et studio acquisiverint suo. Itaque magnis ex ea re obortis inter eos disceptationibus, ne controversiae eiusmodi ad bellum deducerentur, utrique se Alexandri pontificis maximi iudicio staturos spondent. Alexander, tota re cognita, statuit ut, a septentrionibus directa ducta in australem polum linea, quae a Gorgonum insulis tercentena milia passus in occasum distaret, quae pars orbis in Oceano ad occidentem solem esset, ea Hispaniae regibus cederet; quae ad orientem spectaret, iuris Lusitani censeretur. Ita orbis terrarum, ab ea Oceani ora in duas divisus partes, duobus regibus perquirendus et obtinendus est traditus. Ad quam quidem certe rem magna uterque diligentia consequendam se dedit.

7   Sed Hispanis ulteriora temptantibus terra est obiecta continens, paulo minus decies centena milia passuum ab Hispaniola protenta meridiem versus; atque in ea populi sub rege bellum cum finitimis gerente occurrerunt; quorum feminae virum passae nullam partem corporis praeter muliebria, virgines ne illam quidem tegebant. Regem ii suum honoris gratia sublime in humeris ferunt. Tum alii deinde populi, capillo promisso et liberali aspectu, auro atque gemmis culti. Vino ii utuntur albo nigroque, ex quibusdam confecto fructibus, sapore delectabili. Post hos item alii, qui certa-

for the most part in a golden age. They know no boundaries to their fields; they have no courts or laws; they have no use for writing or trade; they live not for the future but from day to day.

During the course of these investigations, King João of Portugal protested through his ambassadors to the Spanish court that the sovereigns were attempting to get possession of his shores and his lands; the islands they had discovered belonged to him as owner of the Western Isles, and it was his ancestors that had ventured to cross the Ocean before anyone else. The Spanish sovereigns said in rebuttal that what no one had previously acquired was open to anyone. They were doing no one an injury if by their labor and effort they had won lands unknown to others. And so a great dispute over this matter arose between them, but to avoid the quarrel ending in war, both parties undertook to abide by the decision of Pope Alexander. Alexander made a thorough investigation of the matter and decided to draw a line from the north to the south pole 300 miles west of the Cape Verde islands. What lay in the Ocean to the west of the line he granted to the Spanish kings; what lay to the east was to be regarded as under Portuguese jurisdiction.[4] The world from the shore of Ocean being thus divided into two parts, it was handed over to the two rulers for exploration and possession. And certainly both of them bent themselves to doing so with a will.

But when the Spaniards pressed on further they encountered a mainland, a little less than a thousand miles south of Hispaniola. There they were faced by tribes under a king who was at war with his neighbors. Their women who have known a man covered no part of the body except the genitals, the virgins not even that. They carry their king aloft on their shoulders as a mark of honor. Then they came across other peoples with long hair and a noble appearance, who adorned themselves with gold and jewels. They enjoy white and red wine made from a number of fruits, which has a delicious flavor. After them they met yet others who dyed

rum se herbarum coloribus pullo et purpureo inficiunt aspectuque sunt in pugna eam ob rem taetriore ac horribiliore. Demum gens inventa agilis admodum, et item nuda, genitalibus tantummodo cucurbitula vel marina testa inclusis. Cadavera ibi regum et magnorum hominum desiccata in domibus asservantur, eaque in honore magno habent. Est etiam, ubi arida facta conterant eoque pulvere in epulis et poculis honoris causa utantur.

8   Postremo autem, ad meridiem audacius in dies iter flectentibus Hispanis, cum vertex se subducere noster coepit, tum e regione alia quaedam magnopere splendentium quattuor stellarum forma atque series extitit, quam esse australis verticis faciem crediderunt. Visi post haec homines nostris longe proceriores et magno ad obeundas pugnas animo. Tum flumen refertum insulis, immani latitudine—patet enim amplius passuum milia centum—et silvae arborum, quae materiam habent ad tingendas lanas idoneam, aliarumque ita procerarum, ut eas viginti hominum extremis se manibus contingentium capere complexus saepe nequeat. Siliquas hae producunt longitudine palmari, pollice crassiores, lanae mollissimae concisaeque plenas; quae quidem ob tenuitatem et brevitatem deduci in subtegmina fusis non possit, sed ad farcienda strata culcitrasque magnopere sit idonea. Animal eae silvae nutriunt cuniculi magnitudine, gallinis infestissimum, quod quidem femina loculum habet e pelle utero adnexum, quasi uterum alterum, fecundum uberibus, in quo catulos secum gestat emittitque cum vult. Itaque si animal noxium videt, si venatores adesse intelligit, loculo illos recipit et inclusos fugiens aufert; idque tamdiu facit, quoad catuli per se et quae sibi usui ad victum sunt quaerere et vitam tueri possint.

9   In ea terrarum parte homines impuberes in omni aetate sunt prope universi, neque ullos habent pilos. Iidem magnopere natandi artem callent, tum mares tum feminae, eique rei ab parvulis insuescunt. Filios ex sororibus sibi heredes instituunt, quoniam non

themselves with black and crimson colors of certain herbs, making themselves more fearful and terrible to look at in battle. Finally they found a nimble and energetic tribe, likewise naked, with their genitals alone wrapped in a little gourd or sea-shell. There the dried bodies of their kings and potentates are kept in their houses and held in great honor. There is even a place where they grind them up when they have become desiccated and use the dust in food and drink to honor them.

In the end, as the Spaniards turned their course to the south 8 with ever growing boldness, our celestial pole began to be hidden, while opposite it another arrangement of a set of four very bright stars appeared, which they believed marked the southern pole.[5] After that they saw men far taller than ours and possessed of a fine fighting spirit. Then an immensely broad river — more than a hundred miles wide — which was full of islands, and forests with trees which give a wood good for dying wool, and others so large that they frequently exceed the grasp of twenty men with out-stretched arms. The latter produce pods as wide as the palm of a hand and thicker than a thumb, and filled with very soft and short fibers. These are too slender and short to be spun into thread on spindles, however, but are perfectly good for stuffing mattresses and pillows. The forests support an animal the size of a rabbit which is a bitter enemy of hens; the female has a pouch of skin with copious teats next to the stomach, like a second stomach, in which it carries its young and from which it lets them out as and when it wishes. And so if it sees a dangerous animal or senses hunters nearby, it takes them into its pouch and escapes with them inside. It continues to do this until the young are able to hunt for food and defend themselves on their own.

In that part of the world almost all the men are beardless 9 throughout their lives, nor do they have any body hair. They are highly skilled at swimming, the females as well as the males, and they become accustomed to it from an early age. They make their

dubie suae gentis sunt. Mulieres adolescentes parere servile ducunt esse. Itaque si praegnantes fiunt, herba ad eam rem idonea abortum faciunt. Cum vero aetatis flos exaruit, tum pariunt ac proli student. Sed quae regio sunt sanguine, negare aliquid ulli viro qui ex nobili sit genere in turpibus habent rebus. Fere semper cum rege mortuo uxor una et altera sepeliri vult, eo cum ornatu quem vivens adamavit; tum servi etiam et clientes. Ita enim se cum illo apud superos tota tempora victuros putant. Nonnullae gentes deorum imagines filiorum suorum infantium spargunt sanguine. Mitiores aliae sacerdotes ita habent institutos, ut barbam, si quam habent, aut capillum neque tondeant neque pectant totius vitae tempore. Quibusdam in locis propter paludes incolae domos in arboribus aedificant easque inhabitant cum uxoribus et liberis.

10   Atque omnibus fere in continentis regionibus aurum ex fluminibus colligunt, aut ex vicinis fluminibus locis, non magna tamen diligentia — neque enim nummos cudunt — minutis plerumque cum terra globulis, sed saepe etiam librali pondere, ac nonnumquam multo maioribus. Gemmas vero maximeque margaritas ii habent populi qui Cubagae et Cumanae et Terarequi insulis (sic enim eas appellant), in septentrionem versis, paulum a media caeli conversione declinantibus, sunt proximi, ubi eas urinatores expiscantur, tanta cum mari adsuetudine, ut semihorae interdum spatium conchis margaritarum conquirendis sub aqua se contineant. Earum magna vis, ab incolis regibus Hispanis tradita, nobilium feminarum mundum facile auxit. Atque ea quidem omnia ante hos plane annos, quibus haec a nobis conscribi coepta sunt, contigerunt. Nam quae proxime gentes bello ab Hispanis sunt devictae, eae porro et vestium cultu et oppidorum nobilitate et bellandi studio et hominum frequentia et finium ac regnorum amplitudine re-

sisters' sons their heirs, since they can be sure they are of their
own family. They think it is dishonorable for adolescent women to
give birth, and if they become pregnant, they induce abortion with
a suitable herb. But when the bloom of youth has faded, that is
the time that they give birth and are eager to have offspring.
Women of royal blood think it is wrong to deny anything at all to
any man of noble rank. One or two of his wives almost always
wish to be buried with a dead king, along with the ornaments they
held dearest in life, and so too with the slaves and retinue. In doing this they think they will live with him in heaven forever. Some
tribes sprinkle the images of the gods with the blood of their new-
born children. Other, gentler tribes have priests whose custom is
never to cut or comb their hair, or beards if they have them,
throughout their life. In certain places the inhabitants build their
homes in trees on account of the swamps, and live there with their
wives and children.

In almost every part of the mainland they collect gold from   10
rivers or places near them—but with no great assiduousness, since
they do not mint coins—for the most part in tiny grains mixed
with soil, but often in lumps of as much as a pound, and occasion-
ally much larger. But the peoples who live near the islands of
Cubagua, Cumana, and Terarequi (as they are called)[6] a little way
to the north of the equator, do have gems, and pearls especially.
There divers fish for them, men so at home in the sea that on occasion they stay underwater for the space of half an hour as they
search for shells with pearls in them. The great abundance of
those pearls delivered to the Spanish sovereigns by the natives has
greatly enhanced the elegance of noblewomen. All of this, of
course, happened many years before I took up writing this account: the nations most recently conquered by the Spaniards in
war far outstrip all the others of the region in their fine clothing
and noble towns, their enthusiasm for war, size of population and
extent of their lands and realms.[7] Some of them worship the sun

liquis earum regionum omnibus multum praestant. Quorum nonnulli solem et lunam uti virum et uxorem colunt; neque impuberes
plane sunt, venusta etiam forma et probis moribus feminae, tum
ornatae gemmis, praeter cetera, extremas quoque suras ad talos
usque. Auro autem sic abundant, ut parietes templorum ac domo-
rum reges eo vestiant; et vasis ad victum domesticum prope omnibus, uti nos ab aëneis aut testaceis, sic illi aureis utantur. Itaque
victi magno auri pondere Hispaniam referserunt. Cum iis quos su-
perius diximus populis Messicum, Temistanae regionis oppidum
egregium in lacu salsae aquae situm, sub cancro fere ad conversionem positum, numerare nos oportet, cum plerisque non oppidis
modo, sed etiam regionibus ac magno terrarum spatio vectigale
factum. Quod si quas etiam terras ad australem verticem positas
Hispaniae imperio adiecerint aestimabitur, nullus prope antiquorum hominum labor eorum industriam aequaverit.

11   Alia ex parte Lusitani, classe ab rege comparata, in austrum
ab Hesperidibus conversi, Africaeque promontorio quod Bonam
Spem appellant traiecto, Aethiopici oceani se primum ostendenti-
bus litoribus, ad continentem nigrorum hominum terram quae appellatur Cephala naves appulerunt, auro divitem (quod interiores
eo important populi, ut res alias contra mercentur, nullo id pondere aut mensura, sed tantum frustis ex oculorum fide atque arbi-
trio permutantes, ut qui accipiunt saepe lucrum centupli faciant),
atque ibi arcem condiderunt. Deinde ad Mogambicem regionem
delati, portu egregio et advenarum frequentia nobilem, arce item
posita, eius sunt imperio potiti. Labrum inferius hi sibi homines
perforant ossulaque aut gemmas foraminibus appendunt, cultus
honestioris gratia. Quiloae deinde regem bello devictum expule-
runt eumque tenuerunt. Oppidani domus nostro more habent
exaedificatas, colore ipsi inter nigrum albumque, vestibus liberaliter induti. Aliis post hos relictis populis, mare rubrum ingressi,

and moon as man and wife. The men are not completely beardless, the women are of pleasant appearance and good character, their limbs adorned with jewels, even on the lower calves as far as the ankles. They have so much gold that their kings adorn the walls of temples and homes with it, and almost all their dishes for domestic use are made of gold, just as ours are made of copper or clay. The result is that Spain has been stuffed full of the gold of the conquered. Along with the peoples mentioned above, we ought to include Mexico, a fine town of the Tenochtitlan region which is situated on a salt-water lake almost on the tropic of Cancer. Like many other towns, and whole regions making up a great expanse of land as well, it was made to pay tribute to the Spanish. But if one also takes into account the lands toward the southern pole that they added to the Spanish empire, scarcely any venture of the ancients can match their achievement.

In a different sphere, the king of Portugal had a fleet fitted out, 11 and the Portuguese, heading south from the Western Isles, rounded the African cape called Good Hope, the coast of the Ethiopian ocean now revealing itself for the first time. They made landfall on the continent at a place called Cephala,[8] a land of black men and rich in gold. This the peoples of the interior bring there to trade for other goods, making the exchange without weighing or measuring it but with nuggets judged only by eye, so that those who get them often make a hundredfold profit. There the Portuguese established a fort. Next they reached the region of Mozambique,[9] a place well known for its excellent harbor and crowds of foreigners, where they also planted a fort and took the town. These people perforate their lower lip, with little bits of bone or jewels hung from the holes as decorous adornments. Then the Portuguese defeated the ruler of Quiloa[10] in battle, drove him out and occupied the town. The townspeople have homes built in our fashion; they themselves are of a color between black and white, and wear fine clothes. After these, they left other peoples aside and entered the

complures nigrorum item et bonorum hominum ac bello fortium civitates adierunt; qui natis statim feminis naturam consuunt, quoad urinae exitus ne impediatur; easque, cum adoleverint, sic consutas in matrimonium collocant, ut sponsi prima cura sit conglutinatas atque coalitas puellae oras ferro interscindere; tanto in honore apud homines barbaros est non ambigua ducendis uxoribus virginitas.

12   Ac Lusitanis mediam rubri maris partem transgressis, Zides se oppidum obtulit amplo cum portu, ad quod quidem Indici populi suas merces convehebant. Eas Aegyptii, qui eo loci mercaturae causa quotannis convenire consueverunt, camelis imponebant Alexandriamque perferebant. Quas quidem Veneti merces, stato anni tempore eam ad urbem adnavigantes, coemebant, domumque convectas omnium gentium mercatoribus, ea se de causa vulgo petentibus, venditantes, incredibili auri proventu civitatem locupletabant suam. Sed postea quam ad eas regiones Lusitani venerunt, magna rerum commutatio est consecuta. Quicquid enim fere mercaturae causa ex omnibus Arabiae Indiaeque locis <in> mare[1] rubrum importabatur, ipsi emere domumque convehere coeperunt. Qua adductus necessitate, rex Aegyptius, anno ab urbe condita millesimo octogesimo, Zidensium in portu, qui quidem in intimi eius maris sinu sunt, classem magno sumptu comparavit, ut ab Indiae maris navigatione Lusitanos averteret. Sed ab illis ad Dium, in ostio Indi fluminis oppidum, victus, classe capta atque incensa, rem inchoatam reliquit. Zidenses nullam postea vel omnino modicam rerum Indicarum advectionem habuerunt. Ita Aegyptios Venetosque instituta antiquitus mercaturae ratio, quae intercipi nullo posse tempore videbatur, alio conversa prope deseruit.

Red Sea, reaching many communities likewise of blacks, good people and brave in war. These men sew together the reproductive organs of girls as soon as they are born, just far enough to allow urination. When they have matured, they give them in marriage stitched up in this manner, and it is the groom's first concern to sever with a knife the girl's labia thus joined and grown together: so high a value do the barbarians place on unambiguous virginity when taking a wife.

When the Portuguese had sailed half way through the Red Sea, 12 they encountered the town of Jeddah with its ample harbor, to which the peoples of India transport their products. The Egyptians were accustomed to go there every year for purposes of trade, and they would load these goods onto camels and take them to Alexandria. At a certain time each year the Venetians would sail to that city and buy the goods, carry them home, and sell them to merchants from all round the world, who regularly resorted to them for the purpose. In so doing they enriched their city with an amazing quantity of gold. But after the Portuguese reached those parts, the situation was greatly altered. They began to buy up practically everything that was imported by way of trade into the Red Sea from all of Arabia and India, and to take it home themselves. To meet this difficulty, in the year 1080 from the foundation of the city, the sultan of Egypt fitted out a fleet at great expense 1501 in the port of the Jeddans, who live in the innermost bay of the sea, so as to keep the Portuguese from sailing the Indian Ocean. But being defeated by them at Diu, a town at the mouth of the Indus river,[11] and with his fleet captured and burned, he abandoned the enterprise unfinished. Thereafter the people of Jeddah had no further supplies of Indian goods, or at any rate very little. Thus a system of trade that was established in antiquity and which it had seemed could never be usurped, was diverted elsewhere, and effectively lost to the Egyptians and Venetians.

13   Neque hercule propterea Lusitani finem progrediendi fecerunt, sed ad complures Arabici, Persici, Indicique insulas Oceani, atque ad innumeros continentis portus conventusque hominum profecti, silvis felicibus, odorum omni genere, ebore, argento, auro, gemmis beatos, se contulerunt; et Colocuete, oppido propter affluentem earum rerum quas imprimis quaerebant atque adamabant copiam maxime omnium opportuno, proeliis secundis factis et munitionibus institutis in potestatem redacto, eas regiones tenuerunt; Taprobaneque² insula multorum mensium itinere post tergum relicta, quo nemo umquam penetravit sui regis signa audacissime felicissimeque intulerunt. Tametsi maiore omnino audacia, felicitate autem numquam alias audita, si vixisset, Ernandus Maglaianes Lusitanus fuit. Qui, Hispaniae regum opibus classe comparata, viae initio in austrum se flectens, atque ultra mediam caeli conversionem propter continentis terrae oras dextrorsum velificans, magno spatio ad polum versus peracto, ut illum longius altiorem quam nobis noster sit eo in itinere habuerit; et freti quod nunc Maglaianis appellant angustiis trecentorum milium passuum in longitudinem decursis, iterum ad medium caeli spatium se convertit. Deinde ad aurorae populos atque insulas odoratarum arborum plenas quas Molucas appellant, medium complexus globi solidi spatium, pervenit ibique pugnans interiit.

14   Postremo illius comitatus, per Lusitanorum partis Oceanum labore plurimo universi orbis terrarum navigatione triennio confecta, in Hispaniam rediit. Cumque totius itineris enumeratis diebus rationem quam in tabulis habebat repetisset, uno sibi annos illos die longiores factos de dierum nominibus domi audiens reperit. Qui omnino anni, si se is ad orientem, domo profectus, convertisset, ac contra solem usquequaque currens illud ipsum iter

Nor did this mean an end to Portuguese advances. Far from it! 13
They carried on to a good many islands in the Arabian, Persian
and Indian oceans, and made their way to countless ports and human communities on the mainland, places blessed with thriving
forests, aromatic spices of every kind, ivory, silver, gold, and gems.
Following some military successes and the establishment of defense works, they brought Calicut under their control, an ideal
town for them in view of the abundant supply of the things they
were after and specially coveted, and so made themselves masters
of those parts. After a voyage of many months, they left behind
the island of Ceylon and with the utmost daring and good fortune
took their king's flag to a place where man had never penetrated.
But it is true that the Portuguese Ferdinand Magellan was a man
of altogether greater daring and, had he lived, his success would
have been unparalleled. Having got a fleet ready at the expense of
the Spanish sovereigns, he turned south at the beginning of his
journey and after the equator sailed to the right along the shores
of the continent. He travelled a long way toward the southern pole
star, so that it appeared to him a good deal higher in the sky than
our pole star is to us. Passing through the narrows of what is
now called the Strait of Magellan, 300 miles in length, he turned
back again toward the equator. Having traversed half the world,
he reached the peoples of the East and the islands known as
the Moluccas, which are full of aromatic trees, and there died in
battle.

His crew at length returned to Spain through the part of the 14
Ocean under Portuguese sway, having completed with great difficulty a three-year circumnavigation of the entire world. And they
counted the number of days the whole voyage had taken by consulting the reckoning they had in their logs, and when they were
informed of the days entered at home, they found that each of
their years had been longer by a day. Naturally, if they had turned
east on leaving home, and had made exactly the same voyage run-

universum confecisset, uno breviores die redeunti sane fuissent. Semper enim tanto citius orienti soli occurrens, quanto plus itineris post se circumvectus reliquisset, emenso demum totius terrae globo die uno prius solem sibi orientem quam, cum viae se dederat, profecto habuisset.

15 Eodem fere tempore quo legati Pascalici litterae ad senatum venerunt, Aloisius rex Gallorum Tridenti, per legatum suum cardinalem Rotomagensem, cui Mediolano proficiscenti (illi enim urbi atque regno praeerat) Georgium Cornelium, Brixiae magistratum, reginae Cypriae fratrem, senatus legavit, pacem cum Maximiliano imperatore certis condicionibus fecerat; quarum illa erat maxima, ut is se regem Mediolani appellaret, ipse in corona ex qua Maximilianus iure imperator dici posset, more institutoque maiorum a pontifice maximo Romae tradenda, auctoritate opibusque suis praesto ei esse teneretur. Cardinali per fines reipublicae cum magno comitatu eunti et redeunti sumptus est publice factus. Sed Barbadici, quem vita functum dixeramus, loco Leonardum Lauredanum, plurimis necessitudinibus et propinquitatibus atque adfinitatibus fultum, civitas sibi principem declaravit. Eo comitia primum habente, aedis Marciae procuratio, quo in magistratu Philippus Tronus, cuius pater Nicolaus annos sex civitatis principatum obtinuerat, illis ipsis diebus erat mortuus, Benedicto Pisauro, classis praefecto, magno favore civitatis est delata. Eiusdem vero aedis procurationem eam, ex qua Lauredanus summum locum inierat, Marinus Garzonius alteris comitiis est adeptus.

16 Classis interim Gallica itemque Lusitana, quas uterque rex, ut reipublicae auxilio essent, sese receperat missurum, non uno tempore altera Corcyram, altera Zacynthum adveniunt. Tametsi neu-

ning constantly counter to the sun, the years would each have been one day shorter on their return — since they would always meet the rising sun more quickly as they put more of their journey behind them in their circumnavigation, when they had at last circled the entire globe, they would of course have the sun rising a day earlier for them than when they had set out on their journey.

At about the same time that the letter of the envoy Pasqualigo reached the Senate,[12] through his ambassador the cardinal of Rouen,[13] King Louis of France made peace with the emperor Maximilian at Trento, on certain conditions. The Senate had sent their ambassador Giorgio Corner (the governor of Brescia and brother of the queen of Cyprus) to the cardinal as he set out from Milan, where he was governor of the city and duchy. The most important of the conditions was that Maximilian should recognize Louis as duke of Milan, while the king would be required to help with his authority and wealth in the matter of the coronation which would legitimize Maximilian as emperor — according to ancestral custom and usage the crown had to be conferred by the pope at Rome. The cardinal's expenses as he came and went through the Republic's territory with his great retinue were borne by the state. In place of Barbarigo, whose death I mentioned above,[14] the city declared Leonardo Loredan its doge, with the support of his many friends, family, and relations. When he held the first meeting of the Great Council, the Procuratorship of St. Mark's was conferred upon Benedetto Pesaro, captain-general of the fleet, to great popular acclaim, Filippo Tron, whose father Niccolò had been doge for six years, having just died in the office. At the second Council meeting, Marino Garzoni acquired another such Procurator's office, which Loredan had held before his elevation to the top post.

Meanwhile the French and Portuguese fleets, which their respective kings had promised to send in aid of the Republic, arrived at different times, the latter at Corfu, the former at Zante. Nei-

tra omnino earum ulli reipublicae usui fuit. Galli enim priores
apud Zacynthum cum essent, Pisauro non exspectato, quem Aus-
ter ventus Corcyrae, multos dies perincommode flans, detinuerat,
Rhodum versi profecti sunt. Sed naves illas Aloisius ad Federicum
regem Neapolis regno expellendum, inita cum Hispaniae regibus
societate, comparaverat. Itaque pulso illo, ac divisis regni regionibus ex foedere, ut Apulia Calabrisque Consalvo eorum duci traditis, reliqua omnia Aloisius obtinuerit, classem, cuius praeterea non
magnopere indigebat, iuvandae ad speciem reipublicae illo misit.
Lusitani autem paulo post, a Pisauro Corcyrae perliberaliter ac-
cepti, cum ille ab eis petiisset ut secum aut ad Dyrrhachium recuperandum aut ad insulam Leucadiam oppugnandam accederent,
neutro negotio suscepto, quod dicerent suum sibi regem mandavisse ut contra classem Thraciam una cum Veneta omnem belli
fortunam experirentur, ab oppidis obsidendis aut omnino tempt-
tandis abstinerent, quo itinere venerant domum discesserunt. Ea
erat classis navium onerariarum una de triginta; quarum quinque
satis magnae, reliquae pusillae; sed omnes magna tormentorum vi
et numero militum pulcherrime instructae, tum opertis singula-
rum tegumento versicolore puppibus, ut late aquam tentoria tan-
gerent fluctibusque verrerentur; quoniam in nostris classibus id
non fit, praeterquam in navibus longis, neque illo impendio, sed ad
usum tantum, inusitatam atque egregiam classis faciem praebuerunt.

17   Illis destituti patres classibus rogationem iusserunt, ut triremes
in Creta insula decem armarentur, eisque triremibus, quo libentius
civitates imperata facerent, praefecti Cretenses imponerentur.
Itaque triremes ex navalibus, pecunia in stipendium ex aerario est
in Cretam missa. Latum etiam, ne quid intemptatum patres relin-

ther of them, however, proved of any use to the Republic. The French having arrived at Zante before him, they did not wait for Pesaro, unfortunately delayed at Corfu by a south wind that had been blowing for many days, and set off toward Rhodes. Louis had in fact raised the fleet with a view to driving King Federico of Naples from his kingdom in alliance with the Spanish sovereigns. Once Federico was driven out, therefore, and the parts of the kingdom apportioned according to their agreement, Apulia and Calabria being handed over to their general Gonzalo and Louis getting all the rest, he sent the fleet to Zante, having no great need of it anyway, ostensibly to help the Republic. A little later, on the other hand, the Portuguese were heartily welcomed by Pesaro at Corfu, as he had asked them to come to help him recover Durazzo or attack the island of Lefkada. But they would take on neither mission, saying that the king had ordered them to try their luck in war only against the Turkish fleet, alongside the Venetian fleet, and to refrain from besieging towns or making any attack on them at all; and so they left for home the way they had come. The Portuguese fleet consisted of 29 merchantmen; five of them were of considerable size, the rest tiny. But all of them were fitted out very handsomely with a good stock of artillery and quantities of infantry. The stern of each boat was then draped with coverings of various colors, so that the spread-out fabrics reached the water and trailed in the waves. Since this does not happen in our fleets, except in warships, and then not in such a costly fashion but for practical purposes only, they gave the fleet an unusual and distinguished appearance.

Deserted by those fleets, the senators issued an order to have ten galleys fitted out on the island of Crete, and (so that the subject towns would do their bidding with greater enthusiasm) to have Cretan captains put on them. Galleys were therefore sent to Crete from the Arsenale, and money for pay from the treasury. So as to leave nothing untried, the senators also passed a measure

17

querent, ut Franciscus Capellus, cui, legatione apud Aloisium functo, Dominicus Trivisanus, Hieronymus Donatus, de regno Neapolitano sub eius imperium redacto gratulatum a senatu missi, successerant, ad Henricum Britanniae regem, socium atque amicum reipublicae, proficisceretur, auxilium in Turcas postulatum. Tametsi nuntii venerant Baiasetem, a rege Pannoniae bello lacessitum, suas vires eo convertisse, navium aedificatione intermissa. Nam e Pannonia litterae ad senatum datae certiores patres fecerant Turcas equites, cum Danubium flumen traiecissent, ut in fines hostium incursiones facerent, a regio exercitu fusos, duobus milibus interfectis, revertisse; tum transmisso ab eodem exercitu flumine, Turcas, duobus itineribus interclusos maleque habitos, partem suorum non spernendam una cum duce filioque ducis amisisse.

18   Pisaurus profectis Lusitanis, uti classe Gallica se coniungeret, omnem diligentiam adhibuit. Itaque eam demum ad Maleam nactus, muneribus et commeatu largiter praefecto classis missis, ad Mitylenem expugnandam prope invitus una se contulit, cum Galli nihil ea de re antea cum illo communicavissent, neque quid sui consilii esset ab eo petiissent. Nihilo tamen secius omnibus in rebus suam illis[3] operam praestitit. Itaque tormentis expositis Galli nostrique oppidum aggressi, muro deiecto, repulsis atque occisis propugnatoribus, magno impetu ipsum ceperunt. Arcem oppidi autem, sine qua teneri oppidum non poterat, cum iam Veneti turri deiecta signa in muros intulissent, idemque Ligures ex classe Gallica Venetis proximi fecissent, tamen capere non potuerunt, quod duorum praefectorum interitu, quos hostes interfecerant, Galli perterriti se in castra receperunt. Erant autem ex Armoricis finibus plerique qui suorum ducum dicto audientes non fuerunt. Eos se

that Francesco Capello should go to King Henry of England, an ally and friend of the Republic, to seek his aid against the Turks — Capello had served his turn as ambassador to Louis and been succeeded by Domenico Trevisan and Girolamo Donato, who were sent by the Senate to offer their congratulations on his bringing the Kingdom of Naples under his sway. And yet news came that in the face of military provocation by the king of Hungary, the sultan Bayazid had directed his efforts to that quarter and left off building ships: a letter had come to the Senate from Hungary informing the senators that Turkish cavalry had crossed the Danube in an attack on enemy territory, but had been routed by the king's army and had turned back with 2,000 men slaughtered; when the Hungarian army then crossed the river, the Turks' retreat was cut off on two fronts and they were roughly handled, losing a substantial number of men, along with their general and the general's son.

After the departure of the Portuguese, Pesaro exerted himself 18 to join the French fleet. Having finally reached it at Cape Malea, he sent generous gifts and provisions to the commander of the fleet, and somewhat against his will went with them to storm Mytilene, the French having given him no advance warning on the matter, nor had they sought his views on it. Notwithstanding, he gave them every assistance he could. And so when the artillery had been put ashore, our men attacked the town alongside the French, and once the walls were demolished and the defenders driven back and killed, they took it in a great onslaught. But as for the citadel of the town, without which it could not be held, although the Venetians had already knocked down the tower and raised their flag on the walls, and the Ligurians from the French fleet, who were next to the Venetians, had done the same, they were nevertheless unable to capture it, because the French withdrew in panic to their camp following the death of two officers killed by the enemy. There were besides many men from Brittany who disobeyed their captains' commands. As they retreated, all the rest followed, and

recipientes ceteri omnes subsecuti oppugnationem reliquerunt. Ita victoria iam plane parta, si suum Galli munus obiissent, interpellata pedem rettulit.

19   Accidit autem ab Thracibus ea in oppugnatione res permira, quae virtutem illorum atque animum ostenderet. Nam cum tot navibus oppidum obsideretur, tot hostium milia circumfusa ad muros stationes haberent, una in biremi et tribus navigiolis milites trecenti, a Baiasetis filio e Magnesia, cui praeerat, auxilio missi, in arcem se inferre velle non dubitaverunt. Sed ab Gallis intercepti, cum se fortissime defendissent, reliquis interfectis viginti eorum, Gallos elapsi, quo intenderant tenuerunt atque in arcem recepti sunt. Praefectus classis, ea spe deiectus, Pisauro relicto discessit; tempestate turbidissima deprehensus ad Cytheram insulam, navi sua elisa, ex hominibus quingentis qui in ea erant, ipse perpaucique, qui se in parte navis fracta scopuloque infixa continuerunt, evaserunt. Navis ex huius classe altera cum sexcentis hominibus interiit.

20   Pisaurus, multis diebus ad bellum gerendum idoneis Gallorum causa frustra consumptis, hieme praecipiti se ad Melum insulam contulit. Forte ibi Ericus Thrax, qui piraticam multos annos exercuerat plurimaque damna Venetis hominibus intulerat, quod ex Africa veniens naufragium ad insulam fecerat, captus a Meliis in custodia tum erat. Id simul est Pisauro nuntiatum, Ericum ad se adduci imperavit; proptereaque quod is aliquot ante annos civem Venetum, Ambrosium Contarenum, Francisci filium, cum quo mercaturae societatem inierat, nihil ab eo metuentem, cum eius navi per insidias contra iurisiurandi religionem apud Thessalonicam a se captum, igni excruciatum necaverat, vivum comburi iussit.

the attack was abandoned. In this manner a victory that was already plainly assured, had the French done their duty, was cut short and dwindled away.

Now in the course of that attack the Turks did something quite 19 marvelous that showed their courage and spirit. At a time when the town was under siege from so many ships, with so many thousands of the enemy in place spread out all along the walls, Bayazid's son sent 300 infantry as reinforcements from Magnesia, which he governed, in a small galley and three tiny boats, and they did not hesitate to try and force their way into the citadel. But they were caught by the French, and after putting up a most courageous defense, though the rest were slain, twenty of them escaped the French, carried on to their goal and were taken into the fort. With his hopes disappointed, the captain of the French fleet abandoned Pesaro and left. Caught in a very violent storm near the island of Cythera, his ship was dashed to pieces, and of the 500 men who were in it, only the captain and a very few others, who had remained in a shattered part of the ship that was stuck on a rock, made their escape. A second ship from his fleet was lost with 600 men aboard.

Having wasted many days that could have been used on prose- 20 cuting the war, thanks to the French, Pesaro made his way to the island of Melos as winter advanced. By chance Eric the Turk was being held captive there by the Melians, having been shipwrecked on the island on his way from Africa; he had been engaged in piracy for many years and had caused the Venetians grave damage. As soon as Pesaro heard this, he gave orders for Eric to be brought before him. Some years earlier Eric had entered into a trading partnership with a Venetian citizen, Ambrogio di Francesco Contarini, who had no cause to fear anything from him. But in violation of his solemn oath, Eric had captured him and his ship in a surprise attack at Thessalonica, tortured him with fire and killed him. On that account Pesaro had him burnt alive.

21   Haec dum foris administrantur, domi, quod pecunia publice deerat, senatus decrevit uti quam ipse legem prius, deinde comitia huius belli initio iusserant, ut magistratus omnes provinciales atque urbani mediam stipendiorum partem reipublicae remitterent, ea in annum unum prorogaretur. Itaque primis anni diebus cum in comitio Lauredanus quique illi adsident sexviri et quadragintavirum magistri eam legem pronuntiavissent, Ioannes Antonius Minius, civis in dicendo satis audax, qui omnem suam aetatem — erat enim iam senex — causis agendis in privatorum patrocinio consumpserat, eiusmodi contionem habuit.

22   "Non ignoro, cives, magnam me rem et multorum invidiae propositam suscepisse, qui sim contra senatus praeiudicia, contra magistratuum voluntatem pro vestris commodis et vestra incolumitate libere quae sentio dicturus. Neque dubito quin me plerique arroganter facere existiment, quod ea quae patres conscripti iampridem iusserunt, vosque ipsi rata esse voluistis, nunc patribus iterum iubentibus, ego unus, tamquam plus omnibus provideam, improbaturus surrexerim. Sed me praestat omnem invidiae aleam atque pericula subire, dum vos decipi et reipublicae muneribus spoliari, quoad potero, non patiar. Legem hoc bello quod cum rege Thracio gerimus in senatu latam, vestris sententiis sancitam, praeteritis expletam mensibus prorogare patres decreverunt, uti magistratus omnes qui per nos creantur mediam stipendii partem annum reipublicae remittant. Itaque senatu approbante ad vos veniunt, ut eam ratam et sanctam habeatis. Quid est hoc aliud quam velle vos, qui liberos, qui uxores, qui domos familiasque vestras, qui vos ipsos beneficio reipublicae magistratibus obeundis sustinetis, quando annum iam omnibus in difficultatibus confecis-

While these matters were unfolding abroad, at home, in view 21
of the depletion of state funds, the Senate decided to extend for a 1502
year the law they themselves had originally enacted at the outset
of the war, as it was subsequently by the Great Council, that all
magistrates in the provinces and in the city should remit half their
pay to the Republic. At the very beginning of the year, accordingly,
the law was announced by Loredan, the six ducal councillors who
assist him, and the Heads of the Courts of Forty in a meeting
of the Council. Thereupon Gian Antonio Minio, a citizen very
forthright in stating his views, one who had spent all his life (he
was now an old man) in arguing the cases of private citizens in
court, delivered the following speech.

"I am not unaware, citizens, that I am taking on a large task 22
that will arouse much hostility, since I am going to freely speak my
mind in your interests and for your security, and against the settled views of the Senate and the intentions of the magistrates. Nor
do I doubt that I shall be widely thought to be acting in an arrogant manner, as if I were wiser than everyone else, in rising to oppose on my own something that the Conscript Fathers long ago
commanded, that you yourselves have decided to approve, and
which the senators have now commanded again. But I would willingly run the risk of hostility, and undergo any danger, as long as I
can stop you from falling into error and losing the Republic's advantages. The law that all the magistrates appointed by us should
give back to the Republic half of their pay for a year was passed in
the Senate in the course of the war we are waging with the Turkish sultan, and ratified by your votes. It has expired in the last few
months, and the senators have now decided to extend it. The Senate approving the act, they have therefore come to you to have
your ratification and sanction. You support your children, your
wives, your homes and households, your own selves by taking on
magistracies for the good of the Republic, and now that you have
completed a year in the midst of all these difficulties, is this not

tis, alterum non habere annum, unde inopiam levare et vitam tolerare vestram queatis? An, quoniam divitibus ea lege parum iri nocitum vident, reliquos, qui re angusta utuntur, non respiciunt? Estne id alteros tamquam se ipsum diligere, quo uno mediusfidius praecepto omnis humana societas continetur? Ego vero, cives, sic existimo, quod contra hostes nihil prospere gerimus, adversa vero multa et misera singulis diebus nuntiantur, hoc ex fonte manare, quod ipsi inter nos non amamus, neque quisquam alteri consultum vult; nemo qui opibus pollet ei qui debilior est prospicit. Dii profecto immortales, qui acta et cogitationes nostras perspiciunt, irati nobis infensique sunt conatusque nostros frustra suscipi evanescereque omnes sinunt; hostibus virtutem et consilia subministrant.

23   "Tria sunt omnino hac in urbe civium genera: unum locupletum atque potentium; aliud eorum qui sunt dignitate opibusque tenuissimis; mediae inter hos fortunae tertium. Primum illud atque summum propter potentiam in tributa saepe nihil dat, propterea quod nemo principes viros cogere audet, qui plerumque in magistratibus sunt remque publicam administrant. A mediis, quae imponuntur publice onera, multi magistratus exigunt, ab infimis plane universi, nam ab iis minime resistitur. Ita fit ut qui rei minus habent, plus in aerarium conferant, illi qui omnia possident nihil tribuant, nisi cum libet, tamquam reliqui serviant, ipsi regnent atque imperent. Quod si divites fisco quae debent etiam dependant, nihil sit necesse curarum et laborum vestrorum obeundis magistratibus mercedem reipublicae condonari, ut in bellum pecunia suppeditet. Ea summa omnis pro parte media tercentum auri libras non exsuperat. Locupletum et potentium reliqua si ratio subducatur, tantundem decies aut plus etiam conficient. Illa exi-

simply to deny you a second year in which you can relieve your poverty and ameliorate your life? Or is it rather that, since they realise that this law will do little harm to the rich, they have no regard to the straitened circumstances of the rest? Heavens above, is this what it means to love others as you love yourself, the one precept by which all human society is held together? My own view, fellow citizens, is this: the fact that we are having no success against the enemy, but instead have news of many grievous setbacks each and every day, derives from this source, that we do not love each other, nor will anyone take any thought for his neighbor. None of the powerful looks out for his weaker fellows. Almighty God, who scrutinizes our thoughts and actions, is surely angry and hostile, permitting all our efforts to come to nothing and fail of effect, while to the enemy he supplies courage and counsel.

"There are in general three sorts of citizens in this city: one of 23 the rich and powerful, another of those with the most modest means and standing, and a third with middling fortunes between these. In virtue of its power, the first and highest class often pays nothing in taxes because no one dares to force the magnates to do so, being for the most part those who occupy the magistracies and govern the Republic. Many magistrates impose payment of the public tax burdens on the middle class, and certainly all of them do so from the lowest class, for they put up the least resistance. So it comes about that the less one has in the way of wealth, the more one pays into the treasury, while those who possess everything pay nothing except when they feel like it, as if the rest were slaves and they were princes and rulers. But if the rich too were to pay what they owe to the public purse, there would be no need to give the Republic the wages of your labor and pains in filling magistracies in order to fund the war. The entire sum for that does not amount on average to more than 300 gold pounds. If the outstanding accounts of the rich and powerful were reckoned up, they would come to ten times that amount, or even more. Let those of you

gite, qui praepositi estis pecuniae publicae magistratus; neque vos
fisco debentium auctoritas deterreat, ne quid facere contra ipsorum voluntatem audeatis. Abunde vobis aderit quod quaeritur;
neque tenuiorum sed bonorum tamen civium sudorem aut potius
sanguinem exsugere cogemini. Quid autem? nonne, cives, illud
etiam vos impellere ad legem repudiandam potest, quod multi magistratus, ut sit unde se liberosque suos alant, non tam iustitiam in
iurisdictionibus agitare, quam servire quaestui et studere lucro sta-
tuent, dum ea quae iniuria sibi erepta existimabunt quoquo modo
sarciant? Quamobrem omnia passim erunt venalia, neque imme-
rito, quoniam ita senatus et civitatis principes decreverunt.

24   "Animus mihi, cives, eo anno, tum cum primo lex est lata, suadebat ut eius lationi contradicerem. Sed me senatus auctoritas
continuit, quod existimabam ea vestra incommoda annum tantum
duratura, neque legem tam iniquam iri prorogatum verebar. Ita me
meae cogitationes fefellerunt. Nunc eo res est perducta, ut in vestra manu atque sententiis tamen sit totius rei exitus. Quod si vos
legem iterum iusseritis, quid erit causae, quare non aut eam opti-
mates singulis annis ferant, aut vos, quod secundo probavistis, ter-
tio etiam et quarto sanciatis? Ita res in exemplum cesserit. Vos,
cum rumor belli aliquis paulum excitabitur, statim plectemini. Ea
semper erit magistratibus opportuna erogandae pecuniae ratio;
semper reipublicae beneficio spoliabimini quod esse vestrum soli-
dum atque proprium debuerat. Quare censeo ut legem reiciatis, ne
vestra quae sunt, ipsimet proiciatis, neve ullis ab hominibus ludi-
brio vobis libentibus habeamini."

25   Haec cum esset Minius contionatus, magna perturbatio comi-
tium tenuit, quoad quis ei responsurus esset sciri potuit, Lauredano principe sua se e sella sublevante; qui stans dicere sic est

magistrates who are in charge of public funds demand those sums, and do not let the prestige of those who owe the state money deter you from being brave enough to cross their will. You will have what you seek in abundance, and will not be forced to suck the sweat, or rather the blood, of poor yet honest citizens. Then again, fellow citizens, is this too not an inducement to reject the law, that in order to find the wherewithal to feed themselves and their children, many magistrates may decide to pursue profit and aim for wealth rather than deal with their jurisdictions with justice and equity, so long as they can somehow or other make up what they will think of as unjustly snatched from them? In that case everything everywhere will be up for sale, and quite rightly so, since the Senate and the leading citizens would have it so.

"I was minded to oppose the passage of the law at the time 24 when it was first promulgated. But the Senate's authority held me back, because I thought that you would be disadvantaged for no more than a year, and I had no fear that such an unfair law would be extended. In this my calculations played me false. Now things have come to the point that the upshot of the whole matter lies after all in your hands and your votes. If you once again enact the law, what will there be to keep the leaders of the Senate from passing it every year, or you from ratifying it a third time likewise, and a fourth, once you have approved it twice? In this way a precedent will have been set. At the slightest rumour of war you will at once be punished. That will always be sufficient reason for the magistrates to exact money from you; you will always be robbed of what should have been your own secure possession to benefit the Republic. For these reasons I think you should reject the law, in case you throw away what is yours and become a laughing-stock to other men of your own volition."

When Minio had delivered this speech, the Council was 25 gripped by great excitement while they waited to find out who was going to respond to him, as Doge Loredan raised himself up from

exorsus: "Valde me hodie, cives, a mea de Ioanne Antonio Minio spe atque opinione deceptum fateor, qui, cum mihi heri esset dictum, contra legem quam ferimus, verba illum apud vos velle facere, non credidi, neque enim persuadere mihi poteram, huiusce civitatis hominem, quattuor et sexaginta annos natum, qui aliquando rempublicam attigisset, tam aequam, tam etiam necessariam rogationem, quam senatus ipse frequens probavisset, esse impugnaturum. Quamquam fuere qui dicerent, quoniam Minius ad senectutem sine ulla dignitate pervenerit, semel tantum anno superiore in magistratu adolescentulis mandari solito fuerit, id illum cogitavisse: si causam tenuiorum civium suscepisset, qui stipendio munerum reipublicae fraudari se magnopere indignantur, fore ut favorem sibi atque suffragia illorum ad magistratus adipiscendos conciliaret. Quod quidem ego, ut reliqua, falsum esse facile putavi. Vos, qui melius haec cognoscitis, quid sibi is hoc suscepto negotio voluerit vobiscum reputatote.

26   "Tu vero, Mini, solusne es omnium qui quo impliciti bello duos iam annos versemur, quantas in eo impensas fecerimus, quantas facere necesse sit, quibus in difficultatibus cogendae pecuniae dies totos solliciti, noctes insomnes conficiamus, ut hoc imperium ab hoste omnium acerrimo tueamur, nescias? Remigum, militum, praefectorum navium nostrarum, quos innumeros alimus, stipendia immane auri pondus requirunt. In arcium et oppidorum praesidiis multum pecuniae insumitur. Navalia urbana, tot classibus exhausta, magni aeris singulis mensibus indigent, ut naves, ut tormenta, ut reliqua quae bello usui sunt nostris imperatoribus subministrent. Regi Pannoniae, ut cum nostris hostibus bellum gerat, mille auri librae ternis curationibus sunt ex foedere quotannis dependendae. His tot atque tantis impensis pecunia suppeditari qui

his chair. When he was standing, he began to speak as follows: "I confess, citizens, that I have been very wrong in my expectation and estimation of Gian Antonio Minio. When it was mentioned to me yesterday that he wished to speak to you in opposition to the law we are promulgating, I did not believe, indeed could not persuade myself, that a man of this city, sixty-four years old, who had at some point taken part in its governance, would oppose a bill so fair, so necessary even, which a crowded Senate itself had approved. Although there were those who said that since Minio has reached old age without having had any political position, and has only once, last year, occupied a magistracy usually given to youths, he had dreamed up this plan: if he were to take up the cause of the poorer citizens, who are enraged at being defrauded of the salary of state office, he would inevitably win their support and votes in acquiring magistracies. This, like the rest, I gladly regarded as false. You who understand these things better should consider among yourselves what his intention was in taking up this matter.

"Can you, Minio, really be the only person who is unaware 26 what a war we have been tied up in for two years now, how great the sums expended on it and how great those we must still expend, with what difficulty we gather in funds, spending all our days in worry, all our nights without sleep, in order to defend our empire from the fiercest of all enemies? The salaries for our oarsmen, our infantry, the captains of our ships, whom we support in numbers past counting, require a massive amount of gold. Much money is consumed in the garrisoning of citadels and towns. The Arsenale, which has been emptied of so many fleets, needs considerable subvention each month to provide our commanders with ships, artillery, and the other requisites of war. To the king of Hungary 1,000 gold pounds must be paid each year in three installments so he can make war on our enemy, in accordance with our treaty. How can money be found for such huge expenses?

potest? Cives enim nostri, tributis innumerabilibus persolutis, amplius quod tribuant non habent. Provinciales, nova pecunia imperata agrisque suis praeter morem censui addictis, conqueruntur; neque quicquam, nisi coacti, fortunisque suis divenditis, in aerarium conferunt. Vectigalia reipublicae, portoriis propter bellum impeditis, anguste redimuntur. Mercatores nostri ad exteras nationes, exteri ad nos mari commeare non permittuntur. Itaque nisi nos, quorum maxime interest, quibus possumus rationibus reipublicae, belli fluctibus iactatae, opem ferimus, quis omnino erit reliquorum hominum, qui ferat? Omnes enim nobis alieniores sunt, quam nos ipsi.

27   "Nummi autem nervi bellorum sunt; sine iis bellum gerere nulla natio potest. Nos quidem, cives, quos huic urbi atque imperio praeesse voluistis, reliquique magistratus qui nobiscum una rempublicam administrant, hanc inviti legem, magnoque nostro cum dolore, ad vos ferimus, propterea quod urbes nostras ab hostibus capi, dirui, teneri, regiones vastari, populos dissipari, cives nostros aut interfici aut in servitutem abduci multo peius est quam hanc munerum mercedis portionem pro sua quemque parte reipublicae remittere. Quae adhuc mala et acciderunt, et deinceps accidere necesse est, nisi bellum magno apparatu, magnis opibus gesserimus. Opes autem hae pecunia comparantur. Minius, qui vobis ut legem repudietis suadet, illa suadet ut perpetiamini, dum ne pecunia comparari possit nititur efficere. Ego vero huius sum animi atque sententiae, ut a fanorum et templorum adytis aurum atque argentum sacrum omne nummis cudendis auferamus, quibus bellum commodius administrari possit, potius quam ea quae commemorata sunt perferamus, remque publicam periclitari atque hoc imperium proteri ab hoste impurissimo deterrimoque permittamus; idque nos, diis ipsis libentissimis quorum templa spoliabun-

After paying innumerable taxes, our citizens have nothing further to give. The people of the provinces are complaining of fresh demands for funds and of their lands being subject to taxes as they were not in the past, nor do they contribute anything to the treasury except under compulsion and after selling off their property. The revenues of the Republic make good the shortfall only in scant measure, customs duties having dried up because of the war. Our merchants are prevented from traveling by sea to foreign nations, and foreigners to us. It is we who have the greatest stake in this, and if we do not bring aid to the Republic as it is buffeted on the waves of war, by whatever means we can, who on earth will do so? Nobody, after all, is more sympathetic to us than we ourselves are.

"Money, moreover, is the sinews of war; no nation can wage 27
war without it. Citizens, it is we whom you have wished to govern this city and empire, and together with the other magistrates who administer the Republic, it is we who are putting this bill before you, reluctantly and in great distress of mind, because to have our cities taken, plundered, and occupied by the enemy, our lands laid waste, our peoples scattered, our citizens killed or taken into slavery—all this is much worse than for each of you to give the Republic that portion of the salary of his office. The troubles we have had so far must also recur in the future, unless we fight the war on a grand scale and with large forces. But those forces require money. In urging you to reject the law, Minio is urging you to undergo those hardships as he attempts to bring it about that the money cannot be raised. My own view and feeling is that, rather than suffer the misfortunes I mentioned and allow the Republic to be placed at risk and the empire to be overthrown by an abominable and wicked enemy, we should take from the sacristies of chapels and churches all the ecclesiastical gold and silver to coin money so as to prosecute the war more easily. And I think that we should do so with the entire approval of God himself, whose

tur, facturos puto. Verum adhuc quidem ad id nos descendere nulla res cogit, modo vos hoc, quod multo est aequius quodque vobis facere nulla religione impeditis licet, quod ordo amplissimus probavit, vestris hodie sententiis, vestra in patriam liberalitate pietateque iubeatis. Nam quod Minius deos nobis esse iratos commemoravit, mihi quidem dubium non est quin, qui male atque perperam agunt, ii deorum sibi iram pariant. Itaque praefecti nostri qui improbe rempublicam gesserunt partim interierunt, partim exilio ignominiaque multati deorum numen suis infensum rebus dignitatibus rationibus habuerunt. Vos, si quae decet, quae tempus exigit, quae status reipublicae turbulentus, quae pecuniae cogendae difficultas in praesentia postulat, statueritis, nihil ab diis immortalibus timetote; prospera vobis omnia ab illis secundaque advenient.

28 "Quid, quod vos iniustitiae Minius insimulat, quos lege iussa in magistratibus obeundis iurisdictiones vestras ad quaestum conversuros putat? Coniecturam scilicet de aliorum moribus a se ipse capiens, qui linguam atque ingenium, ex quo primum loqui coepit usque ad hos annos atque senium, in lucro et quaestu semper habuerit atque opes sibi amplas ea tantum ratione compararit. Quasi nesciat qui natura boni sunt, magistratibus initis in rebus difficilibus meliores porro fieri; qui pravi et mali, eos a triumviris, vel qui ad urbem sunt, vel quos querelis populorum cognoscendis in provincias mittitis, ad urbana iudicia deduci, quibus a iudiciis improbe factorum poenas luant. Ita fit ut aut suopte ingenio cives duris in rebus afflictati tamquam in cote virtutem subigant et exacuant suam, aut metu iudiciorum a maleficiis nullo non tempore aut rerum casu absterreantur.

churches will be pillaged. But so far at least, nothing compels us to descend to this, provided that by your votes today, by your generosity and sense of duty toward your city, you enact this measure — a measure which is much more just and something you may do unimpeded by religious scruple, something the highest body of state has approved. As for what Minio has brought up about God's wrath against us, I for my part have no doubt that those who do evil and wrong bring down the wrath of God on themselves. Some of our commanders who mismanaged the business of the Republic have in consequence died, others who have been punished with exile and disgrace have found the divine power adverse to their goods, their career, and their affairs. If you settle on the right course of action and what the times require, what the Republic's troubled situation and the present difficulty of collecting funds demand, you have nothing to fear from God. All that flows from Him will bring you prosperity and success.

"What of Minio's charge of unjust behavior against you? If this 28 law is enacted, he supposes you will turn your jurisdictions to profit when you hold office. Obviously he is basing his estimate of the character of others on his own: from the time he began to speak till today, right into his old age, he has always exercised his tongue and his mind for money and profit, and has acquired an ample fortune by that means alone. As if he did not know that those who are naturally good become still better when they take on magistracies in difficult circumstances; those who are corrupt and evil are taken before the Venetian courts by the state attorneys, either the attorneys in the city or those you send into the provinces to listen to the complaints of the populace, and at the hands of the courts they pay the penalty for their misdeeds. So it comes about that when they meet with difficult situations, either our citizens of their own wit grind and sharpen their courage as on a whetstone, or they are deterred from wrongdoing by fear of the courts at all times and under any circumstances.

29   "Ausus etiam tu quidem es, Mini, tria esse genera nostrorum civium dicere, locupletum mediocrium tenuiorum; atque haec inter
se dissidere ostendisti, dum a divitibus in tributa nihil penditur, a
reliquis onera omnia sufferuntur. Regnare etiam illos dixisti, hos
servire, atque in ea civitatae quae, ex quo nata est, libera et sui iuris semper fuit. Id te non puduit in contione esse mentitum? Hoc
quidem, esse tria genera, nihil impedio. Id enim omnibus in civitatibus accidere consuevit; neque aliter propemodum se habere hominum conventus ullus atque societas potest. Divites vero nihil
conferre, ceteros omnia, hoc falsum et iniuriosum est. Nulli enim
homini parcitur; omnes peraeque quod fisco debent etiam solvunt;
aut, si id per se non faciunt, ab iis qui praesunt facere coguntur.
Quaere a fisci magistratibus rationes; subduci iube; reliqua civium
inspice; nihil eorum reperies quae dixisti. An, quod bona locupletum minus hastae subiciuntur, mediorum autem et tenuiorum cottidie, propterea tu divites conferre nihil existimas, reliquos omnino
unos omnia? Male tu quidem urbis nostrae mores et rerum condicionem dispicis, aut te dispicere simulavisti. Divites, quia solvendo
sunt, sua distrahi non sinunt, sed in aerarium sponte conferunt.
Quod cum reliqui non faciunt, saepe fit ut eorum insulas fundos
praedia magistratus ad licentes transferant. Sed quid illud tandem
est, quod tu servitutis et regni nomina in hanc rempublicam in-
duxisti, alteramque civium partem in alterius invidiam trahere his
impiis vocibus excogitavisti? An, qui ab urbe condita uni atque iidem semper fuimus, nunc ut dissideamus inter nos, ut secessiones

"You have also ventured to say, Minio, that our citizens are 29 made up of three classes, the rich, the middle class, and the poor, and you have indicated that these are at odds with one another, for while the wealthy pay nothing in taxes, the whole burden is borne by the rest. You have even said that the former rule while the latter are in a state of servitude, and this in a city which from its foundation has always been free and independent. Were you not ashamed to tell this lie in a public forum? To the idea that there are three classes, I have no objection. That is generally the case in all states, and human communities and societies can hardly exist in any other way. But to say that the wealthy contribute nothing, and the others everything, that is untrue and damaging, for no man is spared and all actually pay what they owe to the treasury equally; or if they do not pay up on their own account, they are compelled to do so by those in charge. Ask for the accounts from the magistrates of the treasury, bid them be reckoned up, examine the arrears of the citizens, you will find that none of what you have said is true. Is it perhaps because the goods of the rich are seldom auctioned off, but those of the middle class and poor are every day, that you think the wealthy contribute nothing and the rest on their own everything? You have a poor understanding of the character of our city and the way things are, or you pretend to. The wealthy are able to pay and so do not allow their goods to be sold off, but make their contributions to the treasury of their own free will. And since the others do not do this, it often happens that their houses, farms, and estates are delivered by the magistrates to those who bid for them at auction. And why is it, finally, that you introduced our Republic to the words 'servitude' and 'kingship', and contrived to make one set of citizens envy the other with these dreadful words? Or do you alone think it is desirable and advisable that we should now be at odds with each other, that divisions should begin to grow up between us, when we have always been one and the same people from the foundation of the city? Is

facere incipiamus, tibi uni esse optabile et conducibile existimas? Id vis, id postulas, id efficere conaris?

30 "Vos appello, magistri decemvirum, qui sedetis, cui antiquitus magistratui cives improbos coercendi omnis est potestas attributa, vos ab eo huius rei causam reposcite. Bello quod cum Liguribus quartum gessimus, Italis populis atque in reipublicae temperatione constitutis, aerario exinanito maiores nostri edixerunt, si quis rempublicam pecunia iuvisset, eum se civitate et iure comitiorum muneraturos. Itaque bello confecto eam ob causam triginta homines ad rempublicam admiserunt. Ii totidem familias in nobilitatem intulerunt; quae nostro iure, nostris muneribus, nostro imperio deinceps sunt usae. Nobis hoc tempore bellum cum barbaris nationibus, cum gente a nostra vitae ratione, a nostris moribus alienissima, cum rege infestissimo ferocissimoque gerentibus, vos huius reipublicae alumnos, ut patriae laboranti succurratis, eius pecuniae qua una cum magistratibus ab ipsa republica donamini, mediam partem eidem reipublicae pigebit restituere? Illi suam civitatem, nobilitatem, iura, imperia in exteros, propterea quod in aerarium contulissent, libentes transfuderunt; vos vestrorum stipendiorum partem vestrae patriae, vestris aris atque focis, vestris liberis cedere gravabimini? Nam nunc quidem, ut vestri liberi ne serviant, est a vobis cautio atque curatio adhibenda. Quis hoc in animum, nisi huius urbis, horum templorum, huius comitii atque curiae hostis et eversor, posset inducere? Inventus tamen est Minius, qui hoc vobis suadere sit conatus. Sed illum sua mens, suus animus, sui mores punient.

31 "Vos autem cives, vos, inquam, cives, quos scio vestrae dicionis atque imperii, quemadmodum semper estis participes, ita numquam non amantes fuisse, ne desinite, quod semel libentissime fecistis, legem iterum velle iubere, iterum pro vestra in patriam caritate hoc, quicquid est incommodi, alacri animo annum alterum

that what you want, is that what you are really asking for, is that what you are trying to bring about?

"I call upon the Chiefs of the Ten, you who are sitting here, to 30 demand from him the reason for his intervention, since your magistracy has from ancient times been granted plenary power to punish the wrongdoing of citizens. When the coffers were empty in the fourth war that we fought against the Genoese (an Italian people and one with a republican constitution), our ancestors proclaimed that anyone who gave the Republic financial help would be rewarded with citizenship and noble status. At the end of the war, accordingly, 30 men were on that account admitted into the polity, and with them 30 families entered the nobility, which thereafter availed themselves of our law, our offices, our empire. At this time we are waging war on a barbarous people, against a race wholly alien to our way of life and customs, against an extremely aggressive and bellicose king. Will you children of the Republic bridle at returning to her half the money that she herself has given you along with your offices, to help out your country in its difficulty? Our ancestors gladly showered on foreigners admission to their citizenship, nobility, civic rights, and military commands for their contributions to the treasury. Will you object to giving up part of your salaries for your own country, your altars and hearths, your children? For you must now take the greatest care that your children do not end up as slaves. Who could have dreamed this up except an enemy and destroyer of this city, these churches, this Council chamber and Senate house?[15] Yet Minio has appeared to try and persuade you of this course of action. But his own mind, his own heart, his own character will be his punishment.

"But you citizens, yes, you citizens, since I know you have al- 31 ways loved your sovereignty and your empire, just as you have always taken your share in them, do not now fail to approve the law for a second time, something you were very glad to do once. Out of affection for your country, do not shrink from cheerfully meet-

sufferre et perpeti, dum haec reipublicae procella decedat, quae longinqua esse, nisi me meus fallit animus, non potest. Confirmate vestris sententiis illud quod eorum qui ad gubernacula reipublicae sunt positi sententiis optimum esse factu videtis. Statuite hoc iudicio, quam cuique cara esse debeat suae patriae libertas, cum ipsi vestrae libertatis causa vestra vitae praesidia reipublicae condonetis. Ostendite provincialibus atque iis qui vestris legibus parent quid ipsi facere debeant, quando vos, qui ceteros cogere potestis, communis omnium utilitatis causa leges vobis unis detrimentosas imponitis. Nemo erit hac in urbe, nemo in reliquis, ubi nomen Venetum viget, qui non nos summis laudibus efferat atque omnibus regendis populis et gentibus dignos putet, cum intelliget nihil vos muneris aliis praecipere, quin prius alterum tantum, eoque multo amplius, vobismet imperaveritis."

32 Hac a Lauredano contione habita, ubi ille consedit, lex est ferri coepta. Erant omnino in comitio iudices mille quadringenti quadraginta duo. Ex iis mille octoginta octo legem probaverunt, trecenti quadraginta septem reiecerunt; quibus non liqueret fuerunt septem. Itaque magno consensu civitatis lege iussa, Lauredanum omnes laudare, bonum esse principem dicere, cui respublica curae esset. Postridie autem eius diei Minius ob contionem seditiosam a decemviris condemnatus est ut in Arba, Illyrici insula, quoad viveret, exularet, triginta auri libris ei quicumque illum extra insulam captum magistratibus tradidisset ex eius bonis constitutis; eique rei bona sunt pignori addicta, ipsi, ut laqueo vitam finiret, poena addita.

33 Illis diebus ignominiae notam, qua Pisaurus in triremium praefectos quinque usus fuerat, patres in foro promulgari voluerunt. Ea nota erat eiusmodi. Dum classem Gallicam Pisaurus consequi cuperet, Paulus Nanus, Georgius Trivisanus,[4] Marcus Antonius De-

ing and enduring whatever inconvenience is involved, until this storm that shakes the Republic subsides, which, if I am not mistaken, cannot be far off. Let your votes confirm what you see from the votes of those placed at the helm of the Republic to be the best course of action. Let this judgment declare how dear each man should hold his country's liberty, since for the sake of your liberty you are giving the Republic the safeguards of your livelihood. Show the inhabitants of the provinces and those under your laws what they should themselves do, when for the sake of the common good, you that have the power to make others do your will impose on yourselves laws that disadvantage you alone. There will be no one in this city, no one in other cities where the name of Venice flourishes, who will not praise us to the skies and think us fit to rule over all peoples and races, when he realizes that you enjoin no duty on others without first imposing on yourselves another just as great or even considerably greater."

After Loredan had delivered this speech, he sat down and the 32 passage of the bill began. There were altogether 1,442 voting members in the Great Council. Of those, 1,088 approved the measure and 347 rejected it, with seven abstentions. With the law thus enacted by a large majority of the citizenry, Loredan was universally praised and hailed as a good doge who had the Republic's interests at heart. On the following day, the Ten condemned Minio for his seditious speech to exile on Arba, an island in Dalmatia, for the rest of his life, with 30 gold pounds from his own funds offered to anyone who captured him outside the island and handed him over to the officials. His property was confiscated as security for this, with the further penalty of death by hanging for Minio himself.

In that period, the senators decided to publicize in St Mark's 33 Square the disgrace which Pesaro had inflicted on five of his ship captains. The punishment came about in this fashion: while Pesaro was trying to reach the French fleet, Paolo Nani, Giorgio Trevisan, Marcantonio da Canal, and Niccolò Barbarigo (all from

canalis, Nicolaus Barbadicus e colonia Cretensi, Petrus Capitellus Apulus, eius missu ad Maleam profecti, quod Galli esse illis in locis dicebantur, in biremes Thracias septem inciderunt, quae navem onerariam hominum Cretensium a se captam remulco trahebant. Ea re animadversa, biremes aggredi communi consilio statuerunt. Itaque incitatis remigibus ad illas contenderunt. Sed cum eis appropinquassent, timore impediti remiges inhibuerunt seseque turpiter a congressu dimicationeque continuerunt. Accidit autem paulo post ut naves triremes aliquot e classe Gallica, quae non longe aberat, idem conspicatae biremes Thracias magno animo aggrederentur. Quae quidem res auxit illorum dedecus, quod eos reipublicae hostes quos propter formidinem ipsi dimiserant, Galli, quorum minus intererat, virtute essent atque animi praesentia consecuti. Ob eam imbecillitatem atque formidinem Pisaurus annos quinque a praefecturis omnibus illos removit stipendiaque ab iis emerita fisco addixit.

34 Iisdem diebus Gabrielem Maurum, Andream Fosculum senatus legatos creavit, qui Ferrariam proficiscerentur, Lucretiae Borgiae, Alexandri filiae, quam pater Alfonso Atestino, Herculis filio, in matrimonium spoponderat, Roma ad illum venienti, et ipsi soceroque eis de nuptiis reipublicae nomine gratulatum. E Pannonia vero crebriores allatae litterae Turcas pluribus locis fusos a regiis ducibus, occidione et praeda ingenti facta, senatui attulerunt. Neque tamen ob eas res classis curam ulla ex parte Baiasetes intermittebat. Quam quidem curam cum magnopere agitaret, reficique naves veteres suis ducibus mandavisset, atque id ei tardius negligentiusque agi ab illis atque administrari videretur, arcum sibi afferri et sagittas imperavit; quibus adductis stantem ante se illum

the colony of Crete) and Pietro Capitello of Apulia had set out for Cape Malea on his orders, since the French were said to be in those parts, when they came upon seven small Turkish galleys towing a merchantman belonging to the Cretans which they had captured. When they saw this, they decided by common agreement to attack the galleys, and so driving on the oarsmen they made for the Turkish boats. But when they had got in close, they were hampered by fear and made the rowers back water, holding themselves back from an assault and a fight in a cowardly fashion. Now it happened a little later that some large galleys from the French fleet, which was not far off, saw the same scene and launched a very spirited attack on the Turkish galleys. The fact that, although there was less at stake for them, the French had pursued with courage and presence of mind enemies of Venice which the Venetians themselves had let go out of fear, only added to their disgrace. On account of this weakness and timidity, Pesaro debarred them from all offices for five years and assigned the salaries they had earned to the treasury.

At around the same time the Senate appointed as its envoys to 34 go to Ferrara Gabriele Moro and Andrea Foscolo. Pope Alexander had betrothed his daughter Lucrezia Borgia to Alfonso d'Este, Ercole's son, and she was coming there from Rome to meet him. Moro and Foscolo were to congratulate Lucrezia, Alfonso, and her father-in-law in the name of the Republic on the occasion of the marriage. From Hungary, on the other hand, fairly frequent letters brought the Senate word that the Turks had been routed in several places by the king's generals, with massive carnage and plunder. Still, Bayazid by no means relaxed his care for the fleet on that account. Indeed, he was strongly pressing on with his concerns about the fleet, and gave his officers orders to have the old ships repaired. When he formed the view that they were carrying out the work too slowly and with insufficient care, he ordered a bow and arrows brought to him, and when they were, he shot in a

ipsum ducem qui priore apud se erat loco indignabundus trans-
fixit. Restituerat idem rex paulo ante ad libertatem cives Venetos
quos, belli initio Byzantii in vincula coniectos, in turri ad fretum
servandos miserat. Ii se libris auri centum redemerunt. Quorum e
numero Andreas Grittus Idibus Martiis ad urbem rediit, eique est
universa civitas gratulata. Attulit is ab Admete, Baiasetis duce, litteras ad senatum cum mandatis, ut si bello quod inter ipsos et
Baiasetem vigebat vellent finem imponere, mitterent Byzantium
aliquem ad pacis condiciones tractandas; ei se adiutorem futurum.

35   Interea Caesarem, Alexandri filium, augendi regni cupiditas
magnum in scelus et proditionem impulit. Nam cum Guidi
Ubaldi, Metaurensium ducis, regnum, quod unum ei deerat ad
omnem Flaminiam obtinendam, propter mirificum populorum in
illum amorem aggredi aperto bello non auderet, neque Venetos
sibi permissuros ut illum expelleret arbitraretur, neque ullam haberet suscipiendi belli causam, Guido Ubaldo omnibus in patrem
suum obsequiis, in se officiis beneuolentissimi coniunctissimique
hominis plane functo, velle se bellum Camertibus inferre simulavit, ut ad fines Urbinatium, qua iter erat ei faciendum, sine Guidi
Ubaldi suspicione tamquam alio tendens cum exercitu accederet.
Atque ut bono se in illum esse animo fidem ei maiorem faceret et
suis eum opibus exueret, ne tueri sese posset communitior, a
Guido Ubaldo ut auxiliares ad id bellum copias cum tormentis
muralibus ad se mitteret pro amicitiae iure per legatos postulavit.
Iis impetratis atque missis, cum ad fines regni venisset, repente in
illos hostiliter irrupit, et magna celeritate adhibita, quod neminem
obvium habebat, Urbinum contendit, parumque abfuit quin Guidum ipsum Ubaldum caperet. Sed is paucarum horarum beneficio

rage the very captain who was the chief of all his officers as he stood before him. A little earlier, the sultan had also restored to liberty the Venetian citizens that he had imprisoned at Constantinople at the outset of the war and had sent to be kept in a tower on the Bosporus. They ransomed themselves for 100 gold pounds. One of their number, Andrea Gritti, returned to Venice on 15 March[16] and was congratulated by the entire city. He brought with him from Bayazid's general Admete a letter to the Senate with a proposal that if they wanted to end the war which existed between them and Bayazid, they should send someone to Constantinople to negotiate peace terms, in which Admete would support him.

Meanwhile Alexander's son Cesare Borgia was driven to com-   35 mit a crime of great treachery by his desire to increase his realm. The people of Guidobaldo, Duke of Urbino, had a remarkable affection for him, and on that account Borgia did not dare to wage open war on the duchy, all that was lacking to his taking total control of Romagna. He also thought the Venetians would not allow him to drive Guidobaldo out, nor did he have any reason to begin hostilities, since Guidobaldo had always shown complete loyalty to Borgia's father, and had patently been a very close and friendly ally to Borgia himself. For all these reasons, Borgia pretended that he wanted to make war on Camerino, to enable him to take his army into the territory of Urbino, through which his route lay, without arousing Guidobaldo's suspicion, as though he were heading elsewhere. In order to increase his trust in his good intentions toward him, and to strip him of his resources so that he would be in a weaker position to defend himself, he asked Guidobaldo through envoys to send him auxiliaries and siege artillery for the campaign in virtue of their friendship. With these granted and sent, when he reached the borders of the duchy, he launched a sudden attack on it, and having no one in his way, marched with all speed to Urbino, coming close to capturing Guidobaldo himself. But with the advantage of a few hours Guidobaldo fled on farm horses

in iumentis agricolarum, et veste rustica, itineribus deviis, quod
omnia nota loca per Caesaris milites obsessa tenebantur, fugiens
Ravennam se recepit atque inde Mantuam est profectus; quam ad
urbem paulo ante uxor eius Elisabeta, Francisci Mantuanorum ducis soror pudicissima lectissimaque, se contulerat, cum officii
causa, Alexandri postulatu, Lucretiae Borgiae ad maritum proficiscenti comes itineris fuisset.

36   Ea re permotis patribus, equites quingenti, pedites mille Ravennam sunt missi, ut, cum iis copiis quae ibi erant coniuncti, oppidi
praesidium augerent, si quid a Caesare consilii, cui fides haberi
nulla poterat, contra rempublicam iniretur. Neque multo post
Anna Candala, natione Aquitana, Aloisii regis Gallorum propin-
qua, ad Vladislaum Pannoniae regem, cui erat nuptui per legatos
tradita, proficiscens Venetias venit cum magno utriusque regis comitatu. Ei fines reipublicae ingressae sumptus est publice atque
largiter factus. Ad urbem ubi fuit, omnia in illam liberalitatis et
benevolentiae officia profuse collata, ut, cum exacto mense discederet, Lauredano principi dixerit tum primum se reginam sibi ipsi
visam, cum apud illum fuit; postea vero quam in Pannonia regiam
exercere dignitatem coepit, amica et benevola reipublicae omnibus
in rebus semper fuerit. Interim Aloisius rex domo discesserat, ut
in Italiam se conferret, Neapolitano bello, quod cum Hispaniae regibus propter finium controversiam gerebat, auxilia comparaturus.
Eo Mediolani finibus appropinquante, senatus Bernardum Bembum, patrem meum, e praetura Veronensi, qua in praetura tunc
erat, legatum misit, ut Aloisio, reipublicae nomine salvere iusso, de
adventu gratularetur. Is regi ad Vegevenum oppidum occurrit
estque apud illum commoratus, dum is Mediolani fuit. Sed, rege

dressed as a peasant, keeping off the roads because all the generally known places were blockaded and occupied by Borgia's soldiers. Guidobaldo withdrew to Ravenna and from there went to Mantua, whither his wife Elisabetta [Gonzaga], the chaste and excellent sister of Francesco, Duke of Mantua,[17] had made her way a little before (at the request of Alexander and as a courtesy, Elisabetta had been the traveling companion of Lucrezia Borgia as she went to meet her husband).

The senators were greatly disturbed by these events, and sent 36
500 cavalry and 1,000 infantry to Ravenna to strengthen the town's garrison by joining the forces already there, in case Borgia, absolutely untrustworthy as he was, should make any hostile move against the Republic. And not much later Anne de Candale of Gascony,[18] a relative of King Louis of France, came to Venice on her way to meet King Ladislas of Hungary, to whom she had been betrothed through envoys, in the company of a considerable retinue of both kings. Her entry into Venetian territory was liberally funded at public expense. While she was in the city, she was showered with every token of generosity and good will, so that on her departure a month later she remarked to Doge Loredan that she had felt herself a queen for the first time when she was his guest. After she took up her royal position in Hungary, she proved to be in every respect a constant friend and well-wisher to the Republic. In the meantime King Louis had left home to make his way to Italy, intending to bring reinforcements to the war in Naples which he was fighting against the Spanish sovereigns over a disputed boundary. As he approached the territory of Milan, the Senate sent, from the governorship of Verona that he then held, my father, Bernardo Bembo, as their ambassador to greet Louis in the name of the Republic and congratulate him on his arrival. He met the king at the town of Vigevano and remained with him while he was at Milan. When the king left for Liguria to send his reinforce-

in Liguriam profecto ad auxilia in regnum Neapolitanum mari transmittenda, Veronam rediit.

37 Dum haec domi administrantur, a Pisauro, apud Chrysopolim atque in sinu Thessalonico depositis militibus, damna sunt plurima illata praedaeque ingentes factae; tum in Aegaeo captae naves onerariae duodecim, biremes undecim. Atque is ad Maleam cum venisset, naves triremes Rhodiorum tres, onerarias duas, regis Gallorum triremes quattuor ad se missas reperit. Neque multo post Iacobus Pisaurus, Alexandri legatus, suas triremes cum Pisauri classe coniunxit. Erat autem universae classis navium omnis generis numerus ad septuaginta. Quibuscum navibus de legatorum consilio ad insulam Leucadiam oppugnandam se convertit.

38 Eo cum appropinquaret, pontificis legatum praemisit, qui per vada eo ab latere quod ad orientem spectat oppidum aggrederetur. Vadis autem ea parte insula maxime cingitur. Is accelerans, per diorictum in vada sese inferens, duodecim biremes quae ibi stationem habebant, eaque maria percurrentes Venetorum navibus infensissimae diu fuerant, et tunc, ut aditu classem prohiberent, occurrebant, omnes fugavit; pauloque post vacuas hominibus occupavit, cum ii sese raptim in litus eiecissent; quos oppidani fugientes receperunt. Iis captis, quod illis in vadis erat a continenti ad oppidum via aquis tecta sic, ut equites commeare ea possent, ibi naves aliquot disposuit; quibus navibus Thracum turmas equitum tres, qui per illam viam, ut essent oppidanis auxilio, vicinis ex locis adventabant, reppulit, cum tamen antea munitionem pro tempore, quae transitum impediret, media in via effecisset. Ea Thraces munitione retardati, dum perrumpere conantur, tormentis se navium vulnerandos praebuerunt; amissisque perpluribus, duce eorum

ments to the Kingdom of Naples by sea, Bembo returned to
Verona.

While these matters were unfolding at home, Pesaro put his   37
soldiers ashore at Chrysopolis and in the bay of Thessalonica,
causing a great deal of damage and taking a huge haul of plunder.
Then in the Aegean he captured twelve merchantmen and eleven
small galleys. When he reached Cape Malea, he found he had
been sent three Rhodian galleys, two merchantmen, and four galleys of the king of France. Shortly afterwards Jacopo Pesaro, Pope
Alexander's legate, united his galleys with Pesaro's fleet.[19] The
number of ships of all sorts in the fleet as a whole was about sev-
enty. On the advice of the proveditors, he turned with these ships
to an attack on the island of Lefkada.

As he drew near, he sent the papal legate on ahead to attack the   38
town through the shallows on the eastern side (the island is mostly
surrounded by shoals on that side). Putting on speed he burst
through a channel into the shallows, and routed all of the twelve
small galleys that were anchored there—they had long been extremely troublesome to Venetian shipping as they patrolled those
seas, and at that point were forming a blockade to stop the fleet
coming in. Shortly thereafter Pesaro took possession of them,
though there were no men on board, the crew having scrambled
ashore in a hurry; as they fled, they were taken in by the townspeople. In the shallows there was a road from the mainland to the
town which was covered with water, but cavalry could still pass
along it, so he stationed some ships there after the capture of the
Turkish boats. With these he threw back three squadrons of
Turkish cavalry that were coming along the road from places
round about to help the townspeople, although he had already
completed a temporary defensework in the middle of the road to
block their passage. Slowed down by the fortification, the Turks
made themselves vulnerable to artillery fire as they attempted to
break through, and suffered a great many casualties, their captain

equo deiecto, nulla parte munitionis perrupta, unde venerant redierunt. Atque idem interea legatus suorum militum partem, equitesque omnes quos in navibus eam ad rem habebat, cum primo
adventu in terram exposuisset atque ad oppidum contendere iussisset, illi, itinere (quod quidem erat passuum milium quattuor)
celeriter confecto, circumvecti, audacissime pugnantes, eo ipso die
proöppidum capiunt.

39   Pisaurus praefectus, quem mari reliquam classem, ventis non
secundis qui eo die flaverant, circumducere oportuit, postero die
ad oppidum oppugnandum sese contulit ac muros quatere tormentis coepit. Erant in oppido milites Thraces quingenti, qui se
acerrime una cum oppidanis defendebant. Ii cum magna tormentorum vi, oppugnatione non intermissa, premerentur, septimo die
deditionem facere voluerunt. Is fuit dies ad diem tertium Kalendarum Septembris. Sed dum inter se ea de re consulunt, militibus irrumpentibus oppidum capitur; ipsi atque oppidani captivi facti;
praeda omnis viritim divisa. Hostes prima oppugnationis die Gabrielem Superantium, triremis praefectum, interfecerunt, capite
pila ferrea disiecto. Eius frater Hieronymus, adolescens nullo reipublicae munere antea functus, paucis post diebus quam id est Venetias allatum, magno comitiorum favore in senatu adlectus est,
praeteritis quamplurimis qui et magistratus gesserant et aetate
longe praestabant.

40   Patres ut primum ex Admetis litteris in spem pacis venerunt,
propterea quod hiems suberat, Pisauro mandarunt ut, triremibus
viginti apud se retentis, classem reliquam domum remitteret;
atque ad regem Pannoniae litteras dederunt; quibus litteris quid
ab Admete habuissent certiorem illum fecerunt, velleque se suum
hominem Byzantium mittere significaverunt, atque ab eo petierunt
ut et ipse suum hominem eodem mitteret, quo maiore cum digni-

being thrown from his horse. Not managing to break through the defenses anywhere, they returned whence they had come. In the meantime, the legate Pesaro had put part of his infantry and all the cavalry that he had on the ships for the purpose on shore, and ordered them to head for the town with all haste. After a quick four-mile march, they surrounded the town, and fighting with great valor took the outskirts that very day.

The Venetian commander Benedetto Pesaro should have 39 brought round the rest of the fleet by sea, but the winds that were blowing that day were not favorable, so on the following day he took himself off to attack the town and began to batter the walls with his artillery. There were 500 Turkish soldiers in the town, who were putting up a fierce defense alongside the inhabitants. But under pressure from the great artillery barrage and a relentless assault, after six days they were ready to surrender. This was on 30 August. But while they were discussing the matter among themselves, the soldiers burst in and took the town, making the Turks and the townspeople prisoner, and sharing out the booty man by man. On the first day of the attack the enemy had killed the galley captain Gabriele Soranzo, his head blown off by a cannonball. When the news was brought to Venice a few days later, his brother Girolamo, a youth who had held no previous state office, was elected to the Senate by a large majority in the Great Council, many men who had served as officials and were much older than him being passed over.

As soon as the Signoria had its hopes of peace raised by 40 Admete's letter, they ordered Benedetto Pesaro to keep 20 galleys with him, as winter was coming on, and send the rest of the fleet home. They sent a letter to the king of Hungary informing him of Admete's communication. They indicated their willingness to send a representative to Constantinople and asked him to send his own man there, so that peace could be negotiated and concluded with greater authority and on fairer terms. When he was apprised

tate pax aequioribusque condicionibus tractari conficique posset. Vladislaus intellecta re patrum consilium probavit, facturumque quod vellent de legato se recepit. Illi Zachariam Frescum, decemvirum scribam, ire Byzantium iusserunt.

41 Guidus Ubaldus regno amisso ad Aloisium regem Galliae Mediolanum sese conferens auxilia in Caesarem postulatum, ubi nihil in eo probitati et innocentiae contra perfidiam et crudelitatem esse praesidii cognovit, cum uxore Venetias venit. Patres eum libentes exceperunt et, domo pro illius dignitate publice tradita, bono esse animo iusserunt. Qua ex domo paulo post, cum Metaurenses, Caesaris arcium praefectis et militibus interfectis oppidisque aliquot receptis, eius imperio se subtraxissent, suum in regnum facile rediit; atque in eo, ab Ursinae gentis principibus adiutus, devictis hostibus suam dignitatem aliquot menses obtinuit. Ea rerum mutatione plerique se populi reipublicae commendaverunt, orantes ut se in deditionem reciperet. Est in Ariminensium finibus mons excelsus, duplici iugo, qua mare prospicit, praeruptus; alia parte declivitatem habet late in occasum patentem, vinetis et segetibus uberem. Illis in iugis duae arces sunt summa in crepidine, quibus oppidum subiacet civitasque montanorum hominum, qui rempublicam administrant neque ulli regi serviunt. Crepidines Pinnae Marinianae appellantur. Ii, et ipsi ne ab Caesare in servitutem redigerentur cum magnopere timerent, senatui eo tempore significaverunt velle se sub eius imperio esse; mitteret ad se aliquem reipublicae nomine; se illius dicto audientes futuros imperataque facturos. Sed neque hos nec ceteros qui se reipublicae dedere cupiebant patres recipiendos censuerunt.

of the matter, Ladislas approved the Signoria's plan, and said he would do as they wished in the matter of the envoy. The Signoria ordered Zaccaria Fresco, the chancellor of the Ten, to go to Constantinople.

Guidobaldo [da Montefeltro], after losing his duchy, made his 41 way to King Louis of France at Milan to ask for his assistance against Borgia, but when he saw that no help was forthcoming from Louis to aid virtue and innocence against treachery and cruelty, he went to Venice with his wife. The senators were glad to welcome him, and gave him a house befitting his rank at public expense, bidding him be of good courage. But the people of Urbino slew Borgia's commanders and soldiers in the fortress, recovered a number of their towns, and cast off Borgia's rule, and it was not long before Guidobaldo left the house and returned to his duchy without difficulty. With the help of princes of the Orsini family, he there defeated his enemies and recovered his position for some months. This turn of events induced many communities to seek the Republic's protection, pleading to be taken into its power. There is in the territory of Rimini a lofty mountain, a sheer cliff on the side overlooking the sea with two ridges;[20] on the other side it has a slope spreading out broadly toward the west with rich vineyards and arable land. On the topmost spurs of the ridges are two citadels, under which lie a town and mountain community which have a republican government independent of any ruler. These spurs are called the Penne di San Marino. Extremely worried that they too would be enslaved by Borgia, these people indicated to the Senate at that juncture that they wanted to place themselves under their authority. The Senate should send them someone in the name of the Republic whom they would obey and whose bidding they would do. The senators, however, decided to accept neither the people of San Marino nor the others who wished to put themselves under the Republic's protection.

42   Miserant inter haec reges Hispaniae ad senatum Laurentium
Suarem, illum eundem qui legatus eorum bello Gallico apud rempublicam fuerat. Is, clam itinere per Galliam confecto, paucis ante
Kalendas Decembres diebus ad urbem venit. Atque illi auri libra
singulis est mensibus in sumptum a senatu constituta. In primis
apud Lauredanum principem et patres sermonibus Suares, de
Aloisio rege Gallorum questus, quod foederi cum suis inito regibus non stetisset, ut cui neque sua neque aliena satis essent, ab
eius amicitia patres avertere modis omnibus est conatus, illum
affirmans propterea Caesaris rebus tanto studio favisse, ut esset
qui reipublicae finibus immineret neque quiescere illam sineret;
gaudere implicitam esse bello Thracio civitatem. Quam ad eos
classem miserit, ad speciem, non ad ullam reipublicae frugem misisse. Id eventu patuisse, quod obfuerit potius quam ulli usui fuerit. Hispaniae regum voluntatem omni tempore cum reipublicae
voluntate consensisse, quoniam utrique fidem et pietatem colerent.
Si se ii foederibus una firment, neminem nocere eis posse.

43   Haec et his similia de Suare non semel a patribus audita, tametsi vera esse pleraque cognoscerent, illos tamen non moverunt,
ut quod ipsis cum Aloisio foedus intercedebat ulla ex parte viola-
rent. Tantum dicere sese Hispaniae regum fidem atque virtutem et
propensum in rempublicam animum plurimi sane facere semperque facturos; cum Aloisio foederis condicionibus se teneri; moleste ferre bellum inter ipsos exerceri potius quam vigere pacem; si
quid possent ad reconciliandam inter eos gratiam, de eo si admo-
neantur, se non defuturos, amicissimorumque hominum officio in

Meanwhile the Spanish sovereigns had sent to the Senate   42
Lorenzo Suarez, the same man who had been their ambassador to
the Republic during the war with France.[21] Making his way
through Lombardy in secret, Suarez arrived at Venice a few days
before the beginning of December. The Senate fixed payment for
his expenses at one gold pound per month. In his initial discussions with Doge Loredan and the senators, Suarez complained
that King Louis of France had not stuck to the terms of the treaty
he had agreed with his sovereigns, like someone for whom neither
his own possessions nor those of others were enough. He used every means at his disposal to detach the senators from their friendship with Louis, asserting that the reason he supported Borgia's
interests so strongly was to have someone who could pose a threat
to the Republic's territory and allow her no peace. Louis, he said,
was happy that Venice was tied up with the Turkish war, and the
fleet he had sent them was only for show and not intended to help
the Republic. That much was clear from the outcome, as it had
proved to be more of an obstacle than anything useful. The policy
of the Spanish sovereigns was always in accord with that of Venice, since both of them had a high regard for trustworthiness and a
keen sense of their obligations. If they supported one another with
mutual treaties, no one would be able to do them harm.

The senators heard these and similar statements from Suarez   43
more than once, but even though they knew them to be for the
most part true, they were still not in the slightest moved to break
the treaty between themselves and Louis. They only said that
while they of course set great store upon the loyalty and valor of
the sovereigns of Spain and their friendly attitude toward the Republic, and they always would, they were bound by the terms of
their treaty with Louis. They were unhappy that instead of peace
a state of war existed between them, and if they could do anything
toward achieving reconciliation between them, and were told of it,
they would not be found wanting, and would act as true friends

utrumque functuros. Cum Vladislao autem Pannoniae rege, de legati ad Baiasetem missione diem ex die ducente, propterea quod, pace cum illo a senatu inita, nisi novae sponsiones intercederent, stipendiis reipublicae carendum ipsi erat, ne res tanta differretur, legati reipublicae pacti sunt, uti mille auri librae, regi annis singulis ab senatu bello Thracio dari solitae, ad tercentum redigerentur, quoad Baiasetes viveret, tribus item pensionibus persolvendas.

44   Alexander cum vidisset Guidum Ubaldum Ursinae gentis studiis regnum suum recuperavisse, orando, territando, magna pollicendo eius familiae principibus in suas traductis partes, foedus cum illis percussit. Simul ab Aloisio missis ad se auxiliiis Caesar magnisque copiis undique comparatis, Guidum Ubaldum, quem quidem sine spe, sine opibus destitutum amici deseruerant, iterum regno expulit, cum tamen ille munitissimum natura totius regni oppidum, misso ad id custodiendum Octaviano Fregosio, adolescente sororis suae filio, cum militibus, et omnium rerum pro tempore copia communitius factum, obtineret. Urbinatibus receptis ad Senogalliam oppugnandam Caesar primis anni diebus recta profectus, ubi civibus sine mora se dedentibus oppido est potitus, Ursinae gentis principes, eos ipsos cum quibus paulo ante foedus percusserat quique secum una venerant omnes in vincula coniecit eaque de re Alexandrum patrem mira celeritate certiorem fecit. Ille statim Baptistam Ursinum cardinalem, qui foederis auctor fuerat, magna apud suos auctoritate, nihil eiusmodi verentem, ad se vocatum custodiae tradidit; qua in custodia paucis post diebus est mortuus. Coniectis ab Caesare in vincula partim nocte proxima, reliquis in Senensium fines adductis, quo Caesar cum exercitu

toward both parties. King Ladislas of Hungary for his part was dragging out from day to day the despatch of an envoy to Bayazid, since if peace was struck with the sultan by the Senate it would entail the loss of his payments from the Republic, in default of a new agreement between them. So as not to put off a matter of such importance, the Venetian ambassadors came to an arrangement with him that the 1,000 gold pounds which the Senate regularly gave the king each year for the Turkish war would be reduced to 300, to be paid in three installments as long as Bayazid lived.

When Pope Alexander saw that Guidobaldo had recovered his 44 duchy with the support of the Orsini family, he brought their leaders over to his side by a combination of wheedling, frightening threats, and extensive promises, and struck a treaty with them. At the same time, having been sent reinforcements by Louis and after assembling a great force from every quarter, Borgia drove Guidobaldo from his duchy again, at a time when he had been deserted by all his friends and was destitute, without hope, without resources. But Guidobaldo nevertheless held on to the town that had the strongest natural defenses of his entire duchy and sent there Ottaviano Fregoso, his sister's young son, making it more secure with a force of soldiers and all necessary supplies, as far as time allowed. After retaking Urbino, Borgia at once set out to attack Senigallia at the beginning of the year . The citizens surren- 1503 dered without delay and Borgia took control of the town, thereupon imprisoning the leaders of the Orsini who had come with him — the very ones with whom he had a short while before struck a treaty — and informing his father of the event with remarkable speed. The latter immediately summoned and imprisoned Cardinal Battista Orsini, who had organised the treaty, a man of great influence among his people who had no suspicion of anything of the sort, and he died in custody a few days later. Of those thrown into prison by Borgia, some were hanged the next night, the rest hanged after being taken into Sienese territory, where Borgia had

contenderat, laqueo gula fracta. Idem vitae finis Venantio et Octaviano, adolescentulis Camertium regis liberis, captis a Caesare Pisauri, datus. Pater eorum, regno amisso clam elapsus, paulo post ad urbem venit.

45   Ob eas Caesaris actiones, qui cum Camertibus Ariminum etiam in suam dicionem redegerat, senatus, uti suos fines magis communiret, Livianum Carracciolumque cum equitibus et militibus Ravennam misit. Guidus Ubaldus, hostem fugiens, cum se Pitilianum in Etruriam contulisset diesque complures ibi fuisset, Caesare Pitilianum bello aggredi velle dictitante, ut illum interciperet, magno cum periculo per Senarum et Florentinorum agrum in fines reipublicae atque ad urbem se recepit. Cui a senatu libra auri dono in sumptum singulis mensibus constituta. Quoniam autem libido ea inter cives creverat, ut quamplurimi sacerdotia, quae habere bonis artibus non poterant, Romae coemerent, qua in urbe eius rei consuetudo facultasque, ab Alexandro instituta, late palamque invaluerat, decemviri sanxerunt, si quis in posterum id faceret, eius bona fisco inferrentur, ipse ab urbe atque urbis finibus quamdiu viveret exul esset.

46   Neque multo post Ioannes Michael, civis Venetus, cardinalis, qui Pauli secundi pontificis maximi sororis filius fuerat, Romae veneno interiit, quod ei Alexander a praefecto Michaelis epularum dari iussit. Causa interficiendi hominem fuit aurum atque argentum quod is habere existimabatur; quarum omnino rerum inexplebilis Alexandri animum cupiditas ad omnem iniquitatem incendebat, uti filio pecuniam exercitibus alendis suppeditaret, quo is Italorum principum regna occupare celerius posset, se iam sene. Minister veneni haud multo post, Iulio pontifice maximo re per

gone with his army. Venanzio and Ottaviano, the young sons of the lord of Camerino[22] who had been captured by Borgia at Pesaro, met the same end. Following the loss of his principality, their father made a secret escape and a short while later went to Venice.

In view of these activities of Borgia, who along with Camerino 45 had also brought Rimini into his power, the Senate sent d'Alviano and Caracciolo to Ravenna with cavalry and footsoldiers to secure their borders. In his flight from the enemy, Guidobaldo made his way to Pitigliano in Tuscany and spent several days there, with Borgia proclaiming his readiness to attack the town in order to catch him. He then retreated at great risk through the lands of Siena and Florence into the territory of the Republic and so to Venice. The Senate decided to give him a gold pound each month for his expenses. Now a passion had sprung up among the citizens whereby a great many of them bought benefices at Rome that they could not have had by honorable means. Alexander had begun the fashion and provided the opportunity for this custom, which had become widespread and unconcealed at Rome. The Ten accordingly ordained that if anyone were to do this in future, his property would be confiscated and he would be exiled from the city and its territories for as long as he lived.

Shortly after that, Cardinal Giovanni Michiel, a Venetian citi- 46 zen who had been the son of Pope Paul II's sister, died at Rome of poison which Alexander had told Michiel's steward to give him. The reason for killing him was the gold and silver he was thought to have. Alexander's mind had indeed been gripped by an insatiable lust for such things and it was driving him into all sorts of iniquity in order that he could supply his son with funds for raising armies and so bring nearer the day when he could take over the realms of the Italian princes, Alexander himself being now an old man. The man who administered the poison was imprisoned not long afterwards, in the reign of Pope Julius, when fresh evidence

indicium enuntiata, in vincula coniectus, quaestione habita sui sceleris poenas persolvit.

47   Baiasetes interim, indutiis cum Sophi Armeniae rege initis,
cum quo sibi atrox bellum intercedebat, ad bellum Venetum solu-
tior factus, animos quos deiecerat sumpsit; deque pace cum republica nihil se facturum dixit, nisi Veneti Leucadiam sibi insulam
restituerent. Patres, de eo per Admetis ad Andream Grittum litteras perque nuntios certiores facti, ne diutius eo bello contereren-
tur, pacem cum Baiasete fecerunt, Leucadiamque insulam, cuius
oppidum magna impensa Pisaurus longe firmius iam communi-
tiusque fecerat, Baiaseti restituendam curaverunt, Pisauro domum
reditione permissa. Ea de pace uti diis immortalibus gratiae agerentur atque auri librae tres dono in sacerdotum[5] collegia distri-
buerentur, senatus censuit. Et quoniam Baiasetes legatum suum
una cum Zacharia, domum redeunte, ad urbem miserat, ut,
quando ipse legato reipublicae iusiurandum dederat fore de pace
uti pollicebatur, ita is dando item a Lauredano principe iuriiu-
rando praesens adesset, senatus Andream Grittum legavit, qui ad
Baiasetem cum eodem legato, reverti properante, proficisceretur.
Cui legato vestis aurea et item serica cum ternis auri libris dono
data. Eadem est pax aliquot post menses a Baiasete cum Vladislao
rege Pannoniae inita.

48   His rebus ita constitutis, ab Aloisio rege Galliae missus ad senatum legatus paucis ante Kalendas Quintiles diebus postulavit
uti novum suo cum rege patres foedus sancirent. Is fuit Ioannes
Lascaris Byzantius, Graecis litteris eruditus. Atque id ea de causa
rex procurandum sibi et contendendum statuerat, ut, quoniam
Consalvus, Hispani dux exercitus in Brutiis, suum exercitum in-
terfecto duce fuderat fugaverat, regnumque Neapolitanum prope

threw light on the matter, and after interrogation he paid the penalty for his crime.

Meanwhile Bayazid had struck a truce with Sofi, the ruler of 47 Armenia, with whom a savage war had been going on in the meantime, and having thus a freer hand for the Venetian war, he regained the fighting spirit he had lost. He said he would do nothing about the peace treaty with the Republic unless the Venetians returned the island of Lefkada to him. Learning of this from letters of Admete to Andrea Gritti and from messengers, the senators made peace with Bayazid so as not to be further worn down in prosecuting the war, and saw to it that the island of Lefkada was restored to him, after Pesaro had at great expense made its town far stronger and more secure. Pesaro was given permission to return home. The Senate voted to give public thanks to Almighty God for the peace, and to distribute three gold pounds among the monasteries as a gift. Bayazid had sent his envoy to Venice in company with Zaccaria Fresco as the latter returned home, so that, just as he had given his oath to the Venetian ambassador that the peace would take place as he had promised, so his ambassador would be present when Doge Loredan likewise took the oath. The Senate accordingly chose Andrea Gritti to go to Bayazid with the same ambassador, who was in a hurry to return. The ambassador was given a gift of a golden robe and another of silk, along with three gold pounds. Bayazid reached the same peace agreement with King Ladislas of Hungary some months later.

Things having been settled in this way, an envoy sent to the 48 Senate by King Louis a few days before the beginning of July asked the senators to ratify a new treaty with his king. This was Janus Lascaris of Constantinople, a scholar of Greek literature. The reason the king supposed he really had to have such a treaty was that Gonzalo, the commander of the Spanish army in Calabria,[23] had shattered and routed his army, killing its commander, and had brought almost all the Kingdom of Naples under

omne sub regum suorum imperio redegerat, renovato foedere Veneti cum Hispaniae regibus bellum una facere tenerentur. Atque ut ad eam rem patres animum inducerent, amplissimae ab Aloisio condiciones proponebantur; quas omnes senatus respuit, veteri se foedere contentum dictitans.

49 Alexander, veneno quod furtim dari Adriano cardinali familiari suo iusserat, cuius in hortis una cum Caesare filio cenabat, per ministri imprudentiam epoto, quinto decimo Kalendas Septembris excessit e vita. Caesar eodem haustu paene absumptus difficilem in morbum incidit. Qua in re deorum immortalium mens et voluntas visa est magnopere adfuisse, cum ii qui plurimos et Romanae reipublicae principes et clientes suos, ut eorum opibus et thesauris potirentur, veneno necaverant, et tunc suum hospitem atque alumnum adiungi ad reliquos necarique mandaverant, eo ipso in ministerio semet pro illo interficerent. Illis diebus Benedictus Pisaurus classis praefectus, vir egregia virtute, cum se ad reditum compararet, valetudine impeditus Corcyrae interiit.

50 Patres ob Alexandri mortem, id quod re evenit existimantes, fore ut multa oppida, malis artibus ab Caesare capta, eius imperium essent detrectatura, praefectis aliquot Ravennam missis, copiarum quae ibi erant numerum duplicaverunt. Pauloque post decemviri Christophorum Maurum, unum ex quinqueviris qui res bellicas in senatu procurant, legatum creaverunt atque in Flaminiam contendere iusserunt, ut, si quod ex Caesaris oppidis sponte reipublicae se dederet, ab eo reciperetur. Cumque complura iam Romanorum principum castella pagique, eiectis aut interfectis Caesaris ministris, ad priores dominos rediissent, Pisaurum Ariminum Camerinum Senogallia, etiam Populonia, cuius regem Caesar expulerat oppidumque ceperat, idem factura dicerentur,

the sway of his monarchs; so if the treaty was renewed, the Venetians would be obliged to join him in making war on the Spanish sovereigns. To incline the senators toward his plan, Louis proposed very generous terms, but the Senate rejected all of them, declaring itself content with the former treaty.

By a mistake on the part of a servant, Alexander swallowed a   49
poison which he had ordered to be secretly given to Cardinal Adriano, one of his household, in whose gardens he was dining with his son Cesare Borgia, and he departed this life on 18 August. Borgia was nearly carried off by the same draught and fell into an intractable illness. The will and intention of Almighty God was thought to have played a large part in this episode: men who had murdered by poison a considerable number of the princes of the Church of Rome as well as their own dependents, so as to get their hands on their wealth and treasure, and had ordered that their own host and protégé should follow the rest on that occasion and be murdered, had by serving up that same poison killed themselves instead of him.[24] At that time Benedetto Pesaro, captain-general of the fleet and a man of outstanding valor, was surprised by illness as he was preparing to return home, and died at Corfu.

With the death of Alexander the senators foresaw what did in   50
fact happen, that many of the towns taken by Borgia's trickery would reject his rule, and accordingly sent some officers to Ravenna, doubling their forces there. Not long after that, the Ten appointed as their proveditor Cristoforo Moro, one of the five men who oversee military matters in the Senate,[25] and ordered him to proceed with all haste to Romagna so he could receive any of Borgia's towns that surrendered to the Republic of their own free will. Already a number of castles and villages of Roman princes had thrown out or killed Borgia's underlings and returned to their former masters, and Pesaro, Rimini, Camerino, Senigallia, even Piombino (a town that Borgia had taken and whose lord he had expelled) were said to be on the point of doing the same.

Guidus Ubaldus, et ipse suum ad regnum recuperandum a popularibus accersitus, triginta auri libris a senatu mutuo acceptis, viae se dedit, eoque adveniens omnibus ab oppidis magna gratulatione est receptus.

51 Caesar, non tam quod esset morbo implicitus quam propter Romanorum civium in sese odia vitae suae metuens, quicquid equitum et militum habebat in Urbem introduxit. Ea re accidit, quod accidere erat necesse, ut cardinales, qui iam prope omnes convenerant ad novum pontificem legendum, ne facere id possent, Caesaris exercitus timore impedirentur. Qua intellecta re, senatus litteras ad eos dedit: si ita opus esse ducerent, se celeriter omnes suas copias Romam missurum, quibus facilius Romanae reipublicae maiestatem et suam dignitatem tueri, et quae ex usu essent administrare libere ac sine metu possent. Antonius etiam Iustinianus legatus coram idem est pollicitus senatus reipublicaeque nomine. Quod quidem illis tam suspecto tempore gratum ac peropportunum fuit. Ea enim re permotus, ne in se rempublicam incitaret, Roma cum suis omnibus egressus copiis, Caesar Vaticanum sacro senatui reliquit.

52 Interim a Guido Ubaldo nuntius ad senatum venit: sese regnum et salutem suam illi acceptam referre; cupere cum equitibus gravioris armaturae centum, levioris qui sagittis uterentur centum et quinquaginta, stipendia reipublicae facere; milites se habere paratissimos numero ad duo milia, quibus sine stipendio mensem eoque amplius senatus uti possit; rogare ut in eius fidem recipiatur. Cognitis his postulatis, satis est ei omnibus in rebus ab senatu factum, atque auri librae centum annuae in stipendium constitutae. Cardinalium collegium, Caesaris abitu liberum factum, cardinalem Senensem pontificem maximum creavit, qui se Pium tertium appellari voluit. Huic, ante mensis exitum vitiatae tibiae doloribus mortuo, successit Iulius secundus Ligurus; quem respu-

Guidobaldo himself was invited by his countrymen to recover his duchy, and having accepted a loan of 30 gold pounds from the Senate, took to the road, all the towns welcoming him on his arrival with great rejoicing.

Fearing for his life, not so much because he was in the grip of 51 illness as on account of the hatred the Romans felt toward him, Borgia brought whatever cavalry and infantry he had into the city. Because of this it inevitably happened that the cardinals, who had nearly all now assembled to elect a new pope, were prevented from doing so by fear of Borgia's army. When this became known to them, the Senate sent the cardinals a letter: if they reckoned there was need to do so, the Senate would quickly send all its forces to Rome so that they could better defend the majesty of the Roman Church and their own position, and carry out what needed to be done freely and without fear. The ambassador Antonio Giustinian also made them the same promise in person in the name of the Senate and the Republic. This proposal was welcome to them, and extremely helpful in a time of such uncertainty. Borgia was very disturbed at this turn of events, and so as not to stir up the Republic against himself, left Rome with all his troops and abandoned the Vatican to the college of cardinals.

In the meantime a messenger came to the Senate from 52 Guidobaldo: to them, he said, he owed his duchy and his life. He wished to enter the Republic's service with 100 heavy cavalry and 150 mounted archers; he had about 2,000 footsoldiers ready to fight, which the Senate could use for a month or more without pay; and he asked to be taken under their protection. Learning of these requests, the Senate gave him everything he wanted, and arranged for him to be paid 100 gold pounds a year. Set at liberty by the departure of Borgia, the college of cardinals elected the cardinal of Siena as pope, who wished to be known as Pius III.[26] Dead before a month was out from the pain and distress of an infected leg, he was succeeded by the Ligurian Julius II.[27] The Republic

blica pontificem fieri maiorem in modum concupiverat eique rei
omnem suam operam adhibuerat.

53   Sed Pio vita fruente, Iacobus Venerius, Ravennae praefectus,
Cesenam ab eius oppidi civibus accersitus, qui se reipublicae dedere volebant, cum militibus noctu se contulit, frustra, propterea
quod non ea quae inter ipsos convenerat sed nocte postera eo venit. Illi autem cum se superiori nocte ad illum recipiendum com-
paravissent neque is se ostendisset, studium et diligentiam remiserunt. Accidit autem ob eiusmodi moram uti Caesaris militibus res
in suspicionem veniret, qui ad portas et in muris stationes habuerunt. Itaque Venerius infecta re Ravennam rediit. Paucis post diebus Petri Remiri Hispani, qui Fori Livii arcem munitissimam Caesari custodiebat, nuntius Ravennam ad legatum venit: si respublica
eam arcem velit, Remirum illam traditurum, modo ei liceat quae
in arce sit suppellex Caesaris Ravennam atque ad urbem asportare;
tum ab senatu praefecturam habeat equitum quinquaginta, totque
in urbe insulas, quibus ex insulis duarum auri librarum fructus annuus ad sese redeat. Ea intellecta re, senatus consultum factum
est: legato licere praefecto arcis fidem dare reipublicae nomine fore
quemadmodum velle se ostendisset, arcemque ab eo accipere,
atque ea de causa Forum Livii accedere cum ea copia quam ex usu
esse reipublicae statuisset; neve quis eam rem enuntiaret, a senato-
ribus omnibus iusiurandum datum.

54   Deinde Romani interregni diebus cum Pandulphum Malates-
tam, qui Ariminum, a Roberto patre traditum, aliquot annos
iniuste regnans obtinuerat, et ab Caesare eiectus oppido fuerat, eo
cum copiis accedentem oppidani reppulissent, Guidus Ubaldus
per legatum suum senatui significavit Pandulphum cupere ut, quo-

had very much wanted him to become pope, and had taken great pains to secure this outcome.

While Pius yet lived, Giacomo Venier, the governor of Ravenna, 53 was invited to Cesena by the citizens of that town, who wanted to surrender to the Republic. With his soldiers he made his way there by night, but in vain, because he arrived not on the night that had been agreed upon between them but on the next one. Since they had been ready to take him in the night before and he had not appeared, their enthusiasm and alertness had abated. In connection with this delay, it happened that the situation came to be regarded with suspicion by Borgia's soldiers, who were standing guard at the gates and walls. Venier therefore returned to Ravenna with nothing achieved. A few days later a messenger of the Spaniard Pedro Remirez, who was guarding the very strong fortress of Forlì for Borgia, came to the proveditor at Ravenna: if the Republic wanted that fortress, Remirez would hand it over, provided he was allowed to carry off to Ravenna and Venice the property of Borgia in the citadel, and that the Senate should give him a command of fifty horse, and as many houses in the city as would provide him with an annual return of two gold pounds. When this became known, a Senate decree was passed to the effect that the proveditor had permission to give his word to the commander of the citadel in the Republic's name that things would be done in accordance with his expressed wishes, and to receive the citadel from him. He was for this purpose to go to Forlì with such force as he determined the Republic needed. All the senators swore an oath to say nothing on the matter.

Later, during the vacancy of the See of Rome, Pandolfo 54 Malatesta was driven back by the townspeople of Rimini as he approached the town with his troops. Rimini had passed down to Pandolfo from his father Roberto, and he had been for some years a harsh ruler of the town until he was expelled by Borgia. Through an envoy, Guidobaldo intimated to the Senate that

niam oppidani adduci non poterant ut ei sese dederent, reipublicae autem imperium magnopere optarent, senatus oppidum reciperet; sperare sibi ab republica non defore vitae pro dignitate traducendae facultatem; itaque, si senatus iubeat, ipsum eam rem curaturum, quo Ariminenses magnopere confiderent. Quamobrem senatus censuit legato respondi oportere: si Guidus Ubaldus uti Ariminum oppidum reipublicae se dederet suo studio et auctoritate quam cum illa civitate habeat effecisset, eam rem senatui gratam fore. Postremo cum Guidus Ubaldus aliquot pagos et castella ex Ariminensium et Cesenatium finibus, valde vel communita vel propter agrorum bonitatem opportuna, vi expugnavisset, et senatui significavisset ea se omnia reipublicae traditurum, modo id se non nolle ostendat, alterum senatus consultum factum est: ea recipi senatui placere.

55 Tum Faventinis civibus aliquot, qui Ravennam ad legatum venerant, reipublicae sese dedere cupientibus, idem uti legatus eis ostenderet imperatum. Et quoniam Arimini Faventiae Forique Cornelii arces munitissimae singulatim a praefectis Caesaris obtinebantur, quorum pars reipublicae eas vendere cupiebat, latum uti de condicionibus cum eorum nuntiis legatus ageret. Russium praeterea in Faventinorum, et Archangelianum ac Savinianum in Ariminensium finibus, pagi frumentarii et magna uterque fertilitate, itemque castellum Urbinatibus finitimum summo in iugo, quod incolae Montisflorem appellant, reipublicae deduntur. Etiam Faventiae ager prope universus una cum arce oppidi egregia, legato cum copiis accedente, in fidem recipitur. Quo fere die allatum est Iulium pontificem maximum esse factum. Itaque in urbe omnes magnopere laetari, oppido egregio ad reipublicae imperium acce-

Malatesta wanted the Senate to take over the town, since the townspeople could not be induced to surrender to him but very much wanted Venetian rule. Guidobaldo hoped he would not be denied by the Republic the chance to live out his life in accordance with his station. If the Senate ordered it, then, he would see to the matter himself, the people of Rimini placing great trust in him. At this, the Senate resolved to make the following reply to the envoy: if Guidobaldo brought about the surrender of Rimini to the Republic through his efforts and in virtue of the authority he carried with the town, the Senate would find it very welcome. Guidobaldo stormed a number of villages and castles in the territories of Rimini and Cesena, which were either well defended strongholds or favorably situated thanks to the fertility of their land, and indicated to the Senate that he would hand them all over to the Republic provided she showed herself not unwilling to have them; and so in the end the Senate passed a second decree, that they were pleased to receive them.

Next some citizens of Faenza came to the proveditor at 55 Ravenna, wanting to surrender it to the Republic, and the proveditor was told to make them the same offer. The very strong citadels of Rimini, Faenza, and Imola were held independently by Borgia's captains, some of whom wished to sell them to the Republic, so a measure was passed that the proveditor should discuss terms with their messengers. In addition to that, Russi in the territory of Faenza, and Santarcangelo di Romagna and Savignano in that of Rimini, both very fertile grain-producing areas, and a fortress on top of a ridge bordering on Urbino, called by the inhabitants Montefiore, were surrendered to the Republic. Nearly all the countryside of Faenza, too, along with the town's fine fortress, were taken under the proveditor's protection as he proceeded there with his troops. Almost on the same day came the news that Julius had been made pope. And so everyone in Venice was delighted at the addition of a fine town to the Republic's dominion and at

dente, et Iulio pontifice, in quem senatus largiter omnia sua studia atque officia contulisset, lecto. Ipse vero Iulius, cum ad eum gratulatum Antonius legatus accessisset, hominem hilariter complexus, omnia se reipublicae debere profiteri; nihil esse, quod de se[6] senatus polliceri sibi[7] non posset. Cumque ab legato sermo de Caesare institutus esset, propterea quod nonnullis ab hominibus praedicabatur illum ab Iulio fotum ac defensum iri, legato uti nihil eiusmodi vereretur fidem fecit. Illud etiam se dixit cupere, ut, quae Caesar possideret in Flaminia oppida, ea illi eriperentur. Quae quidem certe oratio gratissima civitati fuit. Inter haec Pandulphus, nonnullorum factione inter eos excitata, ab Ariminensibus recipitur.

56   Florentini, quod aegre ferrent Faventiam in reipublicae potestatem venire, copias miserant, quae civium parti qui secum sentiebant auxilio essent, ut sibi potius quam reipublicae se dederent. Ea pars milites et agrestes homines in oppidum introduxerat. Ab iis reliqui perterrebantur, ne portas legato aperirent. Itaque milites quos Guidus Ubaldus senatui pollicitus fuerat legatus ab eo accersit; alios comparat et delectum habet; tormenta adduci imperat; equites mittit, qui Florentinorum copias in montibus morentur et repellant.

57   Dum haec foris administrantur, senatus legatos creavit, qui Romam proficiscerentur Iulio pontifici maximo gratulatum, ob propensam in illum reipublicae voluntatem, octo; quod ante eam diem numquam acciderat, ut tot legati ad pontificem non Venetum mitterentur. Florentini cum potiri Faventia non possent, per Franciscum Soderinum, civem suum, cardinalem, egerunt ut is suspectam Iulio rempublicam faceret: omnes eius oppidi fines arcemque oppidi iam in reipublicae potestate esse; oppidum etiam

Julius' election as pope, to whom the Senate had given their un-
stinting support and service. Indeed, when the ambassador Antonio Giustinian went to congratulate him, Julius cheerfully em-
braced the man, declaring that he owed everything to the
Republic, and that there was nothing which the Senate could not
expect of him. The ambassador began to speak to him of Borgia,
since some people were putting it about that Julius would take him
under his wing and protect him, but Julius gave him his word that
they should have no fears on that score. He even said that he
wanted the towns that Borgia held in Romagna to be taken from
him—talk that was certainly very welcome in Venice. Meanwhile
Malatesta was taken back by the people of Rimini after some of
the citizens formed a conspiracy among them.

The Florentines took it hard that Faenza had come under the   56
Republic's sway and sent troops to support those of the citizens
that felt the same way, with a view to having them surrender to
themselves rather than to Venice. That faction had brought soldiers and the country folk into the town—the rest were being
frightened by them into not opening the gates to the proveditor.
The proveditor therefore called on Guidobaldo for the infantry he
had promised the Senate, himself getting others together and
holding a levy of them. He ordered artillery to be brought up and
sent cavalry to hold up the Florentine troops in the hills and drive
them back.

While these events were unfolding outside the city, the Senate   57
appointed ambassadors to go to Rome to congratulate Pope Julius,
eight of them, in view of the great good will of the Republic toward him; never before had it happened that so many ambassadors were sent to a pope who was not a Venetian. When the Florentines found themselves unable to take Faenza, they worked
through their fellow countryman Cardinal Francesco Soderini to
make the Republic an object of suspicion in Julius' eyes. All of the
town's territory and its citadel were now in Venetian hands, he

brevi futurum; id illam, non tam ut ab Caesare male parta extor-
queantur, quam ut sibi acquirat, contendere et tantopere conari;
quod semel Veneti ceperint, numquam eos reddere consuevisse;
ipsum eam rem sero cogniturum, cum iam ii rerum domini eius
permissu fuerint. De eo Antonius legatus certior factus, ut senatum purgaret, Iulium adiit rogavitque ne reipublicae calumniatori-
bus aures tribueret, quos non defore sciebat. Cumque quod visum
fuit in eam sententiam dixisset, Iulius neque se quicquam credi-
disse iis qui maledictis rempublicam insectati essent respondit,
neque in posterum crediturum; scire se amari a Veneta civitate,
eiusque rei permulta habere indicia; et ipsum contra amore
summo erga illam affici; gaudere etiam, cum quis se ob id non Li-
gurem, sed Venetum appellet; quod quidem iam fieret ab iis qui
tantam ipsius et reipublicae coniunctionem et inter ipsos benevolentiam moleste admodum ferunt. Sed quod ad Caesaris regnum
dicionemque attinet, cupere se ut, quae in Romanae reipublicae
imperio ante illum erant oppida, eidem reipublicae restituantur.
Hoc sermone habito, ab se legatum dimisit.

58   Inter haec Pandulphus ad urbem venit. Qui cum vereretur sese
Ariminum propter civium infensam in se voluntatem obtinere diutius non posse, ad id quod per Guidum Ubaldum paulo ante senatui proposuerat rediit, atque Ariminum reipublicae certis condicionibus tradidit. Itaque Dominicum Maripetrum legatum, qui
oppidum, et Vincentium Valerium, qui arcem reciperet, patres
Ariminum miserunt. Pandulpho posterisque eius Citadella, oppidum in Patavinorum finibus, et paulo post civitas cum iure comitiorum ipsi et Carolo fratri eius data. Pandulphus etiam in reipublicae militiam receptus, eique praefectura equitum attributa,

said, and soon the town would be too. Venice was striving with might and main to attain this goal, not so much to wrest from Borgia his ill-gotten gains as to acquire them for herself. And what the Venetians had once taken, they were not in the habit of giving back. Julius would realise this too late when they had become all dominant with his acquiescence. When he was told of this, the ambassador Giustinian approached Julius to clear the Senate's name, and asked him not to lend his ears to critics of the Republic, of whom, as Julius knew, there would never be a shortage. When he had said what he thought appropriate on the subject, Julius replied that he had given no credence to those who heaped abuse on the Republic, nor would he in the future. He knew he was well loved by the citizens of Venice, and he had a good many tokens of that; he, conversely, felt the greatest love toward them. He actually rejoiced when anyone called him for this reason not a Ligurian but a Venetian, as was already happening with people who were enraged at the closeness of the association of himself and the Republic and the good will that existed between them. But as far as Borgia's state and dominion was concerned, he said that it was his wish that the towns which had been under the control of the Roman Church before Borgia should be restored to her. Having delivered this speech, he let the ambassador go.

In the meantime, Pandolfo Malatesta came to Venice. Since he was afraid that he would no longer be able to hold on to Rimini because of its citizens' hostility toward him, he went back to what he had proposed to the Senate a little earlier through Guidobaldo, and with certain conditions, handed Rimini over to the Republic. The senators accordingly sent Domenico Malipiero to Rimini to accept the town, and Vincenzo Valier to take over the fortress. To Malatesta and his heirs was given Cittadella, a town in the territory of Padua, and a little later he and his brother Carlo were granted citizenship and noble status. Malatesta was also taken into military service by the Republic, and given a cavalry captaincy, 58

uxori et fratri Carolo quinque auri librae annuae utrique constitutae; alteri ex liberis duobus sacerdotia liberiora promissa quot petierat. Ipsi datae dono in praesentia auri librae centum. Ea de re per Antonium legatum senatus Iulium certiorem facit. Qui in eo perseverat, ut velle se ostendat, quae fuerint Romanae reipublicae oppida, ei restitui. Itaque petere a senatu, ut auxilio suo atque opibus ad ea recuperanda sese iuvet.

59   Miserat ante illos dies senatus alterum Faventiam legatum, Nicolaum Fuscarenum, ad oppidi oppugnationem maiore studio et celeritate procurandam, lente adhuc administratam existimans. Iusserat etiam ut Nicolaus, copiarum reipublicae praefectus, cum iis Faventiam contenderet. Is statim viae se dedit. Sed antequam Ravennam perveniret, muro tormentis percusso legatisque proponentibus se oppidum ad praedam militibus daturos, si cives deditionem differant, ante diem tertiumdecimum Kalendarum Decembrium[8] Faventia deditur. Venetias ubi de eo est allatum, senatus consultum fit, ne Iulii animus irritetur, nihil oppidorum Caesaris recipi amplius ab legatis oportere; satis in Arimino atque Faventia reipublicae factum. Deinde legatorum alter iussus Ariminum se conferre honestandi oppidi causa.

60   Iisdem diebus Andreas Grittus, quem senatus ad regem Thracium miserat, pacis condicionibus aliquot in reipublicae utilitatem recognitis, ipsa recte firmata domum rediit. At cum paulo post Roma Antonii legati litteris patres intellexissent multorum sermonibus confirmari Iulii permissu Caesarem ad suum in Flaminia regnum propediem reversurum, proximo senatus consulto rescisso, litterae sunt ad legatos ab senatu datae, ut quicquid possent de Caesaris dicione reipublicae addere capereque festinarent. Ea re

while an annual pension of five gold pounds a year each was laid down for his wife and his brother Carlo; to one of his two children were promised all the benefices without cure of souls that he had sought. He himself was made a gift of 100 gold pounds for the time being. The Senate informed Julius of this through its ambassador Antonio Giustinian. Julius continued to make it plain that he wanted restored to Rome the towns that had been hers. He therefore asked the Senate for its support and resources to help recover them.

Before that, the Senate had sent another proveditor to Faenza, 59 Niccolò Foscarini, to secure a more energetic and speedier assault on the town, which they thought had been proceeding too slowly up to that point. They had also ordered Niccolò Orsini, captain of the Venetian troops, to march to Faenza with them, and he immediately took to the road. But before he reached Ravenna, Faenza surrendered on 19 November, its walls having been shattered by artillery and the proveditors threatening to give the town over to the soldiers to plunder if the citizens delayed the surrender. When the news reached Venice, the Senate passed a decree that so as not to provoke Julius, the proveditors should accept no more of Borgia's towns; the Republic was satisfied with having Rimini and Faenza. The second proveditor was ordered to make his way to Rimini to honor the town by his presence.

At about the same time Andrea Gritti, whom the Senate had 60 sent to the Turkish sultan, had adjusted some of the terms of the peace treaty in the Republic's favor and returned home with the peace properly settled. A little later the senators learned from a letter of their ambassador Giustinian in Rome that, according to widespread report, Borgia would soon be returning to his realm in Romagna with Julius' acquiescence. The previous Senate decree was consequently rescinded, and the Senate sent a letter to the proveditors to say that they should make haste to seize whatever they could of the lands under Borgia's sway and add it to the Re-

evenit ut Meldulam in Ariminensi agro, et Tossinianum in Foro
Corneliensi, pagos muris arcibusque communitos, missi ab legatis
equites ad reipublicae imperium libentissimos adiecerint. Post
haec Angelus episcopus Tiburtinus, qui Alexandri legatus aliquot
annos apud rempublicam fuerat, eoque mortuo Romam redierat,
iterum missu Iulii Venetias venit eodem legati nomine. Is primo
adventus sui die salvere ab Iulio Lauredanum principem et patres
iussit, humanissimis amantissimisque verbis; eisque gratias ingentes agere illum dixit, quod in se iuvando, ut pontifex maximus le-
geretur, multum operae studiique contulissent; plurimumque ex ea
se re debere senatui libenter profiteri; neque umquam eius officii
memoriam abiecturum; amare insuper sua sponte Venetam civitatem remque publicam, optimis utentem et institutis et legibus;
itaque omnia ei omni tempore tributurum quae ex dignitate sua
tribui amicissimis hominibus possint. Hoc sermone habito, appel-
latis suo nomine patribus quibuscum priore legatione adsueverat,
discedit, mandata reliqua, quae longioris essent morae, in aliam se
differre diem pronuntians.

61   Ea dies ubi venit, secreto apud illos, decemvirum adhibitis ma-
gistris, proponit velle Iulium et petere uti Ariminum et Faventia,
quae interceperint de Romana dicione oppida, ea ipsi restituantur;
rogare etiam ut ad reliqua recuperanda eum iuvent; decrevisse
enim ne ulla Caesari turricula, cui imperet, relinquatur, sed omnia
eo redeant unde recessere. Patres, questi non esse hoc illud quod
ob suam in Iulium pietatem et studium ab eo exspectarent, rem ad
senatum deferunt. Senatus censuit legato respondi oportere: quod

public. So it came about that Meldola in the Riminese and Tossignano in the Imolese, small towns defended by walls and fortresses, were very happy to be added to the Venetian dominions by cavalry sent by the proveditors. After that, Angelo [Leonini], Bishop of Tivoli, who had been for some years Alexander's nuncio at Venice, returning to Rome when he died, came back to Venice again, sent by Julius with the same title of papal nuncio. On the day he arrived he delivered greetings from Julius to Doge Loredan and the Signoria in the most kindly and affectionate terms. He said that Julius felt enormous gratitude toward them for their exertions and support in helping him be elected pope, and that he was happy to acknowledge the great debt he owed the Senate in the matter, and would never forget the service they had done him. He was besides by nature very fond of the citizens and republic of Venice, enjoying as it did the best of institutions and laws. He would at all times bestow on them every favor that someone in his position could bestow on a people with whom he had the friendliest relations. Having delivered this speech, Leonini gave his personal greetings to those senators with whom he had become acquainted on his previous nunciature, and departed, declaring that he would put off to another day the rest of his commission, which needed more time.

When that day came, meeting them in secret in the presence of   61 the Heads of the Ten, he put before the Signoria Julius' desire and request that Rimini and Faenza, the towns which they had seized from the domain of the Roman Church, should be restored to him. He also asked them to assist him in recovering the rest, as he had decided that Borgia should not be left in control of so much as a tower, and everything should go back to where it was at the start. The Signoria complained that this was not what they expected for their dutifulness and devotion toward Julius, and referred the matter to the Senate. The Senate resolved to give the nuncio the following response: when the Republic took Rimini

Ariminum et Faventiam respublica ceperit, ea ab Caesare homine importunissimo crudelissimoque cepisse, Iulio ipso, antequam pontifex maximus fieret, hortante, facto autem permittente atque adsentiente; eaque oppida, uti a vicariis obtineri solita, rempublicam modo sua fecisse, reliqua non attigisse, quae si voluisset non fuisse difficile capere atque retinere; eorum duorum oppidorum nomine se vicariam Romanae reipublicae velle esse, uti priores domini fuissent. Quid in eo Iulius amitteret? Quare ea sibi esse retinenda statuisse. Quod ad eum ad reliqua iuvandum attineret, suas omnes copias atque opes polliceri; eis ille tamquam suis uteretur. Haec responsi lex. Illud autem, hortatorem Iulium eius negotii fuisse, verissima senatus oratio fuit. Nam cum apud Iulium Antonius legatus Pii pontificis regno in eum sermonem esset ingressus, ut de Caesaris iniustissima Flaminiae possessione quereretur, auctor reipublicae eius magnopere consilii Iulius fuerat.

62   Iis de rebus saepe ultro citroque datis ad legatum Romam litteris et acceptis, Iulio a sententia non recedente, adfirmante interdum potius, quoniam sibi ad bellum cum republica gerendum vires non suppeterent, se a Christianis regibus auxilia contra eam imploraturum, quos sciret Romanae reipublicae opis eorum egenti numquam defuisse; Antonio autem legato ipsum illum ab eo nondum pontifice habitum secum sermonem repetente atque ut eius reminisceretur ab illo postulante, cuius omnino rei Iulius satis idoneam adferre excusationem non poterat, tantum inquiebat, quae non pontifex dixerit, ea se expendere non oportuisse.

63   Annus ad exitum labitur. Itaque prima insequentis anni die Antonius, oratione apposita et leni Iulium satis hilarem aggressus,

and Faenza, they were taken from Cesare Borgia, a man of the utmost perversity and cruelty, with the encouragement of Julius himself before he became pope, and with his permission and agreement afterwards. The Republic had appropriated only those towns that were customarily held by vicars of the Church of Rome, and had not touched the others, though it would not have been difficult to seize and hold on to them had she so wished. Venice wished to be named as Rome's vicar of those two towns, just as their previous masters had been. What would Julius lose in doing that? For these reasons Venice had decided she had to keep them. As for helping him with the other towns, she promised him all her troops and resources: these he could use as his own. Such were the terms of the Senate's reply. As to Julius having encouraged the Venetian enterprise, that was a very true statement on the Senate's part, for when in the reign of Pope Pius their ambassador Antonio Giustinian had in Julius' presence broached the subject and complained about Borgia's iniquitous possession of Romagna, Julius had been a strong supporter of the Republic's plan.

Frequent letters on these matters passed to and from the Venetian ambassador at Rome, but Julius continued to stick to his position. From time to time, indeed, he would actually say that since he did not have the military strength to make war on the Republic, he would ask the Christian monarchs for assistance against her — he knew they had never failed when the Church of Rome needed their help. When the ambassador Giustinian repeated the actual conversation he had had with him before he was pope, and asked him to recall it, he could offer no plausible excuse for it at all, but merely said that he did not have to take into consideration what he had said when he was not yet pope. 62

The year drew to a close. On the first day of the following year, Giustinian accosted Julius, who was in a pretty good mood, with a mild but apt address: he asked him in a friendly manner, since it 63

1504

familiariter petiit ut, quoniam ea die clientibus atque amicis dari munera consuevissent, ipse dono reipublicae tam illi deditae, tam affectae atque amanti daret, ut Ariminum et Faventiam eo libente obtineret, quo ipse vellet nomine. Ad quae subridens Iulius ita respondit: ageret ipse cum republica ut Tossinianum, quod esset in Fori Cornelii finibus, postremo captum ante omnia restitueret; post id de Arimino atque Faventia peteret; aliquid fortasse impetraturum. Hoc Iulii sermone ad senatum Antonii litteris celeriter perlato, dum de eo patres consulunt resque altercatione magistratuum ex die in diem reicitur, Angelus legatus litteras Iulii patribus reddit; quibus litteris omnem illis spem Iulius adimit aliter inter se remque publicam posse convenire quam si ablata restituantur: id ni fecerint, deos se et homines in auxilium vocaturum atque ad omnia descensurum minatur. Tum vero patres magnopere turbari idque se ab Angelo magis quam ab Iulio agnoscere, qui de senatus in illum voluntate perincommode saepe scripserit, cum moderatius atque sedatius agere debuisset, Iuliique animum, quem quidem cum iracundum per se, tum calumniis malevolorum incitatum et succensum restingui bonis verbis oportebat, digna atque indigna congerens malis persuasionibus inflammavisset. Eoque magis indignabantur, quod omnia quae in senatu secreto agitabantur idem cognoscere modis omnibus nitebatur, dabatque operam ut ea quamprimum Iulius intelligeret, odiosasque ad eum litteras dabat.

64   Illud etiam patribus ad hanc molestiam accedebat, quod Iulius suum hominem legatum ad Aloisium regem Galliae miserat ques-

was the day on which protégés and friends were customarily given gifts, whether he would not be glad to give the Republic possession of Rimini and Faenza as a gift, under whatever title he wished, the Republic being so devoted and well-disposed and affectionate toward him. To which Julius replied with a smile that first of all he should negotiate with the Republic the return of Tossignano, the town in the territory of Imola which they had very recently seized. After that he could ask after Rimini and Faenza, and might perhaps get something. This remark of Julius was soon reported to the Senate in a letter of Giustinian, and while the senators considered the matter and wrangling among the magistrates caused it to be pushed back day after day, the nuncio Angelo Leonini delivered a letter of Julius to the senators. In the letter Julius wrecked any hope that an agreement between him and the Republic could be reached without their returning what they had seized. If they failed to do so, he threatened to summon God and man to his aid, and there would be no measure to which he would not resort. The senators were very much taken aback at this, but realized that it came from Leonini rather than Julius. Leonini often wrote very negatively about the Senate's attitude toward Julius, when he should have acted in a more restrained and calmer fashion. While Julius was in himself naturally irascible, he had also been roused and fired up by the lies of those who were ill disposed toward Venice. And when Leonini ought to have been damping down the fires with good advice, he had actually inflamed him with bad arguments that mingled truth and falsehood. They were all the more annoyed at his efforts to find out by any means possible what was being discussed in confidence in the Senate,[28] and his exertions to make Julius aware of it as soon as possible, sending him letters full of hatred toward Venice.

Adding to the senators' vexation was the fact that Julius had 64 sent one of his men on an embassy to King Louis of France to complain about the injuries done him by the Republic, and to ask

tum de reipublicae iniuriis auxiliaque contra illam postulatum. Idemque apud Maximilianum per oratoris ipsius scribam, Iacobum Bannisium, Roma missum, fieri procurarique mandaverat, scriptis ad eum litteris acerbioribus ea de re, decimamque fructuum ex sacerdotiis Germanicis, quam quidem Maximilianus ab eo magno studio petierat, ultro illi deferens, si se iuverit.

65   Apud quem utrumque senatus ab legatis reipublicae facti excusationem adferri iussit: se Ariminum et Faventiam non ab Romanis pontificibus, sed ab latrone omnium taeterrimo avertisse; alterum, ne a Florentina civitate, sibi propter recentem Pisani belli memoriam inimicissima, quae eo suas copias miserat, interciperetur; alterum, permutatione oppidi cum eius regulo facta in reipublicae finibus; ea oppida ante Caesarem per vicarios obtineri consuevisse; si se illorum vicarium fieri senatus velit, nihil novi petere; id pro eius plurimis in rempublicam Christianam meritis aequum esse ei tribui, quod saepe aliis nihil merentibus sit datum; neminem in Flaminia vicarium neque ad eam ipsam reliquaque Romanae dictionis[9] oppida defendenda firmiorem quam senatus sit, neque qui maiori illi usui, si res exigat, possit esse, hac Iulium tempestate habiturum. Quaenam invidia sit, quod temere cuilibet ac sine ullo usu condonatur, id et praeteritis reipublicae promeritis et spei futurorum, cum se occasio dederit, proventuum et commodorum pernegari? Ipsum praeterea Iulium suasorem senatui per legatum abripiendi ab Caesare Flaminiam extitisse; post id, praeter illud cuius ipse hortator fuit, nihil novi accidisse; ut non tam Iulius habere causam, cur a sententia recedat, quam quonam

for assistance against her. He had given instructions that the same should be done at the court of Maximilian through Jacopo Bannisio, the secretary of Maximilian's ambassador.[29] Bannisio was despatched from Rome with a letter to Maximilian on the matter, written in very sharp terms, and Julius' spontaneous offer to him, if his help was forthcoming, of a tithe of the income from German benefices, something for which Maximilian had been pressing very hard.

The Senate ordered that the Republic's ambassadors at both courts should put forward a defense of their actions: they had taken Rimini and Faenza not from the Roman popes but from the world's wickedest brigand; the latter, in case it should be seized by the city of Florence, which had sent its troops there, a state that was extremely hostile to them thanks to the Pisan war which was still fresh in the memory; the former, after making an exchange with its lord of a town in Venetian territory. Before Borgia, the towns had been customarily governed by vicars. If the Senate now wished to become their vicar, it was seeking nothing new. It was only just that, in view of their many services to the Christian commonwealth, they should be granted what was often given to others who were completely undeserving. At this juncture Julius would have no vicar in Romagna stronger for the defence of that region and the other towns of Rome's jurisdiction than the Senate, nor one who could be of more use to him if the need arose. Was it not great spitefulness that something which was randomly and fruitlessly presented to all manner of men was denied both to the Republic's past services and to the hope of success and profit to come, when the occasion should arise? Besides, Julius himself, through his ambassador, had been the chief advocate of the Senate's seizing Romagna from Borgia; after that, no further developments had taken place except for what he himself encouraged. The result was that Julius appeared to have cause not so much to abandon his earlier views as to discover and devise ways in which

65

modo reipublicae noceat, quaerere ac meditari videatur; petere itaque rempublicam ab Aloisio quidem, ne foederis religionem, quod ei cum senatu est, propter Iulium tam iniuste se efferentem violet; a Maximiliano autem, ut amicus reipublicae, quae finitima illi est atque benevola semper fuit, bona in causa malit esse, quam Iulio, qui longe ab eius regno abest, in periniqua, si fides inter homines atque constantia suum ius obtineant. Qua accepta excusatione, uterque, a se reipublicae causam apud Iulium defensum iri liberaliter pollicitus, senatum paulo quietiorem reddidit.

66   Illis diebus, propterea quod Nicolao Ursino, qui Ravennae erat, reipublicae copiarum praefecturae tempus explebatur, ob eius fidem atque constantiam, quod, a compluribus civitatibus et regibus, ut ipsorum stipendia faceret, magnis pollicitationibus invitatus, rempublicam deserere noluerat, per triennium imperatorium ei nomen cum stipendio annuo auri librarum quingentarum senatus dandum censuit.

he could do the Republic harm. And so the Republic asked Louis not to violate the sanctity of the treaty he had with the Senate just because Julius was behaving so unfairly. Of Maximilian, on the other hand, they asked that in a good cause he should choose to be a friend to the Republic which was his neighbor and had always been well disposed toward him, rather than to Julius, who was a long way from his kingdom, in a cause that was quite unjust — if good faith and loyalty still counted for anything among men. When they had heard this justification, both Louis and Maximilian promised that they would wholeheartedly defend the Republic's cause before Julius, and so made the Senate a little calmer.

About this time, the term of office of Niccolò Orsini, the cap- 66 tain of the Venetian troops, who was at Ravenna, was nearing completion. In return for his loyalty and constancy (he had refused to desert the Republic, although tempted with great promises by many cities and rulers to enter their service), the Senate voted to give him the title of captain-general for three years, with an annual salary of 500 gold pounds.

LIBER SEPTIMUS

1   Eodem fere tempore, quod Vincentius Naldius Faventinus, magna
in oppidi finibus gratia, omne studium et diligentiam adhibuisset,
ut Faventia in deditionem potestatemque reipublicae redigeretur,
ei militiae insignia cum veste aurea aurique librae viginti sunt a patribus dono datae; tum quinque in annos singulos constitutae pen-
sionis nomine, immunitate omnium rerum, quam heredes eius se-
querentur, addita; primis quoque proximi ordines militum belli
tempore promissi; eius etiam propinquis quattuor victus annuus
attributus. Neque multo post eaedem honestates, donaque totidem quot in Vincentium senatus contulerat, in Dionysium item
Naldium eius consobrinum sunt collata.

2   Aestate vero inita, cum Guidus Ubaldus Iulii suasu Franciscum
Mariam, sororis suae filium, cui fuerat pater Ioannes, Iulii frater,
Senogalliam obtinens, adoptavisset, eam adoptionem Iulius, de
collegii sententia, magno studio comprobavit. Qua una quidem re
suam in Venetos iracundiam iniustiorem reddidit, cum videri posset, quod illis iuris in Romanae reipublicae oppida tam obstinate
pernegaret, suis facile propinquis tribuisse. Maximilianus autem,
suscepti paulo ante reipublicae apud Iulium patrocinii plane iam
immemor, duos legatos Venetias misit, qui senatum hortarentur
uti Iulio Faventiam atque Ariminum restitueret; eam in primis
curam ad se spectare, suique esse muneris Romanae reipublicae
pontificisque rerum procurationem; id si nolit, causam ad iudicium remittat; se curaturum ut item ab Iulio remittatur; quod si se

BOOK VII

At about the same time, Vincenzo Naldi of Faenza, a man of great influence in the district who had been energetic and assiduous in helping to bring about the surrender of the town and its passage into the hands of the Republic, was given by the senators the insignia of a knight, together with a golden robe and 20 gold pounds. He was granted a further five pounds as an annual pension, and in addition general immunity from taxation, which could pass to his heirs. In time of war he was promised a high rank in the military, next to the highest. Annual living expenses were granted to four of his relatives as well. Not long afterwards, the honors and gifts that the Senate had conferred on Vincenzo were also conferred in the same measure on his cousin Dionigi Naldi.

At the beginning of summer, urged on by Pope Julius, Guidobaldo da Montefeltro had adopted his sister's son Francesco Maria della Rovere, whose father had been Julius' brother Giovanni, the lord of Senigallia. With the approval of the college of cardinals Julius then confirmed the adoption with great enthusiasm. This action alone made his wrath against the Venetians all the more unfair, since it became apparent that he had been ready to grant his relatives rights over towns in the Papal States that he had so obstinately denied to them. Maximilian, on the other hand, evidently forgetting his promise a little earlier to support the Republic before Julius, sent two ambassadors to Venice to urge the Senate to return Faenza and Rimini to the pope. They said that this concerned Maximilian more than anyone else, and that it was his duty to oversee the affairs of the pope and the Church of Rome. If the Venetians were unwilling to do so, they should let the matter go to arbitration, and he would see to it that Julius would do the

arbitrum velint eius disceptationis facere, se non recusaturum et pro rei aequitate sententiam laturum. Iis legatis Lauredanus, consulto senatu, cum omnes eius rei causas, quas quidem Maximiliano civitatis legati antea ostenderant, enumeravisset, unum modo respondit: reipublicae ius illis in oppidis satis esse clarum atque notum per sese; itaque nolle patres id in ambiguum vertere. Eo responso accepto, legatorum alter Romam discessit, altero apud senatum relicto, eique sumptus publice factus, quoad apud patres fuit. Iulius interim arcem Forolivianam, auri libris centum quinquaginta quas ab Caesare acceperat Remiro praefecto traditis, unaque oppidum obtinuit, cum antea Cesenam et Cornelium Forum iisdem prope artibus suae potestatis fecisset. Praefectus arcis Forolivianae cum Caesaris suppellectili Venetias venit.

3   Post haec inter Aloisium Gallorum regem et Maximilianum foedera sunt firmata, cum de eo per legatos diu multumque disceptavissent. Quibus confectis Ioannem Lascarem Byzantium Aloisius iterum ad senatum misit, qui diceret hortari sese patres ut aliquam cum Iulio inirent ad concordiam et consensionem viam; qua inita unanimi omnes studio ea de bello Thracio cogitare possent quae iam pridem cogitanda atque agenda sunt; adderet et illud: sibi cum Maximiliano convenisse, pacemque et benevolentiam inter ipsos esse constitutam, non illam quidem, ut cuipiam nocerent, sed suarum utriusque rerum et regnorum tuendorum causa. Patres, auri libra in sumptum mensibus singulis legato regio a quaestoribus dari iussa, nihil se fecisse reliqui dixerunt orando, pollicendo, ut Iulium placarent; descendisse enim etiam ad illud: tametsi Alexander Faventiam et reliqua oppida Caesari libera im-

same. If they should want him to arbitrate in the dispute, he would not refuse the task, and would deliver an equitable judgment. After consulting the Senate and having rehearsed to them all the reasons for the present state of affairs (which indeed the city's envoys had already made plain to Maximilian), Loredan said just one thing in reply to the ambassadors: the Republic's claim on the towns was in itself perfectly clear and well known, and the senators were accordingly not disposed to have it regarded as open to dispute. On hearing this response, one of the ambassadors left for Rome, leaving the other behind with the Senate; his expenses were paid by the state for the duration of his stay with the senators. Meanwhile Julius took over the fortress and town of Forlì, giving its commander Pedro Remirez 150 gold pounds which he had had from Cesare Borgia, and after he had brought Cesena and Imola into his power by much the same stratagem. The commander of the Forlì fortress went to Venice with Borgia's gear.

After this a treaty between King Louis of France and 3 Maximilian was signed after long and hard negotiations by their ambassadors. With the league concluded, Louis again sent Janus Lascaris of Constantinople to the Senate to say that the king urged them to find some path to reaching an understanding and agreement with Julius. Once they were on that path, they could all with one mind turn to concentrated consideration of matters to do with the Turkish war which had long since needed to be considered and acted upon. Lascaris was also to say that Louis had reached agreement with Maximilian, and peace and goodwill had been established between them, not indeed with a view to doing anyone harm but in order to protect the interests and realms of both of them. The treasurers were told to give the king's envoy one gold pound a month for his expenses, but he was told by the senators that they had done everything in their power to placate Julius by way of entreaties and promises. Things had reached the point that although Alexander had given Borgia Faenza and the other

muniaque dederit, velle tamen se stipendiarios Romanae reipublicae fieri, Faventiae Ariminique nomine; legem ipse stipendiorum diceret, nihil se recusaturos, auroque Veneto recenter signato annis omnibus ea libenter persoluturos; neque quidquam tamen profecisse; ceterum laetari se, duorum tantorum regum animos ab odio exercendo ad pacem et benevolentiam esse conversos; verum, propterea quod in foedere quod reipublicae cum Aloisio intercedebat caput unum erat eiusmodi: neutri sine alterius voluntate foedus ullum cum rege ullo facere licere; scire patres cupere, cur de eo rex nihil antea senatui significavisset. Ad ea legatus cum aliquamdiu siluisset, tandem se scire nihil respondit, nisi unum: ei foederi tempus quattuor mensium esse praestitutum quos uterque velit sibi socios et foederatos nominandi; itaque posse adhuc quidem regem ei foederi inserere rempublicam. Qui legati tamen sermo patrum animos, quibus quidem ea pax, senatu non appellato confecta, suspicionem haud parvam afferebat, nihil leniit.

4   Post haec decemviri, certiores facti servi indicio, qui ab eo vapulaverat, Hieronymum Tronum, qui bello Thracio Naupacti arcem, quam reipublicae nomine custodiebat, hostibus tradiderat eamque ob rem exul aliquot annos fuerat, id quod fecerat de tradenda arce pretio accepto fecisse, Tronum ab exilio domum redeuntem in vincula coniecerunt; pauloque post, quaestione habita, e superiore curiae porticu, quae in foro est, inter rubri lapidis columnas reste suspenso carnifex gulam fregit. Atque ultimis fere anni diebus Ioannes, Pisaurum obtinens, Mathei Teupoli filiam duxit uxorem, nuptiis in urbe per legatos institutis. Tum litterae ex Hispania ad senatum venerunt Isabellam reginam, Ferdinandi uxorem, magno animo excellentique virtute feminam, e vita excessisse; eiusque ge-

towns free of all taxes, the Venetians were still prepared to pay tribute to the Church of Rome on Faenza and Rimini's account. Julius had only to say what the terms of pay were, and they would refuse him nothing, they would gladly make him annual payments in recently-coined Venetian gold; but nothing had come of it. But they were pleased that two such great kings had turned their hearts from hatred toward peace and goodwill. There was, on the other hand, in the existing treaty between Louis and the Republic a clause to the effect that neither was permitted to enter into a treaty with any ruler without the consent of the other party. The senators therefore desired to know why the king had given them no prior notice of the treaty. After a period of silence, the ambassador at length replied that all he knew was that for this treaty, a period of four months had been agreed for nominating those that either side wished to have as allies and confederates, and so it was still possible for the king to include the Republic in the treaty. The ambassador's statement, however, did nothing to soothe the feelings of the senators, in whom this peace agreement aroused no little suspicion, concluded as it was without reference to the Senate.

In the course of the Turkish war, Girolamo Tron, who was 4 guarding the citadel of Lepanto for the Republic, had handed it over to the enemy, and on that account had been for some years an exile. The Ten were now informed, by the testimony of a servant who had been beaten by him, that he had taken a bribe to do what he had done in surrendering it. As Tron returned home from exile they had him thrown into prison. Following an enquiry, he was shortly thereafter hung by a rope from the upper loggia of the Ducal Palace which faces onto St. Mark's Square between the red stone columns, the executioner breaking his neck. Almost at the end of the year Giovanni Sforza, lord of Pesaro, took as his wife the daughter of Matteo Tiepolo,[1] a wedding that was conducted in Venice by his ambassadors. Then a letter from Spain reached the Senate to say that Queen Isabella, Ferdinand's wife, a woman of

nerum Philippum, Maximiliani filium, in Belgis regem, testamenti tabulis permagna Hispaniae terrae parte auctum fuisse. Quibus duabus de causis Vincentius Quirinus, vir in philosophiae studiis clarus, ad Philippum legatus a senatu lectus est, ut illi et de socrus morte reipublicae molestiam ostenderet, et de regni accessione gratularetur. Pauloque post Hercules Ferrariensium dux item moriens Alphonso filio regnum reliquit.

5 Erat in celeberrima urbis regione ad Rivumaltum domus reipublicae perampla, quae antiquitus a Germanis mercatoribus incoli consueverat. In eam illi cuiusquemodi res, quas quidem vendere cuperent, advectas suis ab oppidis inferebant et civitati emendas proponebant; quasque in urbe ipsi coemebant, ut in Germaniam conveherent, eodem congerebant, quoad essent deportandae. Ea domus, ut erat mercium omnis generis plenissima, insequentis anni initio magna cum plurimorum honestorum hominum iactura conflagravit. Quam tamen domum illo ipso anno civitas a fundamentis, fornicibus inaedificatam, ne ignis nocere posset, magnificentiore multo forma commodioreque restituit. Eiusdem initio anni Bartholomaeo Liviano, qui a republica, peracto stipendiorum tempore, patribus non permittentibus discesserat, ut illatas suae in primis genti reliquisque Romanis principibus ab Alexandro atque ab Caesare caedes et vastitatem vindicaret, Hispaniaeque regum militiam fecerat, iterum recipi postulanti praefectura equitum, cum stipendio annuo librarum auri centum quinquaginta, est a senatu data.

6 Cumque Cesenae, Forilivii, Forique Cornelii legati apud Iulium questi essent se, a Venetis magna agri parte spoliatos, angustis uti finibus atque inopia multarum rerum premi, Iulius per Guidum

great spirit and singular excellence, had departed this life. Her son-in-law Philip Duke of Burgundy, the son of Maximilian, had been favored in her will with a very substantial part of the Spanish lands.[2] For both these reasons Vincenzo Quirini, a man distinguished for his philosophical studies, was chosen by the Senate as their ambassador to Philip to express the Republic's condolences on the death of his mother-in-law, and to congratulate him on his accession to the kingship. Shortly thereafter Ercole d'Este, Duke of Ferrara, also died, leaving the duchy to his son Alfonso. 1505

In a very populous district of Venice, around the Rialto, there 5 was a great palazzo belonging to the Republic in which German merchants had been accustomed to live from early times.[3] Into it they would bring goods of all sorts which they imported from their towns for sale at Venice, offering them to the populace for purchase, while the goods that they themselves bought in the city were stored there awaiting transport to take them to Germany. Packed with all sorts of merchandise as it was, the house burned down at the beginning of the following year with the loss of a great many good men. The city reconstructed the palazzo from its foundations that same year, however, built on arches so that fire could not damage it, and on a much grander and more convenient plan. Bartolommeo d'Alviano had without the senators' permission left the Republic on the expiry of his term of military service to avenge the bloodshed and destruction brought on his own people in particular, and on the other Roman princes, by Alexander and Borgia, and had subsequently fought for the Spanish sovereigns. At the beginning of the same year, he asked to be taken back into Venetian service, and was granted a cavalry captaincy by the Senate with an annual pay of 150 gold pounds.

Ambassadors from Cesena, Forlì and Imola had lodged com- 6 plaints with Julius that since the Venetians had robbed them of much of their land, their territory had been reduced and they were suffering from widespread shortages. Through Guidobaldo

Ubaldum Antonio legato proposuit, si senatus eos fines sibi restituat, de Faventia atque Arimino se deinceps verbum non facturum, reique publicae oppida illa in omne tempus uti retineat permissurum. Ea Guidi Ubaldi oratione Antonii litteris ad patres
perlata, senatus, ne cuipiam obstinatior videri posset, Antonio re-
scripsit: si ei Iulius fidem faciat, ita fore uti Guidus Ubaldus ei
dixit, se fines illos restituturum, legatosque quos creasset octo ad
illum missurum, suumque in eum studium et observantiam praest-
aturum. Quo responso accepto, Iulius et Antonio de Arimino
atque Faventia liberaliter est pollicitus, et magnam se ex eo voluptatem cepisse apud suos familiares prae se tulit. Senatus, de eo
certior factus, oppidula decem numero cum eorum finibus uti Iulio restituerentur, censuit; in quibus Cesenae portus, qui est in
maris litore, Savinianum, Tossinianum, Archangelianum fuere.

7   Iis Iulii internuntio, quem ad id in Flaminiam miserat, per legatos reipublicae restitutis, Iulius rem ad collegium deduxit; lauda-
tusque ab omnibus, quod se ad concordiam cum senatu dedisset,
magnum sui consilii fructum tulit. Unus Franciscus Soderinus
cardinalis, cum et ipse Iulium verbis honorificis extulisset, addidit
eo se magis illum laudare, quod quemadmodum fines illos recupe-
ravisset, ita etiam Ariminum ab eo atque Faventiam brevi recupe-
ratum iri confidebat. Legatio postea, de qua supra dictum est, Romam missa ab Iulio libentissimo recipitur. Ii fuerunt: Bernardus
Bembus, pater meus, Paulus Pisanus, Hieronymus Donatus, Nicolaus Foscarenus, Andreas Venerius, Andreas Grittus, Leonardus
Mocenicus, cuius pater Ioannes Venetorum dux fuerat, et Dominicus Trivisanus, templi Marci procurator. Eius legationis Bernardus Bembus propter aetatem principem locum tenuit. Andreas
Grittus et Nicolaus Foscarenus e sexviris qui principi assident le-

da Montefeltro, Julius then proposed to the Venetian ambassador Giustinian that if the Senate restored those territories to him, he would say not a word about Faenza and Rimini in future and would allow the Republic to keep the towns forever. Giustinian relayed Guidobaldo's proposal to the senators by letter and the Senate, not wishing to appear at all obstinate in the matter, replied to him that if Julius guaranteed that what Guidobaldo had told Giustinian was so, they would return those lands and would send him the eight ambassadors they had appointed to render their devotion and obedience. On receipt of this reply, Julius gave Giustinian a generous undertaking on Rimini and Faenza, and professed to his household that he derived great pleasure from doing so. Informed of this, the Senate voted to restore ten small towns to Julius, along with their territories, among them the port of Cesena on the coast,[4] Savignano, Tossignano, and Santarcangelo di Romagna.

When the towns had been returned by the Venetian ambassadors to the nuncio that Julius had sent to Romagna for the purpose, the pope brought the matter before the college of cardinals. There he was universally praised for having devoted himself to reaching agreement with the Senate, and so Julius' plan turned out greatly to his profit. One of the cardinals, Francesco Soderini, lauded Julius to the skies like the others, and added that he praised him all the more because he was sure that he would soon also recover Rimini and Faenza in the same way that he had recovered those lands. After that, the embassy I mentioned was sent to Rome and was received by Julius in a very friendly manner. The members were my father Bernardo Bembo, Paolo Pisani, Girolamo Donato, Niccolò Foscarini, Andrea Venier, Andrea Gritti, Leonardo Mocenigo (whose father Giovanni had been doge), and Domenico Trevisan, a Procurator of St. Mark's. In view of his seniority Bernardo Bembo was the leader of the embassy. Andrea Gritti and Niccolò Foscarini joined the embassy as Ducal Coun-

7

gationem inierunt. Antonio autem, cum diu Romae in ea legatione fuisset reique publicae singulari suo studio atque prudentia magnopere satisfecisset, domum est reditio permissa. Atque haec vere medio eum quem diximus eventum habuerunt.

8   Aestate vero inita, Alfonsus Atestinus, ut Lauredanum principem et patres regni sui initio salutaret, magno comitatu ad urbem venit; honorificeque acceptus, et auri libra diebus singulis in sumptum a senatu donatus, gravi cum patribus benevolentiae foedere amicitiaque artiore constituta, domum rediit. Patres sub haec, de adventu in Italiam Maximiliani, qui Romam velle ire dictitabat, ut imperii insignia a Pontifice Maximo acciperet, saepe consulti, eius legatorum postulatis amice et benevole sunt polliciti. Decembri demum mense de confectis ab Aloisio Gallorum rege Ferdinandoque inter se foederibus cognoverunt. Quae omnino res susceptam ab illis iam antea de Aloisii in sese animo suspicionem facile auxit, propterea quod is nihil ante de ea quoque re senatui significavisset. Ferdinandus quidem per legatum suum patribus ostendit propter nova illa inita cum Gallorum rege foedera nihil se de vetere sua cum ipsis benevolentia diminuere; quam non retinere modo atque alere, sed augere etiam studiis atque officiis in dies singulos cuperet; nullos eventus eam sibi mentem erepturos.

9   Anno insequente, ob nonnullos mare Aegaeum atque Ionium, demum etiam Adriaticum navigantibus infestum reddentes piratas, senatus quamplurimas triremes non uno tempore armandas curavit; quibus a triremibus capti aliquot latrociniorum poenas reipublicae dederunt. Eo tempore Tunetis regis legatus, ad sena-

cillors. Antonio Giustinian, on the other hand, had been an envoy at Rome for a long time and had given great satisfaction to the Republic by his remarkable hard work and practical wisdom, and was accordingly granted permission to return home. Things had reached the point I have described by the middle of spring.

At the beginning of summer, Alfonso d'Este came to Venice 8 with a great retinue to pay his respects to Doge Loredan and the senators at the beginning of Loredan's reign. He was respectfully received and given by the Senate a per diem allowance of a gold pound for his expenses. After he struck a solemn treaty of goodwill and close friendship with the Senate, he returned home. The senators had often held discussions about the arrival in Italy of Maximilian, who was expressing his desire to go to Rome to receive the imperial crown from the pope. Directly after Alfonso d'Este's visit, they responded to the requests of Maximilian's envoys with friendly and benevolent undertakings. Finally, they learned in December of the treaties concluded between King Louis of France and Ferdinand of Aragon—this of course had the effect of greatly increasing their existing suspicions about Louis' attitude toward them, because he had given the Senate no prior hint of the matter. Ferdinand for his part let the senators know through his ambassador that the new treaties he had entered into with the French king would in no way diminish the goodwill he had long felt toward them: not only did he want to retain and cherish it, but he meant actually to enhance it by devoted service to them each and every day, and nothing could happen to change this intention.

A number of pirates had been making the Aegean, Ionian, and 9 in the end even the Adriatic dangerous for sailors, so in the following year, the Senate gave orders for the arming of a great many 1506 galleys on more than one occasion. Some of them were captured by these galleys and paid the Republic the price of their piracy. At much the same time an envoy of the sultan of Tunis was sent to

tum missus, equos mirae pernicitatis, more Punico ephippiatos, quattuor aquilasque aucupio idoneas totidem et canes venaticos patribus dono attulit, petens ut naves longas ad mercatum eo mitterent; velle enim regem suum amicitiam cum republica instituere. Is legatus, liberaliter acceptus domumque cum muneribus remissus, optimam in regem civitatis voluntatem reportavit. Etiam Norimbergenses, ampla et florens atque in primis libera suique iuris in Germania civitas, missis ad urbem legatis, exemplum Venetarum legum a patribus petiverunt, velleque sese eis uti legibus ostenderunt. Quod quidem illis senatus frequens concessit.

10 Petente autem ab senatu arroganter Baiasete rege ut Alexium in Illyrico insulam, bello Thracio captam, sibi restitueret, obstinatis eius atque assiduis postulationibus patres victi, ne is pacem quam cum illo fecerant, si reiceretur, frangeret, ab Alexio incolis omnibus emigrare iussis, aliisque in locis collocatis, rebus asportatis, arce diruta, eam inanem atque vacuam importuno regi relinquendam censuerunt. Erat paucis ante id senatus consultum diebus Marcus Antonius Sabellicus, qui res Venetas conscripsit, ipsa in urbe mortuus, laudaveratque illum Egnatius. Quoniam vero civibus Venetis qui tunc in Aegypto mercaturam exercebant multa incommoda rex Alexandrinus intulerat, auctis praeter morem Indicarum mercium pretiis, ipsorum bonis vi direptis, aliquot in vincula coniectis, senatusque ea de re per legatos apud regem questus fuerat, regis legatus ad senatum venit eius controversiae dirimendae atque componendae gratia, Tangavardinus,[1] homo Hispanus qui multos annos Alexandriae fuisset. Ei est sumptus de mercatorum pecuniis, aequis portionibus aestimatis, datus.

the Senate, bringing the senators a gift of four horses of remarkable speed, saddled in the African manner, and the same number of falcons[5] and hunting dogs, with the request that they should send galleys there to engage in trade, his sultan wanting to reach a friendly understanding with the Republic. The envoy was warmly received and sent back home with gifts, taking back with him assurances of Venice's great goodwill toward the sultan. The people of Nuremberg too, a large and flourishing German city, and one that was above all free and independent, sent ambassadors to Venice to ask the senators for a copy of the laws of the Republic, declaring that they wanted to make use of those laws themselves. A crowded Senate granted their request.

The Sultan Bayazid had made a high-handed request that the 10 Senate should return to him the island of Alessio in Albania, which had been taken in the Turkish war.[6] Beaten down by his insistent and continual demands, and worried that he might break the peace treaty they had made with him if he were refused, the senators voted to leave it barren and empty for the relentless sultan. They told all the inhabitants to leave Alessio and resettled them elsewhere, with all their property removed and the fortress razed to the ground. A few days before this Senate decree, Marcantonio Sabellico, who wrote the history of Venice, died in the city itself, and Giovanni Battista Egnazio delivered his eulogy. Now the sultan of Alexandria[7] had inflicted a good deal of hardship on the Venetian citizens who were at the time engaged in commerce in Egypt, by raising the prices of spices excessively, forcibly seizing their goods, and throwing some of them into prison. The Senate having made a complaint about this through its ambassadors to the sultan, an envoy of his, a Spaniard named Tangavardino who had been at Alexandria for many years,[8] came to the Senate to resolve the dispute and get it settled. His expenses were given him from funds of the merchants, once their fair shares were determined.

11   E Gallia etiam ab rege litterae Iulii litteras ad senatum datas attulerunt; quibus litteris, quoad Iulius viveret, Ariminum et Faventiam retinendi reipublicae facultas dabatur. Eas litteras Iulius ad
regem miserat, ut per illum senatui redderentur, quo maior auctoritas intercederet, quod intelligebat illarum scripto multo minus se
praestare, quam id erat quod pactus cum republica fuisset lega-
toque ipse Veneto suamet oratione confirmavisset. Id ubi patres de
legato regio intellexerunt, magna eos indignatio tenuit, ingrato
animo esse Iulium praedicantes, nullaque constantia, qui tantis receptis finibus, tot ad se missis una legatione civibus, quot nemini
umquam externo, tam insignibus in illum civitate functa officiis,
tamen nunc condicionibus a se uno positis non stet, nisi tenuis-
sima ex parte, atque eius quidem partis rege internuntio, ut illius
auctoritate res, quemadmodum quidem vult, minore negotio trans-
igatur. Eas ob regis litteras coacto biduum senatu, decernitur litteras Iulianas non esse accipiendas.

12   Ferdinandus interea rex classe Neapolim adventabat ut, quoniam ad Philippum generum omnis prope Hispaniae nobilitas
confluebat, atque ipsum pristina populorum gratia dignitasque
apud eas nationes destituebant, id in regnum se conferret cuius ille
particeps non esset. Eam ob rem patres Georgium Pisanum, Marcum Dandulum legatos creaverunt, qui Neapolim ad Ferdinandum proficiscerentur, de eius in Italiam adventu gratulatum.
Atque is neque dum Neapolim attigerat, cum Philippus in Hispania, quo socru mortua mari e Belgio venerat, pituita interiit. Ita
sunt magna incepta spesque ingentes una cum vita iuveni
abruptae. Eam ob filii mortem Maximilianus pater suum in aliud

From France there also came a letter from the king enclosing a 11
letter of Julius addressed to the Senate, in which the Republic was
granted the right to retain Rimini and Faenza as long as Julius
lived. Julius had sent the letter to the king to be forwarded by him
to the Senate so that it might carry greater weight, because he realized that he was offering much less in it than he had agreed with
the Republic and had himself confirmed in his own words to the
Venetian ambassador. When the senators learned of this from the
king's ambassador, they became highly indignant, proclaiming Julius to be an ingrate and completely unreliable. When he had received such large lands from Venice, when he had had more citizens sent to him on an embassy than any foreigner before him,[9]
when Venice had done him so many notable services, now he was
reneging on the terms that he himself had proposed, except in a
minimal way, and using the king as his go-between in that minimum, so that with the king's authority the business might be settled with less trouble in the way he wished. The Senate spent two
days in session over the king's letter, reaching a decision not to accept the letter of Julius.

In the meantime, since almost the entire nobility of Spain was 12
flocking to his son-in-law Philip, and he was losing the favor he
had formerly enjoyed with his people and the position he had held
among them, King Ferdinand was drawing near Naples with a
fleet so as to take himself off to a kingdom in which Philip had no
concern. In view of this, the senators appointed Giorgio Pisani
and Marco Dandolo as ambassadors to go to Ferdinand at Naples
and congratulate him upon his arrival in Italy. Ferdinand had not
yet reached Naples when Philip died of catarrh in Spain, whither
he had come from Flanders by sea on the death of his mother-in-
law. Thus were his great beginnings and the high hopes placed on
him cut short along with his young life. Owing to the death of his
son, his father Maximilian put off his trip to Rome to another

tempus Romanum iter distulit; quique iam praemissi ab eo in Alpibus Germani erant milites, domum revocati redierunt.

13　Iulius autem, qui omnes suos conatus eo intenderat, ut oppidum Bononiam in suam dicionem atque imperium revocaret, cuius quidem oppidi regnum tametsi Romani iuris esset, a Ioanne tamen Bentivolo obtinebatur, comparatis rebus omnibus quae ad bellum usui essent, Roma cum exercitu et collegio in Flaminiam, aestate iam confecta, discesserat, ut illum oppido expelleret. Quod omnino longe facilius, quam hominum opinio ferebat, propter ingens civitatis in illum odium, adductis in fines oppidi quas et ipse habebat et ab rege Gallo acceperat copiis, mense Octobri est assecutus. Ea illi de re ab Dominico Pisano legato, qui Antonio successerat, reipublicae nomine gratulatio est facta; tametsi ipse quoque Iulius suum tabellarium cum litteris ad senatum miserat, quae illum iis de rebus docerent.

14　Ultimis anni diebus, propterea quod saepe fiebat ut, qui impetrare magnam aut difficilem rem aliquam a magistratibus cuperent, regum et pontificum maximorum legatis uterentur, qui eos principi patribusque commendarent, interdum etiam ipsorum regum principumque civitatum ad urbem venientium patrocinio nitebantur, quorum auctoritati patres prope negare nihil poterant, senatus consultum factum est: cui quid a patribus impetrare sit necesse, is neque virum principem neque legatum adhibeat, cuius commendatione apud eos niti possit, poena pro genere hominum iis qui senatus consultum neglexissent constituta.

15　Primis vero ineuntis anni diebus Petrus Barotius, Patavinorum episcopus, moritur, vir politioribus litteris et sacrarum ac multarum disciplinarum doctrina insignis, moribus vitaque sanctiore, quique sublevandis egestate pressis civibus sacerdotii sui fructus omnes largiebatur, ut unius illius liberalitate non parva oppidanorum pars viveret. Itaque mortuo neque nummi neque suppellex

time, and the German soldiers in the Alps that he had sent on ahead were called back and returned home.

Julius, meanwhile, was bending all his efforts to bringing into his power and domain the town of Bologna, the lordship of which was held by Giovanni Bentivoglio, though it was under the jurisdiction of the Roman Church. Julius had made all the necessary preparations for war and, the summer now over, left Rome for Romagna with his army and the college of cardinals in order to expel Bentivoglio from the town. Bringing his own troops into Bolognese territory as well as those he had had from the king of France, Julius accomplished this in the month of October much more easily than people had imagined, owing to the deep hatred the city felt for Bentivoglio. He was congratulated on this achievement in the Republic's name by Domenico Pisani, who had succeeded Antonio Giustinian, though Julius had himself sent the Senate his own courier with a letter to inform them of the matter.

It often happened that people who wanted to win from the magistrates some large or difficult favor would employ the ambassadors of kings and popes to support them before the doge and senators; sometimes they would actually rely upon the advocacy of kings and princes themselves when they came to Venice, their prestige making it very difficult for the senators to deny them anything. In the last days of the year the Senate accordingly passed a decree that if a person needed to ask the senators for anything, he should employ neither a prince nor an ambassador to support him before them, and a penalty was laid down in proportion to their social rank for those who ignored the Senate decree.

At the beginning of the new year Pietro Barozzi, the bishop of Padua, died, a man of distinction in literature, learned in theology and many other disciplines, and of pious character and life. He spent all the fruits of his office on helping citizens oppressed by poverty, so that a considerable part of the townspeople lived only through his generosity; in consequence no money or any sort of

13

14

15

1507

pretiosa ulla inventa, praeter bibliothecam. Eas ob res sepulcrum
ei marmoreum in templo Patavino faciendum publica pecunia patres conscripti censuerunt. Pauloque post, cum cives plurimi Ligures emigrare domo atque urbem velle incolere sese patribus ostendissent, modo tuti publice fierent, si quid in Venetos Ligur
quispiam deliquisset, sua bona ea re non teneri, senatus consultum
factum est, quo eis civitas atque securitas est data, navigatione
mercaturae causa in orientem excepta.

16   Sub idem tempus, Aloisio Gallorum rege in Italiam properante,
ut Genuensium civitati, quae ab eo defecerat seseque in libertatem
vindicaverat, bellum inferret, Dominicum Trivisanum, Paulum Pisanum, Patavinorum magistratum, senatus legatos ad regem de adventu gratulatum misit. Ille autem, recepta paucis diebus Genua,
Mediolanum se contulit, ibique eum legati convenerunt. Sed cum,
in Galliam transalpinam rediens, apud Astam cognovisset Ferdinandum regem, qui Neapoli classe in Hispaniam revertebatur, ex
itinere Genuam appulisse convenireque se cupere, ei praesto ad
Savonem oppidum fuit; magnoque illum honore excipiens, cum
una dies aliquot fuissent,[2] Ferdinando abeunte ipse in Galliam
profectus est; legati domum reverterunt.

17   Cum[3] ob Aloisii tam celerem in Italiam adventum, cum illum,
si inimico esset in rempublicam animo, non longinquitas itineris,
non reges interpositi, non denique Alpes moraturae viderentur,
quin, cum vellet, in citeriorem Galliam parvo negotio traiceret,
tum etiam quod rumor increbuerat Maximilianum in Italiam cogitare, ne respublica ad eiusmodi casus imparatior offendi posset, senatus consultum factum est: in Veronensium finibus eorum qui
arma ferre possent certus agrestium hominum numerus conscribe-
retur, qui rei militari assuefierent; iisque immunitas reliquarum re-

luxury goods were found at his death, apart from his library. The senators[10] accordingly voted for a marble tomb to be erected to him in the cathedral of Padua at public expense. Shortly thereafter, a good number of Genoese citizens wanting to leave home and live in Venice approached the senators to ask for official assurance that they could live peaceably there and not have their goods seized on account of any wrongs that Genoese persons might have done Venetians. A Senate decree was passed giving them that assurance and Venetian citizenship, but excluding them from taking part in the eastern maritime trade.

About the same time, as King Louis of France hastened to Italy to make war on Genoa, which had defected from him and declared its independence, the Senate sent Domenico Trevisan and the praetor of Padua, Paolo Pisani, as ambassadors to the king to congratulate him on his advent. He retook Genoa within a few days, and then made his way to Milan, where the ambassadors met him. But as he was returning to France, he found out at Asti that King Ferdinand, who was returning to Spain from Naples with his fleet, had put in at Genoa en route and desired to meet him, so he attended him at the town of Savona, receiving him there with every mark of respect. After a few days in his company, he set out for France and Ferdinand departed, the Venetian ambassadors returning home.

Louis's rapid descent into Italy (it seemed that if he intended to do the Republic harm, neither the length of the journey, nor the rulers placed in his way, nor even the Alps themselves would stop him from crossing into Lombardy without difficulty whenever he wished), and also the growing rumor that Maximilian contemplated coming to Italy, induced the Senate to pass a decree so as to have the Republic better prepared for such an eventuality: in the territory of Verona a number of countrymen fit to bear arms were to be recruited to accustom them to military service. They were to be relieved of other burdens so as to have them readier to face the

16

17

rum daretur, quo paratiores ad obeunda belli munera essent, et,
cum vocarentur ad signa, e vestigio convenirent. Ea militum ex
agris deinceps institutio ad reliquos reipublicae fines, ut est usus
omnium rerum magister, brevi permanavit. Itaque nunc quidem
cuiusque oppidi vici pagique partem habent suorum, qui ei rei student, ut armati paratique sint, nullo ut interposito temporis spatio
ad bellum prodire reique publicae celerem navare operam possint.
Hosque omnes uno nomine milites pro ordinibus appellaverunt.
Rex post haec Alexandrinus, controversiis quas habebat cum republica fine facto, ad iustitiam et aequitatem sese dedit. Itaque triremes ad mercatum eo remissae cum magistratu Veneto, qui
Alexandriae moram traheret, cumque legato regio, de quo supra
dictum est; cui proficiscenti vestis aurea cum pretiosis pellibus aurique librae decem sunt a senatu dono datae, comitatuique eius
omni indumenta honestiora tradita.

18   Interim a Vincentio Quirino legato, quem ad Maximilianum
patres miserant, acceptis saepe litteris significabatur Maximilianum, spreta quam superiore anno fecerat cum rege Gallorum pace,
neglectisque foederibus, quibus illum non stetisse conquerebatur,
de Germaniae consilio statuisse in Italiam cum exercitu accedere,
ad speciem ut tuto Romam se conferret, re ut Mediolani regno illum eiceret. Senatus novis equitatus et peditatus copiis munire
rempublicam decrevit. Itaque praefecti sunt equitum adlecti quamplures; in iis Vitellius Tifernas, et Guidus Vainus e Cornelii Foro,
cum militibus sexcentis, equitibus quinquaginta ambo; Iacobusque
Siccus e Gallia cisalpina, et Lucius Malvetius Bononiensis, cum
turma equitum uterque gravioris armaturae centum. Tum, ut milites numero ad decem milia conscriberentur, latum, qui sub tribunis et centurionibus in castris versarentur, quique per oppida praesidii causa disponerentur ad quinque milia. Equites etiam levioris

exigencies of war and assemble at once when called to arms. This practise of levying of soldiers from the countryside soon spread to the rest of the Republic's territories, custom being king in everything, and so it comes about that at present the villages and districts of every town have a number of their inhabitants devoted to this purpose, so they can be armed and ready to set out for battle in an instant and give the Republic speedy assistance. All these men were called by the same term, 'regular militias.'[11] After this, the sultan of Alexandria put aside the disputes he had with the Republic and adopted a just and equitable course. The galleys were therefore sent back there to begin trading again, taking with them a Venetian magistrate who was to be resident in the city and the sultan's ambassador, of whom mention has been made above;[12] on his departure, the Senate made him a gift of a brocaded robe decked with expensive fur[13] and ten gold pounds, and all his retinue were given fine garments.

Meanwhile the senators had been receiving frequent letters from 18 Vincenzo Quirini, whom they had sent as ambassador to Maximilian. They revealed that in disregard of the peace he had made with the king of France the previous year, and ignoring the treaties which he complained the latter had not kept to, Maximilian had with the backing of Germany decided to descend into Italy with an army, ostensibly to guard his passage to Rome but in fact with a view to throwing the king out of the duchy of Milan. The Senate decided to protect the Republic with fresh forces of cavalry and footsoldiers. A large number of cavalry captains were accordingly chosen, among them Vitelli of Città di Castello and Guido Vaina of Imola, both with 600 infantry and 50 cavalry, and Giacomo Secco of Lombardy, and Lucio Malvezzi of Bologna, each with a squadron of 100 light cavalry. They then voted to recruit up to 10,000 infantry, who were to be deployed in camp under their colonels and officers, and 5,000 more who would be dispersed through the towns to serve as garrisons. In

armaturae tercentum quadraginta, Nauplia et Zacyntho accersiti, urbano in litore, quo appulerant, a magistratibus lustrati, stipendio accepto se Taurisum contulerunt.

19 Iis rebus confectis, Maximiliani legati tres ad urbem veniunt postulatum, propterea quod rex eorum iter haberet nullum aliud, uti Romam, quo eundum illi erat, per fines reipublicae regi exercituique regio itineris faciendi senatus facultatem daret; recipere Maximilianum, fidemque suam in eo interponere, sese sine maleficio atque iniuria per eos fines iter facturum exercitumque ducturum. Quod si, propter eam quam haberet respublica cum rege Gallorum amicitiam, senatus id se minus recte posse facere existimet, monere patres Maximilianum atque aperte profiteri nullum esse in eo rege fidem, nullam constantiam; id se esse saepenumero expertum; itaque rectius facturum senatum, si nihil in illo sibi praesidii putet esse constitutum; sese patribus foedera quae pepigerit vita sua diligentius servaturum. Ea re ad senatum relata, cum plures sententiae dicerentur, essentque nonnulli ex magistratibus et principibus civitatis qui Maximiliano credi oportere contenderent, vicit tamen ea sententia quae legatis in hunc modum uti responderetur censuit: si Maximilianus pacate sineque exercitu velit iter facere, rempublicam ei quod peteret libentissime concessuram legatosque missuram, qui illum exciperent omnibusque honoribus prosequerentur; sin cum exercitu proficiscatur, a pace quam cum rege Gallo habeat non posse discedere senatum sine perfidiae crimine, itaque nihil ei permissurum.

20 Atque his ipsis nondum ab urbe profectis legatis, Gallorum rex novam legationem ad senatum misit, mentem ac voluntatem reipublicae, si Maximilianus ei bellum inferat, sciscitatum. Magno enim timore afficiebatur, propterea quod fama vulgaverat Germaniae populos Maximiliano ingentes copias subministraturos, ne

addition, 340 light cavalry summoned from Nauplia and Zante were reviewed by the magistrates when they landed at the Lido of Venice, were given their pay and made their way to Treviso.

That done, three of Maximilian's ambassadors came to the city 19 to ask the Senate to give the king and his army their permission to march through the Republic's territory to his destination, Rome, since that was the only route he could take. Maximilian undertook to make his way through their territory at the head of his army without causing any harm or injury, and gave his word on the matter. But if in the light of the Republic's alliance with the king of France, the Senate judged that they could not in justice do this, Maximilian gave the senators warning by openly declaring that there was no trustworthiness to be found in the king, nothing they could rely on, as he himself had often experienced, and so the Senate would be better advised to realise that in Louis they had no safeguard. As for Maximilian, he would guard the treaties he had concluded more jealously than his life. When this was reported to the Senate, although a wide variety of opinions were expressed, and there were some magistrates and leading citizens who argued in favor of trusting Maximilian, in the end the view that they should answer the ambassadors as follows nevertheless won the day: if Maximilian was prepared to make his journey peaceably and without an army, the Republic would very willingly grant him what he asked and would send ambassadors to welcome him and attend him with every mark of honor. But if he set out with an army, the Senate could not depart from the peace accord which it had with the French king without incurring a charge of perfidy, and in that case would give him nothing.

Maximilian's ambassadors had not yet left Venice when the 20 king of France sent a new embassy to the Senate to find out what the attitude of the Republic would be if Maximilian were to make war on him. Having heard widespread reports that the German peoples were going to supply Maximilian with vast numbers of

ab eo tanta in re tam unanimi illarum nationum consensu patres perterriti deficerent, aliorum mores hominum, ut plerumque fit, suorum morum modio atque consuetudine metiens. Senatus autem omnes reipublicae facultates legatis ad regem defendendum est pollicitus; quaeque Maximiliani legati a republica petiissent, quod ad illa responsum habuissent, amico eis animo aperuit.

21 Patres post haec venientem ad urbem Nicolaum Ursinum imperatorem ab ipsis accersitum, ut cum eo et Liviano et Carraciolo, qui utrique iussu eorum venerant, de bello consilium caperent, ei obviam in navi Bucentauro profecti, civitate circumvecta exceperunt; insequentibusque diebus quibus in locis Maximiliano, quamque ante diem copiae reipublicae essent opponendae, una cum his constituerunt; eosque e vestigio reverti, et quam quisque partem reipublicae finium tuendam suscepisset, ad eam illum contendere iusserunt. Certiores enim facti tractari arma in Maximiliani finibus militesque pluribus in locis cogi, nihil sibi reliqui ad exercitum comparandum copiasque partiendas fecerunt, ut in tempore occurri posset.

22 Ubi Maximilianus de legatis suis cognovit nolle senatum ei armato per fines reipublicae iter dare, Vincentium Quirinum ab se dimisit. Profectus ille cum in primis reipublicae finibus subsedisset, ne iniussu patrum propius accederet, senatu permittente domum rediit. Patres, tametsi Decembri appetente mense multis verisimile non fieret Maximilianum Alpes esse cum exercitu traiecturum, tamen Georgio Emo legato ab senatu declarato, qui in fines Veronensium cum copiis accederet, eo se ab latere celeriter munire decreverunt, praesertim quod intelligebant Germanorum militum

troops, the king was very worried that faced with this absolute unanimity of the Germans the senators would take fright and desert him in this vitally important matter, estimating, as is usually the case, the character of others from the limits of his own. For their part, the Senate promised the ambassadors that the Republic would do everything in its power to defend the king, and in a spirit of friendship they revealed to them what Maximilian's ambassadors had asked for and the response they had received.

After this episode the captain-general Niccolò Orsini came to 21 Venice at the request of the senators, so that they might make plans for war with him, d'Alviano, and Caracciolo, the latter two also summoned by them. The senators went to meet Orsini in the Bucintoro and bade him welcome, the citizens accompanying them in their boats. In consultation with these captains, they decided over the next few days where and when the Republic's forces had to be in place to oppose Maximilian. They were ordered to go back at once and make for the particular parts of Venetian territory they were responsible for defending. When they received information that ordnance was being handled in Maximilian's lands and soldiers assembled in many places, the senators left no stone unturned in raising an army and disposing their forces so as to be in a position to confront him in time.

Maximilian learned from his ambassadors that the Senate had 22 refused to allow him to march in arms through the Republic's lands, and he thereupon dismissed Vincenzo Quirini. Quirini left but stopped as soon as he came to Venetian territory, unwilling to go further without the Senate's express permission, on being given which he returned home. Though many thought it improbable that Maximilian and his army would cross the Alps with December coming on, the senators all the same appointed Giorgio Emo their proveditor to take troops into the Veronese, having taken a decision to protect themselves quickly on that front, especially since they understood that a certain number of German infantry

certam iam manum adventare, ut illis ex Alpibus se demitteret. Quae quidem manus, neque dum munitis itineribus et saltibus, facile traiecit, sine ullo tamen reipublicae maleficio, pacataque in Mantuanorum se fines contulit. Ii erant milites circiter mille ducenti. Paucisque post diebus cum, nullo accepto in Italia stipendio, domum redire statuissent, Emusque interea legatus exercitu adducto itinera clausisset, ut reverti eius voluntate sibi liceret ab eo petiverunt. Ille armis depositis iter facere iussit.

23   Sed cum iisdem in locis atque in Vicetiorum saltibus anno insequente inito Germani saepenumero se ostendissent, ut in fines reipublicae irrumperent, omnino neque in eo perfecerunt quicquam ipsi, neque a Venetis ulla est res paulo illustrior gesta, neque oppidum quodpiam nobilius captum aut caedes aut fuga hostium memorabilior facta, tametsi Aloisius rex, qui saepe senatum per legatos oratione magnifica confirmaverat sese eum numquam deserturum, ipsum etiam, si necesse sit, reipublicae auxilio venturum, Triultium cum copiis in castra Veneta misisset, et senatus Andream Grittum legatum magna cum manu eodem accedere iussisset. Nam cum duos uno tempore legatos senatus creavisset, Grittum et Georgium Cornelium, ut alter in Raetos, alter in Carnos proficisceretur (inde enim etiam in reipublicae dicionem velle perrumpere Germanos litteris nuntiisque afferebatur), iis uti sorte imperia partirentur patres permiserunt. Ita Gritto Raeti, Cornelio Carni provincia obtigit. Atque in Raetis quidem hunc unum res eventum habuerunt, ut repressi et repulsi saepe hostes ex reipublicae dicione atque imperio nullum sibi iter patefecerint, nihil omnino ceperint, amiserint autem potius ultimis belli diebus montanum oppidulum Agrestam.

was already on its way with the intent of swooping down from the local Alps. The German force did in fact cross over with ease, since the roads and mountain passes had not yet been fortified, but no harm was done to the Republic, and it made its way peacefully into the territory of Mantua. They numbered about 1,200 soldiers. A few days later, having received no pay in Italy, they decided to return home, but in the meantime the proveditor Emo had brought in his army and closed the roads, so they asked his permission to be allowed to return. He required them to lay down their arms before they made the journey.

At the beginning of the following year, though the Germans had often made an appearance in those places and in the uplands of Vicenza with a view to invading the Republic's territory, they made absolutely no headway there, nor was there any specially notable action on the Venetian side—no important town taken, no remarkable slaughter or rout of the enemy. All the same, King Louis, who had often grandly assured the Senate through his ambassadors that he would never desert them, that if necessary he would come to the aid of the Republic in person, did send Giangiacomo Trivulzio to the Venetian camp with troops, the Senate ordering the proveditor Andrea Gritti to go there too with a large force. The Senate had appointed two proveditors at the same time, Gritti and Giorgio Corner, one to proceed to the Tyrol, the other to Friuli, for reports were coming in by letter and messenger that the Germans wanted to invade Venetian territory from there as well. The senators allowed them to share out the commands by lot, and so the province of the Tyrol fell to Gritti, Friuli to Corner. In the Tyrol all that happened was that the enemy was often worsted and driven back from the lands under Venice's sway. They opened up no path for themselves, made no conquests at all, but on the contrary ended by losing in the last days of the war the little mountain town of Agresta.

23

1508

24   At in Carnis, qua nihilo secius Germani aditum in reipublicae fines temptaverant, Livianus, qui exercitui praeerat, et Cornelius legatus rem sane publicam naviter atque feliciter gesserunt. Nam cum mense Februario rumor increbuisset hostium non parvam coactam in Carnis manum eo ab latere bellum illaturam adventare, Daniel Dandulus Feltriam a senatu missus est, rebus quae ex usu essent procurandis commeatuque exercitui, qui eo venturus erat durissimo anni tempore, locis impeditissimis, subministrando. Gradiscas quoque, castellum apud Sontium flumen arte atque opere communitum, Iustinianus Maurocenus senatu iubente iisdem cum mandatis est profectus. Tum Cornelius et Livianus Bassiano, in Alpium radicibus ad Medoaci ripam sito, quod ad oppidum multis e reipublicae finibus exercitum cogebant, iussi cum copiis ad Germanos reprimendos contendere.

25   Interim repentino hostium adventu, qui per devia asperaque Alpium iuga praecipitesque declivitates ferratis pedibus iter confecerant, centurionem, cum militibus sexaginta Clusae pagi angustias servantem, profugisse Cadorasque oppidulum ad flumen Plavim, quod ab Clusa quinque milia passuum abest, una cum arce et Petro Ghisio praetore in hostium venisse potestatem nuntiatur. Ea intellecta re in castris, Livianus celeritate adhibita cum duobus familiaribus ad vicina hostibus loca sese contulit speculatum, relicto Cornelio, qui cum copiis paratioribus diurnis nocturnisque itineribus subsequebatur. In urbe Donatus Legius a senatu lectus est, qui Cividale Carnicum contenderet daretque operam, ne quid incommodi respublica eo in oppido acciperet. In Foroiuliensibus autem Hieronymus Saornianus, de quo supra commemoravimus, vir egregia fide atque virtute princepsque civitatis, primo paucis cum equitibus e sua familia ad eos fines est profectus, quibus in finibus

In Friuli, however, where the Germans had likewise attempted   24
to break into the Republic's territory, Bartolomeo d'Alviano, in
charge of the army there, and the proveditor Corner acted on the
Republic's behalf with boldness and success. Rumors spread in
February that a substantial enemy force raised in Friuli was coming with the aim of starting a war on that front, and so Daniele
Dandolo was sent by the Senate to Feltre in order to procure
the necessary supplies for the war and arrange for provisions for
the army, which would be coming there at the hardest time of the
year and facing very difficult terrain. By order of the Senate,
Giustiniano Morosini went with the same instructions to
Gradisca too, a fortress on the Isonzo river that skill and hard labor had made very secure. Then, since Corner and d'Alviano were
raising an army near the town of Bassano del Grappa, located at
the foot of the Alps on the banks of the Brenta river, they were ordered to march from there with their troops to drive back the Germans.

The enemy arrived all of a sudden, having made their way along   25
remote and difficult Alpine ridges and over precipitous slopes on
iron-shod feet. At that, it was reported, an officer who was guarding the pass of the village of Chiusa[14] with sixty men, had taken to
his heels and the enemy had taken possession of Pieve di Cadore,
a small town five miles from Chiusa on the Piave, together with its
fortress and Pietro Ghiso its governor. When this became known
in camp, d'Alviano with two of his household took himself with
all speed to the vicinity of the enemy lines to make a reconnais-
sance, leaving behind Corner, who followed with the fitter troops,
marching day and night. In Venice, Donato da Legge was chosen
by the Senate to make for Cividale del Friuli and do his best to
see that the Republic suffered no loss in that town. In Udine,
Girolamo Savorgnan, whom we have mentioned above,[15] the leading citizen of the town and a man of outstanding loyalty and courage, initially set out with a few cavalry from his own household to

hostes impressionem fecerant, magnaque celeriter auxilia reipublicae conventura confirmans, earum regionum incolas labentes iam ad imperataque Maximiliani facienda pronos, in officio continuit. Deinde coactis hominum duobus milibus quingentis, equitatu etiam addito, iter impeditissimum faciebat, ut contra hostes cum legato exercituque reipublicae illa cum manu se coniungeret.

26   Dum haec agitarentur, Lucas Renaldius, Maximiliani legatus, ad senatum venit, illud idem postulatum de quo antea saepe rex egerat, iter Romam per fines reipublicae repetens: regem suum propterea velle armatum incedere, quod se tutum ab suis hostibus aliter fore non confidebat; reipublicae nihil ab eo nocitum iri omnibus illum modis confirmaturum; vel senatus obsides ei daret nociturum esse illi neminem; hoc si praestet, sine armis regem iturum. Ad haec Lauredanus respondit: scire regem quam propensa semper fuerit reipublicae erga Federicum imperatorem, patrem suum, seque ipsum voluntas; quo magis indignum esse bellum ab eo inferri non unis reipublicae finibus, praedas abigi, castella expugnari. De eo se maximo opere conqueri deosque testes adhibere non esse ita de rege meritam rempublicam, sed rem se ad senatum relaturum deque eius sententia responsurum. Nam quod a Cornelio litterae venerant confidere Livianum propeque recipere hostes sibi poenas cito daturos, patres respondendi Maximiliani legato tempus interponere volebant, dum a Carnis aliquid confecti afferretur. Legato autem socii sunt atque custodes dati, ne quis eum alloqui posset cui patres id non permisissent.

that district, where the enemy had made an attack. He assured the inhabitants of the area that substantial Venetian reinforcements would soon arrive and so kept them loyal when they were already wavering and inclining to follow Maximilian's orders. Then he collected 2,500 soldiers, and some cavalry as well, and set out on a march of the utmost difficulty in order to join forces with the Venetian proveditor and army against the enemy.

While all this was going on, Maximilian's ambassador Luca de' 26 Rinaldi came to the Senate to make the same request that the king had often made before, seeking permission once more to pass through the Republic's territory to Rome: the reason, he said, that the king wanted to proceed under arms was that he had no confidence that he would be safe from his enemies if he did not. He was willing to give all manner of assurances that he would do no harm to the Republic. Alternatively, the Senate could give him hostages against any harm being done to *him*, and if they offered to do so, the king would proceed without arms. To this Doge Loredan replied: the king knew how well disposed the Republic had always been toward his father, the emperor Frederick, and toward himself. It was all the more intolerable that war was being made on the Republic in more than one of its lands, booty carried off, fortresses stormed. Of that he complained in the strongest terms and called God to witness that the Republic had not deserved this treatment at the king's hands; but he would refer the matter to the Senate and respond in accordance with their decision. A letter had come from Corner to the effect that d'Alviano was confident—indeed almost guaranteed—that the enemy would soon pay the penalty, so the senators wanted to let some time pass before responding to Maximilian's ambassador, until some concrete success was reported from Friuli. The ambassador was given companions and guards so that no one could speak to him without the Senate's permission.

27   Livianus, adductis ad se militibus mille octingentis, quorum erat dux Petrus Montius, vir magna virtute, equitibusque levis armaturae ex Epiro prope ducentis, quibus praeerant Palaeologus et Busichius, tum ex iis qui sagittis utebantur alteris fere totidem, graviorisque armaturae ex ipsius et reliquorum turmis paulo plus ducentis, Saorniani litteris ac nuntiis de locorum situ, de hostium numero deque belli rationibus admonitus, qui quidem iam adventabat atque ab altera montis parte in trium pontium loco Germanos observare eisque occurrere statuerat, prima luce hostes aggredi constituit. Is erat Martii Kalendarum dies. Sed propterea quod nix ea nocte plurima ceciderat, proelium in aliam reiectum est diem, quod quidem secundissimum postridie fuit. Nam cum Germani, redeundi domum itineribus praesaeptis ad se veniri certiores facti, ne intercluderentur, Venetos aggredi viamque ferro sibi ipsi aperire statuissent, atque in editiorem proximae vallis partem cum impedimentis et tormentis se collegissent, numero ad duo milia quingenti, ut e loco superiore in Venetos subeuntes impetum facerent (erant autem e Maximiliani comitatu quamplurimis centurionibus, viris fortibus, interiecti),[4] ipse acie instructa, per nives recta progressus, proelium audacissime commisit; eosque primo fortiter pugnantes, post impedimentis exutos, tormentisque abreptis, desperatis rebus non magnopere resistentes concidit, praeter illos qui proiectis armis pacem suppliciter petiverunt. Pauci, fuga in montes elapsi, ab Epirotis equitibus eundem casum subierunt, capitaque sunt eorum in castra relata, pro quibus singulis Livianus pecuniam pollicitus interfectoribus fuerat. Ex Venetis desiderati sunt sane pauci.

28   Nocte ea quae secuta est exercitui ad quietem data, Livianus ad Germanos qui arcem Cadorarum custodiebant amplius sexaginta

To d'Alviano had been brought 1,800 infantry, whose captain   27
was Piero del Monte Santa Maria, a man of great courage, and
almost 200 stradiots from Albania under the command of
Palaeologus and Busicchio, and almost as many again mounted archers, and a little more than 200 heavy cavalry, from his own
squadrons and others'. Savorgnan was already drawing near and
had decided that he would wait and meet the Germans on the
other flank of the mountain, at Treponti. D'Alviano had had letters and messengers from him informing him of the geography,
enemy numbers and war plans, and decided to attack the enemy
at dawn. This was the first day of March. But because a great deal
of snow had fallen that night, the battle was put off till the next
day, when indeed it went off very well. The Germans had learned
that their routes for the return home were blocked and that the
enemy was drawing near, so they decided to attack the Venetians
and open up a path for themselves with the sword, in case they
should be cut off. They gathered themselves to the number of
about 2,500 (scattered among them a great many officers from
Maximilian's personal guard, men of valor) on an elevated part of
the neighboring valley with their baggage and artillery, so as to
launch an attack on the Venetians from higher ground as they
came up the valley. D'Alviano drew up his battle lines, advanced
straight through the snow, and with great daring joined battle. At
first the Germans fought bravely, but later, after losing their bag-
gage-train and with their artillery taken from them, they offered
small resistance in their desperation and, with the exception of
those who threw down their arms and humbly begged for peace,
were cut down by d'Alviano. A few, having fled to the mountains,
suffered a like fate at the hands of the stradiots; their heads, for
each of which d'Alviano promised the slaughterers money, were
carried back to the camp. Of the Venetians very few were lost.

The army was given the following night to rest while d'Alviano   28
sent more than sixty men to the Germans who were guarding the

misit, imperans uti arcem traderent. Ii trium dierum spatium ad eam rem sibi dari petiverunt. Livianus, eorum postulatione reiecta, ad arcem expugnandam est profectus. Quam cum diem totum, omni missilium genere tormentisque in adverso iugo positis, continenter oppugnavisset magnamque propugnatorum partem interfecisset, muro etiam propugnaculi subrupto, reliqui postridie deditionem fecerunt. In ea oppugnatione Carolus Malatesta adolescens, saxo ab arce percussus, cum nonnullis viris fortibus interiit. Captivi qui arcem tradiderant, una cum prioribus dediticiis, omnes quingenti armis ceterisque rebus exuti, Liviani permissu domum redierunt. Harum rerum primis in urbe nuntiis acceptis, idem est responsum legato Maximiliani a senatu datum quod superioribus legatis patres antea dederant; neque quicquam cum illo de caede Germanorum communicatum. Ac, ne quid ei redeunti ab armatis in Raetico noceretur, comites sunt ducesque itineris per fines reipublicae attributi.

29 Ubi ex litteris Cornelii legati de proelio deque arcis expugnatione singula ordine civitas intellexit, Livianique et consilium et celeritas et virtus laudari vocibus omnium coepit, patres, ut et illius animum alacriorem in posterum ad belli munia redderent, honorum insignibus et magnitudine praemiorum excitatum, et reliquorum voluntates accenderent ad bene de republica promerendum, cum viderent fortes industriosque viros ab ea fieri plurimi, praefecturam omnium reipublicae copiarum Liviano detulerunt. Ea est amplissima post imperatoris nomen dignitas quae pro eorum meritis ab senatu militaribus viris tribui consuevit. Auctusque est equitum illius numerus, qui erat sexcentorum, ad integrum mille. Auctum quoque stipendium ab auri libris centum quinquaginta ad tercentenas libras. Tum decem in praesentia dono datae cum iis

citadel of Pieve di Cadore, ordering them to surrender it. They asked to be given three days to consider the matter, but d'Alviano rejected their request and set out to storm the citadel. After he had spent a whole day putting it under constant attack with artillery and missiles of every kind placed on the hill opposite, killing a large part of the defenders, and also undermining the wall of the rampart, the rest of them surrendered the following day. In the attack the young Carlo Malatesta was struck by a rock from the citadel and died, along with a number of other brave men. The prisoners who had surrendered the citadel, together with those taken captive before, went home with d'Alviano's permission, all 500 stripped of their weapons and other equipment. When the first news of these events reached Venice, the Senate gave Maximilian's ambassador the same response it had given before to the earlier ambassadors, communicating nothing about the slaughter of the Germans to him. In case he should come to any harm at the hands of the men under arms in the Tyrol as he returned, a bodyguard and guides were assigned to him as he passed through the Republic's territory.

When the city learned from a letter of the proveditor Corner 29 the full story of the battle and the storming of the citadel, d'Alviano's strategic ability, speed and courage began to be praised on everyone's lips. Not only to inspire him to ever greater alacrity in his future military duties, once roused with marks of honor and handsome rewards, but also to fire the minds of others to serve the Republic when they saw the regard in which she held brave and hard-working men, the senators awarded d'Alviano general command of all the Venetian forces. After the title of captain-general, this is the most distinguished rank that the Senate generally gives to military men for their services. The number of his cavalry, formerly 600, was increased to a full thousand. His pay was increased, too, from 150 gold pounds to 300. Ten were given him as an immediate gift, along with the artillery which the enemy had

tormentis bellicis quae hostes e Germania secum attulerant,
quaeque ipse ob rei bene gestae memoriam a patribus sibi dari cupere in sermonibus cum legato habitis ostenderat; Caroli autem
Malatestae uxori ac duobus liberis infantibus illa ipsa pensio an-
nua qua is vivens a republica donatus fruebatur in victum tradita.
Deinde cum patribus nuntiatum esset a Maximiliano copias in
Carnis comparari, tum incursiones in reipublicae dicionem a Gori-
tianis fieri, quod est oppidum in monte ultra Sontium flumen situm, senatus consultum factum est, ut milites ter mille celeriter
conscriberentur atque ad legatum mitterentur.

30   Ceterum quod erant plerique magistratus, qui bellum inferri
Maximiliano censebant oportere atque in eius fines exercitum in-
troduci volebant, Dominicus Maurocenus, templi Marcii procurator, vir re atque cognomine sapiens, aetate valde proclinata (erat
enim annos natus nonaginta), patres monere ac rogare coepit ne id
fieri permitterent: Germaniae civitates, quae liberae suique iuris
essent, aegre ferre a Maximiliano arma contra rempublicam exerceri, cum pace frui possit; eas easdem, si ei bellum inferatur, moleste id laturas neque passuras sui regis nomen dignitatemque
convelli ac proteri; non magnas esse ab illo iniurias in republi-
cam illatas, de iis tamen deorum immortalium benignitate poenas
ipsum reipublicae dedisse: omnem illam in Carnis manum conci-
sam deletamque esse, Cadoras Clusamque recepta, in Raetis nihil
amissum, neque ullam contumeliam acceptam; "quod si eo
contenti," inquit, "erimus," magnum nos fructum continentiae laturos,[5] Germaniae totius benevolentiam, "quae quidem certe Germania commeatibus asportandis mercibusque reciprocandis et rerum plurimarum communicatione ita est coniuncta nobiscum et
consociata, ut magni inde proventus in rempublicam portorii nomine, magnae privatim utilitates in omne genus civium inferantur."
Laudabile profecto esse hostes bello superare, propagare imperii

brought with them from Germany, and which in conversation with the proveditor he had expressed a desire to have given him by the Senate as a memento of his success. Besides that, the wife and two young children of Carlo Malatesta were given the annual pension for living expenses that Carlo had enjoyed in life as a gift of the Republic. When the senators then heard that Maximilian was raising troops in Friuli and attacks were being made on Venetian territory by the people of Gorizia (a hill town on the other side of the Isonzo), they passed a decree that 3,000 infantry should be quickly recruited and sent to the proveditor.

Many of the magistrates thought that they should go to war 30 with Maximilian and wanted to send an army into his lands, but Domenico Morosini, a Procurator of St. Mark's, a man wise in name and nature[16] and of very advanced age (he was ninety years old), began to give the senators advice, asking them not to permit it: the free and independent states of Germany resented Maximilian's taking up arms against the Republic when he could be enjoying peace. Those same states would take it ill if he got involved in a war, nor would they suffer the name and prestige of their king to be undermined and trampled under foot. The damage he had inflicted on the Republic was not great, yet by the grace of Almighty God he had paid the price for them: his entire force in Friuli had been cut down and wiped out, Pieve di Cadore and Chiusa had been taken back, there had been no losses in the Tyrol, nor any humiliation wrought on them. "But if," he said, "we content ourselves with that," we should reap great profit from our restraint, namely, the goodwill of all Germany, "which in the transport of foodstuffs[17] and reciprocal trade in goods and the exchange of all manner of things is so connected and allied with us that the Republic collects a large income from the customs tolls and great private advantages accrue to citizens of every class." It was indeed a laudable thing (he said) to worst an enemy in war, to extend the bounds of empire; but very much more laudable to re-

fines; multo autem laudabilius se ipsos continere ac vincere, ius-
titiae moderationis gravitatis opinionem apud omnes homines
auxisse lateque promovisse. Bellorum eventus a fortuna plerumque
administrari, quae fluxa atque incerta sit; prudentiae consilia stabi-
lem habere exitum, semperque plus proficere constantia et maturi-
tate quam illa impetu <nata quae nullum> usum ex sese prae-
buerint.[6]

31   Haec cum senex sapiens dixisset, ardor ille magistratuum ad[7]
bellum gerendum parumper restinctus est. Itaque nihil latum, nisi
uti ea de re patres amplius consulerentur. Alfonsus post haec, Ferrariensium dux, ad urbem familiariter se contulit patribus purga-
tum, quod suspectus eis fuerat litteras nuntiosque ad Maximilianum misisse, societatem ineundi seque cum illo coniungendi
causa, confirmans nihil se umquam eiusmodi cogitavisse; cupere
autem et statuisse una cum republica omnem fortunam experiri;
neque ullo tempore a senatus auctoritate velle recedere. Patres eam
orationem auribus libentissimis acceperunt; collaudatumque,
atque ut omnia summae benevolentiae officia a senatu exspectaret
confirmatum, domum remiserunt.

32   Interim nulla in Raetico belli cessatione a Maximiliano fieri cognita, in Carnis milites non unis in locis cogi rumore nuntiisque
afferentibus, senatus, suam in illum lenitatem frustra adhibitam
sentiens, pridie Nonarum Aprilium constituit uti bellum omnibus
a partibus Maximiliani finibus inferretur. Itaque non legatis modo
Gritto et Cornelio id senatus consultum celeriter est missum, sed
omnino etiam Hieronymo Contareno, qui cum classe aliquot triremium legatus in Istris tunc erat, litterae sunt a senatu datae, uti
maritima Maximiliani oppida, qua vellet, aggredi capereque conaretur; se alias paucis diebus triremes ad illum missurum. Senatus
consulto ad Cornelium perlato, voluntateque civitatis Liviano reli-

strain and be masters of ourselves, to have augmented and diffused the view all mankind has of our justice, moderation, and seriousness. How a war ends is largely governed by Fortune, which is changeable and uncertain; counsels based on prudence have a sure outcome, and more is always accomplished by fixity of purpose and mature deliberation than counsels born of impulsiveness, from which no benefit derives.

These wise words of the old man rather dampened the magistrates' enthusiasm for war and so no resolution was passed, except that the senators would deliberate further on the matter. After that, Alfonso d'Este, the Duke of Ferrara, made his way to Venice on a private visit, to clear himself before the senators of the suspicion of having sent letters and messengers to Maximilian with a view to entering into an alliance and joining forces with him. He assured them that he had never contemplated anything of the sort, that on the contrary his desire and determination was to take his chances entirely with the Republic, and that never at any time would he fail to respect the Senate's authority. The senators were very glad to hear this declaration. They praised his attitude and assured him that he might expect from the Senate every token of their goodwill, and so sent him home.

In the meantime, there was no sign of Maximilian letting up on his war in the Tyrol, and rumors and reports were coming in of troops being raised in several places in Friuli. The Senate realised that its leniency toward him had been pointless and decided on 4 April to make war on all parts of Maximilian's territory. Not only did the Senate quickly send the decree to the proveditors Gritti and Corner, but they also sent a letter to Girolamo Contarini, then in Istria as proveditor with a small fleet of galleys, to say that he should attempt to attack and seize Maximilian's towns on the coast, wherever he wished; more galleys would be sent him in a few days. When the Senate decree reached Corner and the state's decision was read out to d'Alviano and the other officers, they

quisque principibus declarata, magnum iis studium, magna omni exercitui alacritas innata est belli gerendi. Quamobrem tormentis muralibus adductis, quod oppidum Cormonse citra Sontium flumen, natura atque arte communitum (monti enim impositum, muro praealto cingebatur), opportunum hostibus receptum dabat, omnibus ad id copiis accesserunt, magnaque vi aggressi, deiecta muri parte, celeriter ceperunt. Quod cum diriperetur, Cornelius mulieres omnes, uno in templo compulsas, ab iniuria militum defendit, suppellectilemque sacram, ipsis ab adytis abreptam, fanis et sacerdotibus restituit. Inde ad arcem expugnandam eodem impetu cum perrexissent ac tormentis quatere coepissent, a propugnatoribus deditio est facta. Ea intellecta re, tria se castella sponte legato dediderunt. Portus autem Naonis civitas legatos de deditione ad senatum misit. Eos legatos liberali oratione patres prosecuti ad Cornelium reiecerunt, ut cum illo agerent cui ea omnia mandaverat senatus. Cornelius, cum ad illum legati venissent, oppidum in fidem deditionemque accepit.

33   Eodem tempore Lucas Renaldius, a Maximiliano ad urbem remissus, cum tabellis regis manu subscriptis patres adiit; quibus in tabellis certas Maximilianus indutiarum condiciones reipublicae proponebat. Quarum erat una ut annuas secum indutias senatus faceret, quo tempore de suis cum Gallorum rege controversiis in communi Germaniae concilio disceptari et cognosci posset. Eas patres indutias legato sese paratos esse facere dixerunt, dum eadem indutiarum condicione foederati reipublicae includantur; neque enim sine iis quicquam posse conficere senatum. Renaldius his cum mandatis tantum discesserat, cum, maioribus comitiis haberi coeptis, litterae nuntiique a Cornelio venerunt, qui dicerent: post-

were seized by a great passion to go to war, and equal enthusiasm spread in the army as a whole. On that account they brought up siege artillery and, since the town of Cormons on this side of the Isonzo was affording the enemy a convenient place of refuge (it was well defended by nature and art, being situated on a hill and surrounded with a very high wall), they came up to it with all their troops, and attacking it with great force, swiftly took it after knocking down part of the wall. While it was being plundered, Corner forced all the women into a church and kept them from being harmed by the soldiers. He also returned to the churches and the priests the ecclesiastical furnishings ripped from the sacristies. They then proceeded to storm the fortress in the same assault, and when they began to batter it with artillery, the defenders surrendered. When this became known, three castles voluntarily gave themselves up to the proveditor. The citizens of Pordenone sent spokesmen to the Senate about surrendering, but while the senators received them courteously, they referred them to Corner to negotiate with the man whom the Senate had entrusted with the whole affair. When the ambassadors reached Corner, he received the town's surrender and took it under Venetian protection.

At the same time Luca de' Rinaldi, sent back to Venice by 33 Maximilian, approached the senators with documents signed by the king's hand, in which Maximilian proposed to the Republic certain conditions for a truce. One of them was that the Senate should declare a year's truce with him, during which time there could be debate and inquiry in the common council of Germany[18] concerning his dispute with the king of France. The senators told the ambassador they were prepared to declare such a truce, provided that the allies of the Republic were included on the same terms, for without them the Senate was not in a position to conclude anything. No sooner had Rinaldi left with these instructions and a meeting of the Great Council begun than messengers arrived with a letter from Corner. The letter said that after

eaquam ponte quem hostes resciderant in Sontio flumine celeriter confecto exercituque traducto, Goritianos duabus maximis uno die impressionibus Livianus oppugnavisset, qua in oppugnatione centum milites amisisset, velletque postero die acrius vehementiusque idem facere, oppidanos perterritos sese ei dedidisse. Eae litterae, antequam suffragia inirentur, comitiis recitatae sunt, magnaque ab iis gratulatio patribus est facta.

34   Erat in oppido arx, quam milites ducenti custodiebant. Ii cum pulvere ad tormenta exercenda carerent, neque se arcem tueri posse sine iis confiderent, pro eis armamentis reliquoque commeatu libras auri quadraginta sibi datum iri fide accepta, quatriduo intermisso arcem tradiderunt. Ante quos quidem dies Belgradum facta deditione legati praefectum introduxit; itemque Vipaum, admodum elegans et ipsum oppidulum, quod abest ab Goritia milia passuum viginti Iapidas versus. Contarenus, quattuor triremibus Tergestinos magno animo aggressus, quarum erant duae medii inter bellicas generis atque eas triremes quibus ad mercaturam civitas utitur, quas nothas appellabant, muros tormentis deicere instituit, qua parte mari oppidum alluitur. Ea tormenta eiusmodi tum erant ut, ex aere tota confecta, pedes vicenos binos in longitudinem protenderentur, acclinataque in priore navis parte, sic ut cauda malo proxima ore proram contingerent, pilam ferream librarum centum, si nihil impediret, bis mille atque octingentorum passuum spatium impellebant; itaque muris vicina vehementi eos impetu concutiebant. Id tormenti genus basilium appellabatur, neque sustineri propter pondus, nisi a magnis triremibus aut a nothis, poterat; duasque in partes divisum, ut tractari facilius posset, collectione inter se mutua circumvolutum ita introrsus conglutinabatur, ut esse unum et continens videretur nihilque aeris per spiras admitteret.

d'Alviano had quickly repaired the bridge over the Isonzo which the enemy had destroyed and had taken his army across, he had attacked Gorizia with two great onslaughts in a single day, in which he lost 100 soldiers. On the following day he was going to repeat the assault with even greater ferocity and violence when the terrified townsfolk surrendered to him. This letter was read out to the Great Council before the votes were cast, and the councillors offered the senators their hearty congratulations.

There was a citadel in Gorizia, guarded by 200 infantry. Since 34 they lacked gunpowder for the artillery pieces, and confidence that they could defend the citadel without them, on receiving an assurance that they would be given 40 gold pounds for those armaments and the rest of their provisions, they handed over the citadel after an interval of four days. Prior to that, Belgrade[19] had surrendered and a governor appointed by the proveditor had been brought in. Vipacco followed suit, a rather handsome little town in itself, twenty miles from Gorizia toward Istria. After a very spirited attack on Trieste with four galleys (two of which were of the class called *bastarde*,[20] midway between warships and the galleys used by the city for trade), Contarini began to knock down the walls with artillery at the point where the town bordered the sea. The sort of artillery in use at that time was made entirely of bronze, each piece twenty-two feet in length and laid in the front of the ship so that if one end was next to the mast, the other touched the prow. They could fire an iron ball weighing a hundred pounds a distance of 2,800 paces if there was nothing in the way, and so they struck the walls immediately in front of them with considerable force. This kind of artillery was called a *basilisk*, and due to its weight it could only be carried by great galleys or by *bastarde*. It was divided into two parts for easier handling, and had a reciprocal joint so that when it was screwed together, it held fast and seemed to be a single continuous object, no air being admitted through the join.

35   Ea instituta oppugnatione, Duinum maritimum castellum deditur; quattuorque triremes eiusdem quo priores generis, missae a
patribus, Contareni classem duplicaverunt; senatusque ad Cornelium scripsit, si ei e republica esse videretur, cum exercitu ad Tergeste oppugnandum accederet. Cornelius ea de re Livianum
consuluit; ille, Contareni conatus terrestribus adiuvandos esse copiis magnopere existimans, cum tormentis muralibus quae mari
deportanda curaverat celeriter eo venit; atque ad Contarenum primum omnium navicula perlatus, belli consiliis cum illo communicatis, ad muros oppidi omnibus a terrae partibus demoliendos rediit.

36   Inter haec, propterea quod Aloisius Galliae rex valde se cupere
ostenderat ut in eodem quod secum et cum republica foedus intercedebat Ferdinandus rex Hispaniae particeps esset, novaque cum
illo societas, iisdem tamen legibus, institueretur, res agitari coepta
hanc difficultatem habuit ut, quoniam senatui longum atque impeditum videbatur id quod in priore foedere erat, se nullam pacis
condicionem, quae plerumque in parvis temporum momentis ex-
sisteret, posse a suis hostibus accipere, nisi prius, dum eant in Hispaniam tabellarii dumque redeant, exspectarit, caput illud patres
ita refici censebant oportere, uti qui pacem facere vellet sociorum
modo nomina insereret foederi scribendo, ne multorum dierum
itinere litteris mittendis et responsis praestolandis occasionem pacis amitteret. Verum tamen, ut id regum voluntate fieret, tempus
intermitti placuit, dum id sciri posset. Itaque foederis confectio in
alium reiecta est diem.

37   Contarenus classe aucta, ad quem etiam naves duas tectas patres miserant, quae muris se subicere auderent, iis ab eo latere oppidi maiore multo impetu percussis, aedificiisque nonnullis intra
urbem dirutis, Livianus, parte altera perforatis deiectisque oppidi

Once this attack had been launched, the coastal fortress of   35
Duino surrendered, and four galleys of the same class as before
were sent by the senators to double the size of Contarini's fleet.
The Senate wrote to Corner that if it seemed to the Republic's advantage, he should go with the army to attack Trieste. Corner consulted d'Alviano on the matter. D'Alviano was strongly of the belief that Contarini's efforts should be supported by land forces and
went quickly to Trieste with the siege artillery that he had arranged to have taken by sea. First of all he was taken to Contarini
in a small boat, discussed the battle plans with him, and returned
to demolish the walls of the town on all the landward sides.

Meanwhile King Louis of France had indicated that he was   36
very eager that King Ferdinand of Spain should join the treaty
that existed between himself and the Republic, and that a fresh alliance, but on the same conditions, should be drawn up with him.
Discussions started on the matter, but there was the difficulty that
a clause in the earlier treaty seemed to the Senate laborious and
complicated, providing as it did that they could not accept an offer
of peace terms from their enemies (something that usually had to
be done quickly) until they had waited for couriers to go to Spain
and come back. The senators thought that the clause ought to be
rewritten so that the party wishing to make peace might simply in-
sert the names of their allies in writing the treaty, in case the opportunity for peace was lost by a journey of many days while letters were sent and the replies awaited. Nevertheless, in order to
have this done with the consent of the kings, they decided to allow
an interval for it to become known to them. The drafting of the
treaty was therefore put off to another day.

With his enlarged fleet, to which the senators had further   37
added two covered ships which could venture directly under the
walls, Contarini bombarded the walls on the seaward side with
much greater force, destroying a number of buildings inside the
city, while on the other side d'Alviano was breaching and demol-

moenibus tormentorum impulsione non intermissa, Tergestinos ad deditionem compulerunt. Itaque pridie Nonas Maias una cum arce oppidum receptum est, nulla condicione interposita, nisi ut militibus qui oppidum atque arcem custodierant recedere armatis liceret. Oppidani, ne diriperentur, libris auri centum quinquaginta exercitui persolvendis se suaque omnia redemerunt, Liviano et legatis procurantibus, quibus erat oppidum nobile diripi permolestum. Eius rei litterae laetitia et gratulatione civitatem impleverunt. Livianus, Cornelius, Contarenus, omnium ordinum studiis certatim laudati, quod tantam rem tam celeriter confecissent, magnam sunt ex eo virtutis atque industriae gloriam consecuti. Atque iis statim litterae a senatu datae sunt: in eam cogitationem incumberent ut Pisinum Flumenque, Maximiliani oppida, sub reipublicae imperium redigerentur. Quorum alterum mediterraneum est abestque a litore milia passuum sedecim, multoque maximam inter Istros habet auctoritatem; Flumen, ad mare positum, plurimarum rerum copiam subministrat estque illis gentibus et regionibus opportunissimum. Praetor etiam Tergestinis declaratus Franciscus Capellus, arcis praefectus Aloisius Zanes, Vipao, qui utrumque munus exerceret, Marcus Antonius Erizus, qui Duino, Nicolaus Balbus, qui Cormonsi, Troianus Bonus, paulo post ad magistratus obeundos in provinciam abierunt, cum antea Dominicum Grittum, qui arcem custodiret, senatus Goritiam misisset. Nam oppido Iustinianus Maurocenus a legato datus praeerat.

38   Senatus consulto accepto, cum Pisinum, quod est in monte tribus a partibus valde praecipiti situm, Contarenus classiarios suos et Liviani equitatus peditatusque magnam partem cum tormentis adduceret, castello Trevisa, quod est in via quinque milia passuum

ishing the town walls with an unremitting artillery barrage; together they compelled the people of Trieste to surrender. And so
on May 6 the town was taken into Venetian hands along with its
fortress, no conditions being attached except that the soldiers who
had guarded the town and citadel should be allowed to retreat
without disarming. For fear of being plundered, the townspeople
indemnified themselves and all their property by paying the army
150 gold pounds, the matter being managed by d'Alviano and the
proveditors, men to whom the pillaging of a fine town was deeply
troubling. Letters about the event gave rise to much rejoicing and
congratulation in Venice. All ranks of society competed to praise
d'Alviano, Corner, and Contarini to the skies for having accomplished such an enterprise with such despatch, and in doing so
they won great glory for their courage and hard work. They were
at once sent a letter by the Senate to say that they should turn
their thoughts to bringing Maximilian's towns of Pisino and
Fiume under the sway of the Republic. Of these the first lies inland, sixteen miles from the coast, and is much the most powerful
town in Istria; Fiume is by the sea and extremely productive, an
important centre for the people and districts round about.
Francesco Capello was also made governor of Trieste, and Alvise
Zane commander of the fortress there; Marcantonio Erizzo was
appointed to exercise both functions at Vipacco, Niccolò Balbi at
Duino, and Troiano Bon at Cormons, and they all left to take up
their offices in the province a little later — the Senate had earlier
sent Domenico Gritti to Gorizia to take command of the fortress
there, Giustiniano Morosini already being in charge of the town
on the proveditor's appointment.

Pisino is situated on a hill that is very steep on three sides. 38
Once he had the Senate's decree, Contarini brought up his ma-
rines and a large part of d'Alviano's horse and footsoldiers to the
town, along with their artillery. On the way they stormed and
plundered the castle of Trevisa,[21] which is five miles from Pisino

a Pisino seque magno animo ad defensionem comparaverat, vi capto atque direpto, omnes celeriter ad Pisinenses oppugnandos contenderunt; tormentisque prima vesperi positis, eam muri partem quae una ex quattuor adiri poterat velle deicere coeperunt. Id cum mane postero die acrius continentiusque fecissent ac portae turrim prope aperuissent, oppidani, una salutis condicione impetrata, deditionem fecerunt. In eius oppidi finibus castella erant decem septem, quorum sedecim sub reipublicae dicionem sunt redacta. At cum Vipaum indiligentius custoditum hostes recuperavissent praefectumque cepissent, Vipaenses postea, missis eo militibus, iterum capti ac direpti sunt. Praesidio Pisinensibus relicto, Contarenus ad Phanatici[8] sinus insulas se contulit, atque ex Apsoro Crespa Vegio reliquisque plus mille armatis hominibus naves longas conscendere iussis, ad Flumen oppugnandum rediit; cumque mille passus ab oppido abesset, qui oppidanos uti se dederent postularet misit: si se cingi ab exercitu sinerent, quem postridie adfuturum confirmabat, non fore liberam se dedendi potestatem. Id cum illi magnopere timerent, pacti ne quid ex suis rebus amitterent, eo die Contarenum intromiserunt.

39　　Ea confecta re, quod erat oppidum mediterraneum illis in finibus, non postremae apud Istros auctoritatis, Postoina, Cornelius et Livianus eo exercitum converterunt atque ad vicinos ei oppido pagos equites levis armaturae plus ducentos praemiserunt. Illi, praeda passim abacta, nullis e Postoina exire ausis, cuius ad muros incursionem fecerant, in vico sese proximo receperunt. Ibi cum noctu armis positis sine vigiliis quieti se dedidissent, hostes, Postoina silentio emissi, equites circiter centum quinquaginta, quorum erant duces Bernardinus Rainicher, oppidi praefectus, et Chrystophorus Friapanes, homo ferox acerque, eos inopinantes ag-

and had put up a spirited defense, and then everyone made with all speed to attack Pisino. The artillery was put into position in the early evening and they began to knock down the only side of the four walls that they could get near. The following morning they continued the attack even more fiercely and continuously and had almost breached the gatetower when the inhabitants surrendered, the one condition being that their lives were spared. In the territory of the town there were seventeen castles, sixteen of which were brought under Venetian control. The enemy had recovered Vipacco, which had been guarded with insufficient care, and had taken the governor prisoner, but soldiers were sent there and the town was once again captured and pillaged. Leaving a garrison at Pisino, Contarini made his way to the islands of the Quarnaro Gulf, and had more than 1,000 armed men from Ossero, Cres, Veglia,[22] and other places board the warships and then returned to attack Fiume. When he was a mile from the town, he sent someone to demand the surrender of the inhabitants: if they allowed themselves to be surrounded by the army, which he assured them would be there the next day, they would have no choice as to how they surrendered. This prospect greatly alarmed them and having reached an agreement that they would not lose any of their property, they let Contarini in on the same day.

When that was settled, Corner and d'Alviano turned the army 39 toward an inland town of the region, Postoina, a place of some importance among the Istrians, sending more than 200 light cavalry to the hamlets round about. The cavalry made off with plunder from all over the surrounding area, but since no one dared to come out of Postoina, though they had made an assault on its walls, they retreated to the nearest village. There at nightfall they took off their armor and gave themselves over to rest without posting any watch. Slipping out of Postoina in silence, about 150 cavalry led by the town's governor Bernardino Rainicher and Cristoforo Frangipane, a wild and violent man, took them unawares, killing

gressi partim interfecerunt, partim ceperunt; paucos in fugam coniectos noctis umbra occuluit. Ea re nuntiata Livianus, maiorem
hostium numerum veritus, una cum legato Goritiam exercitum
reduxit.

40   Hostibus eo successu elatis, castellisque omnibus quae circum
se amiserant, nisi ad se redirent, bellum et direptionem denuntian-
tibus, magnus est ab iis concursus ad legatum factus, orantibus uti
se tueretur, neque diripi, propterea quod se reipublicae dedidissent, sineret. Quamobrem, non parvo armatorum hominum numero in Foroiuliensibus celeriter imperato atque ad se adducto,
Cornelius ad Postoinam oppugnandam est profectus. Eo itinere
nondum confecto, iidem illi hostes, Postoina egressi, ad Premium
municipium, quod est in Tergestinorum finibus, animati arma-
tique, id ut caperent atque diriperent, accesserunt. Quod cum se
magno animo defenderet, forte fortuna ignis, tormentorum pulvere succenso, omnem locum atque arcem, qua ex arce propugna-
batur, ita corripuit itaque foedavit, ut Ludovicus Contarenus praefectus, Hieronymusque Saornianus, qui omnibus illis in rebus
totoque bello egregiam operam reipublicae navaverat Premiumque
tunc prope unus defendebat, ne comburerentur aut fumo necaren-
tur, sese hostibus dediderint. Legato post haec et Liviano Postoinam cum pleno exercitu accedentibus tormentisque positis, ubi ea
murum quatere coeperunt, Rainicher praefectus, ne diriperetur, se
atque oppidum tradidit. Cui statim comites dati, qui illum abeuntem in tuto sisterent.

41   Dum haec in Istris geruntur, Pauli Lictestenii suasu, prudentis
in primis hominis, et recti ac temperati viri, qui magna erat apud
Maximilianum regem gratia atque ab eo impetraverat ut se ad pacem cum republica converteret, Tridentinorum episcopus senatum
per litteras certiorem facit cupere Maximilianum indutias cum republica facere; quod si nunc eadem est ei mens quae paulo antea fuit,
mittat aliquem, quicum ipse regis nomine agere quae tractanda

some and capturing others; a few took flight and were concealed under cover of night. On receiving news of this, d'Alviano grew afraid that the enemy was there in greater numbers and together with the proveditor led the force back to Gorizia.

With the enemy elated at this success and threatening war and pillage to all the neighboring castles that they had lost unless they returned to them, the inhabitants came in droves to the proveditor, begging him to protect them and not allow them to be looted for having surrendered to the Republic. When a considerable body of armed men had been quickly mobilized in Friuli and brought to him, Corner accordingly set out to attack Postoina. Before they had finished their march, however, the same enemy combatants left Postoina in arms and with their spirits up and made for the community of Premio in the territory of Trieste, intending to seize and plunder it. The town defended itself with great courage but, as luck would have it, the gunpowder for the artillery caught fire, and the fire burned and ravaged the whole area and the fortress from which they were fighting, so much so that the governor Ludovico Contarini, and Girolamo Savorgnan, who had throughout the course of the war done sterling service for the Republic in every regard and was at that time almost the sole defender of Premio, surrendered to the enemy to avoid being burned or killed by the smoke. Later, the proveditor and d'Alviano arrived at Postoina with the full army and drew up their artillery; as the artillery began to batter the walls, the governor Rainicher surrendered himself and the town to avoid it being plundered. He was at once given a bodyguard to convey him in safety as he left.

While this was going on in Istria, the bishop of Trento wrote to the Senate to inform them that Maximilian wanted to make a truce with the Republic: if they were now of the same view that they had taken a short while before, they should send someone with whom he could negotiate on behalf of the king the matters that needed to be discussed. This was at the instance of Paul von

40

41

erunt possit. Senatus, ea intellecta re, Zachariam Contarenum legavit, qui eo dandis indutiis proficisceretur. Contarenus cum in Raetos venisset, cum episcopo tribusque viris principibus, quibus omnino quattuor eam rem mandaverat Maximiliani iussu Lictestenius, in regis et reipublicae finium loco medio collocutus, causam satis quidem perplexam atque difficilem Gritti legati consiliis explicuit, ut vellent illi trium annorum indutias cum republica facere cumque eius foederatis, Galliae Hispaniaeque regibus, atque iis qui in Italia socii aut ipsius aut illorum regum essent. Nam cum transalpinis uti facerent, adduci nullo modo potuerunt. Id cum senatus cognovisset, adhibitis regum legatis, quaesivit num id illis caput placeret. Quibus adnuentibus, facultate sic conficiendi per litteras celeriter ei missa, Contarenus octavo Idus Iunias, indutiis triennalibus cum rege factis, scribendo adfuit reipublicae nomine. Quod quidem gratissimum senatui fuit, qui pacem quam bellum, et onerum vacationem dari civibus quam ab iis tributa exigi cottidie, malebat. Tum illud etiam verebatur, ne, si Maximiliani oppida capi ac diripi sentiens frenum Germania momordisset, tam forti nationi tantaeque multitudini resisti ab sese, et illarum gentium ferocissimarum bellum respublica defendere sustinereque, non posset.

42   Erant in Raetico exercitu Ioannes Iacobus Triultius, ut supra dictum est, et Giufredus Carolus, consiliariorum Mediolanensium magister, quem praefectus regius Mediolano miserat, rogatus ab senatu ut aliquem regis sui nomine in Raetis vellet conficiendis in-

Lichtenstein, an upright and moderate man of great good sense, who had much influence with King Maximilian and had prevailed upon him to seek peace with the Republic. On learning this, the Senate appointed Zaccaria Contarini their ambassador to go there and arrange the truce. Contarini went to the Tyrol and on neutral ground between the king's territory and the Republic's entered negotiations with the bishop and three other leading citizens, the four having been entrusted with the matter by Lichtenstein at Maximilian's bidding. He laid out the rather complex and difficult case according to the instructions of the proveditor Gritti, with the result that they agreed to make a three-year truce with the Republic and her allies the kings of France and Spain, and with those who were allied to herself or the kings in Italy — they absolutely refused to include any allies of those parties north of the Alps. When the Senate learned of this, they summoned the ambassadors of the kings and asked whether that clause was acceptable to them. With their assent, a letter giving Contarini authority to conclude the matter in this way was quickly sent to him and on June 6 he made the three-year truce with the king, signing in the Republic's name. This was a cause of great satisfaction to the Senate, which preferred peace to war and to relieve the citizens of their burdens rather than demand funds from them on a daily basis. They had another concern too, that if the Germans saw Maximilian's towns being captured and plundered and were to take the bit between their teeth, the Venetians would find it impossible to resist such a strong and populous nation, nor would the Republic be able to avoid or withstand conflict with that warlike race.

In the Tyrolean army were Giangiacomo Trivulzio, as was mentioned above, and Giufredo Carlo, the head of the Milanese council, whom the king's governor had sent from Milan on being asked by the Senate to send someone in the king's name to attend the signing of the truce in the Tyrol. Both of them were unwilling to

42

dutiis adesse. Uterque eas indutias fieri, nisi prius ea de re ab rege litterae venissent, noluerat atque in eo perseveraverat. Itaque foederi scribendo neuter eorum adfuit. Triultius postridie[9] eius diei cum suo comitatu Mediolanum abiit; ei Grittus legatus per omnes reipublicae fines patrum iussu comes fuit. Nonis autem Iuniis, qui dies pridie[10] quam indutiae firmarentur fuit, cum Aloisius rex, in foedere cum Ferdinando rege cumque republica sanciendo, id pertinaciter caput inseri voluerit, se non admonito nullam omnino pacem fieri posse, uti societas ea lege firmaretur foedusque conficeretur, senatus tandem censuit. Pauloque post, quoniam, indutiis in Raetico firmatis, Postoinam in Istris oppidum Cornelius legatus ceperat, uti oppidum Postoina Maximiliano restitueretur, idem senatus petentibus Germanis iussit; interim milites equitesque e Raetis et Carnis in hiberna sunt deducti, oppidaque capta praesidiis communita; muri eorum, quos tormenta deiecerant, atque arces in meliorem multo formam uti reficerentur, cura praefectis tradita. Quorum omnium ratione habita, oppidorum fines centum milia passuum in longitudinem patere Cornelius legatus in senatu dixit. Post quem redeuntem ad urbem Livianum in Bucentauro navi Lauredanus et patres exceperunt. Pauloque post et Portus Naonis oppidum et ius comitiorum ei posterisque eius sunt ob rempublicam bene gestam dono data. Cornelius etiam illum lautioribus in epulis cum principibus civitatis et feminarum nobilissimarum choro diem unum domi suae habuit.

43   Cognitis Aloisius rex indutiis vehementer perturbatus questusque est cum legato reipublicae Antonio Condulmerio:[11] non se id ab ea meruisse, ut responso ab se non exspectato ullas cum Maximiliano senatus indutias faceret; nihil ad se, in Italia foederatos aut amicos illis indutiis esse inclusos, pertinere; unum Mena-

have the truce struck until they had a letter from the king on the matter, and they refused to budge. Neither of them accordingly attended the signing of the treaty. Trivulzio departed for Milan with his retinue on the following day, the proveditor Gritti accompanying him as long as he was in Venetian territory by order of the senators. Before he would ratify the treaty with Ferdinand and the Republic, King Louis persisted in his demands to have a clause inserted to the effect that no peace could be made without his being consulted, and so on 5 June, the day before the truce was concluded,[23] the Senate finally agreed to have the alliance established and the treaty signed on those terms. The proveditor Corner had seized Postoina in Istria after the truce was made in the Tyrol, and so a short while later, at the request of the Germans, the Senate ordered the town to be restored to Maximilian. In the meantime the infantry and cavalry were marched out of Tyrol and Friuli into winter quarters, and the captured towns were secured with garrisons. The governors were charged with rebuilding the walls that the artillery had knocked down in greatly improved form, and the citadels of the towns too. The proveditor Corner told the Senate that when all was reckoned up, the land belonging to the towns stretched for a hundred miles. Returning after him to the city, d'Alviano was welcomed by Loredan and the senators in the Bucintoro. Shortly afterwards he and his descendants were given the town of Pordenone and the status of Venetian nobles as a reward for his great services to the Republic. Corner also entertained him for a day at a fine banquet in his house with the leading men of the city and a group of ladies of the highest rank.

When he heard of the truce, King Louis was greatly upset and 43 lodged a complaint with the Republic's ambassador Antonio Condulmer: he had not deserved such treatment at the hands of the Republic, that the Senate should make a truce with Maximilian without waiting for a response from him. He was not concerned that allies or friends of Venice in Italy had been in-

piorum ducem Maximiliani potentiae non obici se tantummodo voluisse; id ereptum sibi esse ab republica, a qua iuvari in primis debuerit; sibi tamen auri libras esse paratas decies milies; iis illi auxilio se futurum, neque passurum ut foederatorum suorum iniuria opprimi ab ullo possit. Ea oratione iracundiae suae impetu apud legatum pronuntiata, cum se id fecisse paenituisset, ad tranquillitatem se conversum postea simulavit mitioresque sermones habuit, praesertim cum Antonius legatus reipublicae factum excusavisset: senatum id respexisse, ne Maximilianus indutiarum tempore Mediolani res perturbare atque ei molestiam id ob regnum inferre posset; neque cum illo rempublicam ulla alia nisi Italarum rerum causa esse coniunctam. Quid enim ei cum transalpinis? Sed qui iam antea non amico in rempublicam animo esset eiusque secundis rebus magnopere invideret, facile eam ob rem succensus clam ad malas cogitationes sese dedit; tametsi suo chirographo se indutias comprobaturum Antonio legato confirmavisset.

44 Iisdem fere diebus, quibus ea intellecta sunt, Hieronymi Donati, Petri Marcelli, magistratuum Cretensium, litteris patres cognoverunt tantos terraemotus ea in insula fuisse, ut magna aedium et fanorum pars corruerit; ipsorum domos in oppido Candia, tum reliquorum prope omnes, quas modo tremor solo non aequaverit, ea vitia fecisse, ut lapsurae iam iamque videantur; mortuos sub ruinis ad eam diem esse repertos circiter quadringentos, in quibus sint ex coloniae nobilitate non pauci; arcem in Lyctiis deiectam esse; omnes patresfamilias cum uxoribus et liberis sub dio degere, eius rei periculo perterritos. Huic ingenti malo reipublicae illud

cluded in the truce; all he had wanted was for the duke of Guelders[24] to be shielded from Maximilian's violence, something in which the Republic had failed him when they should have been the readiest to help him. Notwithstanding, he had 10,000 gold pounds in ready money which he would use to assist the duke, nor would he suffer anyone to bring him to ruin through the injury done him by his own allies. He delivered this speech to the ambassador in a headlong rage but came to regret having done so. Afterwards he pretended to have calmed down, talking in more measured tones, especially when Condulmer defended the Republic's action: the Senate had been concerned that Maximilian should be prevented from stirring things up at Milan during the period of the truce and from making difficulties for Louis with regard to the duchy. The Republic had allied herself with Maximilian simply on account of the situation in Italy—what had she to do with the people on the other side of the Alps? But Louis had long since turned his mind against the Republic and greatly resented her successes. In his anger over the matter he now gave way to dark and secret thoughts all too easily, though he had assured the ambassador Condulmer that he would sign the truce with his own hand.

At much the same time that this news became known, the sen- 44 ators learned from a letter of the Cretan magistrates Girolamo Donato and Pietro Marcello that earthquakes had struck the island with such force that many of the houses and churches had collapsed. Their own homes in the town of Heraklion, and almost all the others that had not been flattened by the tremor, had suffered such damage that it appeared they might topple over at any moment. About 400 dead had so far been found under the rubble, including an appreciable number of the local nobility; the citadel of Lyktos[25] had fallen down; the heads of households were all living in the open with their wives and children, terrified by the peril they were in. To this huge misfortune of the Republic there

etiam est incommodum adiectum, quod Contarenus cognomine Camalis, triremium et ipse reipublicae praefectus, dum e Corcyra domum reverteretur, duabus ex sua classe navibus, quarum in una erat ipse, tempestate disiectis atque in Piceni elisis litore, una cum quadraginta hominibus periit. Itemque Carratius, militum reipublicae praefectus, homo impiger egregiaque virtute, in agro Veronensi equo insidens ab homine cive suo, de quo nihil verebatur, interfectus est, gladio renibus infixo. De sicario, quem Mantuanorum dux suis in finibus captum magistratui Veronensium tradiderat, poena sumpta. Is, dum ea de re quaestio haberetur, se propterea Carratium occidisse, quod sibi olim male dixerit, magistratui confirmavit. Tanta est homini in hominem tamque diuturna, parvula saepe de re suscepta, iracundiae vis et indignatio.

45   Sub haec aestatis exitu, quoniam magistratibus comitiis maioribus creandis leges iubent, ut ii quibus id sorte munus obtigerit, ut nomen alicuius civis ad honores publicos suffragiis provehendi palam ederent, optimum quemque civem renuntient, ac nonnulli, divites ex civibus qui essent, nonnihil donarent eis qui illos ad suffragia legissent, quo proniores ad eos in posterum renuntiandos fierent, legem decemviri tulerunt: "Qui civi cuipiam qui eum ad suffragia legisset, uti magistratus crearetur, pecuniam aut quid aliud ob eam rem dederit donaverit, qua in insula decemviris placebit, exul esto; eo relicto loco captus, foediore in urbis carcere vitam producito ac relinquito; eam poenam minorem, nisi omnibus ad unum suffragiis, collegium ne facito; qui facere volet, ei decem auri librae multa esto."

46   Paucisque post diebus Maximiliani regis consiliarius Ioannes Raublerius, nullo comitatu, secreto ad urbem venit, Zachariamque Contarenum adiit seque ad illum ab rege missum ostendit, petens

was added a further setback: one Contarini surnamed Camali, who was another proveditor of the Venetian galleys, was returning home from Corfu when two of his ships, one of them with him in it, were scattered by a storm and wrecked on the coast of the Marches, Contarini perishing along with forty of his men. Caracciolo likewise, captain of the Republic's infantry and a man of great energy and courage, was slain by a fellow-citizen of his — a man from whom he had nothing to fear — his kidneys run through with a sword as he sat on his horse in the Veronese countryside. The assassin was captured by the marquis of Mantua in his territory, handed over to the governor of Verona, and paid the penalty. While on trial for the crime, he told the governor he had slain Caracciolo because he had once insulted him: such is the enduring hold of anger and resentment of man against man, often arising from a trivial cause.

Now the laws for the election of magistrates in the Great   45
Council require that those drawn by lot for the task of proposing
the name of some citizen for elevation to public office in the vote
should nominate only the best citizens; and yet some of the richer
sort of citizen were in the habit of making a gift to those who had
chosen them for election so that they would be readier to nominate them in the future.[26] So, following these events, at the end of
summer the Ten passed a law: "Anyone who gives or donates
money or anything else to anyone who has chosen him to be put
to the vote in the election of magistrates shall be exiled to whatever island the Ten choose; if he leaves that place and is captured,
he shall live out the rest of his life in the city's foulest prison. The
Council of Ten may not impose a lesser penalty except by unanimous vote, and whoever wishes to do so shall be fined ten gold
pounds."

A few days later, King Maximilian's councillor Johann Raubler   46
came to Venice in secret and without a retinue. He approached
Zaccaria Contarini and indicated that he had been sent to him by

ut, quemadmodum is indutiis conficiendis paulo ante operam dedisset, ita nunc eadem opera vellet efficere ut aliqua pacis tractatio regem inter atque rempublicam iniretur. Contarenus quae secum regius interpres communicavisset senatui exposuit. Senatus Paulum Pisanum legit, qui quae Raublerius afferret ab eo senatus nomine cognosceret. Nam Contarenus re exposita Cremonam praetor statim abierat. Cum itaque Raublerius cum Pisano ageret, confirmavit velle regem pacem cum republica facere, utque ea fieret, multis rationibus conatus est suadere. Ei Pisanus ostendit salva fide reipublicae, cui cum Aloisio rege firma pax esset, id confici non posse; contraque suadebat eam concordiam pacemque ineundam esse quae Christianis omnibus communis esset.

47   Denique cum Raublerius sibi a patribus responderi peteret, senatus paucis respondit: illum quidem libenti laetoque animo exceptum fuisse, tum regis sui causa, quem respublica unice diligeret atque observaret, quemadmodum etiam cunctos illius maiores amaverat colueratque, tum ob proprias hominis virtutes, verum longe magis ob eam rem ob quam in primis missus fuerat, ut scilicet de pace concordiaque ageretur, quam respublica magis ceteris omnibus rebus semper coluerat, atque hoc tempore multo libentius amplecteretur, si modo omni ex parte ea firma perpetuaque constitueretur, id quod facile evenire posse sperabat; namque exploratum ei erat Aloisii itemque Ferdinandi, Galliae Hispaniarumque regum, sibi sociorum, animos pronos ad pacem esse; quamobrem eum hortari, ut regi suo huiusmodi pacem persuaderet, quae Christianis rebus securitatem dignitatemque esset allatura, regi vero laudem et gloriam sempiternam; tempus maxime ad id opportunum esse; ad eam pacem tractandam omni opera studioque rempublicam paratam esse, modo compertum sit illam communi regum omnium consensu probari; tunc vero constituere,

the king. He asked that just as Contarini had a little earlier exerted himself to bring about a truce, so now he might be prepared to make a like effort to get peace negotiations under way between the king and the Republic. Contarini revealed to the Senate what the king's emissary had vouchsafed to him. The Senate chose Paolo Pisani to find out in the Senate's name what proposals Raubler had brought, for as soon as Contarini had disclosed the matter to them he left at once for Cremona as its governor. In Raubler's consequent discussions with Pisani, he confirmed that the king wished to make peace with the Republic, bringing up a good many persuasive arguments in its favor.[27] Pisani indicated to him that this could not be accomplished with the Republic's good faith intact, since it already had an established peace treaty with King Louis, and he urged him rather to seek a peace concordat that could embrace all the Christian nations.

In the end Raubler sought an official response from the senators and the Senate replied briefly in these terms. They had been very glad to welcome him, both on account of the singular esteem and respect that they bore the king (just as she had loved and cultivated all his forebears), and for his own qualities, but much more on account of the chief object of his mission, namely, to enter negotiations aimed at peace and concord. To this the Republic had always been devoted above all else, and she would now embrace it all the more readily if it could only be put into solid and lasting effect, which she had every hope would come about, for she was sure that the hearts of both Louis and Ferdinand, her allies the kings of France and Spain, were inclined toward peace. The Republic therefore exhorted him to urge upon his king a peace that would bring security and dignity to Christendom, and to the king himself eternal praise and glory. The times were specially propitious for the undertaking, and the Republic was ready to spare no effort in negotiating such a peace once it was sure it met with the united approval of all the rulers. It would then be no hard task to 47

qua ratione quove loco aut quibus arbitris ea tractanda sit, haud magnum negotium futurum.

48   Hunc Raublerii adventum responsumque eidem redditum mandatum fuit Condulmerio, reipublicae legato, ut Aloisio regi declararet, eademque cum Albione, Ferdinandi apud regem legato, communicaret; quae omnia etiam utriusque regis legatis Venetiis agentibus initio declarata fuerant. Censuit enim senatus se legibus amicitiae foederisque quod cum iis regibus percusserat teneri, ut ea faceret. Illa quoque ratio huc accedebat, ut scilicet regum animos ad tuendam pacem magis firmos senatus redderet.

49   Interim, e Flaminia Petrus Landus, Faventiae magistratus, senatui significavit Franciscum Mariam, Metaurensium ducem, Iulii pontificis maximi copias proximis in finibus coegisse, lustrandi exercitum (ut aiebat) causa, itemque Florentinos mandavisse uti sub eorum dicione quilibet paterfamilias, aut omnino quaeque domus, hominem unum armatum legato ipsorum mitteret certum ad locum, ubi essent milites recensendi; neque cur id fieret proponebatur; itaque darent patres operam, ut Faventia communitior fieret, ne quid incommodi respublica, si quid Iulius contra eam moliatur, accipiat. Patres, iis acceptis nuntiis, pecuniam ad milites legendos Petro Lando celeriter mittendam, Lactantiumque Bergomatem, qui se Carnico Istricoque bello fortiter atque amanter gesserat, omnibus militibus quos ibi esse respublica iuberet, praeponendum censuerunt. Equites quoque utriusque armaturae non pauci cum praefectis Faventiam e vestigio contendere sunt iussi.

50   Non me piget inter haec eiusdem temporis rem dignam propter novitatem, quae legentibus nota sit, scribere. Navis Gallica, dum in Oceano iter non longe a Britannia faceret, naviculam ex mediis

settle on the procedures, the place and the negotiators for the peace treaty.

The Republic's ambassador to King Louis, Antonio 48 Condulmer, was instructed to let him know about Raubler's visit and the response he had received, and to communicate it to Albione, Ferdinand's ambassador at the king's court.[28] All of this information had been passed to the ambassadors of both kings at Venice at the outset, the Senate thinking itself duty bound to do so by the ties of friendship and the terms of the treaty it had struck with the kings. There was the additional consideration that the Senate would thereby be strengthening their resolve to preserve the peace.

Meanwhile a message from Emilia came to the Senate, sent by 49 Pietro Lando, the governor of Faenza, to the effect that Francesco Maria della Rovere, the Duke of Urbino, was massing the troops of Pope Julius in neighboring territory for the purpose (as he claimed) of inspecting the army, and also that the Florentines had ordered each head of family in their dominion, or each household at any rate, to send a man under arms to their commissioner at the place where the soldiers were to be reviewed; no reason was given for why this was being done. The senators should therefore endeavor to strengthen the defenses of Faenza in case the Republic should come to any harm if Julius made a move against her. On receipt of this news, the senators voted to send money to Pietro Lando with all speed so that footsoldiers could be recruited, and to put Lattanzio da Bergamo, who had acquitted himself bravely and loyally in the Friulan and Istrian wars, in command of whatever infantry the Republic might require to be there. A sizeable cavalry force, too, both heavy and light, was immediately ordered to make haste to Faenza, along with their officers.

I don't mind writing here of a matter contemporary with these 50 events whose strangeness makes it worthy of note by my readers. A French ship was sailing in the Ocean not far from Britain when

abscissis viminibus arborumque libro solido contectis aedificatam
cepit; in qua homines erant septem mediocri statura, colore sub-
obscuro, lato et patente vultu, cicatriceque una violacea signato.
Hi vestem habebant e piscium corio, maculis eam variantibus. Co-
ronam e culmo pictam, septem quasi auriculis intextam, gerebant.
Carne vescebantur cruda, sanguineque uti nos vinum bibebant.
Eorum sermo intelligi non poterat. Ex iis sex mortem obierunt;
unus adolescens in Aulercos, ubi rex erat, vivus est perductus.

51   Aloisius rex, cupidus imperii sui fines in Italia propagare, intel-
ligensque id se consequi non posse, nisi prius sibi Maximilianum
adiungeret, quocum dissidebat, neque quibus illum artibus, multis
infensum veteribus recentibusque iniuriis, sibi amicum facere posset, omnia cogitans, reperiebat, iis rebus ab legato cognitis quae
patres a Raublerio acceperant, ratusque eam optimam esse occasionem Maximiliani animum sibi conciliandi, ad eum legatos misit, qui, ut illum in rempublicam accenderent, ei declararent se
quidem ab legato reipublicae edoctum fuisse omnibus de rebus
quas Raublerius ad eam attulisset, omniaque consilia sibi patefacta; ex quibus Maximilianus quantum huiuscemodi hominibus
credendum esset, qui illum tam aperte despicerent, ac quo erga
eum animo iidem essent facile cognoscere posset. Totumque hoc
factum rex ex animi sui libidine composuit auxitque, neque ipsum
cogitatio fefellit. Nam ubi ea Maximilianus ab rege excepit, iis omnibus fidem plane adhibens perinde ac si vera fuissent, magnopere
exarsit atque animum, quem in rempublicam benevolum ad eam
diem semper habuerat, his rebus commotus ad Aloisium transtulit. Id cum Aloisius cognovisset, magnis illum pollicitationibus
atque illecebris cottidie captum fovens, agere cum Iulio pontifice
maximo et cum Ferdinando rege coepit, quos quidem, oppidorum
quae respublica ex eorum dicione in Flaminia atque Apulia obtine-

it captured a small vessel made of wicker split down the middle and covered all over with tree-bark. In it were seven men of moderate height and rather dark complexion, with broad and open faces marked with a violet-colored scar. They had on clothing made from fish skin dappled with spots. They wore painted crowns of straw, interwoven with seven little 'ears', as it were. They fed on raw flesh, and drank blood as we do wine. Their speech was unintelligible. Six of them died; one young man was taken alive to the king in Normandy.[29]

King Louis wanted to extend the borders of his empire in Italy 51 but realized that he would not be able to do so without first joining forces with Maximilian, with whom he was at loggerheads. Nor for all his thought on the matter could he find the means of making the man his friend, so hostile was he as a result of the many injuries old and new he had suffered. When Louis learned from his ambassador what Raubler had told the senators, he reckoned this offered the best opportunity of winning over Maximilian. He sent ambassadors to sharpen Maximilian's resentment against the Republic by telling him that Louis had been informed by the Republic's ambassador of all that Raubler had proposed to Venice, and that he was aware of all their plans. From this Maximilian could well judge how much faith was to be placed in such men — who so openly despised him — and what their attitude was toward him. The whole business was made up and embellished at the king's whim. Nor did his plan fail, for Maximilian plainly believed that everything he heard from the king was true. He flew into a rage and in his distress transferred to Louis the warm feelings he had up to that point always entertained toward Venice. When Louis learned of this, he nursed his catch with great promises and enticements on a daily basis, even as he began to negotiate with Pope Julius and King Ferdinand to have them enter an alliance with himself and Maximilian against the Venetians and go to war with them. The Venetians now held towns be-

bat recuperandorum cupiditate alterum magnopere teneri sciebat,
alterum pro animi sui motu ac propensione duci vehementer existimabat (nam Ferdinandus ipse nullam eius rei ostensionem fecerat), uti secum et cum Maximiliano contra Venetos foedere inito
bellum sumerent. Quamquam sunt qui affirment agitatum de eo
ab Aloisio multo antea cum utroque fuisse, et cum Ferdinando
quidem eo maxime tempore quo ei, Neapoli classe in Hispaniam
redeunti, Aloisius in Liguria obviam se obtulit diesque aliquot
cum illo fuit.

52   Utcumque autem illud ceciderit, ea re ab neutro repudiata,
Alberto Pio, homine vafro callidoque, et qui Carpis, oppido cir-
cumpadano, eiectus, quod hereditario iure ad se spectare dictitabat, ad Aloisium regem auxilii petendi causa se contulerat, Galli-
cas partes fovente ac magnopere adnitente, propterea quod, si res
ad exitum perduceretur, sese domum rediturum confidebat, inter
eos omnes foedus est percussum, ultimis Octobris diebus, apud
Cameracum Belgarum oppidum; quo in oppido Margarita, Maximiliani filia, quam Carolus Gallorum rex repudiaverat, caelebs eas
nationes regebat eique rei omne studium adhibuerat. Tametsi non
parvam etiam operam in eo navaverat Georgius Ambosius, Cardinalis Rotomagensis, Aloisii legatus; qui quod, Romae comitiis
pontificalibus Alexandri sexti morte praeteritus, eam repulsam reipublicae acceptam referebat, eximio erat in illam odio; et Nicolaus
Frisius, homo Germanus, Italis imbutus moribus, Maximiliano
perfamiliaris, qui ad utrosque non semel ventitaverat cum mandatis, foederique demum feriendo adfuit Maximiliani nomine.

53   Foederis lex praeter cetera fuit uti omnes uno tempore reipublicae bellum inferrent; quo si Veneti bello victi essent, quae ab iis
ultra Veronae urbis fines dicione tenebantur Gallorum regi cede-

longing to Julius and Ferdinand in Romagna and Apulia, and Louis knew for sure that one of them was burning to get them back, while the other he suspected of wanting to do so — judging from his own inclination and temperament, for Ferdinand himself had given no sign of it. There are those, however, who assert that Louis had discussed the matter with both of them much earlier, with Ferdinand in particular at the time that Louis went to meet him in Liguria as he returned to Spain from Naples by sea, and spent several days with him.[30]

But however it came about, neither of them rejected the pro- 52 posal. The French cause was greatly encouraged and promoted by Alberto Pio, a cunning and clever man. When he was thrown out of Carpi, a town in the Po valley of which he claimed to be the hereditary lord, he had taken himself to King Louis to seek assistance in the sure belief that he would return home if matters were brought to a conclusion. All the parties signed a treaty at the end of October in the town of Cambrai in the Low Countries. From that town Margaret, the daughter of Maximilian, whose hand had been rejected by King Charles of France, ruled over the peoples of the country without a consort, and she had put all her energies into the treaty. But Georges d'Amboise, the cardinal of Rouen and Louis' ambassador, also played no small part in bringing it about. He had been passed over in the papal conclave following the death of Alexander VI and attributed his defeat to the Republic, and so nourished a quite exceptional hatred of her. A close friend of Maximilian, Nicholas Frisius, a German but schooled in Italian ways, had several times gone back and forth between both parties with instructions and he signed in Maximilian's name at the conclusion of the treaty.

Among the other provisions of the treaty, there was one oblig- 53 ing all the signatories to make war on the Republic at the same time. If the Venetians were defeated in the war, they were to surrender to the king of France whatever territory they held beyond

rent; Verona, quaeque ab ea usque ad mare Adriaticum pertin-
gunt, Maximiliano; Flaminiae oppida quae reipublicae tunc essent,
Iulius, Apuliae Ferdinandus obtineret. Tanta vero fuit Gallorum
regis cura, ne quid eorum quae in concilio statuissent enuntiaretur,
ut diu nihil certi resciri potuerit, Aloisiusque ipse Antonio, reipublicae legato, ab eo societatis iure quaerenti ecquodnam Cameraci
foedus percussisset, affirmans dixerit se amicum reipublicae esse
neque quicquam fieri contra illius dignitatem permisisse, Anto-
niusque senatui scripserit, nihil omnino actum quod reipublicae
nocere posset, fidem sibi regem suam non semel interposuisse.

54   Erat Mediolani reipublicae nomine Ioannes Iacobus Caroldius,
senatus scriba; cui fidem regii ministri saepe fecerant, dum in
concilium ab legatis iretur deque ea re sermo frequens esset, regem
omnino numquam ab republica dissensurum, omnibusque rebus
carius reipublicae amicitiam semper habiturum; scire enim eam
coniunctionem magno sibi et usui et ornamento esse. Is, quod
Giufredum Carolum (de quo supra commemoravimus), confecto
statim foedere, inter suos gloriantem dixisse intellexerat sese brevi
sui civis mortem cumulate vindicaturum, deque iis qui eum inter-
fecissent poenas sumpturum—Carminiolam, Venetorum imperatorem, avorum nostrorum memoria publice ab iis ob proditionem
capite multatum, eo involucro verborum designantem (utrique
enim eadem tellus patria fuit)—id quod erat ratus senatui primus
omnium per litteras denuntiavit, eo ab foedere sibi caveret; habere
se, contra rempublicam fuisse ictum, indicia.

55   Sed confecto, ut dictum est, foedere, Iulius, tametsi cupiditate
ferebatur Arimino Faventiaque potiundi, quia tamen et Gallorum
regem magnae per se potentiae multo maiorem suo permissu fieri

the borders of Verona; Verona and all the land between it and the Adriatic was to go to Maximilian; Julius would take over the towns of Romagna then in the hands of Venice, and Ferdinand those of Apulia. The king of France was greatly exercised that none of the decisions taken at the meeting should be published and so for a long time there was no certain information. When Antonio Condulmer, the Venetian ambassador, asked him directly, in virtue of their alliance, whether he had struck a treaty at Cambrai, Louis himself assured him that he was the Republic's friend and had never allowed anything to be done to the detriment of her position. Condulmer wrote to the Senate that the king had more than once given his word that nothing at all had been concluded that could harm the Republic.

Giangiacomo Caroldi, the secretary of the Senate, was at Milan   54
in the Republic's name. When the ambassadors were going into meetings (and the matter was much talked about), the king's ministers had often given him their word that the king would never take a different line from the Republic and would always hold its friendship dearer than anything else, since he knew that their alliance was both a great advantage and a great ornament to him. Caroldi had learned that as soon as the treaty was struck, the Giufredo Carlo we mentioned above[31] had boasted to his people that he would soon take ample vengeance for the death of his fellow citizen and punish those who had killed him—this riddling form of words referred to Carmagnola, the Venetian captain-general, the same soil having borne them both. Carmagnola had been executed by the state for treason in our grandfathers' day. Sizing up the situation as it really was, Caroldi was the very first to warn the Senate by letter that they should be on their guard against the treaty, for he had evidence it had been made against the Republic.

But once the treaty was struck, as mentioned above, despite the   55
fact that Julius was very eager to get control of Rimini and Faenza, he was yet unwilling to have the king of France, already a great

nolebat, et cum illam nationem, tum Germaniae populos in possessionem Italiae venire, optimaeque eius partis atque populosissimae dominos fieri, sibi reliquisque Italis detrimentosum existimabat futurum, ut ab illis Venetos opprimi sineret, adduci prope non poterat. Itaque cum videret ab Aloisio exercitum reliquaque ad bellum idonea per hiemem magno studio comparari, ut primo pabuli tempore Alpes traiceret, seque ab eo per legatos perque litteras sollicitari animadverteret, ut suas et ipse copias paratas haberet ad reipublicae fines eodem tempore a Flaminiae latere infestandos atque in eius dicionem irrumpendum, ne sui colligendi aut omnino resistendi reipublicae facultas daretur, Constantino Cominato Epirotae, non postremae apud Maximilianum auctoritatis, qui Romae tunc erat, quoque ipse familiarissime utebatur, mandavit ut in occulto Ioannem Baduarium, reipublicae apud se legatum, alloqueretur; quaeque ab eo dici vellet ei ostendit.

56   Constantinus, qui a Gallis regno pulsus, quod quidem aliquot ante annis uxorio nomine in Salassis obtinuerat, magno illos odio prosequebatur, adhibita diligentia noctu amotis arbitris legatum alloquitur atque omnia Aloisii regis consilia ei aperit, quaeque reipublicae impendeant proponit. Addit, si senatus Ariminum atque Faventiam restituere Iulio velit, propterea quod is reipublicae vastitatem non aequo animo ferat, confidere sese ab eo impetraturum ut una cum Maximiliano a Gallis desciscat, detque operam ne quid ab illis reipublicae noceri possit. Legatus Constantino collaudato, quod tanta secum de re sermonem habuerit, nihil sibi spei esse reliquum dixit posse se ad id perducere senatum; sed quae ab eo cognoverit, uti ad decemvirum magistros quam celerrime perferantur, se curaturum pollicetur.

power, become greater still with his acquiescence. He thought it would be detrimental to himself and to the rest of Italy to have not just the French but the German peoples too gaining possessions in Italy and becoming lords of its best and most populous part. For these reasons he could scarcely be brought to allow them to attack the Venetians. Julius saw that an army and other military measures were being put together by Louis with great energy through the winter, so as to enable him to cross the Alps when the first grass appeared, and he was aware that he was being pressed by ambassadors and letters to have his own troops ready to attack Venetian territory and invade her domain at the same time from the Romagna side, so as not to give the Republic an opportunity to collect herself or even to put up any resistance. He accordingly gave instructions to Costantino Cominato of Epirus, a man of some considerable influence with Maximilian, who was then at Rome and with whom he was himself on the friendliest of terms, to speak in secret to Giovanni Badoer, the Republic's ambassador at his court; and he indicated to him what he wanted him to say.

Cominato had been driven by the French from the realm at 56 Saluzzo that he had ruled some years before in his wife's name, and he had come to loathe them. Taking great care, he approached the ambassador at night with no witnesses present and revealed to him Louis' plans in detail and the dangers threatening the Republic. He added that if the Senate was prepared to restore Rimini and Faenza to Julius, who was unhappy at the prospect of the Republic's downfall, he was sure he would be able to prevail upon him to desert the French and take Maximilian along with him, and that Julius would do his best to see that the Republic came to no harm at their hands. The ambassador thanked Costantino for the discussion on this vital matter, but said there was no chance that he would be able to persuade the Senate to do what he asked. He promised, however, to see to it that what he had learned from him would be relayed to the Heads of the Ten as soon as possible.

57   Decemviri, qui iam de foederis condicionibus aliunde cognoverant, neque oppida illa ab se dimittere ullam ob causam in animum induxerant, nihil omnino ad legatum, qui ad eos litteras dederat, iis de rebus rescripserunt; sed ad Maximilianum, de quo
porro ad eos afferebatur posse illum adhuc quidem ab amicitia
Aloisii regis abstrahi (nondum enim eam rem ob vetus erga illum
odium plurimasque odii causas in eius animo coaluisse), Ioannem
Petrum Stellam, senatus scribam, qui alias ad Maximilianum ventitaverat eratque illi admodum familiaris, secreto miserunt, ut illum quibuscumque posset modis senatui reconciliaret. Is cum, ob
nimium conficiendae rei studium, immatura festinatione se apud
Maximiliani familiares patefecisset sic, ut eius adventus Aloisii regis legatis qui apud Maximilianum erant celari non potuerit, nulli
reipublicae usui fuit.

58   Leonardus quoque Vicentinus, ex nobili Portorum gente, vir et
clari in bonarum artium disciplina nominis et reipublicae amantissimus, magnis itineribus summa hieme ad amicos suos, Maximiliani familiares, qui se ei obtulerant, a senatu missus, ut per illos
regis animum leniret, nihil profuit. Decemviri enim certas pacis
condiciones, quae ab illis proponebantur, quod ex reipublicae dignitate non essent, re inter ipsos agitata respuerunt. Quin etiam illud accidit. Nam quod erant Romae duo reipublicae legati, Ioannes, de quo dixi, Baduarius, homo lenissimis omnino moribus, et
Georgius Pisanus, morosi admodum ingenii, cum Iulio Centum-
cellas petente Pisanus in comitatu fuit, Baduario Romae ob valetu-
dinem relicto. Ibi cum Iulium, tranquillo mari navicula exhilara-
tum, qua una ille re magnopere delectabatur, Pisanus de eo ipso
reipublicae in Flaminia negotio alloqueretur, "Quin tu," inquit Iulius, "non cum senatu tuo agis, ut is aliquem ex suis civibus mihi
proponat, cui ego Ariminum Faventiamque dem, Romanae reipu-

Having already discovered from another source the terms of the   57
treaty, the Ten made up their mind not to let go of those towns on
any account, and so made no reply at all to the letter the ambassador sent them on the matter. As for Maximilian, they were getting
further reports that he could still be detached from his friendship
with Louis, something that because of his old hatred for him, and
the many grounds of that hatred, had not yet taken firm root in
his mind. They sent Giovan Pietro Stella to him in secret, the secretary of the Senate who had on many other occasions been to
Maximilian and was quite close to him, to try to reconcile him
with the Senate in whatever way he could. In his excessive eagerness to carry out his task, Stella showed up with untimely haste at
Maximilian's court, and since his presence could in consequence
not be concealed from Louis' envoys there, he was of no use to the
Republic.

Leonardo da Vicenza of the noble de' Porti family, a man of   58
great reputation in the teaching of humanities and utterly devoted
to the Republic, had also been sent by the Senate on lengthy jour-
neys in the depths of winter to some friends of his, courtiers of
Maximilian who had offered their services to try to soften the
king's heart, but he got nowhere. For after discussion of the matter, the Ten rejected some of the peace terms that were being proposed by the courtiers as inconsistent with the dignity of the Republic. In fact it turned out quite otherwise: the Republic had two
ambassadors at Rome, the Giovanni Badoer I have mentioned, altogether a man of mild character, and Giorgio Pisani, who was of
a rather captious nature.[32] Pisani was in Julius' retinue as he made
his way to Civitavecchia, while owing to illness Badoer was left behind at Rome. In his little boat on a calm sea, something in which
he took special pleasure, Julius was in a good mood. When Pisani
spoke to him about the business of the Republic in Romagna, Julius said, "Why don't you get the Senate to put forward the name
of one of your citizens to whom I can give Rimini and Faenza to

blicae nomine obtinenda, stipendiariumque illum meum faciam?
Ita et habebitis re vos a me oppida illa, et ego ad speciem non ami-
sero." Ad quem quidem Iulii sermonem Pisanus respondisse dici-
tur non consuesse rempublicam quempiam ex sua civitate regem
facere. Tumque nihil de ea re ad senatum scripsit, neque quicquam
cum collega postea communicavit suo.[12]

59   Ita sive casu, sive fortuna, sive deorum immortalium voluntate,
qui rempublicam, florentem opibus, egregiam et illustrem fama,
pollentem auctoritate, in finitimorum regum invidiam adduxerint,
ut ex adversis eius rebus animos hominum erudirent, quae civitas
quodque imperium annos plus mille octoginta semper creverit,
posse id unius diei spatio vehementer conteri ac debilitari, patres,
pacis spe deposita, ad bellum propulsandum ingenti animo se
converterunt. Itaque uti equites gravioris armaturae supplerentur
numero ad decem milia, levioris ad tria milia quingenti, quorum
essent ab Epiro duo milia, militesque ad milia tredecim conscriberentur, senatus statim iussit. Tum ut ei quoque rei prospiceretur, si
quid reges mari molirentur, naves triremes quindecim, quarum essent nothae quattuor, ut in urbe Cretaque insula armarentur classique reliquae coniungerentur, latum. Missus quoque ab decemviris ad regem Britanniae Andreas Baduarius, qui multos annos ea
in insula fuerat linguamque illam callebat, ut eum reipublicae amicum faceret.

60   Interim et Lascaris, Gallorum regis legatus, patribus valere iussis, ab urbe in Galliam discessit ultimis Ianuarii diebus; et Antonio, legato reipublicae, uti domum reverteretur, regii in Gallia interpretes edixerunt, cum ei prius torquem aureum dono regis
nomine attulissent. Antonius autem, non egere se inimici regis
muneribus pronuntians, torque repudiato viae se dedit. Caroldius
etiam, Mediolano dimissus, cum Triultium discedens salutavisset,
ille vero, "Pudet me," inquit, "Caroldi, huius belli quod parari vi-

rule in the name of Rome and whom I can make my vicar? That way not only will you actually have those towns from me but I shall not appear to have lost them." To this remark of Julius, Pisani is said to have replied that the Republic was not accustomed to making a monarch of any of its citizens.[33] He divulged nothing of this to the Senate at the time, nor did he make any mention of it afterwards to his colleague.

And so whether it was by chance, by Fortune, or by the will of   59
Almighty God, who brought the wealthy, splendid, illustrious, and powerful Republic the ill-will of neighboring rulers so that in her adversity the minds of men should learn that a state and empire that had grown continously for more than 1080 years could be savagely crushed and brought low in the space of a single day,[34] the senators now laid aside all hope of peace and turned with stout hearts to beating back the war. The Senate therefore immediately ordered the heavy cavalry to be increased to 10,000, the light cavalry to 3,500 (2,000 of them to be stradiots), and 13,000 infantry recruited. Then, too, to guard against the kings' making a move by sea, they passed a measure to have fifteen galleys, four of them *bastarde*, fitted out in Venice and on the island of Crete and join the rest of the fleet. The Ten also sent Andrea Badoer, who had spent many years on the island and understood the language, to the king of England with a view to seeking an alliance with him.

Meanwhile Janus Lascaris, the French king's ambassador, also   60
bade the senators farewell and left the city for France at the end   1509
of January; Antonio Condulmer, the Republic's ambassador, was likewise told to return home by the king's ministers in France, having first been presented by them with a gold necklace as a gift in the king's name. But declaring that he had no need of gifts from an enemy king, Condulmer rejected the necklace and took to the road. When Caroldi, too, had paid his respects to Trivulzio on his departure after being dismissed from Milan, the latter actually said, "I am ashamed, Caroldi, of the war I see is about to start. It

deo. Nam iniustum est. Nulla enim in re violatam a vobis Gallorum societatem possumus dicere. Nam quod rex de indutiis queritur, id quidem nihil est; senatus enim illi ob res modo Italas
tenebatur; reliquis in rebus erat liber."

61   Paucis autem post diebus, cum parum esse superioribus senatus
consultis provisum exercitu comparando patribus videretur, additum ad illa est uti equitum levis armaturae mille, militum quina
milia advenarum nationum scriberentur, sagittariique e Creta insula mille, ex Acrocerauniis alteri mille cuiusquemodi armorum
accerserentur. Quodque Genuae atque Provinciae portubus naves
innumerarum amphorarum quattuor triremesque non paucas ar-
mari ab rege patres intellexerunt, naves triremes duodecim, quarum essent nothae duae, prioribus addendas censuerunt. Latum
etiam ut Cremonae arx ad sustinendos hostium impetus longe
munitior fieret. Itaque mille operae, ei rei a magistratibus addictae,
opus ante inceptum bellum perfecerunt. Reliqua etiam eorum
finium oppida castellaque, quibus id usui esset, communitiora fieri
magna cura atque impendio coepta sunt. Ea dum Nicolaus imperator inviseret, Bergomumque adire, quod postremum erat, die
dicta statuisset, re per exploratores Mediolani praefecto nuntiata,
noctu eius equites ducenti cum militibus totidem, quos singuli singulos suis in equis imposuerant, Abdua flumine traiecto, se in sil-
vas abdiderunt, ut imperatorem, qui nihil eiusmodi veritus cum
paucis itineri se dederat, de via interciperent. Quorum de insidiis
cum esset Bergomum per agricolas earum regionum magistratibus
nuntiatum, tabellarii nuntiique, citatis ad imperatorem equis missi
ab iis, parvo illi spatio ex hostium manibus erepto, saluti et incolu-
mitati fuerunt.

is not just: there is no particular in which we can say that you have violated your alliance with the French. As to the king's complaint about the truce, there is nothing in it — the Senate was bound to him only in respect of Italian affairs, while in other matters it had a free hand."

A few days later, however, the senators came to believe that they had not made sufficient provision for raising military forces in their previous decrees, and they made a further order to recruit 1,000 light cavalry and 5,000 foreign infantry, and for 1,000 crossbowmen to be levied on the island of Crete and another 1,000 soldiers of all sorts from Albania. Learning that at Genoa and the ports of Provence four vast ships and a substantial number of galleys were being fitted out for war by the king, the senators decided to add twelve galleys to the existing fleet, four of them *bastarde*. They also gave instructions for the fortress of Cremona to have its defenses greatly strengthened against enemy attacks. A thousand workmen given this task by the magistrates carried out the work before the outbreak of war. Where it was necessary, the other towns and fortresses of the region around Cremona also started to improve their fortifications at great pains and expense. In the course of reviewing them, the captain-general Niccolò Orsini decided to go to Bergamo, the last of the towns, on a particular day. Scouts reported this to the governor of Milan and that night 200 cavalry and the same number of infantry — each of the former putting one of the latter on his horse — crossed the river Adda and hid in the forests, meaning to ambush the captain-general. Orsini had feared nothing of the sort and had taken to the road with only a few men. News of the ambush being brought to the officials at Bergamo by local farmers, they despatched couriers and messengers to the captain-general post-haste, and in a short space of time they snatched him safe and sound from the hands of the enemy.

61

62   Iis rebus foris administratis, domi claro ac sereno die urbanis in navalibus, dum pulverem ad tormenta exercenda confectum in arculas ligneas operae infarciunt, ictu mallei favilla emicuit. Ea ingentem eius pulveris acervum comprehendit; disiectisque immani cum fragore ac tonitru terraeque motu eius conclavis in quo asservabatur parietibus et tecto, ut lateres tegulas asseres tignaque ipsa longo per aera tractu volantia ignis vis atque impetus in diversa tulerit, fumo et caligine urbem totam puncto temporis integens, civitatem perterrefecit; senatusque, qui habebatur, miraculo exterritus in forum frequens descendit. Eo igni, et cadentibus passim iis quae sublime ierant fragmentis, ex fabrum collegio quam plurimi magisterque ipse fabrum et honesti homines aliquot interierunt; habitaque pro ostento res fuit.

63   Regis sub haec Ferdinandi legatus patres adiit: regem suum eo se foedere quod ictum Cameraci esset uno modo capite, quo sit bellum Thracibus inferendum, cum Aloisio rege coniunxisse; velle enim, quod cum republica foedus habeat, in eo amantissime permanere; cupere autem, propterea quod fiat certior ab Aloisio arma in rempublicam parari, scire a patribus, quaenam sit eius rei causa; demum, quicquid aut opibus aut benevolentia valeat, id omne reipublicae polliceri. Eiusmodique item sermonem ipse in Hispania rex cum reipublicae legato Francisco Cornelio habuit, ut senatus ea quae multis auctoribus aliunde cognovisset, de Ferdinandi ab se alienatione, falsa esse crederet. Ita sunt prona hominum ad fallendum ingenia, non quorumlibet modo, sed regum quoque.

64   Ubi patres de insidiis imperatori factis in agro Bergomati ab Gallis equitibus intellexerunt, ea re belli factum initium rati, duos

While all this was going on abroad, at Venice, on a clear and 62
calm day in the Arsenale, workmen were packing gunpowder into
chests when a spark flew off from the blow of a hammer, catching
a huge pile of the powder. The walls and roof of the room in
which it was being kept were blown apart by a massive explosion,
with a huge bang and quaking of the earth. The force and violence
of the blast sent bricks, tiles, posts, and the timbers of the building itself flying through the air in different directions over a wide
stretch of ground. Covering the whole city with a dark pall of
smoke in an instant, it utterly terrified the citizens. The Senate
was in session at the time, and they crowded down into the Square
in terror at this amazing event. Owing to the fire and the debris
that had been blown up falling all around them, a great many of
the carpenters' guild and the master carpenter himself perished,
along with some men of consequence.[35] The incident was taken as
a portent.

Shortly after that, the ambassador of King Ferdinand ap- 63
proached the senators: his king had joined King Louis in the
treaty struck at Cambrai in one clause only, by which war was to
be made on the Turks, as he wanted to stick loyally to the treaty
he had with the Republic. But since he was informed that Louis
was preparing for war against the Republic, he wanted to know
from the senators the reason. Finally, whatever his material resources or goodwill was able to do, he promised it all to the Republic. The king had had a similar conversation in Spain with the
Republic's ambassador Francesco Corner, so that what the Senate
had learned from many sources elsewhere about Ferdinand's alien-
ation from them, they believed to be false. So given to deception is
human nature — and not just the nature of men in general, but of
kings too.

When the senators learned of the ambush made by the French 64
cavalry on the captain-general in the countryside of Bergamo, they
regarded it as marking the start of the war and appointed two

ad id legatos legerunt, illos ipsos qui paulo ante bellum Raeticum Carnicumque administraverant, Andream Grittum, Georgium Cornelium. Atque is, antequam proficisceretur, maioribus comitiis templi Marci procurator lectus est, Dominici Mauroceni, qui mortem obierat, de quo supra commemoravimus, loco. Erat Cornelius annorum quinquaginta quinque. Neque post Franciscum Foscarum, qui dux Venetorum fuerat, quemquam minorem natu illum magistratum esse adeptum constabat. Adeo uni senectuti eo creando fere semper honos fuit. Praefectus quoque a senatu lectus est Epirotis equitibus Iustinianus Maurocenus; quaeque ad eam diem in nobilitatem aditum numquam habuerat, Vicentio Valerio tormentorum cura tradita. Proficiscentibus autem ab urbe legatis, quaestor est exercitui Paulus Nanus declaratus.

65   Quoniam vero magistratus regii edictum Mediolani proposuerant ut, cum eius urbis cives, tum vero etiam Ligures aut omnino Galli, qui in dicione reipublicae eo temporis moram traherent, viginti dierum spatio domum reverterentur, id qui non fecisset, mors ei poena esset eiusque bona publicarentur, qua ex re fiebat ut perplurimi, qui vel mercaturam faciebant vel plebeias artes exercebant domiciliaque in urbe habebant, emigrare cogerentur, legem contra patres iusserunt: qui ea de causa urbem reliquisset, quive illum navicula evexisset aut comes itineris fuisset, eius bona fisco inferrentur, aliquandoque captus annum in carcere taeterrimo conficeret. Ea poena proposita, omnes, quibus quidem aut insulae aut fundi aut omnino res aliqua familiaris esset, emigrare veriti restiterunt. Iis rebus bellicisque apparatibus, et Maximiliani cum Aloisio rege nova ex foedere coniunctione, Germani mercatores qui in urbe erant, permoti, concilio coacto a patribus petierunt, uti se tutos, si quid reipublicae ab suo rege accidat, velint esse. Quod quidem illis patres libentissimi concesserunt; amplissimaque iis facultas est

proveditors for the purpose, the same proveditors who had a little earlier supervised the war in the Tyrol and Friuli, Andrea Gritti and Giorgio Corner. Before he set out, the latter was chosen to be a Procurator of St. Mark's by the Great Council, taking the place of Domenico Morosini who had died and whom I mentioned above.[36] Corner was 55 years old. It was common knowledge that not since Francesco Foscari, who became doge, had anyone younger attained that office, to such an extent was election to the honor reserved for age alone. Giustiniano Morosini was also appointed by the Senate as captain of the stradiots, and the artillery command was entrusted to Vincenzo Valier, something that had never fallen to the nobility up to that point. And as the proveditors left the city, Paolo Nani was declared paymaster for the army.

The king's officials at Milan had promulgated an edict to the effect that as well as Milanese citizens, the Genoese too and the French in general who were resident in the Republic's dominions at the time should return home within twenty days. The penalty for anyone not doing so was to be death and the confiscation of his property. And so a great many people engaged in commerce or artisan work who had homes in Venice were forced to emigrate. In consequence of this the senators passed an opposing law: anyone leaving the city on that account, or who had conveyed anyone by boat or accompanied him on the journey, would have his property confiscated by the state, and if captured at any time would spend an entire year in the worst prison of the city. Once the punishment was published, all those people—or at least those who owned buildings or farms or any personal property at all—were afraid to emigrate and stayed where they were. The German merchants in Venice were extremely worried by these measures and by the preparations for war, as well as by Maximilian's new alliance with King Louis. They sent a deputation to ask the senators for guarantees of their safety, should anything happen to the Republic at the hands of their king. This the senators were very willing to

65

omnia, uti consueverant, in tota reipublicae dicione liberrime agendi tradita.

66 Comitiis deinde maioribus praefectus est classis Angelus Trivisanus declaratus iussusque a senatu quam primum conscendere. Nam praeter eas naves quae a Gallorum rege armabantur, Ferdinandum quoque regem parare classem, quam in Siciliam et Tarentum mitteret, reipublicae apud illum legatus ad senatum scripserat. Tametsi eius legatus patribus fidem faceret Africanarum rerum causa eas opes comparari; nihil omnino esse, quod eo ab rege sibi verendum existimarent, qui esset reipublicae amantissimus. Ea res, et quod Iulius exercitum et ipse in Flaminia ex Etruria et Umbria et Piceno cogebat, et Galli magna manu Alpes iam traiecerant, longe maiore autem una cum rege in dies traiecturi dicebantur, et Maximilianum omnes homines idem per se facturum existimabant (misceri enim et tractari arma ex Germania rumor attulerat), senatum sollicitum fecerat, quonam pacto unus tot tantorumque hostium impetus terra marique sustineret; praesertim cum Iulius Roma suisque omnibus ab oppidis et finibus manum ullam ad reipublicae stipendia venire non permitteret, edictis durioribus interpositis, ut qua ex parte plurimi se duces reipublicae obtulerant, multumque copiarum secum adducturos se receperant, resque publica magno eos usui sibi futuros confidebat, ab ea illam parte spes omnis atque opinio destituerit. Quae cum ita se haberent, praestare patribus visum est uti ad senatum de restituenda Iulio Faventia referretur, si forte illum eo munere avertere ab incepto possent. Verum Georgio Emo rem vehementer refellente, nihil latum.

grant them, and they were given absolute freedom to carry on their business throughout the Venetian dominions, just as they had been used to doing.

Angelo Trevisan was then declared captain of the fleet by the   66
Great Council and ordered by the Senate to embark as soon as possible. For besides the ships which were being readied for war by the French king, the Venetian ambassador to King Ferdinand had written to the Senate that he too was preparing a fleet to be sent to Sicily and Taranto. Ferdinand's ambassador nevertheless gave the senators his word that these forces were being assembled for business in Africa: they had absolutely no reason to think there was anything to fear from the king, who was utterly devoted to the Republic. Added to this was the fact that Julius too was collecting an army in Romagna from Tuscany, Umbria, and the Marches, and that the French had already crossed the Alps with a large force, and were reported to be on the point of crossing with a far larger one and the king himself. Everyone thought that Maximilian was going to do the same on his own account—there were rumors from Germany of arms being massed and manoeuvred. All this caused the Senate much anxiety as to how they might on their own withstand the onslaughts by land and sea of such numerous and powerful enemies, and all the more so because Julius had issued stern edicts forbidding any troops from Rome or any of his towns and territories from entering the pay of the Republic. A great many captains there had offered their services to the Republic, undertaking to bring with them large numbers of troops from which the Republic was sure she would derive great advantage, but from that very quarter all her hopes and expectations were dashed. This being so, the senators thought it best to make a Senate proposal to restore Faenza to Julius, in the hope that the gift would dissuade him from his undertaking. But after Giorgio Emo spoke vehemently against the measure, it was not put to the vote.

67   Legatis Brixiam Cremonamque profectis, templi Marcii altera
procuratio, quo in magistratu Marcus Antonius Maurocenus mortem obierat, Andreae Gritto comitiis maioribus est delata, ut eo
munere ad bene de republica promerendum rebus tam dubiis ac-
cenderetur, Andrea Venerio, cive prudente publicique iuris reti-
nente, octo suffragiis praeterito, qui eo anno patribus auctor fuerat
uti, Aloisii regis societate, suspecta illa quidem ac plane dubia, repudiata, cum Maximiliano, magnopere id efflagitante, se coniungerent. Petrum interim Landum, Faventiae magistratu decedentem,
in Flaminia legatum senatus iussit esse. Is Ariminum profectus,
detecta proditione ab Iulio instituta, qua eius militibus noctu oppidi portam tradi convenerat, de proditore poenas sumpsit. Miserant ad Helvetios superioribus diebus patres Hieronymum Saor-
nianum, societatis instituendae causa. Atque is quattuor eorum
pagis persuaserat uti se cum republica coniungerent; fidemque ab
iis acceperat, si per decennium ducentae quinquaginta auri librae
annis singulis a senatu eis dentur, se cum republica futuros atque
in Galliam transalpinam e vestigio contra regem erupturos. Ea intellecta re, uti ita fieret, a senatu lex est lata.

68   Duo sub haec nuntii Venetias allati magno timore pro belli initio civitatem affecerunt. Quorum alter Franciscum, Mantuanorum
principem, Casale, municipium in Padi fluminis ripa sibi finitimum, collecto equitatu et peditatu, repentino impetu cepisse patres certiores faciebat; ab altero Gallorum magnas copias Abdua
traiecto Trevium oppidum aggressas, cum illis obviam qui in oppido erant equites et milites exissent, omnem illam manum fu-
disse, ex militibus non parvum numerum interfecisse, Paulum Me-
mium praetorem et Iustinianum Maurocenum, una cum filio,
praefectosque tres captivos fecisse atque oppidanos ad deditionem

After the proveditors left for Brescia and Cremona, another 67
procuratorship of St. Mark's was conferred by the Great Council
on Andrea Gritti (Marcantonio Morosini having died in office), so
that the honor would encourage him to give the Republic good
service in its present precarious circumstances, passing over by
eight votes Andrea Venier, a wise citizen and one devoted to the
good of the state. Venier had that year suggested to the senators
that they should repudiate the alliance with King Louis, which
was indeed suspect and altogether uncertain, and join forces with
Maximilian, who was very eager to do so. In the meantime the
Senate ordered Pietro Lando, the outgoing governor of Faenza, to
be their proveditor in Romagna. Lando went to Rimini where he
uncovered a treacherous plot arranged by Julius to have the town
gate handed over to his soldiers at night, and he punished the trai-
tor. Some days before, the senators had sent Girolamo Savorgnan
to the Swiss to make an alliance with them. He persuaded four
of the cantons to join the Republic and he took from them an undertaking that in exchange for an annual gift from the Senate of
250 gold pounds over ten years, they would ally themselves with
the Republic and immediately invade France against the king.
Learning of this, the Senate passed a measure to put this into
effect.

Around this time, two reports about the outbreak of war 68
reached Venice and caused great alarm among the citizens. The
first informed the senators that Francesco Gonzaga, the Marquis
of Mantua, had gathered a force of cavalry and infantry and had
taken Casale in a surprise attack, a town neighboring his territory
on the banks of the Po. The other revealed that French soldiers
had crossed the Adda in large numbers and attacked the town of
Treviglio. When the cavalry and footsoldiers in the town went out
to meet them, the French put the whole company to flight, killing
a considerable number of infantry and taking prisoner the governor Paolo Memmo, Giustiniano Morosini and his son, and three

compulisse confirmabatur. Equites tamen Epirotas ducentos, quibus Maurocenus praeerat, reliquis fusis fugatisque, conglobatos per mediam hostium aciem sese incolumes in tutum recepisse, neque eos lacessere ex hostibus ausum quemquam fuisse, idem nuntius adiecerat.

69   Regis etiam Gallorum praeco ad urbem venit, ut bellum reipublicae indiceret. Ab eo patres, semotis aliis, ne civitas re nova permoveretur, se adiri voluerunt. Itaque porta devia in vestibulo curiae admissus, veste liliis aureis intertexta sese induit; tum curiam ingressus ante patrum subsellium stans, "Bellum," inquit, "Lauredane, Venetorum dux, ceterique huius urbis cives, Ludovicus Gallorum rex indicere me vobis iussit tamquam infidis hominibus, pontificisque maximi et reliquorum regum oppida per vim perque iniuriam capta possidentibus, omniumque omnia dolo malo sub vestram dicionem rapere atque redigere festinantibus. Ipse ad vos armatus ea repetiturus venit." Ad haec Lauredanus, patrum medius sua in sella sedens, ita respondit: "Res haec publica, Galle, quam adiisti, nihil iniuste possidet; nam iure agit neque fidem cuiquam fallit. Quam certe fidem nisi valde plus iusto regi ipsi servavissemus tuo, ille vero ubi pedem in suo poneret in Italia non haberet. Sed praestat nos vel cum periculo esse qui semper fuimus, dum Aloisius aeque arrogantia atque perfidia polleat. Bellum quod denuntias propulsaturi cum diis immortalibus sumus; quos ille vindices habiturus est, aut hic aut apud manes, rupti per scelus foederis." Hoc responso accepto, est dimissus; ac ne quis eum violaret, quos itineris comites a reipublicae magistratibus adveniens habuerat, iidem sunt reducere atque in regis finibus sistere illum iussi.

officers, and compelled the inhabitants to surrender. The same report, however, added that after the others were routed and put to flight, 200 stradiots under Morosini's command had closed ranks and retreated to safety through the midst of the enemy lines, and none of the enemy had dared to challenge them.

The herald of the French king also came to Venice to declare 69 war on the Republic. The senators wanted him to appear before them without others present, in case the citizens panicked at the news. He was therefore admitted by a side door into the vestibule of the audience hall,[37] and put on a garment woven with golden lilies. He then entered the hall[38] and standing before the senators' tribunal, he said, "Doge Loredan and other citizens of Venice, King Louis of France has ordered me to declare war on you as men of bad faith, occupying towns of the pope and other rulers which you took wrongfully and by force, hurrying with malice aforethought to seize and bring into your power everyone's property everywhere. He himself is coming to you in arms to seek restitution." To this Loredan, seated on his chair in the midst of the senators, replied as follows: "None of the possessions of the Republic you have approached, Frenchman, were acquired unjustly; she acts with justice and does not break faith with anyone. Indeed, had we not kept faith with your same king above and beyond the requirements of justice, he would have nowhere of his own in Italy in which to set foot. But it is better for us to remain the people we have always been, even though it entails danger, as long as Louis' strength lies in equal measures of arrogance and treachery. With the aid of Almighty God, we shall defend ourselves against the war that you are declaring on us, and that man will have God take revenge on him for the treaty he criminally broke — either here or in hell." With this for reply, he was dismissed, and to ensure he came to no harm from anyone, the same bodyguards he had had from the Republic's magistrates as he arrived were told to escort him back and leave him in the king's territory.

70   Brixiani, ubi de captis oppidis et praefectis nuntiatum est, concilio civitatis coacto milites sex mille sua pecunia legere decreverunt atque ad legatos mittere. Civisque unus ex iis, Aloisius Avogarius, sexcentos milites se celeriter confecturum magistratibus est pollicitus eosque sine ullo reipublicae impendio menses quattuor in exercitu habiturum. Quod quidem Brixianae civitatis factum, plenum fidei atque benevolentiae, postea Veronenses aemulati quinquaginta auri libras exigi ab sese, atque in milites ad exercitum mittendos stipendii nomine distribui, concilio coacto statuerunt. Galli, eo successu cohortati inter se, Caravagium capere aggressi, ubi oppidanos quique oppidum custodiebant milites apertis exire ad proelium portis, magno cum clamore ingentique tubarum sono, e propinquo viderunt, veste atque argento temere ubi consederant relicto, sese fugae mandaverunt.

71   Domi autem, patribus pecunia in bellum eroganda sollicitis, praeter tributa alia de hoc quoque senatus consultum factum est, et quidem solito fieri superioribus in bellis altero tanto gravius, uti a magistratibus urbanis sex mensium stipendia integra reipublicae remittantur; reliquorum vero compendiorum, quae omnino ex iurisdictione ipsa vel ex portoriis fraudatis vel quacumque alia ex re ad eos redeunt, media pars in aerarium inferatur, quadragintaviralibus iudiciis exceptis. Quibus unis media stipendiorum pars maneat, propterea quod aliunde nihil lucrantur; magistratus autem provinciales et arcium praefecti intra sinum Phanaticum qui sunt mediam stipendiorum partem reipublicae remittant, reliquis in rebus eadem qua urbani lege teneantur. Horum autem magistratuum urbanorum et provincialium omnium iuris interpretes et

When news came of the towns taken and commanders cap-   70
tured, the people of Brescia convened a meeting of the citizens
and agreed to enlist 6,000 soldiers at their own expense and send
them to the proveditors. One of the citizens, Luigi Avogadro,
promised the magistrates that he would quickly get together 600
soldiers and keep them in the army for four months at no cost to
the Republic. This signal act of loyalty and goodwill on the part of
the city of Brescia was later emulated by the people of Verona.
They called a meeting of the citizens at which they decided to
raise fifty gold pounds among themselves and distribute them as
pay among the soldiers that were to be sent to the army. Egging
one another on after their success, the French turned to an attack
on Caravaggio, but when they saw at close quarters the inhabitants
and the soldiers who were guarding the town coming out for battle
through the open gates, accompanied by much shouting and a
huge blast of trumpets, they took to their heels, abandoning clothing and money at the spot where they had rashly taken their
stand.

On the home front, the senators were growing concerned about   71
how to raise funds for the war. In addition to other revenues, they
passed a decree to have the magistrates in the city return to the
Republic their entire pay for six months, something that was twice
as onerous as what they had been accustomed to doing in previous
wars, and that half of the remaining income they received from
their administration of justice or customs duty fines or any other
source should be contributed to the treasury. This last did not ap-
ply to the officials of the Courts of the Forty, who were only to
contribute half their pay as they had no other source of income.
Provincial magistrates and commanders of fortresses this side of
the Quarnaro Gulf would remit half their pay to the Republic, in
other respects being bound by the same law as the urban magistrates. Of all these magistrates, urban and provincial, the legal ad-
visers and secretaries and officials were also to give the Republic

scribae ministrique mediam et ipsi cum stipendiorum partem, tum
compendiorum tribuant reipublicae, Veronae Brixiae Bergomi
Cremae Cremonaeque atque Flaminiae magistratibus item exceptis, et iis qui ultra sinum Phanaticum sunt missi, qui omnes quartam modo partem earum utrarumque rerum conferant (satis enim
magna alteris incommoda bellum esse ipsum allaturum, alteris iter
longum et impeditum iam attulisse), ne aliis etiam oneribus ferendis aeque ac ceteri afflictentur. Eam legem, uti dictum est, cum senatus iussisset, maiora quoque comitia, triduo post habita, pari
studio iusserunt. Latum est etiam, uti exules illatae fortuito mortis
causa, qui una cum quattuor bello idoneis hominibus militiam reipublicae menses quattuor sua pecunia fecerint, ab exilio revocen-
tur.

72   Legatus deinde Bergomatibus est datus Marinus Georgius, Ariminensibus Aloisius Armerius, qui eis in oppidis administrando
bello praesint. Interim cum a Petro Lando patres certiores facti essent ab Iulianis copiis incursiones in reipublicae fines fieri abigique
praedas, et agrestes homines vulgo interfici, vel captos in vinculis
adduci, eadem est in Iulii finibus patrandi exercitui reipublicae a
senatu facultas tradita; Laurentiusque Sagredus, praefectus classis
in Flaminiae Picenique litoribus, suis cum navibus Ariminum
contendere est iussus. Cumque hostium numerus in Cremonae
finibus Abduaeque ripis vehementer augeretur, castellaque ad eos
et pagi aliquot defecissent, uti naves aliae adverso Padi flumine in
Galliam mitterentur, aliae in lacu Benaco armarentur, lex est lata;
praefectique alteri classi Sebastianus Maurus, alteri Zacharias
Lauredanus dati. Gaspar etiam Severinas, qui Cesenae erat seque
reipublicae obtulerat, et Antonellus Neapolitanus cum turmis
equitum ad reipublicae militiam sunt conscripti. Atque hic qui-

not only half of their pay but also half of their revenues, with the exception of the magistrates of Verona, Brescia, Bergamo, Crema and Cremona, and likewise those in Romagna and those who were sent out beyond the Gulf of Quarnaro. All of them were to give only a quarter on both accounts, seeing that the war itself would bring great hardship to the first group, and the long and difficult journey had already done so for the second, so as to ensure that they would not be disadvantaged to the same degree as the rest when they already had to bear these added burdens. After the Senate had passed the law, as mentioned above, the Great Council in session three days later also enacted it with equal despatch. A measure was also passed to the effect that if those in exile for involuntary manslaughter served in the Republic's forces for four months at their own expense, and supported four men fit to bear arms, they would have their exile quashed.

Marino Zorzi was then assigned to Bergamo as proveditor, and 72 Alvise d'Armer to Rimini, to take charge of the conduct of war in those towns. When in the meantime the senators were informed by Pietro Lando that Julius' forces were making incursions into the Republic's territory, booty was being driven off and there was widespread slaughter, capture and imprisonment of the people of the countryside, the Senate gave the Venetian army licence to do the same in Julius' territory, and Lorenzo Sagredo, captain of the fleet on the coast of Romagna and the Marches, was ordered to make for Rimini with his ships. The number of the enemy was growing ever larger in the Cremonese and on the banks of the Adda, and some fortresses and villages had already defected to them. A decree was therefore passed to send some ships upstream along the Po into Lombardy, and to arm others on Lake Garda, Sebastiano Moro being given the captaincy of the first fleet, Zaccaria Loredan the other. Gaspare da Sanseverino, who had offered his services to the Republic at Cesena, and Antonello Napoletano were also enlisted in the Republic's forces along with

dem, quod erat plane dives, confectis in urbe testamenti tabulis, templi Marcii procuratores ex asse sibi heredes instituit atque ad bellum profectus est. Leonardus etiam Pratus e Lupis, Apuliae oppido, ex societate Rhodiorum militum, se ad rempublicam contulit, homo et gentis nobilitate et rei militaris scientia clarus; cui paulo post, ut virtuti eius honos haberetur, equites levis armaturae centum quinquaginta, reliquorumque omnium eiusdem modi equitum praefecturam senatus tradidit. Is quoque Leonardus, cum ad urbem quinquaginta auri libras domo secum attulisset, patribus dixit tanto se auro in praesentia non egere; decemque ex ea summa suos in usus retentis libris, reliquas quadraginta eis obtulit atque, a curia in diversorium abiens, statim misit. Tam prona, in alieno homine atque advena, liberalitas cum benevolentia in rempublicam extitit.

73   Venienti autem ad urbem Hannibali Bentivolo, patribusque pollicenti, si favore suo velint opibusque sibi praesto esse, brevi se una cum fratribus et suorum factione Bononiam ab Iulio aversurum, magnamque illi plagam, qua nihil timeat, inusturum, senatus consulto sunt omnia, uti petierat, permissa; litteraeque ad praefectos in Flaminiam datae, rem omni studio iuvarent; atque ipsi equites quingenti, Hermeti fratri eius milites sunt bis mille, cum pecunia pro re quam parabant traditi. Equiti etiam Vulpio e Cornelii Foro, ob seditiones civitate eiecto, equitum gravis armaturae turma data, Herculique Tiberto, Cesenae item exuli, milites quingenti, spe novandarum rerum suo in oppido ab utroque, quibus revocatus motibus Iulius, suisque rebus timens, ab incepto bello desisteret. Inter haec binas auri libras sacris virginibus patres dono dari a quaestoribus curaverunt, ut preces diis immortalibus tam duro tempore pro republica facerent; perque omnia urbis templa sacer-

their cavalry companies.[39] The latter, being very wealthy, drew up his will and testament in the city, making the Procurators of St. Mark's sole heirs of his estate, and set out for the war. Fra Leonardo Prato from Lecce, a town in Apulia, a member of the order of the Knights of Rhodes, also took himself to Venice, a man as famous for the nobility of his family as for his military skill. Shortly thereafter the Senate gave him 150 light cavalry and the captaincy of all the other cavalry of the sort as a mark of honor for his steadfastness. This Leonardo had also brought with him from home 50 gold pounds, but told the senators that he did not at present need so much gold; keeping ten pounds of that sum for his own use, he offered them the other forty and, leaving the palace for his lodgings, sent them immediately. Such was the ready liberality and goodwill toward the Republic shown by a foreigner and newcomer.

Annibale Bentivoglio came to the city and promised the senators that if they helped him with their backing and troops, together with his brothers and their party he would soon wrest Bologna from Julius and strike him a blow where he was least expecting it. A Senate decree granted him everything he asked for; and letters were sent to the proveditors in Romagna that they should give him every assistance in the matter. He was given 500 cavalry and his brother Ermete 2,000 infantry, along with such money as was needed for the enterprise. Taddeo della Volpe of Imola, who had been expelled from his city for sedition, was given a squadron of heavy cavalry, and Ercole Tiberto of Cesena, likewise an exile, 500 infantry, in the hope that they would overthrow the regimes in their respective towns and that Julius would be distracted by these disturbances and desist from the war for fear of losing his possessions. In the meantime the senators had the treasurers give nuns two gold pounds to offer prayers to Almighty God in the Republic's hour of great need, and in all the churches the priests

73

dotes, a pontifice iussi, numina quorum sub tutela Venetum imperium est votis supplicibus et solemni ritu placare.

74 Verum enimvero cum belli facies cottidie formidolosior fieret, eque Gallia transalpina operae fabrique magno numero Mediolanum Laudemque Pompeii advenissent, pontesque tres diversis locis in Abdua flumine ab hostibus instituerentur, regemque ipsum multo maxima cum manu paucis diebus adfuturum fama nuntiique vulgavissent, atque a Flaminiae latere Iulii exercitus modo Ariminum, modo Faventiam invasurus magnopere urgeret, ob ingentes autem tot tamque praesentibus in rebus factas impensas pecunia rempublicam deficeret, quod profecto malum omnium maximum plerisque videbatur, coacto senatu Lauredanus dux, auri libras decem mutuo se daturum reipublicae pollicitus, cives reliquos quibus non deesse facultatem sciebat idem pro se quisque uti facerent est cohortatus. Itaque eo die posteroque plurimae auri librae, mutuo in aerarium collatae, eo metu civitatem liberaverunt. Tauriso deinde reliquisque dicionis Venetae locis, urbe excepta, restitutus est ab exilio Iacobus Collaltus (cuius exilii damnatus ob necem patrui fuerat), dum is in exercitu reipublicae, quemadmodum quidem patribus se obtulerat facturum, cum turma equitum centum menses quattuor sua pecunia militiam faciat.

75 Erat tunc in sermone civitatis haud modico Faventia; quo in oppido detecta proditio fuerat Francisci Brixiani, equitum turmae praefecti, deque eo poena sumpta; oppidi enim portam noctu Iulianis se militibus aperturum cum eorum interprete pepigerat; atque insigne Iulianum cum quercu aurea et coronis, quod in muris mane poneret, ab eo traditum domi suae custodiebat. Illi autem patefacta re in Faventiae se fines intulerunt, ut oppidum montanum Brisigeliam, cui civitas propter optimum genus militum ex eo educi solitum magnopere confidebat, expugnarent. Iamque Tarta-

were told by the patriarch to propitiate the patron saints of the Venetian empire with prayers of supplication and solemn rites.

At the same time the face of war was looking grimmer every 74 day. Workmen and smiths had come from France to Milan and Lodi in great number, and three bridges had been built by the enemy at different places on the Adda. Rumor and report spread it about that the king himself would be coming in a few days with vastly greater forces. On the Romagna front Julius's army was pushing very hard, ready to attack now Rimini, now Faenza, and owing to the massive expenditure on a great range of urgent matters, the Republic was short of funds, something which to many seemed the greatest misfortune of all. Doge Loredan accordingly convened a meeting of the Senate, pledging that he would give the Republic a loan of ten gold pounds, and urged each individual among the other citizens that he knew had the means to do the same. On that day and the next a great many gold pounds were brought into the treasury as loans, quelling the city's fears. Giacomo Collalto had been condemned to exile for the murder of his uncle. He was now allowed to return to Treviso or anywhere else in the Venetian domain except Venice itself, provided that he did military service, as he had offered to do to the senators, with a squadron of 100 cavalry for four months at his own expense.

There was at that time considerable discussion in the city about 75 Faenza. In that town treason on the part of Francesco da Brescia, captain of a cavalry squadron, had been discovered and he had paid the price — he had agreed with a messenger of Julius' forces to open the town gate to them at night, and he kept at home Julius' badge with the golden oak and crowns which had been given him by the messenger, and which he was to put on the walls in the morning. But when the plot was uncovered the soldiers attacked the territory of Faenza instead, hoping to storm the mountain town of Brisighella, a place well thought of by the Venetians for the excellent sort of soldiers they generally got from there. They

rum, centurionem reipublicae, qui Brisigeliam cum tribus cohorti-
bus praesidii causa se conferebat, insidiis positis interceperant;
pauloque post cum oppidum tormentis cinxissent, eo sunt potiti,
praetore quaeque cum eo erat copia et Ioanne Paulo Manfronio,
equitum praefecto magna virtute, qui tuendi oppidi causa eo cum
paucis equitibus per medios hostes sese inferens venerat, in arcem
se recipientibus. Quos tamen omnes multis oppugnatos proeliis,
arce etiam deiecta, captivos fecerunt; et Faventia frustra temptata,
in Ravennae fines ad Russium oppidulum oppugnandum se
contulerunt.

76   Eas ob res civitate perturbata, cum lentius tributa exigerentur,
senatus censuit ut qui iure comitiorum praediti die sibi praestituta
in aerarium non intulissent, eorum nomina comitiis maioribus re-
citarentur, ut ab universa civitate cognosci posset, qui cives non
amantes patriae essent; quod si ob eam contumeliam alia praestituta die non inferrent, tum vero a senatu atque a collegiis secretio-
ribus, demum ab omnibus reipublicae muneribus arceantur, eorum loco alii subrogentur, ipsi ad ferenda suffragia ne admittantur.
Haec tum fuit nobilitati poena multiplex constituta; plebi vero id
unum, ut in aerarium non inferens a publicis et ipsa muneribus
amoveatur; quae cum plurima quidem sunt, tum certe etiam per-
utilia, ut magna pars civium ea se re alat perliberaliter. Eam legem
maiora comitia primum habita comprobaverunt, acerbitate temporum civium animos frangente, ut quod alias non tulissent neque
umquam latum antea meminissent, tum quidem non perferrent
modo impositum patienter, sed ipsi quoque sibimet imponerent

had already set an ambush and caught Tartaro, a Venetian officer, as he made his way to Brisighella with three companies[40] intended for a garrison, and shortly after that they took the town after surrounding it with a ring of artillery. The commander and the troops that were with him retreated into the fortress, along with Giampaolo Manfrone, a courageous cavalry captain who had come through the midst of the enemy with a few cavalry to defend the town. All of them, however, had come under attack in many battles, and when even the fortress was knocked down, they were taken captive. Julius' soldiers made a vain attempt on Faenza and then made their way into the territory of Ravenna to attack the village of Russi.

The city was much disturbed by this turn of events, and since the tax revenues were coming in too slowly, the Senate decided that those of the nobility who had not made their payment to the treasury by the appointed day would have their names read out in the Great Council, so that the entire city could learn which citizens were lacking in patriotism. If they were not moved by this humiliation to make their contribution by a second fixed day, then they would actually be barred from the Senate and the more confidential councils,[41] and finally from all offices in the Republic. Others would be appointed in their place, and they themselves would not be allowed to vote in elections. Such were the complicated penalties laid down for the nobility, while the commoners had only one, that if they did not contribute to the state funds they too would be removed from public office. These offices are not only very numerous but also carry considerable emoluments, so that a large part of the citizens support themselves very handsomely on them. The law was approved by the Great Council at its first session, for the desperate times were breaking the spirit of the citizens, and what they had not endured on earlier occasions, nor remembered ever having endured, they now not merely bore patiently when it was imposed on them, but were actually imposing

76

perferendum. Lege lata Bergomo litterae venerunt: hostes in oppidi finibus Medelaci castellum magna vi oppugnatum cepisse; omnes qui in eo erant interfecisse; non mulieribus, non infantibus pepercisse, ut civitas perterrefacta tuendi oppidi auxilium a legatis petat.

77   Interim magna ex parte collecto ab imperatore Livianoque reipublicae in Gallia exercitu, ad quem quidem equites Epirotae perplures modo allati se contulerant, magnaque vi optimorum tormentorum a Valerio adducta, cum de Abdua flumine transeundo sententiae ab iis atque ab legatis et reliquis praefectis dicerentur, Livianus autem magnopere transitum probaret—multum enim, si transeant, posse ipsos proficere, nondum collectis hostibus, rege non praesente, populis adhuc in ambiguo utram sequi partem praestet constitutis; audacia et celeritate plurima confici, cum sua hostibus consilia impediantur, ipsis animi augeantur—sed reliquis eam rem non probantibus, quod fines reipublicae hostibus direptioni, si et ipsi Abduam transissent, essent relinquendi, Livianus ad legatos conversus, "Agite," inquit, "si cunctari hic volumus, scribite ad senatum, decies millies auri libras paratas habeat, quibus producere bellum possit." Qua de contentione senatus certior ab legatis factus, petentibus ut quid fieri malit imperet, litteras ad illos dat eam se rem imperatori Livianoque permittere, qui rebus omnibus intersint; et moram se et fluminis traiectum ita probaturos, uti ipsum alterutrum e reipublicae commodo susceperint.

78   Interim Iulius, qui Ursinae gentis duces, ne ad reipublicae militiam accederent, partim minis, uti supra demonstratum est, edic-

it on themselves as something to be borne. After the measure was passed, a letter came from Bergamo: the enemy had attacked with great violence the castle of Medolago in Bergamese territory and taken it, killing everyone inside and not sparing the women and children, with the result that the terrified citizenry were now seeking the proveditors' help.

Meanwhile, the Venetian army had been in large measure assembled in Lombardy by the captain-general and d'Alviano, and had been joined by large numbers of stradiots recently levied and a great quantity of the finest artillery brought in by Valier. There was debate among them, the proveditors, and the other captains about crossing the river Adda. D'Alviano was much in favor of crossing: there would be many advantages if they crossed, he said, since the enemy had not yet assembled, the king was not present, and the populace was still uncertain which side it would be better to take. A great many things could be done with boldness and speed, with the enemy being hindered by their own plans while our own spirits were rising. But the others were against it, because if they crossed the Adda themselves, it would mean that the Republic's territory was left for the enemy to plunder. D'Alviano thereupon turned to the proveditors and said, "Come now, if we are going to linger here, you will have to write to the Senate and tell it to provide another 10,000 gold pounds to keep the war going longer." On hearing of this dispute from the proveditors, who wanted guidance as to the course they preferred, the senators sent them a letter leaving the matter in the hands of the captain-general and d'Alviano, who were there on the spot. They would approve either staying where they were or crossing the river, so long as one or the other was carried out to the Republic's advantage. 77

Meanwhile, Julius had frightened off the captains of the Orsini clan from entering Venetian military service and dissuaded them from the course they had started on, in part by threats (as was pointed out above) and edicts, in part through the entreaties and 78

tisque terruerat, partim per filiam suam Felicem, quae Ioanni Iordano, eius familiae principi, nupserat, precibus et femineis consiliis ab itinere instituto revocaverat, stipendiaque sibi ab reipublicae legatis Romae curata ne restituerent interdixerat, data eis venia iure illa retinendi, fideique praestandae religione sublata; praeter quod exercitum in fines reipublicae introduxisset, ad illud etiam pertinaciter descendit, ut Lauredano principi senatuique omni Veneto et civibus singulis aqua et igni interdiceret, eiusque rei litteras omnibus hominibus vulgandas proponeret, maledictorum et execrationum plenas, nisi die praestituta non Faventiam modo atque Ariminum, sed Ravennam quoque Cerviamque sibi tradiderint; quae quidem oppida centum ferme annos in reipublicae imperio fuerant; neque ullus ea pontifex maximus in dubium revocaverat, quin iure a republica possiderentur. Qua intellecta re, ne plebs eiusmodi litteris plus quam tempora et reipublicae difficultates postularent permoveretur, senatus cavit ne reciperentur, neve qui afferrent admitterentur. Appellavit etiam de eo futurum concilium, missis Romam affixisque in templorum foribus publicae expostulationis litteris, missis etiam in Pannoniam ad Thomam, cardinalem Strigoniensem; nam ei propter patriarchatum Constantinopolitanum, cui praeerat, una cum tribus episcopis concilium cogendi ius potestasque antiquitus erat attributa. Has ob res et belli Gallici pericula supplicatio decreta est, aurique tantundem, uti paulo ante, sacris virginibus publice datum placandi Deum causa.

79   Patres interea, certiores facti edictum Neapoli propositum fuisse, ne quis ad reipublicae stipendia se conferret, cogi vero exercitum a prorege, quicum in Apuliam ad reipublicae oppida expugnanda contenderet, exspectari autem ab eo Roma milites quingentos, quos legatus apud Iulium regius in Urbe conscripserit,

feminine wiles of his daughter Felice, who was married to the head of the family, Giangiordano Orsini. Julius had forbidden them to give back the pay that had already been given them at Rome by the Venetian ambassadors and allowed them to keep it as of right, cancelling the obligation to keep their word. Besides sending an army into the Republic's lands, in his dogged perversity he even descended to excommunicating Doge Loredan, the whole Senate and every single Venetian citizen, and he promulgated bulls to that effect to be published throughout the world, bulls full of abuse and maledictions, should the Venetians fail to hand over to him by a set date not only Faenza and Rimini, but Ravenna and Cervia too. Those towns had been in Venetian hands for almost a century and no previous pope had expressed any doubt as to the Republic's right to possess them. When the Senate learned of the matter, they took care not to accept the papal letters or admit those that brought them, so as to avoid the people becoming unduly alarmed at such a bull beyond what the present situation and the Republic's difficulties demanded. They also appealed to a future Council about this, sending official letters of protest to Rome and posting them on church doors. They even sent them to Thomas cardinal of Esztergom in Hungary, for as the head of the Patriarchate of Constantinople, he had of old been granted the right and power of convening a Council, along with three bishops.[42] On this account and on account of the dangers of the war in Lombardy, it was decided to hold a public ceremony,[43] and the nuns were given from public funds the same amount of gold to propitiate God as they had had a little earlier.

In the meantime the senators got word that a decree had been issued at Naples forbidding anyone to enlist in the service of the Republic. The viceroy there was assembling an army to go into Apulia and capture the Republic's towns, but was waiting for 500 soldiers from Rome which the king's ambassador to Julius had recruited in the city, everything else being ready for him to take to

79

reliqua omnia esse iam parata, ut viae sese det, adhibito legato apud se item regio, ea quae non ambiguis auctoribus intellexerant exposuerunt; questique sunt non esse hoc illud quod saepe reipublicae sit pollicitus. Ille vero confidenter pernegare rogareque patres, ne quid eiusmodi crederent: agi a prorege illa omnia muniendi regni causa, propter Gallorum in Italiam adventum, non autem ut reipublicae bellum inferat, suis cum regibus foedere atque benevolentia coniunctissimae. Quae tametsi patres quorsum dicerentur haud obscure cognoscerent, dissimulanda tamen sibi esse statuerunt, dum de belli exitu cum rege Galliae sciri posset.

80   At cum aliquando de Abdua flumine non transeundo, nisi prius quae oppida et castella Galli iam ceperant ab ipsis expugnarentur, ne post se hostes relinquerent, inter duces Venetos convenisset, aliquot ex iis parvo negotio castellis receptis, Trevium se cum exercitu contulerunt; quod oppidum equites militesque ex optimo Gallorum genere bis mille custodiebant; muroque tormentis celeriter deiecto, hostes ad deditionem compulerunt, nulla condicione interposita, nisi ut iis, equis detractis rebusque reliquis abreptis, ceteris, sacramento ab ipsis dato eo se anno bellum reipublicae non facturos, abeundi facultas permitteretur; duces captivi tam diu essent, quoad eorum quos ex Venetis eo in oppido Galli cepissent cum his permutatio fieret. Ab ea oppugnatione uti Venetos repellerent, Galli, magno numero vicinis ex locis coacti, ad eorum quidem castra venerant; manus autem conserere non sunt ausi; ut paene in eorum conspectu oppidum captum sit; quod quidem Liviani permissu statim direptum atque incensum est. Qua in direptione mulieres virginesque prope omnes, a militibus vim passae ac violatae, oppidi casum inhonestiorem reddiderunt. Eo negotio confecto, Hispaniae regum legatus Lauredanum patresque gratula-

the road. They summoned the king's ambassador to Venice and put to him what they had learned from reliable sources, complaining that this was not what he had on many occasions promised the Republic. All the same the ambassador made a stout and confident denial, and asked the senators not to believe anything of the sort: the viceroy was taking all those actions to strengthen the Kingdom in view of the arrival of the French into Italy and not to make war on the Republic, which was closely bound to his monarchs by treaty and goodwill. Although the senators were perfectly aware of his reasons for saying so, they nevertheless decided that they had to hide their feelings till the outcome of the war with the French king became clear.

The Venetian captains at length reached agreement not to cross the Adda without first recapturing the towns and castles the French had already seized, in case they left the enemy in their rear. They took back some castles with little difficulty and made their way to Treviglio with the army. The town was guarded by 2,000 of the best of the French cavalry and footsoldiers, but the wall was soon knocked down by artillery and the enemy were forced to surrender. No conditions were imposed, except that after they were deprived of their horses and had the rest of their gear taken from them, the common soldiers were to be allowed to depart on giving an undertaking that they would not make war on the Republic that year; as for the captains, they would be held prisoner until they were exchanged for the Venetians that the French had taken in the town. To repel this Venetian attack, the French had gathered in great numbers from the surrounding area and had come to the Venetian camp, but they did not dare join battle and so the town was seized almost before their eyes. With d'Alviano's acquiescence it was immediately plundered and burned. In this sack the assault and rape of almost all the women and girls made the fall of the town even more shameful. When the business was done, the ambassador of the Spanish sovereigns approached Loredan and the

80

tum adiit, scire se affirmans suos reges magnam ex eo voluptatem percepturos.

81   Pauloque post Mantuani ducis equites quatercenti, milites sexcenti Alexio duce ad castellum Casaboldum, quod abest ab Asula oppido in Brixianorum finibus milia passuum quattuor, cum tormentis, id ut caperent, improvisi accesserunt. Pagani qui in eo erant, armis captis, fortiter se defendere coeperunt; simul ad Federicum Contarenum, a decemviris legatum Asulanis praeesse iussum, miserunt auxilium imploratum. Federicus confestim quingentis militibus, quos habebat fortes viros, ut eo contenderent petentibusque opem ferrent, imperavit. Ii celeriter itinere confecto proelium cum Mantuanis commiserunt eorumque partem interfecerunt, partem ceperunt; reliquis in fugam coniectis tormentisque abductis, nullo ex suis desiderato, vulneratis perpaucis laeti Asulam ad Federicum reverterunt. Ea clades, Mantuae nuntiata, magnos luctus excitavit. Erant enim in ea manu honesti cives permulti, quorum pars maior interierant.

82   Veneti, quod Trevio capto oppidum militibus diripiendum tradiderant, haud levem ex ea re iacturam fecerunt. Plurimi enim milites, tribunis et centurionibus relictis, cum praeda vulgo domum profugerunt, ut magna illos perturbatio tenuerit. Eo incommodo ad regem ab exploratoribus perlato, qui Mediolanum Kalendis Maii venerat, pauloque antea ex oppidi et suorum deditione graviter commotus, quo utiliter belli consilia verteret non reperiebat, omnibus suis coactis copiis, Cassianum venit ut cum vellet flumen traiceret. Habebat autem lectissimorum equitum milia quindecim, quibus duces clari nominis praeerant, militum triginta; eorum pars Helvetii, Vascones reliqui erant. Ad haec omnem fere totius Galliae nobilitatem sibi stipendiariam secum ducebat. Post-

senators to offer his congratulations, saying that he knew his sovereigns would take great pleasure in it.

A little later, 400 cavalry and 600 infantry of the marquis of 81 Mantua under the leadership of Alessio [Beccagnolo] suddenly arrived with artillery to seize the castle of Casaloldo, which is four miles from the town of Asola in the territory of Brescia. The local countryfolk who were in the castle took up arms and bravely began to defend themselves, at the same time sending word to Federico Contarini to beg for his assistance — Contarini had been ordered by the Ten to take charge of the people of Asola as proveditor. Contarini at once ordered the 500[44] brave footsoldiers he had to march there and bring them the succour they were seeking. They made the journey quickly and soon joined battle with the Mantuan forces. Some they killed and some they took prisoner, the rest being put to flight and their artillery carried off by the victors. The Venetians, with no losses on their side and only a few wounded, returned in triumph to Contarini at Asola. The announcement of the defeat caused great grief at Mantua, for there had been a large number of respectable citizens in that force, most of whom perished.

By giving Treviglio over to the soldiers for plunder after the 82 town was taken, the Venetians suffered no small loss. A great many of the soldiers forsook their commanders and officers and ran off home with their booty, bringing the Venetians great distress. Spies reported this setback to the king, who had come to Milan on the first of May. Louis had been extremely upset at the surrender of the town and of his men a short while before and could not find out how best to put his war plans into effect. He gathered all his troops together and went to Cassano d'Adda, so that he could cross the river at will. He had now 15,000 elite cavalry under the command of distinguished captains and 30,000 footsoldiers, part of them Swiss, the rest Gascons. In addition to these he brought with him in his service almost the entire nobility

remo quicumque in Gallia citeriore aut princeps suae civitatis, aut ampla familia natus, aut magnis opibus, aut omnino aliquo apud suos loco esset, eos omnes nominatim evocaverat. Quae duae quidem res, ad reliquum equitatum adiectae, et numerum et robur, et certe faciem ac splendorem exercitus maiorem in modum adaugebant.

83   Venetus erat exercitus equitum graviorum milium sex, leviorum quattuor, militum trium et triginta; tametsi neque dum omnino omnes nostrae in castra copiae venerant. Nam et Lucius Bononiensis et Leonardus Apulus, praefectus leviorum equitum reipublicae, suis cum turmis, qui quidem erant Brixiae a magistratibus retenti, ut eos fines tuerentur in quos Mantuanorum dux invasurus putabatur, et equites Epirotae perplures, tum demum appulsis ad urbana litora navibus egressi, et milites non pauci, quos Brixianorum civitas cogebat, exspectabantur. Aberat etiam ex legatis Cornelius; qui paulo antea, calculo et urinae vitio vitae suae diffidens, Brixiam se contulerat.

84   Erat autem is exercitus qui convenerat ita florens etiam sine iis, ita instructus, et animo, ut videbatur, paratus ad decertandum, cum ut rempublicam defenderet, tum vero etiam ut quam Italiae partem Galli occupaverant in libertatem vindicaret (id enim prope palam profitebantur, eiusmodique voces eorum creberrime ab hostibus exaudiebantur), ut nullo tempore aut meliores, paucis equitum ductoribus exceptis, aut omnino ampliores copias respublica suis in exercitibus habuerit. Et nisi duces illis defuissent, nihil omnino videbatur eorum aut claram victoriam aut pacem honorificam fuisse interpellaturum. Constat enim Aloisium regem, ubi is prope se hostium exercitum habuit atque ex captivis et numerum et alacritatem copiarum ad pugnandum cognovit, suis ducibus dixisse numquam se tantas Venetorum opes atque copias existimavisse;

of France. Finally, all the leading men of the communities in Lombardy, all the high-born or wealthy, anyone of rank at all among his people were summoned to Louis by name. And these two elements, when added to the existing cavalry, enhanced both the numbers and strength of the army, and certainly its impressiveness and splendor, to a quite exceptional extent.

The Venetian army numbered 6,000 heavy cavalry, 4,000 light cavalry, and 33,000 infantry, though by no means all of our forces had yet arrived in the field: they were still awaiting Lucio Malvezzi of Bologna and Fra Leonardo Prato of Apulia, the captain of the Republic's light cavalry, with their squadrons of horse, who had been kept at Brescia by the magistrates to defend the territory which the marquis of Mantua was thought to be on the point of invading, and a great many stradiots, who had just then disembarked from their ships on landing at the Lido of Venice, and a substantial number of infantry that the city of Brescia was raising. Among the proveditors Giorgio Corner was also absent; he had made his way to Brescia a little earlier fearing for his life owing to a kidney stone and a urinary infection. 83

But it was true that the army which had been raised was so powerful even without them, so well organized and apparently eager to fight to defend the Republic and to liberate the parts of Italy occupied by the French (they said so fairly openly, and their words to this effect were often heard by the enemy), that the Republic had never had more numerous or better forces, a few cavalry commanders excepted. Had their leaders not failed them, it seemed that nothing at all could stand in the way of a famous victory or an honorable peace. It is known that when he had the enemy army nearby and learned from prisoners of their numbers and readiness to fight, Louis told his captains that he had never imagined the Venetians' strength and military forces were so great, and he was not at all sure that his army would be victorious at that time. He had made the treaty with Maximilian and the other kings in order 84

haud sibi tum sui exercitus victoriam satis exploratam esse; foedus se cum Maximiliano reliquisque regibus ad Venetos eodem tempore opprimendos fecisse; decrevisse, si ita illis videatur, non decertare atque ad legatos Venetos mittere qui nuntiet: posteaquam reliqui foederati nihil in commune conferant, ut se ad bellum iuvent, velle sibi rempublicam amicam esse, cumque ea foedus renovare potius quam congredi; verum ab suis ducibus suasum ut ea de re prolixius sibi esse cogitandum statueret; loco esse propter flumen eiusmodi, ut elici invitus ad pugnandum non possit; semper Venetos eum nuntium libenti animo accepturos; rem in alium diem distulisse. Haec ab illis qui concilio interfuerant patres postea cognoverunt.

85 Cassianum est oppidum in Abduae fluminis ripa, loco paulo editiore; pontemque habet ante portam ad fluminis traiectum plane commodum. Trans flumen locus est ad semicirculi prope formam, quamvis magnarum copiarum capax. Eum omnem locum aqua fluminis in altitudinem pedum sex, in latitudinem circiter viginti, a superiore parte derivata inque flumen rediens, claudit communitque, arboribus etiam impedita, ut introspici non facile possit. Cassiani rex biduo confecto, cuius bidui tempore Mantuanorum dux, ab eo accersitus, cum equitibus quingentis ad illum venerat, flumen magno silentio exercitum traiecit atque in eo quem diximus loco castra posuit. Inter quae et nostrorum castra planities tria passuum milia patebat. In ea planitie parva utrimque ab equitibus proelia fiebant. Quibus in rebus ob Epirotarum celeritatem atque virtutem Galli quam Veneti saepius interficiebantur et capiebantur, aut omnino repellebantur. Verum, propterea quod Galli, tormentis in Cassiani arce positis, illam planitiem longe lateque verberabant, nostri non modo ad hostium castra propius accedere prohibebantur, sed neque, num rex flumen traiecisset, plane cognoverant.

86 His ita constitutis rebus, regi nuntiatur Revolutam oppidum suis ab castris abesse milia passuum paulo plus trium; in eo esse

to launch a simultaneous attack on the Venetians. If they agreed, he had decided not to fight but to send a messenger to the Venetian proveditors to announce that since the other allies were making no contribution to help his war effort, he wanted the Republic as his ally and to strike a new treaty with her rather than engage in battle. But he was persuaded by his captains to give the matter more mature consideration: owing to the river, he had a position from which he could not be drawn out to fight against his will, and the Venetians would always be ready to hear that message. And so Louis put the matter off to another day. The senators got to learn of this discussion afterwards from those who had taken part in the meeting.

Cassano is a town on a slight rise by the banks of the Adda,   85
with a bridge opposite its gate which makes it easy to cross the river. Over the river is a place in the shape of a semi-circle which can hold any number of troops. The whole site is bounded and made secure by a watercourse six feet deep and about twenty wide, drawn off from the river upstream and flowing back into it, and thickly planted with trees so that it cannot easily be spied on. At Cassano, after two days had passed in which the marquis of Mantua with 500 cavalry arrived there[45] at his summons, the king led his army across the river in complete silence and pitched camp in the place just mentioned. Between this camp and ours there were three miles of level ground. On that ground there were cavalry skirmishes on both sides, in which more French than Venetians were killed and captured, or at any rate driven back, thanks to the speediness and courage of the stradiots. But as the French had placed their artillery in the fortress of Cassano and were covering the whole plain with fire, our soldiers were prevented from getting nearer to the enemy camp, and were not even sure that the king had crossed the river.

Things had reached this point when the king was told that in   86
the town of Rivolta d'Adda, slightly more than three miles from

hostium milites ad tercentum; perfacile capi posse, si eo celeriter se conferat. Itaque, de media nocte castris cum exercitu egressus, sese itineri secundum flumen dedit. Livianus, qui neque dum etiam sciebat Gallos Abduam traiecisse, ab exploratoribus certior factus, ex tumultu strepituque carrorum, quem exaudierant, Gallos loco se movisse, atque iter secundum flumen facere, cum equitibus levissimis quatercentis sub lucem castris est profectus, ut quid hostes agerent cognosceret et, si citra flumen essent, moraretur, dum reliquus exercitus accederet. Caligo vero ita dense eo mane campis incubuit, ut Livianus, qui citatus ferebatur, temere in Gallorum incideret agmine, eosque tum demum et Gallos esse et flumen transisse cognosceret. Sed illos lacessere tantis in tenebris non ausus, propere ad Revolutanos, quo regem iturum suspicabatur, misit, qui diceret, si ad se hostes accederent, parumper sustinerent, sese omni cum exercitu confestim adfuturum auxiliumque eis allaturum. His datis mandatis ad imperatorem recucurrit; motisque statim castris aciebusque dispositis, ad Revolutanos, si fieri posset, tuendos exercitui dux fuit. Sed ea in re, quod moram interposuerat, nulli usui cum fuisset (Galli enim, confecto interim itinere tormentisque ad muros positis, parvo temporis spatio deditione municipium ceperant), nostri castra quingentos prope hostes passus suo loco posuerunt; ibique diem alterum uterque se exercitus continuit.

87   Postero die autem, qui dies fuit pridie Nonas Maias, rex, ut Pandinum municipium item caperet, bene mane secundum flumen acie disposita iter facere coepit, ea spe ut, si Cremonae appropinquare ad oppidique muros se ostendere cum exercitu posset, non nihil confideret sese oppidum, civibus tradentibus, quorum volun-

his camp, there were about 300 enemy soldiers, and it would be possible to take it very easily if he went there quickly. He therefore left camp with his army in the middle of the night and marched along the river. D'Alviano, who did not even know yet that the French had crossed the Adda, was informed by scouts who had heard the uproar and noise of the carriages that the French were on the move and were marching along the river, and so he set out from camp just before dawn with 400 of his lightest cavalry, to find out what the enemy was doing, and if they were on this side of the river, to block their path until the rest of the army could arrive. But the fog lay so thickly on the fields that morning that in his haste d'Alviano came upon the French column by accident — then he at last realised that it was the French and that they had crossed the river. But not daring to attack them in such darkness, he made haste to send a message to the people of Rivolta, where he suspected the king would go, to tell them that if the enemy approached them, they should hold them off for a little while; he himself would soon be there with the entire army to bring them support. Having given these instructions, he hurried back to the captain-general. He immediately moved camp and drew up his lines as leader in the field for the defense of Rivolta, if defended it could be. But his efforts were all to no avail, since in the delay imposed by these activities the French had meanwhile completed their march and with their artillery trained on the walls, had in short order taken the town's surrender. Our men took up their own position, pitching camp half a mile from the enemy, and there both armies remained for another day.

The day after that, however, 6 May, the king, hoping to seize the community of Pandino as well, drew up his lines along the river very early in the morning and set out on the march in the expectation that, if he could get close to Cremona and make an appearance with the army before the walls of the town, he could be fairly sure that the citizens, whose feelings he had previously

87

tates antea cognoverat, in suam potestatem redacturum. Qua in re sua illum spes atque opinio fefellisset, si Veneti se continuissent neque proelium commisissent. Erant enim loco editiore ac fere medio regionum earum; quo ex loco omnibus eorum oppidis, ne quid aggredi contra reipublicae voluntatem auderent, una tanti exercitus fama facile prospiciebatur, quamcumque se in partem rex incitavisset. Quem si, ut facillimum factu erat, paucos modo dies elusissent, propterea quod laborare commeatu coeperat, qui ad eius exercitum, Abdua flumine interposito, tum Epirotis equitibus omnia diripientibus atque in castra reipublicae trahentibus, magna difficultate afferebatur, ipsa necessitas flumen iterum traicere Laudemque Pompeii aut Mediolanum nulla re confecta illum reverti coegisset. Quem rerum exitum metuens Triultius, homo iam senex atque in rebus bellicis exercitatus, regi auctor fuerat, ne Abduam exercitum traduceret. Cumque nihil profuisset Gallique transire flumen iam inciperent, inter suos "video," inquit, "hodie" Triultius "Venetos Italiae dominos, nobis imperium tradentibus, fore." Alia ex parte imperator, senex et ipse multaque rerum experientia in bellis eruditus, eundem res eventum habituras tum existimans, modis omnibus, ut a pugna se abstineret, Livianum, quem ardere committendi proelii studio cognoverat, hortabatur, Gallos inopia coactos sua sponte brevi se in suos fines recepturos, confectum bellum et victoriam sine sanguine partam dictitans.

88   Itaque cum esset nuntiatum hostes loco se movisse, Livianusque eorum se consilia sua celeritate anteventurum imperatori recepisset petiissetque ab eo ut, cum ipse ad illum mitteret, cum reliquo exercitu subsequi maturaret, "Minime," inquit imperator, "me accersieris, nisi tam longinquis hostibus, ut congredi non possint.

sounded out, would surrender it and he would take control of it. That belief would have been in vain if the Venetians had only held themselves back and not joined battle. They were on higher ground and almost in the heartland of their own territory. From that location, the mere report of such a huge army should easily have seen to it that none of their towns would dare to try anything against the will of the Republic, whatever the king had egged them on to do. If they had avoided him for just a few days, as could very easily have been done, necessity itself—for he had begun to be hard up for supplies, which reached the army with great difficulty owing to the Adda being in the way and the stradiots' wholesale plunder and removal of them to the Venetian camp—would have compelled him to cross the river again and return to Lodi or Milan with nothing accomplished. Fearing this outcome, Trivulzio, now an old man and experienced in military matters, had argued that the king should not lead his army across the Adda. But he got nowhere and when the French were already starting to cross the river, he said to his men, "I see today that the Venetians will be the masters of Italy, with us handing them the mastery." On the other side, Orsini the captain-general, himself an old man whom much experience had made expert in warfare, reckoned that matters would come to the same conclusion and, knowing d'Alviano was fired with enthusiasm for joining battle, he pleaded with him with every means at his disposal to hold off from fighting. The French, he declared, would soon be driven by lack of supplies to retreat to their lands of their own accord; the war was over and a bloodless victory won.

So when the news came that the enemy had moved from its position, d'Alviano gave an undertaking to the captain-general to thwart their plans by swift action. He asked him to follow with the rest of the army as quickly as possible when he sent him word. But in reply the captain-general said, "You must by no means send for me, unless the enemy are so far off that they cannot join battle.

88

Hoc unum, mi fili, neve te animi magni tui confidentia ulterius quam oportet provehat, etiam atque etiam abs te peto. Si enim gladiis reconditis vincimus, quid nos attinet belli fortunam periclitari?" Haec imperator idcirco dixerat, quod non multum equitatui confidebat; quo in equitatu nonnullos esse praefectos qui Gallicis partibus occulte faverent non obscure cognoverat; eosque pugnam detrectaturos, si esset confligendum, maiorem in modum verebatur. Tum Gallorum naturam eiusmodi esse sciebat, ut primo impetu sustineri aegre possent, multaque recentes conficerent quae spatio interposito non essent praestaturi; fieri enim illis omnia in dies duriora ac difficiliora, quod moram ferre nequeant. Sed profecto longe aliter res quam ipse existimaverat cecidit, propter Liviani cum eo disceptationum atque invidiae suscepta pridem semina; qui non superiorem modo sibi illum esse, sed ne exaequari quidem imperio ac dignitate patiebatur, sumptis ab iis rebus animis quas anno superiore in Carnis atque in Istris gesserat. Itaque, spreto prudentiore consilio, Livianus, tum longissime abiisse hostes confirmans, imperatorem ad insequendum incendit: non cunctando neque sedendo reipublicae consuli, quae se suaque omnia ipsorum fidei commiserit; frustra tantum confectum exercitum, tantos thesauros insumptos, si ante ipsorum oculos imperii municipia nullo defendente capiuntur; suum hoc esse dedecus, non reipublicae.

89 His vocibus impulsus, Nicolaus castra moveri et signa tolli imperat, suoque loco relicto, in demissiores atque impeditiores campos exercitum instructum producit. Quattuor nostrorum erant acies equitum militumque, numero fere pares; quae ita iam processerant, ut prior ab extrema, cui Livianus praeerat, tria milia passuum abesset. Rex de eo certior factus, cum esset inter utrosque

This one thing I beg of you, my son, over and over again. You must not let the confidence born of your great spirit carry you too far. If we can win with swords sheathed, why on earth should we risk the chances of war?" The general spoke in this way because he was not entirely sure of his cavalry, being perfectly aware that there were some cavalry captains who secretly favored the French. He was very much afraid that if they had to enter the field, they would decline to fight. He knew, too, that the French character could scarcely withstand the initial attack, and that they could do much while they were fresh that they would not be able to do as time went on. Everything was becoming harder and more uncomfortable for them each passing day, because they could not endure the wait. But things turned out quite different from what he had imagined thanks to d'Alviano's long simmering disagreements with him and his resentment. D'Alviano found it intolerable that Orsini should even be his equal in command and position, let alone his superior, his confidence being based on his exploits in Friuli and Istria the year before. He therefore rejected the more cautious proposal and assuring him that the enemy was a long way off, he spurred Orsini on to follow after him: the Republic's interests were not best served, he said, by sitting around or delaying. The Republic entrusted herself and all her possessions to their reliability. The vast army would have been fruitlessly assembled, the huge expenses borne in vain, if before their very eyes the towns of the Venetian empire were taken with no one to defend them. The shame was theirs, not the Republic's.

Stung by these words, Niccolò Orsini ordered the camp struck and the standards raised, and abandoning his position, he led the army in formation down to lower and less open ground. There were four divisions of our cavalry and infantry, roughly equal in numbers. These had already advanced so far that three miles separated the first from the last, which d'Alviano commanded. Between the two sides was a very long, deep and wide ditch that the

fossa ab incolis ad derivandas aquas confecta in longum porrecta
terrae spatium, alta lataque, ut traici ab alterutris sine magno discrimine non posset, ad extremam eius partem agmen sistit, atque
ab itinere continet eo usque, ut tres nostrorum acies suum exercitum praetergressas sciret esse. Tum agmen et tormenta retorqueri
atque in ultimam nostrorum aciem impetum fieri imperat;
aciemque pleniorem suam, cui magnopere confidebat, in impeditos
atque inopinantes immittit. Veneti primum omnium frequentes ab
Gallis missas tormentorum pilas exceperunt; interfectisque non
paucis, in quibus fuere legati comites aliquot, qui ante ipsum dis-
iecti eius modo sanguine os non resperserunt, ut temporis exiguitas patiebatur, conversi quantum poterant pugnaverunt. Sed quod
erat magna eorum pars ex proördinibus, neque multum rei militaris usum habebat, facile omnes interfecti fugatique sunt. Erant autem numero ad milia quattuor.

90   Apud hos ea in acie cum esset Petrus Montius, de quo supra
dictum est, cum militibus qui sub eo merebant mille, is, hostium
impetum excipiens, cum fortissime et quantum humana vis poterat pugnavisset magnumque hostium numerum interfecisset, reliqui fessi vulneribus iam cederent, submissis ab rege multis optimorum militum[13] milibus, qui proelium restituerunt, cum octingentis
suorum in media hostium acie confossus occubuit. Erant apud illum Saccoccius Spoletinus cum septingentis militibus, Citolusque
Perusinus cum fere totidem, viri et ipsi magna excellentique virtute. Horum alter interfectus est; Citolus, multis vulneribus acceptis, in hostium potestatem venit. Ex reliquis ea in acie qui erant
militibus, perpauci Gallorum impressionem paulisper sustinuerunt.

91   Livianus pugnae initio, proelium commissum conspicatus, alio
ab latere cum sua turma in hostes se iniecit; atque ab ipsis, equo

local people had made for drainage: neither side could cross it without putting themselves at great risk. When the king heard of the Venetian move, he halted his men at the far end of the ditch, and kept them there till he was informed that three of our columns had passed his army. Then he ordered his men and artillery to turn back and launch an attack on our last column, sending in his larger force, in which he had great confidence, against our unsuspecting and encumbered troops. The Venetians first of all took a broadside of artillery fire from the French. Not a few were killed, among them some of the proveditor's company, who were dispersed in front of him and narrowly missed spattering his face with blood. As far as they could in the little time at their disposal, they turned and fought. But because a large part of them consisted of the local militia[46] and they had little military experience, they were all easily slain and put to flight, to the number of about four thousand.

Among the men in that column was the Piero del Monte mentioned above, with a thousand soldiers serving under him. Facing the enemy attack, he had as far as was humanly possible put up a brave fight, killing a great number of the enemy. The others with him were now weak from their wounds and began to give way as the king sent in many thousands of his best soldiers to take up the battle afresh. With 800 of his men, Piero fell in combat, run through in the midst of the enemy lines. With him was Saccoccio da Spoleto with 700 infantry and Citolo da Perugia with almost the same number, themselves men of outstanding military prowess. The former was killed; after taking many wounds, Citolo fell into the enemy's hands. Of the remaining footsoldiers in the company, only very few withstood for a short while the pressure of the French assault.

At the outset of the fighting, when d'Alviano saw the battle had been joined, he threw himself and his squadron on the enemy from the other side. He had dismounted from his tired horse to

90

91

defesso, ut in recentem se inferret, cum desiluisset, vulnere sub oculis accepto captus est. Captique, qui cum illo proelium inierant, fortes viri et claro loco nati sane plurimi. Apud quos Francus Burgius, equitum sagittariorum turmae praefectus, acriter pugnans occubuit. Reliquus equitatus, cum praefectorum proditione, tum timore pugnandi, nulli omnino reipublicae usui fuit; neque ulla ex tribus aciebus quae antecesserant pugnanti quartae auxilium attulit. Ita parvo temporis spatio Galli, quos quidem, magna hostium exercitus formidine affectos, paulo ante valde paenituerat bellum reipublicae intulisse, quos timuerant in fugam coniecerunt (nemo enim ex omni reipublicae copia, fusis fugatisque iis, se continuit), ingentique optimorum tormentorum vi, quam Vincentius Valerius praefectus ministrique incustoditam mediis in campis fugientes praedae hostium reliquerant, sunt potiti.

mount a fresh one when he took a wound on his face under his eyes and was taken captive by them. Also taken were quite a large number of brave and nobly born men, who had entered battle with him. Near them was Franco dal Borgo, captain of a squadron of mounted crossbowmen, who fell after a fierce fight. The rest of the cavalry proved to be completely useless to the Republic thanks to their captains' treachery and their own fear of fighting, nor did any of the three companies that had gone ahead bring aid to the fourth as it engaged in battle. And so within a short time the French, who not long before had been very fearful of the opposing army and had come greatly to regret making war on the Republic, now put to flight the men they had feared—not one of the entire Venetian force stood his ground once the first company had been routed and put to flight. They also took possession of a huge quantity of the very best artillery, which the captain Vincenzo Valier and his aides had abandoned as they fled, leaving them un-guarded in the middle of the fields for the enemy to plunder.

LIBER OCTAVUS

1 Ubi nuntii litteraeque de ea re ad senatum venere, tantus repente dolor omnes tenuit, numquam ut alias patres maiorem animo aegritudinem contraxisse civitas meminerit; fereque omnes tam inexspectatum reipublicae casum graviter dolebant. Nam ex Liviani litteris, qui eos bono animo esse iusserat, et laeta prosperaque multa non semel fuerat pollicitus, victoriam de Gallis prope certa spe animo conceperant; quam si essent consecuti, neque Iulium, qui in ipsos nova interdicti forma usus fuerat, neque omnino quemquam timuissent. Nunc se victos, exercitumque reipublicae fusum et profligatum esse, gravissime ferebant; et reflantem patriae fortunam, et difficultates in quas incidere posset respublica, animo volutabant. Quamquam, aliis super alias acceptis litteris, neque imperatorem neque legatos cum multo maiore exercitus parte proelio interfuisse cognovissent, tamen quod eisdem quoque litteris admonebantur omnium mentes timore prosternatas iacere, peditesque in primis, qui retineri non poterant quin vulgo dilaberentur seque a signis subtraherent, difficile omnino videbatur reipublicae oppida vel a victore rege, vel a Iulio posse defendere.

2 Erat in templi Marcii procuratorum collegio Paulus Barbus, civis sane prudens diuque multa cum laude in republica versatus. Is, quod erat senio confectus, a publicis muneribus abstinens, domi suae aliquot se menses continuerat. Huic Lauredanus princeps misit, qui cladem exercitus nuntiaret et senatum cogi diceret ipsumque adesse, si posset, hortaretur. Quod ubi senex audivit, vestem senatoriam poposcit, atque ita in curiam membris

BOOK VIII

When messengers and letters about the event reached the Senate, 1
all were seized by such grief that the citizens could not remember 1509
the senators ever having suffered greater heartache. Nearly everyone was extremely upset at the great blow the Republic had
suffered. From the letters of d'Alviano, who had told them not to
worry and had more than once made free with cheerful and opti-
mistic promises, they had expected victory over the French to be
more or less certain. If that had been achieved, they would have
had nothing to fear from Julius, who had used an unprecedented
form of excommunication against them, nor indeed anyone else.
But as things were, they took the defeat and the overwhelming
rout of the Venetian army very hard, going over in their minds
this reversal of their country's fortunes and the difficulties which
the Republic might face. From letter after letter they had learned
that neither the captain-general nor the proveditors with the large
majority of the army had taken part in the battle. But those same
letters warned that everyone was mentally prostrate with fear, the
infantry in particular, who could not be stopped from abandoning
the standards and widespread desertion. So it seemed that it
would be a matter of the utmost difficulty to defend the Republic's
towns from the king after his victory or from Julius.

One of the Procurators of St. Mark's was Paolo Barbo, a truly 2
wise citizen who had won much praise in his long service of the
Republic. Old age had made him frail and he had for some
months stayed at home without taking part in public life. Doge
Loredan sent a man to him to inform him of the defeat of the
army and to tell him that the Senate was being convened, urging
him to attend if he could. When the old man heard this, he called
for his senatorial robes and so hauled himself to the Ducal Palace

trementibus sese trahens, orationem quam tempora poscebant habuit: venisse in senatum sese corpore infirmo, nullis viribus, ut eam sententiam diceret quam praesens rerum status pateretur; quotum enim quemque esse, qui in tanta tam repente offusa urbi caligine possit quid fieri expediat recte dispicere. Gravem esse reipublicae casum, illius opes fractas debilitatasque esse; exterorum auxilia unde peti possint, non videri; verum esse deos immortales, quos ruptis foederibus hostes violaverunt, eosque neque arma hominum vereri neque posse decipi ab iis qui nos, in necessitudine ac fide illorum requiescentes, plurimisque nostris maximis atque perpetuis benevolentiae officiis constantiaque fretos, prodiderunt; eos tanti sceleris vindices futuros reique publicae auxilium laturos se confidere.

3   Haec ille cum dixisset, ad ea quae essent procuranda atque statuenda orationem convertit. Quod idem multi magistratus fecerunt. Pluribus igitur dictis sententiis, ut in tam dubiis rebus cuique aliquid fore usui succurrebat, primum omnium pecunia legatis, qui se ex fuga apud Brixiam receperant, ad exercitum instaurandum decreta est. Nam Cornelius, ex morbo paulisper recreatus, dum in castra se referret, clade audita una cum fugientibus eo redierat. Tametsi eis, e stipendio ante proelium exercitui dato, non minimum pecuniae supererat.

4   Deinde ad Dominicum Grimanum et Marcum Cornelium, Georgii legati filium, qui utrique in cardinalium collegio Romae tunc erant, datae litterae, uti Iulio ea quae ipsemet petierat edicto suo ex reipublicae dicione oppida, intra eos quos praestituerat dies, iri ei traditum senatus nomine pollicerentur; rogarent ne rempublicam conteri a barbaris exercitibus permitteret; quam si unam pessum dabunt, tutum illum reliquosque deinceps Romanos pontifices ipsa in urbe non futuros; id quam saepe alias experta

with trembling limbs and delivered the speech the times demanded. He had, he said, come to the Senate with infirm body and drained of strength in order to voice a view suited to the present state of things. How few there were who could see the right course of action when such a thick and sudden fog had descended on the city! It was a serious blow to the Republic, and her strength had been shattered and dissipated, and it was not clear whence they could seek foreign help. But there was Almighty God, whom the enemy had outraged by breaking the treaties, and He had no fear of mortal arms nor could He be deceived by those who had betrayed us—we who had been secure in their trustworthiness and the bonds that tied them to us, who had relied on our innumerable and constant acts of goodwill and loyalty toward them. He was confident that God would avenge this monstrous crime and would come to the Republic's aid.

That said, he turned to the measures and decisions that needed to be taken, as did many of the magistrates. A wide range of views were expressed as each man came up with something to help in this perilous situation: first of all funds to rebuild the army were voted for the proveditors, who had fled to Brescia—Giorgio Corner, having recovered somewhat from his illness, was returning to camp when he heard of the defeat and went back there with them as they escaped. They had all the same a substantial sum left from the payroll funds given to the army before the battle. 3

A letter was then sent to Domenico Grimani and Marco Corner, son of the proveditor Giorgio, both of them cardinals then at Rome. They were to promise in the Senate's name that the towns belonging to the Republic that Julius had sought in his edict would be handed over to him within the period he had prescribed, and to ask him not to permit the annihilation of the Republic at the hands of barbarian armies. If they did destroy her, Julius and all subsequent Roman pontiffs would not be safe even in Rome; no one indeed was unaware how often this had happened at Rome 4

Roma sit, nescire porro neminem; decere ipsum, qui in Italiae
praeclara parte natus caelum hauserit, reliquos Italos tueri potius
quam exterarum nationum plusque nimio per se appetentium vires
opesque, quibus vastitatem Italiae inferant, augere. Latum etiam,
ut Antonius Iustinianus, qui Cremam legatus a senatu lectus
proficiscebatur, ad Maximilianum recta contenderet et cum illo, si
posset, pacem quantumvis duris condicionibus faceret; Terges-
teque oppidum et Portum Naonis, reliquaque municipia quae respublica ex eius dicione superiore anno ceperat, senatum ei para-
tum esse restituere, ac quae oppida ex Romanorum imperatorum
dicione in Carnis et Gallia et Venetia republica possideret, ea se
omnia illi tamquam accepta relaturum nuntiaret; nisi enim ab altero eorum aliquid auxilii afferatur adversus Gallorum audaciam
atque impetum, nullum satis firmum obicem futurum esse vere-
bantur.

5   Demum lecti legati ad exercitum duo priorum legatorum loco
Georgius Emus, Paulus Capellus, legationibus renuntiatis propter
alios magistratus quos obibant, ex quibus magistratibus ad alia
munera invitos evocari non licebat, magnam senatus, magnam totius civitatis invidiam subierunt. Neque eorum loco quisquam sub-
lectus postea fuit, quod iam, de priorum legatorum diligentia,
quae senatus vellet nuntiarentur. Rogatio tantum in decemvirum
collegio lata, ne cui deinceps ulli ullam ob causam adversis reipublicae rebus cuipiam sibi delato muneri reiciendi facultas sit. Lecti
post haec legati duo, Petrus Duodus, Christophorus Maurus, quorum qui plura suffragia tulisset Brixiae, Veronae alter praeesset.
Horum prior clare, senatu audiente, pronuntiavit se id vehementer
cupiisse, ut suam reipublicae tam tristi eius tempore navare operam posset, quando laetiora non dabantur; itaque legationem li-

in earlier times. He himself, who was born and drank in the light of day in a famous part of Italy, should come to the defense of fellow Italians rather than increase the power and wealth of foreigners who were already excessively acquisitive, resources they were using to lay waste to Italy. A motion was also passed that Antonio Giustinian, who was on his way to Crema as the Senate's proveditor, should go straightaway to Maximilian and make peace with him, no matter how harsh the terms, and should tell him that the Senate was ready to restore to him Trieste, Pordenone, and the other communities in his dominion which the Republic had seized the previous year, and would return all the towns under imperial jurisdiction that the Republic possessed in Friuli, Lombardy, and the Veneto as though they had been held of him. They were afraid that unless some assistance were brought by one or the other of them against the daring and violence of the French, they would find no serious obstacle in their way.

Lastly, Giorgio Emo and Paolo Capello had been chosen as re-   5
placements for the previous proveditors to the army but they declined the offices as being engaged in other magistracies, from which they could not be summoned to other duties against their will. This action brought them great resentment on the part of the Senate, and indeed of the whole citizen body. Nor was anyone subsequently elected in their place, as the Senate was already getting the information it wanted about the performance of the previous proveditors. The Council of Ten merely passed a proposal that no one afterwards should for any reason be given the right of refusal to any office conferred on them in the hour of the Republic's need. After that, two proveditors were chosen, Piero Duodo and Cristoforo Moro, the one with the more votes to govern Brescia, the other Verona. The former declared in the Senate's hearing that he greatly desired the task so that he could help the Republic in such dark times, as more pleasant offices were not being given out; and so he would take on the office of proveditor

bentissime obiturum. Maurus autem, ante Lauredani subsellium progressus, patribus dixit post Deum immortalem suam se vitam reipublicae devovisse; ea, uti vellet, uteretur; laeto se illam animo patriae, a qua acceperit, redditurum. Quorum oratio ab omnibus laudata, multorum senatorum patriae caritate implente dulcedine animos lacrimas elicuit. Atque ii statim profecti sunt. Dionysio autem Naldio, qui proelio interfuerat, cuiusque centuriones militesque perplures et capti a Gallis et interfecti fuerant, ipse fortiter pugnans repulsis hostibus se receperat, omnium reipublicae militum praefectura est a senatu tradita.

6   Auxere patrum dolorem inter haec e Flaminia nuntii: Ioannem Graecum, hominem impigrum et spectata fide, equitum sagittariorum turmae praefectum, cum ea quae Ravennae erat manu hostes aggressum, ut eos ab obsidione Russii averteret, quod abest municipium ab Ravenna passuum milia quindecim diuque ab Iulianis oppugnabatur, equi lapsu captum fuisse; eoque ab hostibus ad murum oppidi producto, Russianos una cum praetore sese illis dedisse; eorum exercitum iam iamque ad Ravennam oppugnandam adfuturum. Eiusmodique nuntiis alii e Raetis nuntii successere, qui dicerent manus illis in locis et Maximiliani finibus cogi; tormenta Tridentum afferri; commeatus comportari; certam esse famam bellum inferri a Maximiliano reipublicae. Ex Carnis item et Tergeste patres certiores fiebant milites ad octo milia in Alpibus prope conscriptos esse, qui reipublicae dicionem aggrediantur.

7   Ex castris quoque ab legatis litterae afferebantur regem Caravagio esse potitum, Iacobumque Siccum, eius oppidi municipem, equitum reipublicae praefectum, eo cum suo equitatu contendisse, regique sponte se atque illos tradidisse; nullum vicinorum munici-

very willingly. Moro for his part went forward to Loredan's throne and told the senators that, after Almighty God, he had devoted his life to the Republic. She might use it as she wished: he would cheerfully give it back to the homeland from which he had received it. Their speeches won universal praise and called forth tears from many senators as love of country filled their hearts with sweetness. They set out at once. And the Senate entrusted the command of all the Republic's infantry to Dionigi Naldi, who had taken part in the battle and many of whose officers and soldiers had been captured or killed by the French; he himself had battled bravely, retreating after fighting off the enemy.

The senators' distress was increased in the meantime by news 6
from Romagna. The captain of a company of mounted crossbow-men, Giovanni Greco, a doughty fighter of proven loyalty, had attacked the enemy with the troop that was at Ravenna to try to divert them from the siege of Russi, a community fifteen miles from Ravenna and long under attack by Julius' soldiers. He had been taken captive after his horse fell, and when he was led by the enemy to the town walls, the people of Russi had surrendered to them along with their governor. The enemy army was going to attack Ravenna at any moment. These messages were followed by others of the same sort from the Tyrol to the effect that troops were being levied in the region and in Maximilian's territory; artillery was being brought to Trento and provisions were being laid in. There were reliable reports that Maximilian was making war on the Republic. From Friuli also and Trieste the senators were informed that about 8,000 soldiers in the Alps had been all but recruited to attack the Republic's domains.

Letters also came from the camp, sent by the proveditors to say 7
that the king had taken control of Caravaggio, and that Giacomo Secco, a citizen of the town and a captain of Venetian horse, had hurried there with his cavalry, voluntarily surrendering them and himself to the king. None of the nearby communities was waiting

piorum exercitum Gallorum exspectare; omnes illas regiones in timore magno esse; Brixianos, qui antea et fidem et audaciam reipublicae praestabant, timere suis rebus et diffidere coepisse, quod scirent praetores suos uxores et liberos et suppellectilem domesticam ad urbem misisse (quae res vehementer reprehendebatur). Itaque sese in difficultate plurima versari rerum omnium. Milites enim vel imperia recusare, vel accepto largiter stipendio tamen perfugere; tormenta eis deesse, quibus oppidum tueri possint, si rex eo veniat; quamobrem vereri ne Veronam se recipere cogantur.

8 Sed quod ad Caravagianos attinet, eam rem postea intellectum est ita cecidisse. Nam quod oppidani, ne diriperentur, statuerant regem, qui cum exercitu aderat, recipi ab ipsis oportere, Ludovicus Michael, arcis oppidi praefectus, qui se celeriter et militibus et commeatu communierat, praetore in arcem recepto, se ab Gallis magno animo defendebat. Galli cum triduum tormentis innumerabilibus arcem continenter verberavissent neque multum profecissent, accidit ut ignis, in cellam qua tormentorum pulvis asservabatur temere illatus, omnem illam defendendae arcis facultatem praefecto puncto temporis ademerit. Qua re milites perterriti se atque arcem et praefectum et praetorem regi dediderunt; ipsisque est, ea tantum condicione interposita, salus data. Cives autem ii Veneti duo, iussi se ad mortem comparare, a sacerdote Franciscino precibus regi suppliciter adhibitis (nam ei cum rege in Gallia familiaritas intercesserat), vitam modo non amiserunt, atque in Galliam captivi missi sunt, in custodiaque diu habiti.

9 Patavini cum viderent rempublicam omnibus a partibus premi, concilio civitatis convocato, rogationem tulerunt, ut quingentae auri librae confestim exigerentur atque ad urbem mitterentur, om-

for the French army, and all those areas were in a state of great trepidation. Brescia, which had previously shown loyalty and courage in the Republic's regard, had begun to fear for its property and to lose heart, knowing that their governors had sent their wives, children, and household goods to Venice, something that was strongly criticized. And so the proveditors were in great difficulties on every front: the soldiers were refusing to obey orders or had taken to their heels, despite being generously paid. They lacked the artillery to defend the town if the king were to go there, and on that account they feared they would be compelled to retreat to Verona.

As for the people of Caravaggio, it was later learned that matters had fallen out as follows. To avoid being plundered, the townspeople had decided that the king, who was there with his army, should be admitted by them. The commander of the citadel, Ludovico Michiel, quickly strengthened his position with soldiers and provisions, and taking the governor into the citadel, defended himself against the French with great spirit. The French kept up a barrage of innumerable artillery pieces against the fortress for three days running, but they had made little progress when it chanced that a spark randomly entered the chamber where the gunpowder was kept and deprived the commander in an instant of any means of defending the citadel. At this, the terrified soldiers surrendered themselves to the king along with the citadel, the commander, and the governor, the only condition being that their lives were spared. Two Venetian citizens, who had been ordered to prepare themselves for death, narrowly escaped with their lives after a Franciscan friar pleaded with the king (with whom he had been on friendly terms in France) on their behalf. They were sent to France as prisoners and kept in custody there for a long time.

When the people of Padua saw the Republic under pressure from all sides, they convened a citizen council. There they passed a proposal to collect 500 gold pounds without delay and send it to

niaque se facturos ad eam iuvandam quae imperarentur quaeve
ipsi per se cognoscerent profectura legati statim legendi patribus
renuntiarent. Quae res sane grata illis fuit, non tam quidem, quod
ea magnopere levarentur, quam propterea quod exemplo aliis civitatibus esse poterant amanter se in rempublicam gerendi. At cum
ad urbem venisset Gasparis Severinatis scriba, exposuissetque patribus magna illum difficultate propter Iulii edictum ad vicinos
Cremonae oppidi fines sese unum in veste pastorali contulisse,
quaesissetque quid illum facere patres vellent, responderunt uti,
quantum posset, ipsorum ad exercitum suum adventum maturaret; statutum enim sibi esse Liviani equites ei tradere. Ille vero,
spreta reipublicae condicione, ad regem Galliae postea se contulit
rogatum uti se Maximiliano commendaret, peteretque ab illo ut in
Citadellae principatum, quem pater suus obtinuerat, se restitueret;
scire enim nihil illi Maximilianum negaturum. Ferrariae vero prodominus Aloisius Mula patribus significavit, clade exercitus reipublicae cognita, magnae voluptatis signa cives illos misisse, ple-
bemque omnem vocibus procacioribus et tympanorum sonis
laetam atque hilarem per oppidum cucurrisse; Alfonsum autem
ducem, quem ipse adierit, nolle se tutum sua in urbe praestare,
propterea quod dicat incitatae plebis studia non posse contineri,
itaque illi ut discederet suasisse; redire postea posse, cum belli fer-
vor et interdicti Iuliani acerbitas atque iniuria resederit. Quibus rebus cognitis, Mula, senatus consulto revocatus, medio e magistratu decedens domum rediit.

10   Iamque regi omnibus fere populis se dedentibus, quod a reipublicae copiis nullum eis praesidium afferebatur, senatus iussit uti

Venice, and to appoint ambassadors at once to tell the senators that they would do everything to help her that might be commanded of them or which they might on their own find to her benefit. This was naturally welcome to the senators, not so much because it would greatly relieve their burdens as for setting an example to other cities of loyalty to the Republic. Then the secretary of Gaspare da Sanseverino arrived in Venice to tell the senators that Gaspare had with great difficulty, thanks to Julius' edict, made his way on his own to the neighboring territory of the Cremonese dressed as a shepherd. He asked what the senators wanted Gaspare to do and they replied that he should come and join their army as quickly as he could, as they had decided to give him d'Alviano's cavalry. But Gaspare rejected the Republic's terms of service and later made his way to the king of France to ask him to recommend him to Maximilian and to request that Maximilian restore Gaspare to the lordship of Cittadella, which his father had ruled; for he knew, he said, that Maximilian would deny Louis nothing. At Ferrara, meanwhile, the *visdomino*[1] Luigi da Mula reported to the senators that the citizens there had evinced every sign of pleasure at news of the Venetian army's defeat, and the common people had run through the town in a happy and festive mood, with shouted insults and beating of drums. When he went to see Duke Alfonso d'Este, moreover, he said he could not guarantee da Mula's safety in his own city, because once aroused the passions of the crowd could not be curbed, and so he had urged him to leave: he could return later, when the heat of war and the bitterness and sense of injury caused by Julius' excommunication had subsided. On receipt of this information, da Mula was recalled by Senate decree and he returned home, leaving his magistracy in mid-term.

And now, with no protection afforded them by the Republic's forces, almost all places were surrendering to the king. In view of this the Senate ordered that some 10,000 infantry should be re-

milites ad decem milia, quo celerius fieri posset, conscriberentur, quorum tribuni centurionesque partim a magistratibus in civitate, reliqui in castris legerentur; equites ad tria milia utriusque armaturae conficerentur. Ea postea res, quod nullum prope habitura exitum in tanta rerum omnium perturbatione videbatur—nam neque in urbe qui vellent dare nomina reperiebantur, imperatoris autem et legatorum iussa vulgo despicebantur, pleraque omnia privatim administrabantur—patres, veriti brevi fore ut omnis Italiae continentis pars quam tenerent ipsi a republica deficeret, ad urbem tuendam et commeatibus classibusque muniendam animum adiecerunt. Confirmavit hoc eorum consilium cum Brixianorum civitas, quae copias reipublicae intra oppidum recipere noluerat, quod diceret nolle se ab exercitibus conteri, satis sibi ipsos praesidio futuros; tum quod intelligebant classem a Ferdinando rege in Sicilia Calabrisque esse comparatam, qua ab classe frumenti ad urbem convectiones facile prohiberi posse videbant, nisi respublica maiores ad resistendum opes obiecisset. Itaque latum ut classi supplementum adderetur, ut essent omnes ad triremes quinquaginta.

11   Ab annonae quoque magistratu edicta sunt proposita, quibus frumenta facilius omnibus a locis ad urbem comportarentur. Litteraeque ad Cyprios datae, ut quantum maximum possent frumenti numerum navibus imponerent; navesque perplures ad eos missae, ne navigiorum indigentia convectiones tardarentur; imperatumque ut quae ab insula naves sale onustae iam solvissent, ubicumque essent, eius salis iacturam facerent et in Cyprum reverterentur frumentoque complerentur. Missae etiam in Epirum cum mercatoribus, pretiaque iis qui adduxissent ampliora lege facta. Latum etiam ut quae leges prohiberent ne advenarum navibus frumenta reliquique commeatus Venetias afferrentur, quo civium naves

cruited as quickly as possible.² Some of their commanders and officers were to be chosen by the magistrates in Venice, the rest in the field. About 3,000 cavalry, both heavy and light, were also to be mustered. But afterwards, because this action on their part seemed likely to have very little effect amid the general upheaval — men willing to enlist were not forthcoming in the city while the orders of the captain-general and the proveditors were commonly disregarded, and almost all the war effort was being conducted on a private basis — the senators feared that all their Italian *terraferma* possessions would soon defect from the Republic and so turned their attention to defending the city and making it secure with supplies and ships. This strategy of theirs was borne out on the one hand by the city of Brescia, which refused to admit Venetian troops into the town because, as they said, they did not want to be crushed between the armies, and they would look after themselves; and on the other because the senators learned that King Ferdinand was getting a fleet ready in Sicily and Calabria, which they saw might well hinder shipments of grain to Venice unless the Republic put up greater forces to stand against it. And so a proposal was passed to supplement the fleet, making it 50 galleys in all.

Ordinances were also proposed by the magistrate of the grain   11
supply to facilitate the shipping of grain to Venice from anywhere in the world, and a letter was sent to the Cypriots directing them to load on ships as much grain as they could. A great many ships were sent to them in case the shipments should be delayed for lack of vessels. It was further ordered that ships that had already set sail from the island loaded with salt should dump it wherever they were and return to Cyprus to take on grain. Ships were sent to Albania as well with merchants, and a law was passed to increase prices for those who imported grain. It was also decided that laws prohibiting the importing of grain and other provisions to Venice by foreign ships (to allow greater profit for the ships of citizens)

maiora lucra facerent, eae leges abrogarentur, dum de bello decernatur, liceretque quibuscumque hominibus suis cum navibus commeatuum causa ad urbem sine ancorario accedere.

12   Iisdem diebus Ferdinandi legatus patribus exposuit regis se litteris in Hispaniam revocari. Qua de re coacto senatu, lex est lata, avertendi ab inferendo reipublicae bello eius regis causa: ut legato Lauredanus princeps diceret senatui placere quae haberet in Apulia respublica oppida regi oblatum iri; patres missuros qui ea, cum volet rex, eius ministris tradat. His cum mandatis legatus postero die abiit. Alfonsi etiam legatus salutatis patribus domum rediit.

13   His permoti rebus patres, et quod exercitu redintegrando omnia eos deficiebant, neque multum in Nicolao imperatore spei repositum, diminutis eius copiis, ad rempublicam tuendam habebant, rogationem iusserunt, ut certus homo ad Prosperum Columnam mitteretur (is in finibus regni Neapolitani tunc erat), qui ei nuntiaret, si reipublicae velit praesto esse, senatum ei nomen imperatorium cum stipendio auri librarum sexcentarum singulis annis daturum, modo is equites mille ducentos secum adducat; rogare uti et condicionem acciperet et profectionem, quantum posset, maturaret.

14   Interim rex a Brixianis intra moenia recipitur; arcibusque duabus, quas ii dolo a praefectis interceperant, suos ministros praeficit. Sebastianus Iustinianus praetor, quod in oppidanos magna continentia et moderatione usus fuerat, cum una cum reliquis magistratibus captivus factus esset, publica civitatis commendatione a rege libertati restitutus, Gallorum comitatu in castra ad legatos sese contulit. Cremenses quidem cum oppidum haberent munitis-

should be suspended until the war was decided, and that anyone should be allowed to bring their ships to the city for provisioning without paying anchorage.

In the same period, Ferdinand's ambassador revealed to the 12 senators that he had been recalled to Spain by a letter from the king. The Senate was summoned to discuss the matter and, to stop the king making war on the Republic, a decree was passed that Doge Loredan should tell the ambassador that the Senate had decided to offer the king the towns that the Republic held in Apulia. The senators would send someone to hand them over to the king's ministers whenever he wished. Armed with these instructions, the ambassador left the next day. The ambassador of Alfonso d'Este also paid his respects to the senators and returned home.

The senators were much disturbed by these developments. 13 Lacking any means of replenishing the army and having no great confidence in the captain-general Orsini's ability to defend the Republic with his diminished forces, the senators passed a proposal to send a man to Prospero Colonna (then in the territory of the Kingdom of Naples) to tell him that if he agreed to come to the Republic's aid, the Senate would grant him the title of captain-general with pay of 600 gold pounds a year, provided he brought 1,200 cavalry with him. They asked him to accept the contract and come as soon as possible.

King Louis meanwhile had been let inside the walls by the 14 people of Brescia. He put his officials in charge of the two fortresses there, which they had taken from their commanders by trickery. Because the governor Sebastiano Giustinian had treated the townspeople with great mildness and moderation, when he was taken captive along with the other magistrates, the king gave him his liberty on the city's public recommendation, and he went on his way to the proveditors in camp accompanied by a French escort. Though they had a very well fortified town, the people of

simum, iam ante hos omnes Sonzini Benzonii, eorum municipis
turmaeque equitum reipublicae praefecti, suasu in Gallorum partes transierant. Nam cum in clade exercitus Grittus legatus, qui eo
se recipere cogitaverat, Benzonium Cremam praecurrere iussisset
civitatique nuntiare bono animo ut esset, se iam iamque adfuturum eique praesidio futurum, ille ad cives suos advolans, uti portas
legato clauderent, neque illum neque quemquam Venetum intro-
mitterent, oratione sua, dedecoris perfidiaeque plena, et auctoritate qua pollebat perfecit.

15   Quibus intellectis rebus, imperator legatique Pischeriae, municipio in Mintii fluminis ripa ubi e Benaco exit posito, equitibus levis armaturae trecentis, militibus nongentis ex itinere praesidio relictis, Veronam se recipiunt; castrisque in campo qui appellatur
Martius ad muros oppidi positis, rerum exitum exspectare consti-
tuunt. Omnes equitum ad quina milia, milites mille quingentos
redacti. Nam quod rex edictum vulgaverat, omnes ex Gallia, quam
ipse ceperat, qui reipublicae militiam facerent, nisi ad suam
quisque patriam decem dierum spatio rediissent, eorum se bona
publicaturum atque ipsos hostium loco habiturum, praeter cetera
plurimi eam ob rem etiam legatis permittentibus discesserant. Eorum adventu sollicita civitas, ut plebs ad exercitum iuvandum pro-
nior fieret, portorium frumento molendo exigi vetuit, quoad bellum esset confectum. Ad id ut senatus voluntas accederet, cum
eadem civitas per legatos petiisset, patres in eius gratiam portorium in omne tempus sustulerunt.

16   Iisdem diebus templorum aliquot urbanorum sacerdotes, edicti
Iuliani metu, quo iis omnibus aqua et igni interdicebatur, nisi e dicione reipublicae recederent, atque in primis Georgiani, quorum
est celeberrimum in insula e regione comitii fanum, cum suppel-

Crema had gone over to the French before all of these at the urging of Soncino Benzoni, their fellow townsman and captain of a cavalry company of the Republic. Following the defeat of the army, the proveditor Gritti had contemplated retreating there. He ordered Benzoni to go on ahead to Crema, rally the citizens, and tell them that he would soon be there to protect them. But the man rushed to his fellow citizens, and by the force of his utterly shameful and treacherous oratory and the great authority he had among them, prevailed upon them to close the gates against the proveditor and refuse to admit him or any Venetian.

On learning of this, the captain-general and the proveditors retreated to Verona, leaving behind en route 300 light cavalry and 900 infantry as a garrison at Peschiera, a community located on the banks of the Mincio river at the point where it leaves Lake Garda. Pitching camp on the so-called Campo Marzio before the walls of the town, they decided to await events. They were reduced to about 5,000 cavalry and 1,500 infantry in all. The king, having taken Lombardy, had made a public proclamation that everyone from there who was serving in the Venetian forces would have their property confiscated by him and be considered an enemy if they did not return to their own towns within ten days. A great number had left for that reason, in addition to other factors, even being given permission to do so by the proveditors. The citizens of Verona were alarmed at their arrival and to encourage the people to assist the army more readily, they lifted the collection of duty on the milling of grain for the duration of the war. When the town through its envoys requested the Senate to support the move, the senators abolished the duty in perpetuity out of gratitude for their action.

At that time the priests of a number of Venetian churches had taken fright at Julius' edict, which excommunicated them all unless they left the Republic's domain, especially those of San Giorgio, who have a very famous church on an island opposite the Council

lectili aurea argenteaque Ferrariam atque in Mantuanum agrum
profugerunt, ut urbs eo genere hominum paene destitueretur, civitasque in primis rei divinae assueta magnam ex eo molestiam caperet. Antonii etiam Iustiniani litterae ex Alpibus datae senatum certiorem fecerunt Tridenti episcopum se audire noluisse, quod
diceret ab aqua et igni interdictorum sermonem atque aditum esse
defugiendum. Itaque paucis post diebus, cum nihil impetrare potuisset, senatus permissu domum rediit.

17   Miserant in Flaminiam patres Ioannem Iacobum Caroldium,
uti Ravennam urbem et Cerviam et Ariminum et Faventiae arcem
(nam oppidani se dediderant) reliquaque Venetae dicionis in Flaminia municipia, abductis tormentis receptisque iis quos bello
captivos hostes fecerant, senatus auctoritate Iulii ministris trade-
ret. Ii cum, fide scripto data sese et tormenta asportari permissuros et captivis libertatem donaturos, et praeter haec, quod erat primum atque maximum, uti e vestigio interdictum antiquaretur
curaturos, oppida ipsa recepissent, in nullo eorum quae pepigerant
perstiterunt, retentis tormentis et captivis Romam missis, non iis
modo qui bello capti fuerant, sed illis quoque qui praefecti oppidorum atque arcium illa ipsa pacate tradiderant, civibus Venetis
undecim, quos in ipso negotio circumventos in vincula coniece-
rant, et interdicto non rescisso. Ea Iulii fides, ea pietas in supplices
fuit, atque omnino in illos eosdem qui paulo antea Romae, ut is
pontifex maximus fieret, omnes suas opes, omnem auctoritatem,
gratiam, studia publice contulissent.

18   Non absimili iniuria Alfonsus Ferrariensium dux Rhodigianos,
apud Padum flumen positos, quod oppidum bello Ferrariensi Ve-

chamber.[3] They fled to Ferrara and the countryside of Mantua with their gold and silver furnishings, with the result that the city was almost devoid of such persons, something that caused the citizenry, extremely devout as they were, great distress. A letter sent from the Alps by Antonio Giustinian also informed the Senate that the bishop of Trento had refused to give him a hearing, because he said that conversation and contact with persons under interdict had to be avoided. Having proved unable to get anything at all from him, he accordingly returned home a few days later with the Senate's permission.

The senators had sent Giangiacomo Caroldi to Romagna to   17
hand over to Julius' officials under the Senate's authority the city of Ravenna, Cervia, Rimini, the fortress of Faenza (the townspeople had already surrendered), and the other communities controlled by Venice in Romagna, once the artillery had been removed and the prisoners taken by the enemy in the war returned. But despite having given their word in writing that they would allow the artillery to be taken away and would free the prisoners, and on top of that, by far the most important point, would see to it that the excommunication was lifted, when the officials had taken back the towns themselves, they reneged on everything they had pledged. They kept the artillery and sent the captives to Rome—and not only those who had been taken in war but also the commanders of the Romagnol towns and citadels who had handed them over peacefully, eleven Venetian citizens that they had surrounded and thrown into chains while the business was actually being carried out—nor was the bull of excommunication rescinded. Such was the word of Julius, such his compassion toward suppliants, and indeed toward those very men who at Rome a little earlier had publicly brought to bear all their resources, all their authority, influence, and efforts, to have him elected pope.

In a not dissimilar act of injustice, Alfonso d'Este, Duke of   18
Ferrara, led a small troop to the town of Rovigo near the river Po

neti ceperant atque ex pacis foedere postea tenuerant, parva manu eo adducta, in deditionem recepit. Qua intellecta re, Antonio Bragadeno praetori, qui se in oppidi arcem intulerat, patres per litteras mandaverunt ut tormentis abductis arcem duoque reliqua eius regionis municipia Alfonso restitueret. Sed is, antequam eae ad eum litterae perferrentur, captus ab hostibus una cum arce Ferrariamque perductus, paucis post mensibus in custodia interiit. Itemque ad Sebastianum Maurum, qui cum decem et septem navibus in Athesim missus fuerat, litterae sunt a senatu datae, ut in tutum se reciperet. Is cum ab agricolis in reditu ab utraque ripa omni telorum genere premeretur, ac propter siccitates contractiore aqua minus se subducere celeriter posset, eiectis aliquot in flumen tormentis gravioribus incitatisque remigibus, Bebiam rediit.

19   At in superiore Padi fluminis ripa Cremonenses, Gallis equitibus et militibus in oppidum admissis, sese regi tradiderunt. Eoque biduo nuntius ad senatum venit Pischeriam municipium rege oppugnante captum; milites oppidanosque ad unum caesos; Andream Ripam, arcis praefectum, reste ad arborem exanimatum fuisse. Ea re audita, Zacharias Lauredanus, in Benaco praefectus, simul quod omnia eius lacus municipia partim ad regem, partim ad Maximilianum deficiebant, trireme et bireme quibus praeerat incensis, una cum suis omnibus, hostibus adventantibus se subripuit. Patres ob haec, perspecta difficultate quidquam in Gallia atque in Raetis oppidorum retinendi, legatis mandarunt ut in agrum Patavinum exercitum reducerent; Veronensibusque permiserunt, si Maximilianus ad eos mitteret, qui uti se dederent postularet, ne recusarent. Cumque Taurisani, tumultu civitatis et plebis excitato plerisque non idem sentientibus, per legatos quid se vel-

and took its surrender. The Venetians had taken the town in the war of Ferrara and had subsequently held it in accordance with the peace treaty. On learning of this, the senators sent a letter to the governor Antonio Bragadin, who had taken refuge in the fortress, instructing him to remove his artillery and return the fortress and two other communities in the area to Alfonso. But before the letter reached him, he was captured by the enemy along with the citadel and taken to Ferrara, where he died in custody a few months later. The Senate also despatched a letter to Sebastiano Moro, who had been sent along the Adige with seventeen ships, telling him to retreat to a place of safety. He was hard pressed on his return by the countrymen throwing missiles of all sorts from both banks, and could not extricate himself quickly because of the low water level due to the drought, so he threw some heavier artillery pieces overboard into the river, urged on his rowers and returned to Bebbe.

Further upstream on the banks of the Po river, the people of 19 Cremona admitted the French cavalry and infantry and surrendered to the king. In the space of two days the news reached the Senate that the town of Peschiera, under attack by the king, had been taken; soldiers and townspeople had been slain to a man; Andrea da Ripa, commander of the citadel, had been hanged from a tree.[4] Zaccaria Loredan, the commander on Lake Garda, heard of this, and since all the communities on the lake were defecting at the same time, some to the king, some to Maximilian, he set fire to the galley and a smaller boat that he commanded and escaped from the approaching enemy with all his men. Realizing the difficulty of holding on to any of the towns in Lombardy and the Tyrol, the senators instructed the proveditors to take the army back into the Padovano, and if Maximilian were to send someone to demand surrender of the Veronese, they allowed them to accede to the request. The citizens and common people of Treviso were in uproar with many of them in disagreement. When they asked

lent patres facere a senatu petiissent, id unum, quod conducere sibi ipsi existimarent, legatis responderunt. Scripsere etiam ad suos in Carnis atque Istris magistratus, ut quae oppida superiore anno e Maximiliani dicione respublica ceperat, ea omnia, armamentis commeatibusque publicis abductis, regiis petentibus ministris restituerent.

20   Postremo, quod ab ea cogitatione non longissime aberant, ut urbi quoque ipsi timendum putarent, docti a praesentibus rebus, quantam reipublicae diuturnitas et incrementum in se unos omnium regum invidiam atque odium concitavisset, decemviri duodecim legerunt cives dignitate praeditos, qui vada urbana atque litora, adhibitis eius rei peritis hominibus, diligenter inspicerent, ut aditus, si qui essent apertiores, castellis munirentur. Tum auctus operarum publicarum numerus; iussumque ut omnes insulas et domos vicorum magistri perlustrarent, quantaque esset in urbe advenarum multitudo, quanta armorum privatim ab his comparatio, cognoscerent. Edictumque poena capitis propositum, ne quis armatus incederet. Vigiliaeque noctu vicatim et praefecti cum militibus dispositi, ne quis temere tumultus exoriri posset. Etiam lex lata, ut triremes octo urbis praesidio armarentur. Missusque multo maximus frumenti numerus ab annonae magistratu ad molas farinarias in Taurisanos fines, domi molitus adservandus, ne, si eae ab hostibus molae interciperentur, civitas farinae inopia laboraret. Molaeque aliquot, quas naves sustinebant, e Pado Athesique ad urbem perductae; cogitatumque ut molae aliae, quas vertere ventus quiret, in suburbanis insulis fabricarentur; puteique perplures in portus litore foderentur ut, si a fluminibus aqua propter hostes circumfusos peti non posset, iis puteis civitas uteretur. Missi etiam publice lecti cives ad arborem in Medoaci ripis caedendam atque

the Senate through their envoys what the senators wanted them to do, they were told that they should do only what they judged to be in their own interest. The senators also wrote to their magistrates in Friuli and Istria that the towns in Maximilian's dominions which the Republic had seized the previous year should all be restored to the king's officials upon their request, after the armaments and public provisions had been removed.

The senators were coming to the view that they should also 20 begin to fear for the city itself—recent events had taught them the depth of the resentment and hatred that every ruler felt for them on account of the Republic's long expansion. The Ten accordingly chose twelve well-respected citizens who were to make, with the help of experts, a thorough inspection of the city's canals and coastline in order to strengthen the approaches with fortifications if any were too exposed. They then increased the number of public works, and ordered all buildings and houses to be surveyed by the district officials to ascertain how many foreigners there were in the city and how much private provision of weapons there was among them. An edict was published that no one should carry a weapon in public on pain of death. Night watches and officers with soldiers were stationed in the neighborhoods to put a stop to any random disturbances. A law was also passed to fit out eight galleys for the defense of the city. A very large quantity of grain was sent by the magistrate of the grain supply to flour mills in the territory of Treviso, to be stored on the home front once it was milled, so that the city would not want for flour if the mills were taken by the enemy. Some other mills placed on ships were brought from the Po and the Adige to Venice, and consideration was given to constructing some additional mills on the islands around the city, ones that could be powered by wind. Many wells were dug on the harbor shore so that if enemy occupation prevented water being got from the rivers, the city could use those. Certain citizens chosen for the purpose were also sent at public

ad urbem devehendam, ut materia civibus ad munitiones in propugnatione suppeteret, et hostibus ad oppugnandam vel obsiden-
dam urbem deficeret.

21 Dum haec domi administrantur, Vicentini cum intellexissent
Veronae se urbem Maximiliano dedisse, omniaque in Alpibus castella et municipia, eius civitatis praeiudicium secuta, idem fecisse,
neque a senatu impedirentur, quominus consilium pro tempore et
pro necessitate caperent, ad Leonardum Trissinum, civem suum,
quem Veneti exulem fecerant, quique a Maximiliano praemissus in
eorum fines se intulerat, miserunt: se paratos esse deditionem facere. Cumque is ad oppidum paucis cum militibus accessisset, certis condicionibus interpositis, sese regi dediderunt.

22 Patavini autem, quorum erant nonnulli cives qui rebus novis
magnopere studebant, coactis inter se privatim conciliis, eidem se
regi dedere statuerunt. Itaque magistratibus primum quidem nolle
se exercitum qui adventabat intra moenia recipere denuntiaverunt,
portasque ipsi, eiectis qui in statione erant, tenuerunt. Deinde ut
abirent domum neque plebis impetum exspectarent eos monue-
runt. Postremo agrestes homines armatos in oppidum introduxe-
runt, ut illi, senatu primo iubente, post etiam nolente, discedere
cogerentur. Quamobrem patrum iussu exercitus, Patavium prae-
tergressus, et ponte in Medoaco, decem milia passuum supra eum
locum ubi munitione ad naves transportandas a maris aqua flumen
discluditur, navibus imposito traductus, atque ad Mestre municipium progressus, ibi castris positis substitit. Patavini, ad Leonar-

expense to cut timber on the banks of the Brenta and transport it to the city, so as to supply the citizens with material for defense works and to deny it to the enemy for use in attacking or besieging the city.

Such was the activity on the home front. The people of Vicenza 21 meanwhile learned that the city of Verona had surrendered to Maximilian, and that all the castles and communities in the Alps had followed the example of that city and done the same. Nor was the Senate standing in the way of the Vicentines adopting that plan as a temporary expedient taken under compulsion. They therefore sent word that they were ready to surrender to their fellow citizen Leonardo Trissino, whom the Venetians had exiled, and who had entered their territory after being sent on ahead by Maximilian. When he approached the town accompanied by a few soldiers, they surrendered to the king when certain conditions had been met.

The people of Padua, for their part, some of whose citizens 22 were set on revolution, held their own private meetings among themselves and decided to surrender to the king. They accordingly told the magistrates in the first place that they would not admit the approaching army within the walls, and they seized control of the gates themselves, throwing out those who had been stationed there. Then they warned the magistrates to go home and not to wait for the people to attack them. Finally, they brought armed peasants into the town so that the magistrates were forced to depart, at first at the Senate's request but later whether they liked it or not. By order of the senators, therefore, the army bypassed Padua and crossed over a bridge of boats on the Brenta, ten miles above the spot where the river is divided from the sea by an embankment for hauling ships, and proceeded to the town of Mestre, where they halted and pitched camp. The Paduans sent emissaries to Leonardo Trissino and surrendered to him when he arrived at

dum Trissinum missis interpretibus, ei Patavium cum honesto comitatu venienti se tradiderunt imperataque fecerunt.

23   Interea cum Roma litterae ab Grimano et Cornelio patribus significavissent, nisi novam legationem ad Iulium misissent, nihil spei esse illum a sua in rempublicam pertinacia recessurum, senatus sex legatos creavit ex principibus civitatis: Dominicum Trivisanum, Leonardum Mocenicum, Paulum Pisanum, Hieronymum Donatum, Paulum Capellum, Aloisium Maripetrum; qui Romam proficiscerentur ab Iulioque peterent ut ea quae reipublicae polliciti eius ministri fuerant repraesentaret. Quibus de rebus nonnulli ex civibus, dolore affecti in eos qui senatum regebant, voces plenas querelarum privatim iaciebant, fortasse non percipientes huiusmodi decreta bonis rationibus facta esse, ac ne populi qui reipublicae parerent, eorumque urbes et regiones hostium praedae exposita essent, quorum viribus impetuique eo tempore cedere e re omnium esse videbatur; laetioremque fortunam exspectandam; ea flante, recipi tunc posse quae vitandarum populationum causa desererentur, quemadmodum, dis bene faventibus, evenisse postea compertum est.

24   Hi igitur, qui non satis probe rem intelligebant, spargere: non adeo timide rempublicam administrari oportuisse, non tot egregia oppida tradi hostibus ita facile debuisse; neque enim maiores nostros tantis impensis, tot exercitibus, tantis suis laboribus et sanguine, tot annorum longinquitate ea imperio adiecisse, ut paucis post diebus sponte amitterentur; errare qui mitiores futuros hostes crederent, propterea quod respublica tam facilis in illos fuerit ut, quae nulla certa cum spe maximisque sumptibus bello agere statuerant, pacate ab iis propeque nictu oculi sint confecta; augeri po-

Padua at the head of a distinguished company, and they did his bidding.

In the meantime, a letter from Domenico Grimani and Marco 23 Corner at Rome informed the senators that unless they sent a new embassy to Julius, there was no chance that he would soften his obstinate attitude toward the Republic; so the Senate elected six ambassadors from among the leading citizens, Domenico Trevisan, Leonardo Mocenigo, Paolo Pisani, Girolamo Donato, Paolo Capello, and Alvise Malipiero. They were to leave for Rome and ask Julius to give immediate effect to the promises his ministers had made to the Republic. On these matters some citizens were disaffected from those who controlled the Senate and began to make many private complaints about them,[5] failing perhaps to see that measures of this sort had been taken for good reasons and so that the subject peoples of the Republic and their cities and lands should not fall prey to the enemy. It appeared at present to be in everyone's interest to yield before the violence of the enemy's onslaught and to wait for an upturn in their fortunes. Once Fortune was on their side, they would be able to take back what was given up for the sake of avoiding destruction, just as was later found by God's grace to have happened.

Those people, then, who did not properly understand the situa- 24 tion were putting it about that the Republic ought not to be run so timidly and that all those fine towns should not have been so easily given up to the enemy. Our ancestors had not attached them to the empire at such expense, with so many armies, with such effort and bloodshed on their part and over such a span of years that they should be deliberately parted with in the space of a few days. Those people were mistaken who believed that the enemy would be more merciful because the Republic had been so easy on them that they had accomplished peacefully and practically in the blink of an eye what they had reckoned on doing in arms, with no certain hope and at very great expense. This fact on the contrary

tius ea re eorum audaciam, quod debiliorem multo ad resistendum armis rempublicam offenderint quam putarant; itaque invitari eos iam allicique tanta confecti belli celeritate ad maiora appetenda; id effectum esse huiuscemodi decretis formidine plenis, ut vereri amplius et peiora praeteritis timere nunc cogantur. Quod si regi Gallorum propter exercitum victorem cedendum fuit (quamquam, si maiorum pristina virtus in viventium civium animis resedisset, non is tam propitios habuisset sane deos), quid attinuit vel Maximiliano, nullos exercitus contra rempublicam mittenti, tot oppida ultro dedisse? vel Iulii exercitum, antequam ille pactis stetisset, reipublicae oppida in Flaminia, firmata munitionibus propugnatoribusque, recepisse? Nunc etiam legatos esse ad illum Romam mittendos, ut et ab republica suppliciter adiri se permittat et interdictum abrogare velit?

25   Haec et his similia cum iactarentur, una Mathei Prioli[1] sententia, quam in senatu dixerat, a prudentioribus repetebatur atque iis opponebatur. Ea erat eius modi: quemadmodum gubernatores boni atque industrii solent, qui cum vim tempestatis ferre nequeunt, naufragiique periculum propter mercium quas in navi habent pondus gravitatemque imminet, iacturam partis earum faciunt ut, navi e fluctibus emergente, ipsam reliquasque res et vitam una suam tueantur; sic in reipublicae turbulentis his temporibus fuisse faciendum, ut quando, eius exercitu fortunae magis turbine quam telis hominum disiecto, populi municipiaque omnia quibus praesidia mitti non poterant arma hostium timerent, dederent ipsi per se patres traderentque illis ea quae captui essent propiora atque opportuniora, ut ea re illorum cursum atque impetum siste-

increased the boldness of the enemy, as they encountered a Republic much less able to offer armed resistance than they had thought. In this way the very speedy conclusion of the war was leading them on and inviting them to go after greater things. Such had been the effect of panic measures of this sort[6] that they were now obliged to entertain greater and graver fears than they had in the past. Even if it was necessary to yield to the French king and his conquering army (though if the old valor of our ancestors had remained in the hearts of the citizens alive today, the king would surely not have enjoyed such divine favor), what was the point of voluntarily giving up so many towns to Maximilian when he had sent no armies against the Republic, or allowing Julius' army to take back the Venetian towns in Romagna with their strong defenses and defenders before he had stood by his promises? Were ambassadors really to be sent to him at Rome now to see if he would grant the Republic an audience for their plea and be prepared to cancel the bull of excommunication?

With these and similar sentiments being expressed, the wiser   25
sort countered them by recalling a remark that Matteo Priuli had once made in the Senate to this effect: when good and conscientious helmsmen are unable to withstand the violence of a storm, and the danger of shipwreck looms because of the weight of goods they have on board, they tend to jettison some of them so that the ship can rise above the waves, and they can save it, the remaining cargo, and their own lives all at the same time. And that is what had to be done in such turbulent times for the Republic as these. With her army broken, more by the whirlwind of Fortune than by human arms, and all the peoples and towns to whom reinforcements could not be sent fearful of the enemy's armoury, the senators should of their own accord give up and surrender whatever was closer to them and more liable to be captured. By this means they would check the progress of the enemy's onslaught rather than vainly meet it head on with their already enfeebled forces and

rent potius quam, frustra suas vires iam infractas opponentes, tamen illa ipsa una cum libertate imperii amitterent.

26   Inter hos sermones et querelas legati a Foroiuliensibus ad senatum venerunt auxilium rogatum, quo se tueri, si quid hostes molirentur, et bellum propulsare possent; velle enim omnes a reipublicae imperio non recedere. Ad quos Epirotarum equitum turmam militesque ab exercitu legati patrum iussu statim miserunt. Idem Iustinopolitanis postulantibus milites trecenti sunt ad eos missi, equitesque centum quinquaginta qui illis diebus ab Epiro venerant. Requie exercitui ad Mestre municipium data, libras auri septingentas a quaestoribus urbanis senatus legatis curari iussit; utque ii, recognito copiarum omnium numero, stipendioque eis dato, quas esse idoneas ad bellum gerendum, et virtute ac fide praeditas cognoscerent, eas omnes retinerent, reliquas dimitterent imperavit. Triremes quoque uti quattuor in Illyrico armarentur, cura est a magistratibus adhibita, Crepsa videlicet, Aschrivio Iadera Pharo. Itaque et naves vacuae cum armamentis, et stipendium et praefecti eo ab urbe missi.

27   At in navalibus nulla cessatio fiebat: materia undique convecta importabatur; triremes novae biremesque instituebantur, veteres reficiebantur; navigia humiliora viginti tormentis per vada ferendis aedificabantur; cratesque ex malis navium contexebantur; scaphae cum festucis ad palos in aestuariis figendos, qui munitiones sustinerent, accelerabantur; ipsa ex aere fusili tormenta magno numero, armamenta omnis generis, tela omnia parabantur; fabri, qui suppeterent, ex urbis officinis privatisque navalibus accersebantur; etiam machinationes ad molas frumentarias vertendas inchoatae plurimae perficiebantur. In his agendis ab omnibus diligenter administrabatur, ut ne festis quidem diebus quicquam eorum intermitterent.

28   Bassiano Maximiliani interpretibus tradito, Scala, in Alpibus castellum quod Federicus Michael praefectus timore animi incus-

still lose those same towns in any case, along with the liberty of their empire.

Amid these discussions and differences of opinion, ambassa- 26 dors came to the Senate from Friuli to ask for help to defend themselves and repel any hostile move on the part of the enemy, as none of them had any desire to leave the Republic's dominion. By order of the senators, the proveditors at once sent them a company of stradiots and footsoldiers from the army. When the people of Capodistria made the same request, 300 infantry were sent to them, and 150 cavalry that had lately arrived from Albania. While the army was rested at the town of Mestre, the Senate told the city treasurers to pay the proveditors 700 gold pounds, and ordered the proveditors to find out the total number of troops and give them their pay: they were to retain all those they found to be brave men and true and good for fighting, and discharge the rest. The magistrates took charge of fitting out four galleys in Dalmatia as well, specifically at Cherso, Cattaro, Zara, and Lesina.[7] Unmanned ships with weaponry were accordingly sent there from Venice, along with pay and captains.

Work went on constantly in the Arsenale: timber was brought 27 in from all over, new galleys large and small were constructed and old ones repaired; twenty shallow-draught vessels were built to carry artillery over the lagoon; rafts were made of ships' masts; skiffs with pile-drivers were hurriedly prepared for sinking piles in the lagoon to support defense-works; a great quantity of artillery pieces of cast bronze was got ready, and all manner of armaments and weapons. The artisans needed for the job were brought from the city workshops and private shipyards, and the machines already taken in hand for turning the grain mills were finished off in great numbers. Everyone bent to these tasks with a will and even on holidays all the work went on without interruption.

Once Bassano del Grappa had been surrendered to 28 Maximilian's men, Scala, a castle in the Alps that the governor

toditum reliquerat, regis insignia sustulit. Quod ubi Feltrini cognoverunt, praetore ipsorum Federico Mauroceno item profecto, ne diriperentur, idem fecerunt.

29 Senatus, certior factus Taurisanorum civitatem praeter paucos, qui Maximiliani partes sequebantur, in officio cum republica velle esse, litteras ad eos dedit, quibus litteris immunitas omnium rerum annos quindecim civitati dabatur portoriumque frumento molendo removebatur. Iis rebus cognitis, cives plebsque omnis in primis, magna voluptate affecti, ad propugnandum summo se studio confirmaverunt. Quam eorum voluntatem Petrus Duodus legatus, quem senatus Verona Vicetiaque abeuntem eo miserat, magnopere auxit, tabulis in quibus fisci rationes et civium reliqua erant scripta publice abolitis atque in foro plebe aspectante igni absumptis. Pauloque post milites quingenti, ab exercitu senatus iussu ad eos praesidio missi, cupidissimis omnibus in oppidum recepti sunt. Quod autem etiam Cividale Belunianum Maximiliano nolle se tradere perseverabat cumque republica omnes casus experiri statuerat, senatus consultum factum est, uti Epirotae equites ducenti, Paulo Contareno praefecto, Cividale mitterentur. Non tanta in rempublicam, cuius stipendia faciebat, virtute ac fide Pandulfus Malatesta est usus, qui, non salutatis legatis Cittadellam profectus, in partes Maximiliani sese transtulit.

30 Alfonsus autem Ferrariensium dux, Ateste municipio, a quo antiquitus originem ducebat, quodque abest Patavio passuum milia quindecim, in suam potestatem redacto, omnibus probris rempublicam afficere est aggressus, eius insignibus e foro aliisque locis foede abreptis, et fundis domibusque Venetorum civium sub hasta positis. Idem tamen haud ita multo post, quod ab Gallis suo ipse

Federico Michiel had left without a garrison through want of spirit, raised the king's flag. When the people of Feltre learned of it, they did the same after their own magistrate Federico Morosini had likewise left, in case the town was sacked.

The Senate was informed that the citizens of Treviso, apart   29
from a few who sided with Maximilian, wished to remain faithful to the Republic, and it sent them a letter in which the town was granted immunity from all taxation for fifteen years and the duty on the milling of grain removed. When they learned of this, the citizens, and the common people in particular, were overjoyed and stiffened their resolve to defend themselves with might and main. Their willingness to do so was greatly increased by the proveditor Piero Duodo, whom the Senate had sent there on his departure from Verona and Vicenza. Duodo officially destroyed the ledgers in which the treasury accounts and debts of the citizens had been set down, burning them in the town square in the sight of the people. Not long after that, 500 infantry were sent from the army to protect them by order of the Senate and were welcomed into the town by an enthusiastic populace. Belluno for its part persisted in its refusal to surrender to Maximilian and decided to stick with the Republic, come what may, so the Senate passed a decree to send 200 stradiots there under the command of Paolo Contarini. Pandolfo Malatesta showed no such courage and loyalty toward the Republic which employed him, but went to Cittadella without taking leave of the proveditors and threw in his lot with Maximilian.

Alfonso, Duke of Ferrara, on the other hand, having regained   30
control of Este, a town fifteen miles from Padua from which his family originally came, set about heaping shame and ignominy on the Republic, disgracefully tearing down her flags in the piazza and elsewhere and putting the farms and homes of Venetian citizens up for auction. But not so long afterwards, saying that he had feared for his duchy at the hands of the French—though in fact

regno timuisset, eiusque rei suspicio sermonesque non infimorum hominum in vulgus emanaverant, quas sui milites domos Venetorum civium Rhodigii atque Ateste diripuerant atque diruerant, eae uti publice restituerentur imperavit; litterasque a domesticis suis dari ad amicos quos in urbe habebant voluit; quibus litteris certiores eos facerent Alfonsum ducem quae in Venetos hostiliter egisset timore Gallorum coactum atque invitum fecisse; animo autem esse in rempublicam, uti semper fuerit, amico; deque adversis eius rebus molestiam capere, quod sciret detrimenta reipublicae in universam esse Italiam atque in omnes bonos brevi recasura.

31   Miserat ad regem Galliae senatus unum ex iis qui captivi ab exercitu reipublicae Caravagio recuperato facti Venetiasque perducti fuerant, ut cum rege ageret ut, si vellet suos omnes dimitti, unum Livianum restitueret. Is ab rege tum redierat cum mandatis eiusmodi: ut certos cives Venetos et tribunos ac praefectos, ex captivorum quos habebat numero, pro suis se dimissurum rex diceret, de Liviano nullam se condicionem accepturum confirmaret. Aiebat is etiam in eo quem secum rex habuerat sermone regem sibi dixisse singularem in proelio Venetorum militum fuisse virtutem; quam si equites praestitissent, pelli se atque superari parvo negotio potuisse; aut etiam si a pugna Veneti paucos se dies continuissent, futurum fuisse ut ipse non sine ignominia Mediolanum recederet; magno enim timore multo maximam sui exercitus partem perculsam a dimicatione abhorruisse.

32   Citolus quoque Perusinus, tribunus militum, ab iis qui eum in pugna multis vulneribus paene confectum ceperant nummis traditis dimissus, secundo Padi flumine ad urbem venit. Quem quidem patres omni studio curari mandaverunt; neque dum enim vulnera coaluerant. Huius de proelio sermo, apud Lauredanum habitus, cum sermone Galli congruebat: Gallos pugnae initio fugae sese

because his action had fallen under widespread suspicion and adverse comment by respectable men — the same duke ordered the homes of Venetian citizens that his soldiers had plundered and destroyed at Rovigo and Este to be restored at public expense. He desired members of his household to send letters to friends they had in Venice informing them that the duke had been forced to take hostile measures against the Venetians from fear of the French and against his will, that he was well disposed toward the Republic, as he had always been, and was distressed at her setbacks, because he knew that the Republic's losses would soon be visited on all of Italy and all good men.

One of the prisoners taken to Venice after the recapture of   31
Caravaggio by the Venetian army had been sent by the Senate to the king of France to treat with the king about the release of d'Alviano alone, in exchange for the return of all his men. He came back with the following message: the king said he would release certain Venetian citizens and commanders and captains from among the prisoners he had in exchange for his own men, but assured them that on no account would he release d'Alviano. The man also said that in their conversation, the king had told him that the valor of the Venetian infantry in battle had been quite exceptional. Had the cavalry shown such valor, he might well have been driven back and defeated with little difficulty; or if the Venetians had simply held off fighting for a few days, he would have retreated to Milan in some disgrace, for the great majority of his army had been gripped by panic and had shrunk from the conflict.

Citolo da Perugia, an infantry commander who, after money   32
passed hands, had been released by those who had taken him in battle, almost done for by his many wounds, came down the Po to Venice. The senators gave orders that he should receive the very best treatment, since his wounds were not yet healed. The man's report of the battle, delivered in Loredan's presence, agreed with the Frenchman's account: the French had decided at the outset of

dare decrevisse; idque futurum sine dubio fuisse, non modo si Veneti equites, uti debuerant, depugnavissent, sed omnino etiam si se loco non movissent; eorum temere fuga coepta fieri, hostes retentos se confirmavisse; atque ita non tam ulla sua virtute, quam ingenti equitatus Veneti formidine atque perfidia vicisse. At senatus, ea quam supra commemoravimus de captivis accepta condicione, quos habebat ex Gallis regi restituit; atque ille quos pollicitus fuerat ex Venetis missos fecit, in quibus Naldius, Braccius, Vitellius fuerant.

33 Patres interea cum statuissent reipublicae exercitum esse omni cura atque impensa retinendum, et quod eius missis ad Taurisanos et Belunienses praesidiis decreverat, esse reponendum, centurionibus non paucis, qui post proelium e Gallia, quique post restituta Iulio oppida e Flaminia redierant, uti novos milites conscriberent mandaverunt. Verum enimvero, propterea quod, magna civium parte in tributa non conferente, pecunia eos deficiebat, decemvirum decreto decem cives lecti sunt, qui exigendae pecuniae omni cum potestate atque imperio praeessent, eosque qui maiori eorum parti solvendo esse latis suffragiis censerentur modis omnibus cogerent ad stipem conferendam; in reliquos mitius quidem agerent, aliquid omnino tamen etiam ab iis consequerentur. Atque ii peracto magistratu, qui quidem esset annuus, quo tempore senatoriam dignitatem exercere eis liceret, annum alterum in senatu essent. Eaque re pecuniae postea exigendae ratio patribus aliquanto facilior atque explicatior fuit.

34 Rogaverant illis diebus dimississime Antonii Grimani exulis liberi Bernardum Bembum, patrem meum, Marinum Iustinianum, Aloisium Gradonicum, triumviros ex advocatis reipublicae, vellent, ob reliqua totius patris sui vitae in rempublicam officia et studia, eum civitati aliquando tandem restituere, ut qui esset iam concla-

the fighting to take to their heels, and that doubtless would have happened, not just if the Venetian cavalry had fought as they should have done, but even if they had not moved an inch. Once their precipitate flight was under way, the enemy had held back and recovered their resolve, and in this way they had proved victorious not so much by any prowess on their part as by the great panic and disloyalty of the Venetian cavalry. On hearing the terms on exchange of prisoners mentioned above, the Senate returned to the king the French soldiers they held, and he effected the release of those he had promised to them, including Vincenzo Naldi, Bernardino Braccio, and Vitello Vitelli.

The senators, meanwhile, had decided that they had to keep 33 the Republic's army, whatever the effort and whatever the cost, and to replace the troops they had sent to garrison Treviso and Belluno. They therefore told the officers who had returned from Lombardy after the battle and from Romagna after the restitution of towns to Julius to recruit new infantry. But since a large part of the citizens were not paying their taxes, money was short, and so ten citizens were given full authority by decree of the Ten to take charge of collecting funds. Those who after a majority vote were reckoned by them to be in a position to pay were to be compelled to make their contribution; the rest were to be dealt with more leniently, but all the same something would be forthcoming even from them. At the end of their year in office, during which they were allowed to have senatorial rank, they would remain in the Senate for a second year. This measure made the system of collecting funds subsequently somewhat easier and less complicated for the senators.

At about that time, the children of the exiled Antonio Grimani 34 humbly requested my father Bernardo Bembo, Marino Giustinian, and Alvise Gradenigo, the three state attorneys, to agree at last to restore his citizenship in view of their father's other acts of service and devotion to the Republic over a lifetime, so that in his griev-

mata senectute in patria saltem sepeliri sua posset. Quam quidem rem adiuvabant Dominici cardinalis adhibitae Iulio pro republica assiduae diligentissimaeque preces, tametsi adhuc quidem, propter naturae illius illiberalitatem atque inclementiam, parum profuissent. Tum perturbatis atque adeo tantopere inclinatis civitatis rebus, ad lenitatem dari sese profecto aequissimum magistratibus videbatur. Itaque triumviris legem maioribus comitiis ferentibus, ante diem decimum quintum Kalendarum Quintilium Antonius ab exilio frequentibus sententiis revocatus reique publicae restitutus, paucos post dies Roma, ubi aliquot annos fuerat, domum rediit, cum illum patres etiam nunc absentem in sexvirum qui rempublicam in senatu procurant collegium pluribus quam ceteros suffragiis adoptavissent.

35 De legatis a senatu lectis qui ad se venirent, et nuntium Iulius laeto animo accepisse prae se tulit, et litteras de ea re ad Aloisium et Maximilianum statim dedit; quibus litteris eos certiores faciebat velle se rempublicam in eam quae ante bellum secum intercedebat necessitudinem benevolentiamque recipere. Id autem ea de causa scire eos voluit, ne quid amplius contra illam cogitarent, sibi ipse suisque rebus, si ii rempublicam oppressissent, posse idem accidere non temere existimans. Quod si id minus erat extimescendum, omnino se coactum iri imperata eorum facere, subactis deletisque Venetis, pro explorato ducebat. Senatui autem per Dominicum et Marcum cardinales significavit, ubi legati Romam venissent, se interdictum remoturum. Quamobrem a senatu iussi sunt naves triremes quam primum conscendere Anconamque proficisci, ut Flaminiam evitarent, quam respublica turpiter amiserat.

36 At apud Mestre Cornelius legatus, certior factus in Taurisanis civibus esse nonnullos, qui tum quoque novis rebus studerent, eo cum quingentis equitibus Epirotis profectus, duodecim eorum in

ous old age he might at least be able to find burial in his own country. The matter was assisted by the constant and earnest entreaties that Cardinal Domenico Grimani[8] made to Julius on the Republic's behalf, although up to that point they had made little headway owing to the pope's ungenerous and unbending character. The city's circumstances being in disarray and so much changed for the worse, the magistrates thought that the fairest thing was to take a lenient line. The three therefore proposed the measure to the Great Council and on 17 June Antonio was recalled from exile and restored to the Republic by a large majority of the votes. A few days later he returned home from Rome, where he had been for some years, though while he was still absent the senators had elected him by a plurality of votes to sit on the board of six who supervise the Republic's business in the Senate.[9]

Julius was ostensibly glad to hear the news about the ambassa- 35 dors appointed by the Senate to attend on him, and at the same time at once sent letters on the matter to Louis and Maximilian, informing them that he was ready to resume the close and friendly relationship that had existed between them before the war. He wanted them to know this so that they would not make any further plans against Venice, quite rightly judging that if they overthrew the Republic, the same thing could happen to himself and his state. Even if that was an unreal fear, he regarded it as certain that, with Venice crushed and destroyed, he would be forced to do their bidding in general. He also intimated to the Senate through the cardinals Domenico Grimani and Marco Corner[10] that he would set aside the excommunication when the ambassadors came to Rome. For this reason they were told by the Senate to take ship and leave for Ancona as soon as possible, in order to avoid Romagna, which to its shame the Republic had lost.

At Mestre the proveditor Giorgio Corner was informed that 36 some of the citizens of Treviso were still set on rebellion, so he went there with 500 stradiots, had twelve of them clapped in irons

vincula coniectos ad decemvirum collegium misit, munireque oppidum instituit. Pauloque post, ex tribus legatis qui erant in exercitu, Gritto, Cornelio, Mauro, Cornelius a senatu revocatus domum rediit.

37 Concupiverat Aloisius rex Maximilianum regem alloqui, ut illum in rempublicam accenderet. Valde enim deliberatum ei erat
quidquid esset reliqui ex reipublicae dicione in continente urbemque ipsam, si res procederet, capere. Id autem sine Maximiliani voluntate quibus posset modis, quibus artibus consequi, non
videbat. Itaque ut hoc illi persuadere coram posset, suum interpre-
tem, Cardinalem Rotomagensem, Tridentum ad illum misit, qui
ab eo peteret ut de magnis utriusque rebus colloqui secum vellet.
Tempus et locum ipse diceret; se, qua die quoque loco vellet congredi, ad illum venturum. Maximilianus, qui neque hominem
amaret, et maiorem ac potentiorem nollet fieri, satisque haberet
quae respublica superiore anno dicionis suae oppida ceperat sibi
restitui, et se praeter haec Verona, Vicetia, Patavio esse potitum,
cum quamobrem colloquium peteretur haud dubie cognosceret,
fictis quibusdam abeundi causis, colloquio evitato interius in regnum se recepit; perque suum legatum questus apud Aloisium est
pagos nonnullos et municipia in Veronae finibus quae ad se spectarent illum occupavisse. Quibus intellectis rebus, Aloisius, Pis-
cheria, quam munire coeperat, discedens in Brixianos fines rediit.

38 Cremonae interim arx, militum qui in ea erant scelere atque
perfidia, Gallis deditur, Aloisio Mula, Zacharia Contareno, urbis
praetoribus, Sebastiano Maripetro quaestore, qui in eam se receperant, Marco Lauredano, Andrea Dandulo, arcis praefectis, in
praedam hostibus traditis Mediolanumque abductis. Quae sane
res magno dolori civitati fuit. Nemo enim verebatur, quin omnem
Gallorum impetum et obsidionem, si modo viri essent, quam diu-

and sent to the Council of Ten, and ordered the fortification of the town. Not long afterward, of the three proveditors who were with the army, Gritti, Corner, and Moro, Corner was recalled by the Senate and went back home.

King Louis had wanted very much to speak to King 37 Maximilian to rouse him against the Republic, for he had conceived a strong desire to seize all that remained of the Republic's dominion on the mainland, and Venice itself, if things went well. But without Maximilian's acquiescence he could not see the means or methods of bringing this about. To persuade him of this in person, he sent the cardinal of Rouen as his emissary to Maximilian at Trento to ask him to agree to a meeting to discuss matters of importance to them both. Let Maximilian name the time and the place: he would come to him whenever and wherever he wished to meet. Maximilian did not like the man, nor did he wish him to grow in importance and power. He was satisfied with getting back the towns that the Republic had seized from his territory the previous year and with gaining control of Verona, Vicenza, and Padua besides. Doubtless understanding why this meeting was being sought, he invented a number of reasons for leaving, and avoiding the encounter, withdrew further into his kingdom. Through his ambassador to Louis he lodged a complaint that the king had occupied some towns and villages belonging to him in the Veronese. On learning of this, Louis left Peschiera, which he had begun to fortify, and returned to the territory of Brescia.

Meanwhile the fortress of Cremona was surrendered to the 38 French, thanks to the misdeeds and treachery of the soldiers in it. Luigi da Mula and Zaccaria Contarini, the governors of the city,[11] and Sebastiano Malipiero the treasurer, who had taken refuge there, and Marco Loredan and Andrea Dandolo, the commanders of the fortress, were handed over as prizes and taken off to Milan. This was certainly a great blow to the citizenry: no one had the slightest doubt that they would have been able to hold out for a

tissime sustinere potuissent. Ea capta rex Cremonam se contulit. Illis diebus, quod venerant Bassianum milites e Germania quattuor mille (id autem est oppidum in Medoaci ripa sub Alpium iugis, abestque Patavio passuum milia viginti quattuor), Maurus legatus, cum parte exercitus in Taurisanos fines profectus, ea loca tutiora et quietiora reddidit. Aloisius, Cremonae dies paucos moratus, cum ibi Triultium oppidi praesidio reliquisset, Galeatium Palavicinum Brixiam, Antonium Mariam, eius fratrem, Bergomum, Palitiae principem Cremam misisset, Mediolanum rediit.

39   Iulius, Aloisio profecto exercituque eius prope dimisso, nihil iam gravius ab illo metuens, neque Maximilianum per sese magnum quidquam atque arduum contra rempublicam ausurum existimans, per Dominicum Grimanum suadere senatui coepit, ut Taurisum et Forum Iulii, quae duo quidem oppida ex foedere quod is cum Aloisio percusserat ad illum spectarent, pacate ac libentes ei traderent, potius quam bello atque inviti paulo post amitterent tamen. Id an propterea sit aggressus, quod cuperet nihil reipublicae reliqui in continenti esse, ne vires, ad illa recuperanda quae ipse ex eius dicione in Flaminia ceperat, redintegrare posset, an ut Italiae cladibus ea re finis imponeretur, quo facilius bellum in Thraces, perdiu illud quidem cogitatum atque adeo sermonibus agitatum, unanimi omnium regum consensu opibusque sumi posset, quod unum prae se ferebat, quia nobis nihil liquet, in ambiguo relinquimus. Sed omnino patribus molestissima ea Iulii suasio fuit, qui saepius iam qua via eorum oppidorum quae Maximiliano se dediderant recuperari aliquod posset, quam ut ex iis quae habereent in continente reliqua quicquam ei traderent cogitabant. Itaque legatis, qui, Anconam classe appulsa, iter Romam pedibus facie-

very long time against any attack or blockade of the French, if only they had been men. Once the fortress was taken, the king made his way to Cremona. At about that time, in view of the fact that 4,000 soldiers had come from Germany to Bassano del Grappa (a town on the banks of the Brenta beneath the Alps, twenty-four miles from Padua), the proveditor Moro left for the territory of Treviso with a part of the army and secured and pacified the locality. After staying at Cremona a few days, Louis returned to Milan, leaving Trivulzio behind to protect the town, and sending Galeazzo Pallavicino to Brescia, his brother Anton Maria to Bergamo, and the marshal of La Palice[12] to Crema.

After Louis had left and his army had been practically dis- 39
banded, Julius now had nothing much to fear from him, and judging that Maximilian would not venture on any major or difficult move against the Republic on his own, he began to urge the Senate through Domenico Grimani to hand over to him Treviso and Udine (towns that belonged to Maximilian[13] under the treaty he had struck with Louis), voluntarily and without a fight, rather than reluctantly lose them in war a little later anyway. It is not at all clear to us why he made this approach, so we must leave the matter uncertain: perhaps he wanted the Republic to have nothing left on the mainland, so that she would be unable to recover her strength to take back the Romagnol territory he had seized from her, or perhaps he intended by doing so to put an end to Italy's calamities so as to facilitate the war against the Turks with the unanimous consent and united resources of all the rulers — the latter was his only professed reason, and had indeed been contemplated by him and even debated in conversation for a very long time. But Julius' proposal was certainly extremely unwelcome to the senators. At this point, their attention was more directed to how they could recover some of the towns that had surrendered to Maximilian than to handing over to Julius any of their remaining possessions on the mainland. They therefore wrote to the ambassadors, who

bant, scripserunt: darent operam, cum ad Urbem essent mandataque reipublicae confecissent, ut ab ea cogitatione Iulium abducerent. Ioannes interim Baduarius, Georgius Pisanus, qui legati Romae fuerant, domum redierunt.

40 Patres cum ab Gritto intellexissent, propter Maximiliani milites qui Bassianum venerant, aliosque permultos qui pluribus in Alpium municipiis civitatibusque cogebantur, atque ipsum in primis Maximilianum, quem cum exercitu Feltriae appropinquare nuntii venerant, tutius futurum, si copiae reipublicae Taurisum ducerentur, ita uti fieret censuerunt. Praemissique Taurisum sunt virtute et fide praediti ac probati patribus viri e plebe tres cum suis quisque militibus, qui tribus oppidi portis praeessent easque ad omnes casus custodirent. Ad Castellum Novum autem, quod est in Alpibus supra Taurisanos fines in regione Querio appellata, natura et artificio communitum, milites Germani cum venissent et tormentis murum quatere coepissent, atque Andreas Rimundius praefectus, qui eum locum sibi tuendum a senatu sumpserat, turpiter se fugae mandavisset, castello sunt potiti. Maximilianus Feltriam venit.

41 Ea re ad Maurum legatum per cives Patavinos amicos reipublicae confestim delata, qui illi magnum esse Germanorum militum cum rege numerum significaverant, Maurus nocte intempesta, omni cum ea manu quam habebat, ad imperatorem, qui Mestre nondum abierat, se recepit; Castellumque Francum, quo in municipio erat Maurus, regi se e vestigio tradidit. His interiectis diebus, dato ab omnibus iure iurando se in fide atque officio cum republica futuros, exercitus Mestre eductus Taurisumque perductus est. Quo tubicen Maximiliani venerat, petens ut regi se oppidani traderent, nisi diripi atque interfici mallent. Ei consulto senatu ab legatis est responsum datum: velle se oppidum tueri reipublicae

were traveling overland to Rome after the fleet had put in at Ancona: when they were at Rome and had carried out the Republic's instructions, they were to do their best to dissuade Julius from his plan. Meanwhile Giovanni Badoer and Giorgio Pisani, who had been ambassadors at Rome, returned home.

The senators learned from Gritti that it would be safer to have   40
the Republic's forces march to Treviso, on account of the arrival of Maximilian's soldiers at Bassano and the great many others gathering in the Alpine towns and cities, and above all because Maximilian himself had been reported to be nearing Feltre with his army, and they accordingly voted to have this done. Three commoners whose courage and loyalty were well known to the senators were sent on ahead to Treviso, each with his own soldiers, to take charge of the town's three gates and safeguard them against all eventualities. At Castelnuovo, which is in the Alps above the Trevigiano in the region called Quer, a place well fortified by nature and human handiwork, the German soldiers came and began to pound the wall with their artillery. When the commander Andrea Rimondo, who had taken over the defense of the place from the Senate, ran away in cowardly fashion, they took control of the fortress. Maximilian arrived at Feltre.

This was quickly reported to the proveditor Moro by Paduan   41
citizens friendly to the Republic, who told him there was a large number of German infantry with the king. In the middle of the night, Moro took all the troops he had and withdrew to the captain-general, who had not yet left Mestre. Castelfranco Veneto, the town where Moro had been, at once surrendered to the king. Some days after that, everyone swore an oath of loyalty and obedience to the Republic and the army was led out of Mestre and on to Treviso. Maximilian's herald had come there, demanding that the townspeople surrender to the king, unless they preferred to be plundered and killed. After consulting the Senate, the proveditors gave him the following response: they wanted to defend the town

atque in eo cives omnes consensisse; neque direptionis aut mortis
metu absterreri posse, ne fidem praestent quam semel pepigerunt;
virtuti nullam vim fieri, nullum incuti timorem iis qui honeste oc-
cumbere quam turpiter vivere satius atque prius putant. Iisdem legatis deinde certioribus factis hostium copias ad Citadellam convenire, ut in illas impetum faceret, Grittus Tauriso cum Leonardo
Apulo cumque Epirotis equitibus ad vicina ei municipio loca sese
contulit.

42   Andreas interim Fusculus, qui Byzantii reipublicae negotia pro-
curabat, patres facit per litteras certiores, clade reipublicae cognita,
regem Thracium sibi ostendisse magnam se ex ea re molestiam accepisse; questum etiam apud illum fuisse, quod non secum de hostium consiliis apparatibusque communicarit atque auxilium in
tempore petierit; quod quoniam factum non sit, suas nunc opes
terra marique amico se animo atque benevolo reipublicae polliceri;
petere, ut id quam primum Lauredano principi significet.

43   Vix eae litterae in senatu recitatae sunt, cum ab legatis Roma
item litterae perferuntur, in quibus erat scriptum: ubi ipsi ad urbem appropinquavissent, misisse Iulium, qui diceret velle se eos
Romam noctu ingredi sine ulla obviam itione civitatis, neque eis[2]
sacra ministrari, quoad se convenerint; ipsum autem Iulium statim
se Hostiam contulisse, ut illi interim in contemptu et squalore
diutius manerent; cum autem is ad urbem aliquot post dies rediis-
set, uno ex legatis Hieronymo Donato ad se vocato ostendisse placere sibi uti foederis quod Cameraci percussum sit capita omnia
impleantur: si Taurisum Forumque Iulii respublica Maximiliano
tradiderit; si iuri, quod in Ferrariae urbis dominatu quodque in
sinu Adriatico habeat, portorii, ab omnibus qui eo mari navigent

for the Republic, and all the citizens were agreed on that. Nor could they be deterred by fear of plunder or death from showing the fidelity they had pledged once and for all. To those who think it better and nobler to meet their death with honor than to live in shame, no violence can be done to valor, no fear can be struck into them. Upon the proveditors' then being informed that the enemy troops had massed at Cittadella, Gritti made his way with Leonardo Prato and the stradiots from Treviso to the vicinity of the town to attack them.

Meanwhile Andrea Foscolo, who looked after the Republic's 42 business in Constantinople, sent the senators a letter informing them that the Turkish sultan had made it clear to him that he was extremely upset at the news of the Venetian defeat. He had even complained to Foscolo that he had not shared information with him about the enemy's plans and preparations and sought his assistance in time. Since that had not been done, he now pledged his resources on land and sea to the Republic in a friendly and kindly spirit, and asked that he should pass this on to Doge Loredan as soon as possible.

Scarcely had this letter been read out in the Senate, when an- 43 other letter couched in the following terms arrived from the ambassadors at Rome: when they had got near Rome, Julius had sent word that he wanted them to enter by night without any citizens[14] going to meet them, and he did not want them to take part in the Mass until they met him. Julius himself had immediately gone to Ostia, so that in the interim they had remained for quite a while ignored and in discomfort. When Julius returned to Rome some days later, he summoned one of the ambassadors, Girolamo Donato, and told him he wanted all the clauses of the treaty struck at Cambrai fulfilled: if the Republic handed over Treviso and Udine to Maximilian; if she renounced the right which she exercised in the domain of Ferrara and in the Adriatic gulf to have customs duties paid at Venice by all who sail that sea;

Venetiis solvendi, renuntiarit; si sacerdotia non modo provincialia, sed etiam urbana pontificibus maximis remiserit, ipsa nullam eorum partem tributis exigendis interceperit; si se in ipsum deliquisse fassa fuerit, eiusque rei veniam subiectissime petierit; tum se interdictum remoturum; eorum si quid facere senatus recusarit, suas se copias Maximiliano traditurum, regemque Galliae idem facturum, uti rempublicam opprimat. Adiuvisse autem eam rem totam eiusdem regis Galliae magnopere legatos, qui ab Iulio diligentissime petierant ne ad se legatos Venetos admitteret, neve interdictum aboleret aut rempublicam sublevari pateretur; ita enim illum reliquis Italis principibus, et regum ceterorum omnium animis et cupiditatibus arbitratu suo moderaturum, si reipublicae non frenum modo, sed etiam vincula iniecisset.

44   His recitatis litteris, nullus ordo in senatu fuit, qui non Iulium omnibus probris et maledictis fuerit prosecutus; nemo, qui non se ipse magnopere damnaverit, quod legem de legatis ad illum mittendis suo suffragio comprobarit: ea lege sex civitatis principes reliquis civibus, qui captivi contra fas, contra pactiones, contra fidem datam Romae sint, adiectos in reipublicae ludibrium, Iulii iracundiae traditos; itaque omnes magistratus ira indignationeque ardere; reliquos fremere atque in illos invehi; neminem profecto scire iam, quid agi, quid temptari oporteat. Unus Laurentius Lauredanus, Leonardi principis filius, clara voce, "Cur non," inquit, "ad regem Thracium, qui nobis sese obtulit, legatos statim mittimus, auxilium contra istum, non pontificem maximum, sed carnificem omni crudelitate praeditum, imploratum?" Hac a plerisque sententia probata, nonnullis mitius et temperatius agendum statuentibus, neque fine consiliorum reperto, iussis patribus ea in re diligenter cogitare quid praestaret, senatus dimittitur.

if she resigned to the popes the benefices not only in her provinces but even in Venice itself, and appropriated no part of them for herself when taxes were being collected; if she admitted to having wronged him and humbly asked his forgiveness — if all this were done, then he would set aside the excommunication. If the Senate declined any of these conditions, he would give his troops to Maximilian, and the king of France would do the same, so that Maximilian could crush the Republic. Moreover (they wrote), the whole business was stoked up by the ambassadors of the king of France, who had insistently asked Julius not to give the Venetian ambassadors an audience, nor to lift the excommunication or allow the Republic any relief. In this way, they said, Julius would control at will the other princes of Italy and the intents and desires of the kings elsewhere, if he fastened on Venice not just a harness but chains as well.

When this letter was read out, every section of the Senate 44 heaped insults and curses on Julius' head. Each of them roundly condemned himself for voting for the measure to send him ambassadors, whereby six of the foremost Venetians had joined the other citizens imprisoned at Rome in contravention of the law, of understandings, of pledges given: surrendered to the wrath of Julius, they had brought the Republic into contempt. And so all the magistrates burned with anger and indignation, the rest grumbled and criticized them. No one indeed knew what they should do now, what course to try. One man alone, Lorenzo Loredan, son of Doge Leonardo, said in a loud voice, "Why not send ambassadors at once to the Turkish sultan, who has offered his services to us, to implore his aid against this man — no pope, but a butcher of infinite cruelty?" This view met with wide approval, but some reckoned that more cautious and less drastic action was called for. Their deliberations having reached no conclusion, the senators were told to give careful consideration to the best way forward, and the Senate was dismissed.

45   At in Carnis, oppido Sacilio ab hostibus, qui primo id impetu ceperant, civitate eos expellente recuperato, Ioannes Vitturius, civis egregia virtute, a patribus statim praesidio cum militibus et equitibus est illo missus. Ab Gritto etiam legato Franciscus Beraldius Patavinus, equitum reipublicae centum quinquaginta praefectus, qui ad hostes perfugerat, aliique item praefecti equitum tres, quorum erat unus Busichii Epirotae fratris filius, capti ad urbem in custodia perducuntur. Nam cum Epirotae prope trecenti, ab legato praemissi, hostibus, qui Cittadella exierant, appropinquavissent, fuga simulata in apertos ante villam Cornelianam campos et planitiem eos pertraxerunt. Tum repente conversis equis impetuque in illos facto, quinquaginta ex iis interfecerunt, sexaginta captivos fecerunt. Duces reliqui, Mercurius Bua, Ranerius Saxeta, Pandulfus Malatesta, fugere perseverantes se in tutum receperunt. His rebus agitatis, propterea quod ab amicis reipublicae patres cognoverant Maximilianum cupere ut senatus civem aliquem ad se mitteret, quicum agere de communibus utriusque rebus posset, Aloisium Mocenicum, unum ex quinqueviris senatu regendo, legerunt, qui ad illum proficisceretur. Litterae quoque ad eos qui creandi Romanorum imperatorem ius habent, tum ad liberas Germaniae civitates datae sunt; quibus litteris senatus petebat ne Maximilianum saevire contra rempublicam, quae in illum tam liberalis fuisset, ulterius permitterent.

46   Neque tamen propter haec intermittebant patres in eam cogitationem incumbere, ut Patavium, quod plane oppidum ante oculos esset civitatis, improviso magis et repentino incursu quam aperto bello recuperarent. Accendebat eorum animos illorum magnopere avaritia qui Patavium regebant, quod nulli Venetorum civium qui in eo agro fundos possessionesque habebant, qui quidem erant plurimi, fructus suos evehendi facultas ab iis permittebatur, sed ipsi eos inter se pro libidine distrahebant. Multae in oppido in-

In Friuli in the meantime, the town of Sacile was recovered 45
from the enemy, who had captured it at the first assault, the citizens driving them out. Giovanni Vettori, a citizen of remarkable
valor, was immediately sent there by the senators with infantry
and cavalry to defend it. The proveditor Gritti also captured
Francesco Beraldo of Padua, who commanded 150 of the Venetian
cavalry and who had fled to the enemy, and three more cavalry
captains likewise, one of them the nephew of Busicchio the Albanian, who were sent off to prison in Venice — nearly 300 stradiots
had been sent on ahead by the proveditor and when they got
near the enemy, who had come out of Cittadella, they pretended
to flee and drew them out onto the open fields and level ground
in front of the villa Corner. Then they suddenly turned their
horses around and charged them, killing fifty and taking sixty captive. The other enemy commanders, Mercurio Bua, Rinieri della
Sassetta, and Pandolfo Malatesta, continued their flight and retreated to safety. Following these events, the senators learned from
friends of the Republic that Maximilian wanted them to send
him a citizen to negotiate on matters of common interest, and so
they chose one of the five Sages for Mainland Affairs,[15] Alvise
Mocenigo, to go to him. Letters were also sent to the Electors of
the Holy Roman Empire and to the free German cities, asking
them to put a stop to Maximilian venting his rage on the Republic
which had been so generous toward him.

Not that all this stopped the senators dwelling on plans to re- 46
cover Padua, a town that lay spread out before their eyes, by some
sudden and unexpected sortie rather than open warfare. They
were much incensed at the greed of the regime in Padua, because
none of the Venetian citizens who had farms and properties in the
countryside there — and there were a great many of them — were
being allowed to take their produce away, but the Paduans split it
up among themselves as they pleased. Many tenement blocks and
houses in the town, which had been privately bought by Venetians

sulae domusque, quas iure et more maiorum privatim Veneti ab oppidanis emerant, aut ipsi aedificaverant, ab illis direptae possidebantur. Multa praedia villaeque alienissimis hominibus vulgo donabantur.

47 Itaque patres, antequam ad alia descenderent, Franciscum Capellum, quem quidem virum Leonardus Trissinus (de quo supra commemoravimus), quod in legatione Gallica aliquot ante annos in eius comitatu adolescens fuerat locumque apud illum paene filii obtinuerat, magno cultu prosequebatur, Patavium miserunt, ad speciem ut legatus ad Maximilianum proficisceretur, re ut Leonardum conveniret eique polliceretur, si Patavium reipublicae restituat, exilii se legem rescissuros; tum ei, liberis posterisque eius civitatem et ius comitiorum, et Cittadellam municipium, quod Pandulfus Malatesta proditione amiserat, cumque iis praefecturam ipsi equitum ducentorum rempublicam dono daturam. Capellus Patavium subvectus, dum oppidum ingreditur cognitus ab iis, qui portam custodiebant, ab oppidanisque retentus, alloqui Trissinum secreto non potuit. Cumque se apud eos legationis iure defenderet, suffragiis egerunt, num illum interficere, quod Patavium furtim venisset, an domum remittere deberent, quod legati munere fungeretur. Octo erant ex nobilitate cives, octo ex plebe, qui suffragium ferebant. Septem ex iis Capellum condemnaverunt, novem absolverunt. Ita in magno vitae periculo a fortuna versatus, tantuloque discrimine sententiarum ab eadem servatus, multis ab civibus pro eius dignitate ac nomine ad oppidi portam, qua venerat, flumenque perductus, conscendit, ad urbemque rediit.

48 Patres, eo consilio depulsi, ad aliam se cogitationem converterunt. Nam quod erant eo in oppido cives duo, centurionis reipublicae fratres, quibus ambobus cum portae oppidi praefecto

from townspeople in a lawful manner and in accordance with ancient custom, or had been built by themselves, had been plundered and taken over by them. Many estates and villas were being indiscriminately given to complete strangers.

Before attending to other matters, therefore, the senators sent 47 Francesco Capello to Padua. Capello was received with great honor by the Leonardo Trissino we mentioned above[16] because, as a young man some years previously, he had been on an embassy to the French in his company and had become almost like a son to him. He was sent on the pretext that he was going as ambassador to Maximilian, but in reality it was to meet Trissino and promise him that if he restored Padua to the Republic, the senators would rescind the decree that sent him into exile, and the Republic would give him, his children, and descendants the privileges of citizenship and noble status, and the town of Cittadella (which Pandolfo Malatesta had lost by reason of his treachery), and along with all that, the captaincy of 200 cavalry for himself. Capello was conveyed to Padua, but he was recognized at the gate by the guards as he entered the town and taken into custody by the inhabitants, so he was unable to speak to Trissino in private. When in his defense he claimed ambassadorial privilege, they took a vote to see whether they should put him to death for entering Padua by stealth or send him home in his quality of ambassador. The votes were cast by eight citizens of the nobility and eight from among the commoners. Seven of them convicted Capello, nine acquitted. So, with Fortune putting him at great risk of his life and also preserving him by that slightest of differences in the verdicts, in view of his rank and fame he was accompanied by a crowd of citizens to the town gate by which he had come in and so to the river, where he took ship and returned to Venice.

After the failure of this plan, the senators turned to another 48 scheme. There were two citizens in Padua who were brothers of an officer in the Republic's army, both of them on very friendly

summa necessitudo intercedebat, petiit ab iis per occultos inter-
nuntios centurio, darent operam, ut ea porta legato reipublicae
aperiretur. Re complures dies agitata, cum demum inter ipsos
convenisset, Aloisius Molinus, quinquevir senatu regendo, patribus proposuit tantas hostium iniurias ulterius non esse perferen-
das; sperare sese atque confidere, si Patavium exercitus de improviso mittatur, civibus iis portam tradentibus qui se reipublicae
obtulerunt, oppidum capi facile posse; neque enim satis esse communitum; itaque ad Grittum legatum scribi oportere, ut eam rem
quam primum suscipiat.

49   Ad ea Lauredanus princeps videri sibi periculosum respondit,
Aloisio rege Galliae reipublicae nervis ac sanguini magnopere im-
minente, Iulio pontifice maximo ad civitatis perniciem atque interitum omnia moliente, Maximiliano mediis in imperii finibus vis-
ceribusque crassante,[3] Ferdinando Hispaniae rege, quasi quarto
scriptis tabulis herede, in possessiones reipublicae se inferente, Patavium velle recipere; quam quidem paulo ante urbem una cum
aliis plerisque oppidis et municipiis, ut huius belli tempestatem a
suo capite averteret, senatus Maximiliano tamquam de manu tradidit; valde enim se timere, id si fit, ne hostes reipublicae, qui, ea
senatus liberalitate victi, nihil ultra prope cogitant, magnam redin-
tegrandi belli causam se habere statuentes, iterum in rempublicam
universi convertantur, neque Patavium modo brevi recipiant, sed
reliquam imperii partem quae in continente est etiam suam faciant; nam vires ad eos repellendos reipublicae suppeditaturas, neminem tam stultum esse, qui sperare audeat; neque esse credendum, qui pares illis integri non fuerint, fractos ac debilitatos
superiores fore.

terms with the commander of one of the city gates. The officer sent his brothers secret messages to ask them to do their best to have the gate opened to the Venetian proveditor. After many days considering the matter, they finally came to an agreement. Alvise Molin, one of the five Sages for Mainland Affairs, put it to the senators that such great wrongs on the part of the enemy were no longer to be tolerated. He hoped and believed that if an army was sent to Padua unexpectedly, the citizens who had offered their services to the Republic would hand over the gate, and the town, with its inadequate defenses, could easily be taken. They should accordingly write to the proveditor Gritti to see to the matter as soon as possible.

To this proposal Doge Loredan replied that he thought it dangerous to try to recover Padua when King Louis of France was posing such a threat to the very sinews and life-blood of the Republic, Pope Julius striving might and main to ruin and destroy the city, Maximilian running riot amid her empire's territory and heartlands, and King Ferdinand of Spain imposing himself on Venetian possessions as though a will had made him the fourth heir. Not long ago the Senate had handed over Padua to Maximilian as if on a silver platter, along with many other towns and communities, in order to protect itself from the storm of war. Loredan was very much afraid that if Padua were retaken, the Republic's enemies — at present pacified by the Senate's generosity and pretty much without further hostile plans — might decide that they had good reason to start up the war again, and would one and all turn on the Republic once more, and not only recapture Padua in short order but also make the remaining part of our *terraferma* empire their own. Surely no one was so foolish as to imagine that the Republic would have sufficient strength to drive them back, nor could they hope that their forces which were not equal to the enemy when they were whole would prevail in their present broken and enfeebled state.

49

50   Civium privatim iacturam, qui fructus suorum praediorum in agro Patavino amittant, tantam non esse, ut rempublicam periclitari malint, si amantes patriae sint; quod si alia mens eorum est, non esse in civium habendos loco qui rempublicam sua potiorem carioremque non habeant. Maiores ipsorum opes suas maritimis auxisse rebus, atque imperium longe lateque ea tantum ratione promovisse; si ad illum unum maris exercendi morem atque consuetudinem redeundum sit, bene cum ipsis fortunam agere omnes recte sentientes existimaturos, quod quae artes imperio constituendo profuerunt, eisdem etiam usquequaque vel crescat propageturque artibus imperium, vel optime tutissimeque retineatur. Cum ea ita se habeant, tamen Taurisum Forumque Iulii adhuc quidem in reipublicae dicione contineri; ea ne amittantur, magis providendum ipsis esse, quam ut aliquid acquiratur; id autem facile fieri moderatione, si iis contenti sint; neminem enim iam reipublicae magnopere invidere illam partem. Quod si Patavium receperint, verendum in primis esse — dicatne, an sileat? sed non silebit quae praevisa omnibus multumque cogitata debent esse — ne, cum fines in continente reliquos amiserint, urbs quoque ipsa, parens altrixque civitatis, de qua paulo ante ipsi non obscure timuerint, in hostium suorum potestatem, quod dii omen obruant, redigatur; saepe enim accidisse ut qui nimia pertinacia in iis quibus carerent appetendis rebus essent, etiam earum quas habebant, quibusque pacate frui poterant, amissione plecterentur, suaeque eos intemperantiae vehementer paeniteret.

51   Hac oratione ab Lauredano habita, plerique magistratus in eius facile sententiam abierunt. Pauci cum Molino, rei bene gerendae

The private deprivations of citizens who might lose the produce 50
of their estates in the Padovano, he said, were not so great as to
make them prefer that the Republic should be placed at risk, provided they were patriots. And as for those who took a different
view, men who did not reckon that the Republic was more important and precious than their own affairs were not to be accounted
citizens at all. Their ancestors had grown wealthy by maritime
trade, and the boundaries of their empire had been pushed forward far and wide by that means alone. If they had to go back to
that single style and manner of life, plying the seas, every sensible
person would think that Fortune looked on them with favor, as
the same habits that had stood them in good stead in forming the
empire would see to it that it would either increase and enlarge itself on all fronts or would remain as it was, perfectly safe and
sound. Be that as it may, Treviso and Friuli nevertheless still remained in the Republic's dominions, and they should take care not
to lose them rather than try to make acquisitions; and that was
easily done by exercising self-restraint, if they would just be content with those places, areas that nobody nowadays greatly be-
grudged the Republic. But if they recaptured Padua (should he say
it or remain silent? But he could not pass over in silence a prospect that everyone should contemplate and devote a good deal of
thought to), the main thing they had to fear would be that once
they had lost their remaining territory on the mainland, Venice
herself—the parent and nursemaid of the citizenry, for which they
themselves had been distinctly fearful not long before—would also
fall into the enemy's hands, God forbid. It had often come about
that people who were too tenacious in pursuit of things they had
been deprived of lost the very things they had, which they could
have enjoyed in peace, and came to bitterly regret their want of restraint.

After Loredan had delivered this speech, many magistrates 51
readily came round to his view. A few continued to side with

occasionem non esse amittendam, perseveraverunt. Nonnulli tam dubia in re, quid probarent et eligerent, prope ipsimet se nescire fatebantur. Itaque, magna inter eos altercatione orta, cum finis rei nullus reperiretur, Molinus ad senatum conversus eiusmodi orationem habuit: non tam se quidem ea re angi ac dolore confici, quod hoc tempore fortuna, quae plerumque res humanas administrat, plures potentioresque quam umquam antea hostes in rempublicam armaverit—fato enim id necessitateque accidisse, itaque moderate esse ferendum—quam propterea quod ipsa sibi respublica desit, quodque ex iis qui eam regunt nonnulli sint qui, dum immodico terrore opprimuntur, plus detrimenti civitati important, quam ii qui ei bellum intulerunt. Quid autem se potissimum commemorare ac conqueri? quattuorne Flaminiae oppida communita Iulii ducibus aperire portas iussa, interdicto non rescisso? civesne perplures eorum atque arcium praefectos proditos atque abductos in servitutem? sexne legatos, principes civitatis, ultro Romam missos in dedecus reipublicae? an vero Apuliae optimam fertilissimamque partem Ferdinando, antequam de ea verbum faceret, condonatam? an Vicetiam atque Patavium, praeclaras nobilissimasque urbes, Maximiliano non petenti, nihil armorum paranti, traditas et inculcatas? nam quod Taurisum retentum sit, id virtute factum atque constantia eius oppidi civium; qui, soli ferme et destituti, ob eorum tamen in rempublicam studium manere in fide atque officio voluerunt.

52   "Ego vero," inquit, " — o patres, qui tantopere formidatis, ad vos nunc tantum orationem me convertere operae pretium est—maris quidem artes atque studia deserenda nobis esse non existimo, sed omni studio diligentiaque percolenda, dum ne id imperium quod in continente maiores nostri suis laboribus, suo nobis sanguine pepererunt nostrorum animorum debilitate amittamus. Quod qui-

Molin's belief that such a fine opportunity was not to be lost. Amid this considerable uncertainty, some more or less admitted that they did not know what course to prefer or follow. And so while debate raged and no resolution was in sight, Molin turned to the Senate and delivered a speech along these lines:[17] for his part, he was not so much distressed and pained at Fortune's having on this occasion armed against the Republic enemies greater in number and in power than ever before—Fortune governs human affairs in general, and this had happened by fate and of necessity, and so must be borne with resignation—as at the Republic's letting itself down: there were some among its rulers who were in the grip of an unreasonable terror and brought more harm on the citizenry than those who made war on them. What should he remind them of first—and deplore? that four strong towns in Romagna had been told to open their gates to Julius' captains without the interdict being lifted? that a great many of their citizens and commanders of their fortresses had been betrayed and taken off into slavery? that six of their leading citizens had voluntarily been sent to Rome as ambassadors, to the Republic's shame? or that the best and most fertile part of Apulia had been given up to Ferdinand, before he said a word about it? or that Vicenza and Padua, those famous and noble cities, had been surrendered and trampled on when Maximilian was not even asking for them, nor taking any military measures at all? The fact that Treviso was still theirs was due to the courage and fidelity of its citizens. Almost alone and abandoned, they nevertheless preferred to remain loyal and obedient, thanks to their devotion to the Republic.

"Senators," he said, "—it is worth my addressing directly only those of you who are now in the grip of such panic—I by no means think that we should abandon our seafaring arts and interests. They must indeed be pursued with passion and drive, as long as we do not lose by our weak-mindedness the empire on the mainland that our ancestors won for us by toil and blood. And if

dem certe malum semel nostro vitio si contractum est, an nunc etiam a nobis, cum ex parte corrigi potest, neglegatur? Ac obloquendi occasio hac ratione omnibus hominibus facile praestetur, non tam fortunae vi atque impetu nos, quam nostra ipsorum imbecillitate victos esse? At etiam additis civium privatim damna tanti non esse, ut ea de causa respublica in periculum adducatur; quod si una cum privatis rebus salva esse potest publica, nonne ad id multo iustius accendamini, quam si rei quidem publicae saluti esse valeamus, privatae nequeamus? praesertim cum privatae nostrorum civium opes maxime ad rempublicam pertineant, quae suorum civium pecunia maxima ex parte bella regere et sustinere consuevit. Atque hoc eo libentius dico, quod nulla mihi praedia in Patavino agro sunt, ne quisquam meis me commodis ductum existimet ad legem ferendam, ut Patavium recipiatur. Res me publica impellit, quae mihi est mea vita carior; ad quam unam cum meorum civium commoda atque utilitates adiungantur, quid est quod aut me aut quemquam civem bonum atque industrium deterrere a suo suffragio probanda lege debeat?

53   "Superest pars illa plena formidinis: ut negotio capessendo desistamus, ne, si ea re hostes nostros irritaverimus, illi inter se ad reliqua nostrae dicionis adorienda iterum parati atque animati conveniant; quasi aut facillimum eis sit tantos exercitus comparare atque cogere; aut ex regia dignitate videatur esse Aloisium, qui suum in regnum se recipit, statim in Italiam recurrere, ut Maximiliano praesto sit; aut ignoremus Ferdinandum, nostris potitum oppidis, ne unum quidem nummum ulterius in bellum insumpturum; aut Maximilianus abundare thesauris consueverit ad copias contrahendas, qui duorum mensium spatio pauculas cohortes prope nudas, ad Veronam Vicetiam Patavium tuendum, vix aegreque miserit; aut Iulius, quo demissius atque abiectius cum illo

that misfortune has indeed arisen through our fault, should we now leave it as it is when we can to some extent rectify it? And is everyone to get from this an easy chance to abuse us for being brought low not so much by a violent onslaught of Fortune as by our own weakness? Ah, but you also add that the private losses of citizens are not so grave as to justify placing the Republic in danger. But if the commonwealth can be saved alongside private wealth,[18] should we not be all the keener to do so—and with greater justice—than if we were able to save the Republic alone but unable to save private possessions? Especially since the private wealth of our citizens is of the greatest importance to the Republic, which is used to waging and sustaining wars largely from the money of her citizens. I say this the more readily because I have no estates in the Padovano, in case anyone thinks I have been led to propose a bill to have Padua retaken from self-interest. What drives me on is the Republic, which is dearer to me than life itself. When the advantages and benefits of my fellow citizens are joined to those of the Republic alone, what is there in this bill that should stop me or any good and hard-working citizen from voting for it?

"There remains the argument that causes most fear, that we should avoid taking on the task in case we stir up our enemies against us by doing so, and they once more join forces, ready and eager to attack the rest of our dominions—as if they found it the easiest thing in the world to raise and recruit armies of such size; as if Louis, as he withdraws to France, would think it consonant with his royal dignity to scurry back immediately to Italy to support Maximilian; or as if we are unaware that Ferdinand will not spend a single penny more on the war once he is in possession of our towns; as if Maximilian is habitually rolling in money for raising troops, when in the space of two months he has scarcely managed to send miserable little companies, and those practically unarmed, to defend Verona, Vicenza, and Padua; or as if Julius

53

agimus, eo non maiores sumat in nos spiritus, duriorem seque atque implacabiliorem multo praebeat; quod si intelliget Patavium receptum, nobisque pristinam inesse virtutem ac vim sentiet, non despiciet tam arroganter eos quos obesse sibi posse aliquando verebitur.

54   "At etiam veremini haec ne urbs, parens nostra, in hostium nostrorum potestatem redigatur. Quid, vos quaeso, interest, urbsne ipsa in potestate sit hostium, an eius incolae ac cives, quique illam regimus, omnia quae hostes nostri velint atque optent statuamus? Optabile illis est Patavium non recipi, ut eo ipsi oppido una cum reliquis pacate frui possint; optabile etiam est ut Taurisum Iuliique Forum, tractumque hunc Venetiae qui nobis reliquus est ipsis, ut alia multa tam praeclara dedimus, etiam tradamus; vos eis morem gerere vultis. Hocne hanc urbem servire non est? hoc non est eam suorum hostium esse factam? non est libertatem reipublicae, quae una cum huius urbis parietibus semper crevit, quam maiores nostri nobis integram atque intactam reliquerunt, prorsus atque omnino perdidisse?

55   "Si maiores iidem nostri, ab ea caeli regione in qua beatissimi sempiternam vitam agunt, hic exsistant, atque ad vos conversi eiusmodi sermonem habeant: 'Nos urbem vobis dedimus cum liberam, tum eo situ et natura loci ut, nisi ipsi vobis desitis, nemo cogere vos possit; cur quae hostes vestri optant facere didicistis, homines maxime omnium qui hodie sub caelo degunt liberi? cur imperium pulcherrimum quod vobis constituimus tam formidolose regitis? cur Patavium, male ab hostibus custoditum, quod paene vestris sub oculis est, vosque appellat atque obtestatur, non recipitis?' quid illis, obsecro, respondeatis? Primum scilicet uni vos servisse tempori, quodque tempus postularit, id fecisse. Iam istud vobis omnes concedimus; tempori enim hostium perpulchre inser-

doesn't become ever more imperious toward us and show himself much harsher and more implacable the more meekly and submissively we deal with him. On the contrary, if he learns that Padua is retaken and hears that we have regained the courage and power we had of old, he will not look down so arrogantly on those he fears may one day stand in his way.[19]

"You are also afraid that this city, our parent, may fall into the hands of our enemies. But I ask you, what difference does it make whether the city herself is in the power of the enemy, or her inhabitants and citizens and we who govern her carry out everything our enemies wish and hope for? They do not want Padua to be recaptured, so they may have peaceable enjoyment of the town along with the rest. They also want us to hand over Treviso and Friuli and the stretch of the Veneto still left to us, just as we have given them so many other fine possessions — and you want to oblige them. Is this not to enslave the city? Is this not to make her an enemy possession? Is this not the complete and utter destruction of the Republic's liberty, which has always grown along with the buildings of this city, which our ancestors left to us whole and intact?

"Suppose those same ancestors of ours were to appear here from the tract of heaven where they lead lives of eternal bliss, and turned to you and said: 'We gave you a city that was not only free but so situated and placed by nature that unless you fail yourselves, no one can compel you with force. How have you learned to do what your enemies desire when you are the freest of all men living under heaven? Why do you rule so timidly this fine empire we made for you? Why do you not take back Padua, poorly defended by the enemy as it is and almost within eyesight, as she calls out to you and implores you?' How, I ask you, would you reply to them? First, no doubt, that you have been the slaves only to circumstance and have done what circumstance demanded. This we all readily grant you right away, for the enemy's circumstances

54

55

vitum est. De hac urbe autem timere vos ne amittatur dicere non audebitis; neque, opinor, tam timide in senatu locuti essetis, nedum etiam apud illos ipsos maiores vestros, optimos fortissimosque viros, qui sciunt urbem hanc capi non posse, eiusmodi proferre quicquam audeatis; reposcent enim statim vos repetentque a vobis parta gravibus verbis; quodque tam pusillo animo fueritis conquerentur, qui ne hoc imperii domicilium vestris ab hostibus tueri possetis pertimueritis.

56   "Sed de eo plura me dicere minime necesse esse arbitror; urbs enim pro se ipsa satis loquitur, quae, obsessa vadis undique, neque a iustis classibus, neque a terrestribus exercitibus adiri se permittit. Itaque ad vos omnes revertar, patres; tota enim haec vestra causa est. Nam propterea quod imperio retinendo timidiores nos, quam par erat, praestitimus, aequum est nunc in recuperando acres atque fortes esse, ut eam infamiam quam formidine contraximus animi robore atque praestantia deleamus. Aloisium regem copiis dimissis Galliam ulteriorem petere certiores facti sumus. Maximiliano quam prompta sint quae in bellum requiruntur, sane cognoscimus. Iulius in alios quam sit largus, quam munificus, satis superque exploratum nobis est. Quam hinc longe absit Ferdinandus, etiam videmus. Qui tamen ipsi si velint, si festinent bellum nobis facere, ut Patavium recuperent, aestas abierit; ita hiemis beneficio res in annum alterum differetur. Quid vultis amplius? quam occasionem aptiorem, opportuniorem a diis immortalibus postulatis? quod tempus ad hanc rem paratius atque accommodatius esse potest? Quamquam, quae simultates odiique semina in illorum regum animis iamdudum insita radices altas habent, quae fortunae ac rerum humanarum vices sunt, sperandum nobis est neque illos amplius conventuros, et nos brevi magnam reliquorum

have been served quite nicely.[20] You cannot bring yourselves to say that you were afraid of losing the city, nor, I think, would you have spoken so timidly in the Senate, much less would you dare to utter anything of the sort before those ancestors of yours, the best and bravest of men, who know that the city cannot be taken: they will at once ask and demand of you in strong language the return of the things you had from them, and they will complain that you were so feeble of spirit as to be terrified that you could not defend this seat of empire from your enemies.

"But I hardly think I need say more on this subject; the city   56
speaks well enough for herself, being surrounded by shallows on all sides and so permitting no approach of regular ships or land forces. And so I return to all of you, senators, for this is your concern. Since we have behaved in a more cowardly fashion than we should have done for holding on to our empire, it is only right that we should now be vigorous and brave in recovering it, so we may expunge the stain of infamy that our timidity has brought on us by our firmness and excellent spirit. We have been informed that King Louis has discharged his troops and is heading for France, and we know very well how easy Maximilian finds it to lay his hands on the requisites of war. We are perfectly well aware how generous and bountiful Julius is toward others. We also see how distant Ferdinand is from here. But even if they should want to, if they hurry to make war on us to get Padua back, the summer has gone by, and so thanks to winter the matter will be put off till next year. What more do you want? What better occasion or more advantageous circumstances can you ask of Almighty God? What time could be more opportune or better suited to dealing with this business? Although considering how deep-rooted are the animosity and seeds of hostility long since planted in those rulers' hearts, and the fortunes and vicissitudes of human affairs, we must expect that they will not join forces again and that we shall quickly and easily recover a large proportion of the other towns. Our enemies

oppidorum partem facile recuperaturos. Ita enim cum his civitatibus ac populis quos a nobis habuerunt hostes se nostri gerunt, nihil ut malint iam, quam illorum iugum suis a cervicibus excutere, nostramque in se benevolentiam indulgentiamque requirant.

57 "Est autem prudentiae vestrae, patres, haec, si deorum beneficia sunt, qui nobis ea quae foederatorum nostrorum scelere perfidiaque amisimus, reddere statuerint, sive temporis, quod illorum dominatum in satietatem atque invidiam subiectorum populorum verterit, plane non despicere; semel aut iterum homines, ad regendum imperium natos, maximis in rebus timide lapsos esse, humanum fortasse sit veniaque non indignum; usquequaque autem sine causa eosdem illos omnia vereri, neque dignum venia est nec excusatione; ad interitum enim tendit qui id agit. Satis obdormivimus reipublicae; satis longos dies in pavore inertiaque iacuimus; expergiscamur iam, timoremque hunc nostrum, nocturnum atque umbratilem, aliquando tandem exuamus. Copias, quantis opus est, habemus proximas atque paratissimas. Agrestes homines universi nobis favent, nos exspectant, morari conqueruntur. Oppidani etiam accersunt nos, rogantque ne sui obliviscamur, neve se barbaros perpeti dominos addiscere servitutis longinquitate cogamus. Patavium vero ipsum eiusmodi est, ut, si receptum semel sit, amitti amplius prope non possit, cum et custodire ipsi illud municipium, tamquam domum suam quilibet, ob propinquitatem facillime queamus; et ob reipublicae utilitates, quas ex eo percipere consuevit, et facti laudem atque gloriam maxime debeamus, et propter privata civium commoda fructuumque copiam, et villarum amoenitates, magis ut velimus adducamur honestissime.

58 "Unum, patres, moneo, ut ne tempus ullum rei gerendae interponatur, ne, si parumper distulerimus, hostes se interim muniant,

have behaved toward the towns and peoples they have taken from us in such a way that they now want nothing better than to shake off their yoke from their necks, and they are looking for goodwill and leniency from us.

"It is for you in your wisdom, senators, not to disdain these opportunities, whether they be the gift of God, who has decided to restore to us what we lost through the criminality and perfidy of our allies, or of the times, which have turned their tyranny into disgust and resentment among the subject peoples. It may be human and forgivable for men born to rule an empire to have once or twice made mistakes in matters of great moment out of timidity, but for those same men to have a constant baseless fear of everything deserves neither forgiveness nor excuse. Those who behave in this way are doomed to destruction. We have been asleep for the Republic long enough, and we have lain prostrate in fear and inertia for a sufficient length of days; let us now awaken and at last cast off this fear of ours, a thing of night and shadow. We have all the troops we need nearby and in high state of readiness. All the countrymen are on our side, awaiting us and complaining of the delay. The townspeople too invite us in, and they ask us not to forget them, not to force them to learn to endure barbarous masters by long years of servitude. Then again, Padua itself is the sort of place that once it is retaken, can scarcely be lost again, since protecting the town is something that we can very easily do owing to its proximity, just as someone would protect his own home. And it is something we really ought to do, both on account of the benefits the Republic has traditionally derived from Padua and for the renown and glory of the action. The private advantage of citizens, the abundance of produce, and the delights of the villas all draw us on to desire this end, to our great credit.

"I give you a warning, senators, that you should let no time pass before taking action, in case, if we delay just a little, the enemy reinforce themselves in the meantime and all our efforts are

57

58

atque ab iis conatus nostri omnes retundantur. Nihil est in bello celeritate conducibilius, nihil omnino victoriarum efficientius. Ea et qui utuntur alacriores facit, quod in hostes imparatos impetum se facturos vident; et hostes ipsos imbelles reddit, propterea quod saepe imprudentes nec opinantes offenduntur, ut arma capiendi seque defendendi tempus facultatemque non habeant. Postremum est ut deos omnes orem, teque in primis, Marce, urbis huius parens et conservator, cuius templum inauratum atque augustum ante curiam maiores nostri antiquitus aedificaverunt omnique pietate semper coluerunt, quodque nunc persancte ipsi adimus atque incolimus cottidie, ut, si ipsi hanc mihi mentem dederunt, ut legem ad vos ferrem Patavium recipi e republica esse — neque enim aliunde recta hominibus consilia, quam a dis immortalibus veniunt — et vos eam, patres conscripti, vestris suffragiis hoc vesperi sanciatis, et ipsi mihi et vobis ac civitati et reipublicae totum negotium faustum felix fortunatum velint esse."

59   Hac oratione habita, cum nonnulli magistratus ad Molini se sententiam adiunxissent, lex est perlata, ut ad Patavium recipiendum Grittus legatus e vestigio contenderet; datumque omnibus iusiurandum, ne quid eius quis enuntiaret. De ea re perlatis statim ad Grittum senatus litteris, ille, cum equitibus mille, militibus item mille Tauriso profectus, medio itinere ad Novale municipium se continuit. Eodemque die decemviri cumbas suas cum armatis hominibus ad omnia itinera diligenter custodienda miserunt, ne quis Patavium eius rei nuntius ab urbe mitti posset.

60   Postero die autem, qui fuit dies decimus sextus Kalendarum Sextilis, noctu reliquo itinere confecto, legatus ante lucem prope oppidum substitit. Interim carri aliquot frumento imposito, quos legatus ad id praeparaverat, cum bubulcis ante portam se contulerunt atque, ut sibi aperiretur, paulisper exspectaverunt. Apertis

blunted by them. There is nothing of more advantage in warfare than speed, nothing at all that brings more victories. It lifts the spirits of those who employ it because they see that the enemy will be unready when they attack; and it renders the enemy themselves cowardly because they are taken unawares and unexpectedly, so that they have neither the time nor the ability to take up arms and defend themselves. My last task is to pray to God and all the saints,[21] and above all to you, Mark, the father and defender of this city, whose gilded and august basilica our ancestors built of old before the Ducal Palace and have always held in reverence with every mark of devotion, and which we ourselves now devoutly attend and abide in every day: if God and the saints themselves have put it into my mind to propose a motion to you that the Republic's interests are best served by retaking Padua — for right counsel comes to men from God alone and nowhere else — and if you, Conscript Fathers,[22] enact it by your vote this evening, may it please them to have the whole enterprise turn out favorably, felicitously, and fortunately, for me and you, for the citizenry, and for the Republic."

On delivery of this speech, some of the magistrates went over 59 to Molin's view and the law was passed instructing the proveditor Gritti to proceed with all haste to retake Padua. Everyone took an oath to say nothing about it in public. The Senate's letter on the matter was at once taken to Gritti, and he left Treviso with a thousand cavalry and another thousand footsoldiers, halting in midcourse at the town of Novale. On the same day the Ten sent their boats with armed men to keep careful watch on all the roads, so that news of the venture could not reach Padua from Venice.

On the following day, 17 July, making the rest of the march by 60 night, the proveditor stopped before dawn near the town. Meanwhile some oxcarts loaded with grain, prepared by the proveditor for the purpose, arrived outside the gate and waited a short while for it to be opened for them. The gates stand at the first branch of

portis quae ad priorem Medoaci fluminis alveum sunt, quo tum alveo naves permeabant, ac demisso ponte, et carris in transmissu commorantibus, legati pedites levissimi adveniunt portamque capiunt. Pauloque post legatus cum reliquo agmine in oppidum irrumpit; profectusque ad interiorem oppidi portam, qua murus item alter, postremo longe altior atque solidior, una cum altero Medoaci alveo tamquam circino circumductus, urbem reliquam tuebatur, ea refracta ad forum omnes magno cum clamore ac tubarum sono recta contendunt. Quibus obviam progressa gens Parmensis (id erat fratrum illorum ac centurionis familiae nomen, quae se ad hoc ea nocte comparaverat), armata cum legato laeta atque hilaris se coniunxit.

61   Eo tumultu excitus, Brunorus Saregius Veronensis, clara gente natus, qui stipendia Maximiliani faciebat eoque biduo Patavium venerat, cum turma equitum ducentorum Venetos, qui forum iam omnesque vias atque aditus obsederant, repellere aggressus, amissis perplurimis ex suis, ab iis capitur. Germani quoque milites, ad praetorium qui erant, cum praefectis regiis eodem accurrerunt. Sed commisso proelio repulsi, se in arcem oppidi fugientes intulerunt. Oppidani magna pars se legato, qui eorum praetor summa cum laude paulo antea fuerat, gratulantes dediderunt. Ita parvo temporis spatio Patavium recipitur, eo ipso die quo primo captum fuerat anni ab urbe condita nongentesimi octogesimi secundi, cum binos et quadragenos dies in Maximiliani partibus fuisset.

62   Miserant ea nocte decemviri magnam armatorum hominum manum, cum ex plebe urbana et navalibus, quorum omnes prope operas eduxerunt, una cum eorum praefecto Nicolao Pascalico, qui eas regeret, tum ex suburbanis municipiis, Torcellio Maiorbio Buriano Muriano, evocatam suis cum naviculis, ut, Medoaco flu-

the river Brenta, down which ships used to pass at that time.
When they were opened and the bridge lowered, the carts delayed
their crossing while the proveditor's fastest infantry arrived and
seized the gate. Soon after that, the proveditor broke into the
town with the rest of his troops and went to the inner gate of the
town, where a second wall defends the rest of the city: it is much
higher and stronger than the outer wall and follows the course of
another branch of the Brenta as if drawn by a pair of compasses.
Breaking open that gate, they all made straight for the town square
with a great cry and blaring of trumpets. The da Parma clan came
out under arms to meet them (this was the family name of the
brothers and the Venetian officer, who had prepared themselves
for this action overnight),[23] and with high and happy spirits joined
up with the proveditor.

Roused by the uproar, Brunoro da Sarego of Verona, a man of   61
high birth who was in the service of Maximilian and had come to
Padua two days before, tried to drive back the Venetians with a
company of 200 cavalry. The Venetians had now blockaded the
town square and all the streets and approaches, and after Brunoro
lost a great many of his men, he was taken prisoner by them. German soldiers stationed at the town hall also dashed there with the
king's captains. But once battle was joined, they were driven back
and fled to take refuge in the citadel. The townspeople for the
most part were glad to surrender to the proveditor, who had been
their much admired governor not long before. And so in a short
span of time Padua was retaken, on the very day when it had been
first taken in the 982nd year from the foundation of Venice;[24] it
had been on Maximilian's side for 42 days.

That night the Ten sent a great band of armed men drawn both   62
from the people of the city and the Arsenale, nearly all of whose
workers they had taken there, with their officer Niccolò
Pasqualigo in charge of them, and from the outlying communities,
Torcello, Mazzorbo, Burano, Murano. These men were told to

mine superato, Patavium legato auxilium ferentes mane accederent. Ii celeritate adhibita, turri etiam quae in Strata pago flumini
adiacet expugnata (is abest pagus a Patavio milia passuum
quinque), a qua remulco subvehi, Germanis militibus qui in ea
erant lapides et tela conicientibus, non permittebantur, progressi,
in oppidumque recepti una cum legati militibus, Iudaeorum faene-
ratorum domos, valde quidem plenas, quarum erat magnus numerus, universas spoliaverunt; a quibus digressi nonnullas etiam eorum civium qui reipublicae adversissimi fuerant, vitae
inquilinorum parcentes, diripuerunt. Verum edicto legati propo-
sito, ut praedandi finis fieret, et luminibus singulis in domibus e
fenestris tota nocte ardere iussis, ne tenebrae licentiam peccandi
adderent, stationibusque in foro atque ad portas dispositis, ipso
etiam legato cum militibus oppidum perambulante, non tamen
quorundam Venetorum civium, qui spe praedae privati Patavium
venerant, audacia comprimi potuit, quin cum armatis direptiones
exercerent, atque in legati milites, a quibus prohibebantur, impetum facerent. Ea de re ab legato ad decemviros datis litteris, quod
statuere ipse in cives Venetos non auderet, Hieronymum Quirinum, magistrum suum, Marinum Maurocenum, triumvirum ex
advocatis reipublicae, decemviri Patavium celeriter miserunt. Hi,
retentis nonnullis atque in vincula coniectis, tumultum sedave-
runt.

63   Proximo vero die, tormentis ad arcem oppidi positis, et magna
circumfusa armatorum multitudine, demum parte propugnaculi
deiecta, dum de deditione hostes agunt, milites, superatis per ruinas muris, arcem capiunt; in qua captivi facti Leonardus Trissinus
praefectus, vulnere in capite accepto, et Manfredus Facinus, vir
egregia virtute, qui complura stipendia multisque in exercitibus

bring their boats so that they could sail up the Brenta and reach Padua in the morning with reinforcements for the proveditor. Making all speed, they actually took a tower beside the river at the village of Stra (five miles from Padua), which was preventing their being towed along the river, the German infantry in it throwing stones and missiles at them. They advanced to the town and were taken into it along with the proveditor's infantry. They looted all of the Jewish moneylenders' well-stocked homes, of which there was a great number, and moved on to plunder a number of homes of those citizens who had been most opposed to the Republic, though sparing the lives of the inhabitants. The proveditor issued an edict to put an end to the looting, and ordered that torches should be lit in the windows of each house all night long so that the darkness should not give assistance to the criminal activity. Guards were stationed in the square and at the gates, and the proveditor himself even patrolled the town with his infantry. But all the same certain reckless Venetian citizens, who had come on their own account to Padua in hopes of booty, could not be restrained from carrying on looting with armed men and attacking the proveditor's infantry when they tried to prevent them. The proveditor sent a letter about the matter to the Ten, not daring to take it upon himself to adjudicate against Venetian citizens, and they quickly sent to Padua their Head, Girolamo Quirini, and Marino Morosini, one of the state attorneys. These two arrested some of the looters and threw them into prison, and so put an end to the disorder.

On the following day, with artillery in position by the town fortress and huge numbers of soldiers surrounding it, part of the fortification was at last knocked down and the enemy were negotiating surrender when the infantry crossed over the walls through the rubble and took the fortress. There they captured the commander Leonardo Trissino, who suffered a headwound, and Manfredo Faccino, a man of great courage who had done the Republic ster-

63

reipublicae magna cum laude meruerat; et Germani viri fortes et
claro loco nati sex, civesque Patavini tres; iique omnes patrum
iussu sunt ad urbem missi, Facino excepto; quem Grittus legatus
cum magnopere diligeret, liberaliter appellatum castigatumque,
quod cum tot annos reipublicae militiam fecisset, tam duro eius
tempore in hostium numero esse voluisset, nullo accepto incommodo, statim dimiserat.

ling service in numerous campaigns and in many armies, as well as six Germans, brave men of high birth, and three citizens of Padua. All of them were sent to Venice by order of the senators, with the exception of Faccino. As he held him in great affection, the proveditor Gritti summoned Faccino and gently upbraided him for being prepared to side with the enemy in such a crisis for the Republic, though he had been in Venetian service for so many years and had suffered no harm at her hands; he then immediately let him go.

Note on the Text and Translation

The Latin text of Bembo's *Historia Veneta* was first published in 1551, four years after his death, in both Venice and Paris; the Italian version appeared in 1552. There were subsequent Latin editions in 1722 (Leiden) and, in editions of his *Opera*, in 1556 (Basel), 1567 (Basel), and 1611 (Strasbourg). Both versions are included in parallel columns in the edition of his *Opera* of 1729 (Venice). Both versions were subjected to censorship by the Council of Ten and the *Riformatori* in Padua before the initial publication, causing excisions, rewriting, and additions in a few places. The manuscript of the Latin version has remained lost, but Bembo's original of the Italian version was finally published at Venice in 1790, enabling a comparison with the censored version and the archival record of the deliberations of the Ten about the passages that were altered (see the studies by Teza and Lagomaggiore cited in the Bibliography). These changes are indicated in the Notes to the Translation. It should be noted that Bembo's vernacular was altered in the original printing, mostly in passages that were being changed for their content, but in some other passages as well, so that his particular stylistic preferences for the *volgare* are not always observed. I have consulted both versions in preparing my own English version.

The text presented in this volume is not a critical edition, but a working edition to serve as a basis for the translation. It is based upon the edition of Venice, 1551, incorporating the Errata (which stop in Book IX), with additional minor corrections from the edition of Venice, 1729. The latter are indicated in the *Notes to the Text*. The first edition is not divided into paragraphs (except by capitalizing the first word of some sentences); the divisions of the later edition have mostly been retained, and others added. Capitalization and punctuation have been modernized, as has been Bembo's orthography, with the exception of proper names. In the case of the latter Bembo's spelling is given in the Latin text but the modern English or Italian form of the name in the translation.

ABBREVIATIONS

A   Petri Bembi cardinalis historiae Venetae libri XII. Venice: Manutius, 1551.

B   Della historia vinitiana di M. Pietro Bembo cardinale volgarmente scritta libri XII. Venice: Gualtero Scotto, 1552.

C   Opere del Cardinale Pietro Bembo, ora per la prima volta tutte in un corpo unite. Venice: Francesco Hertzhauser, 1729.

D   Bembo, Pietro, Della istoria viniziana di M. Pietro Bembo, cardinale, da lui volgarizzata, libri dodici, ora par la prima volta secondo l'originale pubblicati. Ed. Jacopo Morelli. Venice: A. Zatta, 1790.

Notes to the Text

BOOK V

1. sacerdotium *AC*

2. Prodonum *A, corrected in C*

3. *thus AC: one should perhaps read* cum

4. *thus AC: I should prefer* ad se

5. Euripi *AC*

6. lactu A, *corrected in C*

7. totidem *A,* totidem, an itidem? *A (Errata),* itidem *C*

8. quadrin | tas *A, corrected in C*

9. et *omitted in AC* (ed in Ancona *BD*)

10. sacerdotium *AC*

BOOK VI

1. in *omitted in AC*

2. Tapobraneque A, *corrected in C*

3. illi A, *corrected in C*

4. Trivisianus A, *corrected in C*

5. sacerdotium *AC*

6. *thus AC, scil.* de Iulio

7. *thus AC, scil.* senatui

8. a venti di di Novembre *B*

9. dicionis *C, perhaps rightly*

BOOK VII

1. Tanguardinus *C*

2. fuisset *A, corrected in* C

3. eum *A*

4. interiectis *A, corrected in* C

5. *thus AC: one should perhaps read* laturi sumus *so as not to interrupt the direct statement*

6. *Words seem to have dropped out in AC, here supplemented to conform to B:* che quelli non fanno, che impetuosamente nascono

7. ab *A, corrected in* C

8. *thus AC for* Flanaticum. Fanaticus sinus *was the reading of the early editions of Pliny (NH 3.129) on this stretch of water*

9. *thus AC: one should perhaps read* pridie

10. postridie *AC: see note to the English text*

11. Condolmerio *A, see 48 below*

12. *C does not end the paragraph here, but after the next sentence, which ends with* debilitari, *as in* A

13. militibus *AC*

BOOK VIII

1. Priol *A, corrected in* C

2. ei *AC*

3. *Humanist spelling of* grassante, *as corrected in* C

Notes to the Translation

BOOK V

1. A gold 'coin' (*nummus*) in the Latin, specified as a florin in *BD*.

2. *Rettori* in *BD*.

3. Andrea in *D*.

4. Now the Greek prefecture of Aitolia and Akarnania; *Romania* in *B*, omitted in *D*.

5. See 4.52 above.

6. Lit., a public ceremony of prayer; in *B*, "processions for our Lord God" (*supplicazioni* in *D*).

7. *D* adds "due to lack of courage, and cowardice"; excised by the censors, as in *B*. From this point on to 13 below, a number of changes were made by the censors; see Teza, pp. 81–83.

8. In *D*, "he did not dare to."

9. In *D*, "since they had realised that Grimani was afraid."

10. In *D*, "Antonio and the proveditors sent our soldiers, or rather their captains, not so much as a boat or dinghy, ultimately no help at all. And so they were killed. . ."

11. *D* adds "the other of the two islands across from Methoni."

12. In *D*, "borne along by no good fortune, they spent two painful days getting back there, to such an extent were they scattered hither and yon by the iniquity of their superiors, a panic lacking any orderliness, and a stupid disregard of instructions."

13. This sentence does not appear in *D*.

14. Castel Tornese (modern Chlemoutsi), on the westernmost promontory of the Peloponnese facing Zante (Zakynthos); see Frederic C. Lane, "Naval actions and fleet organization, 1499–1502," in J. R. Hale, ed., *Re-*

naissance Venice (London, 1974), p. 153: "new skirmishes followed on August 20th and 22nd opposite Castel Tornese."

15. In D, "moved by shame, the Venetians finally roused themselves."

16. The words "by some ill chance" are not in D.

17. In BD, "the timbers of the poops."

18. In D, "After this the French, when they had freely criticized the worthlessness of our men as having derived everything from Fortune, and nothing from their own spirit and courage, . . ."

19. In D, "it was this Antonio who was lashed by the curses of the magistrates and the Senate and the citizenry, and of the people at large: nor was there a single person among this great number who did not think he was worthy and deserving of every penalty and every punishment. . ."

20. D continues, "and he had thrown away the glory and splendor of a fine victory that was already very nearly won, due to his poverty of spirit and to the very great damage of the Republic."

21. In place of this last sentence, D gives a fuller account of the content of their vituperation: "Now he himself had handed the enemy a not inconsiderable part of the empire. He had not destroyed their fleet, which was surrounded and could not escape, nor had he provided any assistance to the men of of Lepanto. While all of this was being complained of and condemned by universal reproof and remonstrance, the death and loss of Andrea Loredan and Albano d'Armer, and of 800 men with them, moved the entire city to grief, along with unbounded hatred for him. To none of them had Grimani sent any assistance when he saw their ships on fire. If he had sent them some galleys, they would easily have been able to tow the two ships away from the Turkish vessel. And even if he had not been able to do that, certainly the captains and some others could have been saved. Grimani had given more to the enemy than they would have dared to dream of. For which of them could ever have dared hope that he would not come to the aid of his men, when he could easily have done so?" See Teza, pp. 82–83.

22. *Avogadori di Comun*: see above, 2.6, n. 2.

23. See 9 above.

24. The *Zonta*.

25. In *D*, "with the friends and relations . . . toiling to obtain either that he should be absolved. . ."; see Teza, pp. 83–84.

26. Literally, "his case was pled in chains", which *BD* interpret as "his case was discussed in the Great Council, he himself, however, being kept in the prisons".

27. Now Cres and Lošinj off the Croatian coast.

28. Actually only in 2.24; see also 3.37.

29. 25 November 1499.

30. The principality of Imola and Forlì had passed to Girolamo Riario, nephew of Sixtus IV (died 1488), as the dowry of his bride Caterina Sforza, having previously been under Sforza control.

31. I.e. the one that had remained at Milan while the other went off with Cesare Borgia (19 above).

32. *D* adds this: "that it was a very bad practice to put old men in command of fleets, for they are bereft of blood and passion owing to their length of years, and so unwilling to try anything. A man in his prime abounds in vigor and strength of spirit and good counsel; citizens consumed by age should be reserved for the home or the grave. The previous summer, when Grimani could easily have increased and extended the Republic with eternal glory and a vast advance of its borders, he had delivered to the city and the fatherland a disgrace it would never live down, together with great losses, through his cowardice and want of spirit. Now Trevisan too was making war with much the same negligence. There was no vigor in him, either for venturing on anything instantly when opportunity and the occasion offered, or in giving counsel. When you are waging war, most actions depend on speed, and if generals do not use it, no good can come of it"; excised by the censors, as in *B*, see Teza, p. 84.

33. For the apparent coinage *prooppidum*, *BD* have *borgo*, "suburb".

34. *BD* have 10 August.

35. I.e., the Bosporus.

36. See above, 2.11.

37. I.e., the *savi agli ordini*, the Sages for Maritime Affairs.

38. See above, 34, though they are not named there.

39. The Roman *iugerum* was actually an area of 240 x 120 Roman feet, about two-thirds of an acre. The Italian merely says "for every field", *per ogni campo*.

40. The Bojana forms the border at the coast of modern Albania and Montenegro.

41. Bembo's mother was a Morosini (Elena).

42. Alessio (Lezhë) is on the Drino in Albania, but not an island.

43. *BD* specify the Castel Sant'Angelo as the place he was kept. See also 3.19, 61 for Astorre Manfredi.

44. The date is given as 8 May in the margin of C.

45. Bembo's original word "shame" was softened by the censors to "setback"; see Teza, p. 78.

46. In *BD* the number is given as 150.

47. Ulcinj in the far south of Montenegro, then in Venetian hands.

BOOK VI

1. Lit., the ocean of Mauretania and Gaetulia, Roman provinces of north Africa.

2. Bembo's source is Oviedo, by his own admission in a letter to him from Venice, 20 April 1538 (no. 1928 in *Lettere*, ed. E. Travi, vol. 4 (Bologna, 1993), pp. 6–7): ". . .I have again read your *History of the Indies*, in which I have not only discovered the marvel of the unheard-of things of the regions there described; but in addition to this, your considerable learning and wisdom in measuring the sky and land and its sites. All of which, collected and published by you, will make that history, in my opinion, perhaps the most pleasing that has ever come into the hands and the reading of man . . . My homeland and this Republic having for some years now given me the task of writing in Latin the history of its affairs, I have briefly inserted a summary of those discoveries of yours of

the New World and of its Indies, the one and the other becoming thus necessary to be known." This appears to contradict the statement of Eric Cochrane that Bembo is independent of books for this information; see his *Historians and Historiography* (Chicago, 1981), p. 323: "Obviously, Italian historians were not wholly dependent upon what was published in one or another of their own states. Pietro Bembo, for instance, did not have to consult any books at all in order to fill up the some twenty [? actually seven] pages of Book VI of his history of Venice dedicated to the flora, fauna, and geography of the New World: he obtained the information he needed either orally from Navagero, then Venetian ambassador to Spain, or from his correspondence with Oviedo. . .".

3. See 4.3 above.

4. By the famous bull "Inter caetera" of 4 May 1493.

5. That is, *Crux* or the Southern Cross, only seen in the tropics and southern hemisphere.

6. Cubagua is an island off the north coast of Venezuela; Cumana is not an island, but a mainland town near Cubagua; but Terarequi (Tararequi in D) or San Miguel is the principal island of the Pearl Islands in the Gulf of Panama; there is, however, a Lago de Tacarigua on the coast near Cubagua and Cumana.

7. No doubt Bembo has in mind the Incas of Peru and Aztecs of Mexico, conquered by Pizarro and Cortés.

8. Probably Sofala (Beira) in modern Mozambique; Zefala in D, Tefalà in C.

9. Mogambice in BD.

10. The sultan of Kilwa (on the southern coast of modern Tanzania).

11. Diu is actually near, not at the mouth of the Indus, and closer to the mouth of the Narmada river.

12. See 1 above. The narrative now resumes.

13. Georges d'Amboise.

14. See 5.61 above.

15. I.e., the Hall of the Great Council and the Ducal Palace.

16. 13 March in BD.

17. Francesco Gonzaga was in fact the fourth *marquis* (usually termed *princeps* by Bembo in the Latin), his son Federico becoming first duke in 1530.

18. Anne de Foix, daughter of Gaston II de Foix, Comte de Candale, married Ladislas II, King of Hungary and Bohemia, as his third wife on 6 October 1502.

19. See 5.56 above.

20. I.e., Monte Titano in San Marino; *D* has "two peaks like two horns," *B* corrects this to "three peaks like three horns" and three citadels.

21. See 2.28 above.

22. Giulio Cesare da Varano.

23. Gonzalo Fernández de Córdoba; see 5.39–44.

24. The host of the Borgias was Card. Adriano Castellesi. Bembo gives the impression that Cesare too died in this episode but (as we see below) he was active for many months afterwards, eventually dying in Spain in 1507.

25. I.e., the five *savi di terraferma*, the Sages for Mainland Affairs.

26. Francesco Todeschini Piccolomini, died 18 October 1503.

27. Giuliano della Rovere, elected 31 October.

28. *D* continues at this point: "There were in the Senate a number of men whose view was that it would be best for the Republic to seize the whole of Romagna. When he found this out, Leonini wrote malicious letters to Julius on the subject, as if he wanted to inform him not so much about the debate in the Senate, but the arguments of each and every senator, and almost their very thoughts." Excised by the censors, as in *B*; see Teza, pp. 84–85.

29. The Dalmatian Jakov Banicevic, a long-time diplomat in the service of Maximilian and later Charles V; see *Contemporaries of Erasmus*, s.v. Bannisio.

BOOK VII

1. *B* adds "a Venetian nobleman," not in *D*; the daughter's name was Ginevra, see below, 10.59. Sforza's marriage to Lucrezia Borgia had been annulled in 1497.

2. "Philippe le Beau" reigned as King Philip I of Castile, 1504–1506, in virtue of his marriage to Ferdinand and Isabella's daughter Juana ("the Mad"). Ferdinand continued as King of Aragon.

3. The Fondaco de' Tedeschi.

4. I.e., Cesenatico.

5. Lit., eagles suitable for hunting; one of the objects of Lipsius' scorn (see vol. I, pp. xix–xx above, and 4.54).

6. Modern Lezhë, actually a mainland town.

7. Kansawh al-Ghawri, the Mamluk Sultan of Egypt 1501–16.

8. I.e. the dragoman Taghri Berdi, probably of Spanish birth.

9. He means the embassy of eight citizens giving Julius the city's obedience mentioned in 7 above.

10. Lit., "conscript fathers," another phrase criticized by Lipsius (see above, vol. I, p. xviii) but in fact rarely used by Bembo.

11. *proördines;* in *B, soldati delle ordinanze,* "soldiers of the ranks" (i.e. 'regulars', not mercenaries) but in *D,* "Ciernite" (select?); another term criticized by Lipsius (see above, vol. I, p. xx), used only here and in 89 below.

12. See 10 above.

13. In *BD,* "of brocade lined with sables."

14. Perhaps Chiusaforte in Friuli, but that is not five miles from Pieve di Cadore; Chiusa (Klausen) is even further away.

15. See 1.11 above.

16. I.e., he had the title of *savio* or 'Sage' in the government.

17. Negatively interpreted in *BD:* "the carrying off by her of our provisions."

18. The Reichstag.

19. In *BD*, "the castle of Belgrade," presumably Biograd on the coast SE of Zara.

20. *galea bastarda* or *bastardella* (Frederic C. Lane, *Venetian Ships and Shipbuilders in the Renaissance*, [Baltimore, 1934]).

21. Trviz in modern Croatia: in *AC* Trevisa; in *BD*, Prevesa.

22. Kvarner, Lošinj, Cres, and Krk in Croatia.

23. The Latin text of *A* reads "the day after," as does *D*, corrected in *B* to "the day preceding."

24. Charles of Egmont, who had rebelled against Maximilian.

25. Modern Xydas in the Prefecture of Heraklion; *BD* have "ne' Litti."

26. *D* reads as follows: "since, in the election of magistrates in the Great Council, those who were rich gave to those who elected and nominated them money, or worked gold and silver, so that in the future they and others would be even more inclined to elect and nominate them; and for this reason, those to whom this lot fell, that they were to put forward the name of some citizen, put forward not the best, as the laws ordain, but the richest and most powerful, so as to have from him a bigger gift"; revised by the censors, as in *B*, see Teza, p. 85.

27. Beginning with this sentence, *D* has a quite different text: "… For Contarini, having spoken to the Heads of the Ten, left to go to Cremona as governor. These things having been learned from Paolo, and announced to the Senate, because they were such that there were contained in them what King Louis intended to do to destroy the Republic, and what part of the empire he promised to give to Maximilian to be his ally, and in addition what Maximilian's intention was toward King Louis, and what he wanted the Republic to do; the Senate wrote about this to King Louis, and made him understand all these things in order." The censors replaced this with the present text (through 48), as in *B*; see Teza, p. 86.

28. Joan Albió, Aragonese diplomat.

29. Lit., to the Aulerci, ancient tribes in northern Gaul; in *BD*, Rouen.

30. See 16 above.

31. See 42 above.

32. The characterization of Pisani has been softened by the censors from Bembo's original, as indicated by D, "of an unpleasant nature and quite arrogant." See Teza, p. 86.

33. Here D adds: "And perhaps to him, given the ferocity and implacability of his nature, it would have been a vexation to see any Venetian citizen placed in such a position; nothing of this. . ."; see previous note.

34. In BC, the sentence thus far is treated as a complete sentence, and in the latter edition it is included in the previous paragraph. In D it begins a new paragraph as here and is joined to the following.

35. According to Marin Sanudo, Diarii, VIII.6, the master carpenter was Francesco Rosso, foreman of the Arsenale.

36. See 30 above.

37. in vestibulo curiae; in BD, "into the Palace" (the usual meaning of curia in this work).

38. curiam; in BD, "sala dell'audienza."

39. Antonello Napoletano is unidentified; perhaps Altobello da Napoli (d. 1510).

40. In BD, 300 infantry.

41. Presumably the Pien Collegio, Doge's Council, and the Council of Ten; in BD, "the secret colleges."

42. Tamás Bakócz, archbishop of Esztergom, cardinal of S. Martino ai Monti, titular Latin patriarch of Constantinople since 1507.

43. In D, literally translated as "supplications"; in B, "processions."

44. In BD, 600.

45. ad illum; not "to him," as it is preceded by ab eo. But D reads "summoned by him, had come to him," where B has "summoned by him, came there."

46. I.e. they were locally raised troops, not professional mercenaries. See note 11 above.

BOOK VIII

1. *prodominus*; another coinage criticized by Lipsius (see above, vol. I, p. xx); in *BD* *vicedomino*, "vicelord."

2. Lipsius criticizes this as imitating an Italian idiom contrary to Latin usage.

3. In *BD*, "located across from the part of the Palace where the hall of the Great Council is."

4. Lit., strangled by a rope at a tree.

5. *D* does not contain the following passage, down to (24) "were putting it about:. . ."; it reads instead: "against those who ruled the city they privately made great objection and complaint: this was no way to govern the Republic; so many noble cities should not be rashly given to the enemy. . ."; revised and added to by the censors, as in *B*; see Teza, p. 87.

6. The phrase is rather stronger in *D*: "what Doge Loredan and the other magistrates have brought about by their cowardice and fear is that they are constrained now to fear more and expect an even worse outcome than in the past." See previous note.

7. Modern Cres, Kotoro, Zadar, and Hvar.

8. One of Antonio's sons.

9. I.e., the *savi grandi* or Great Sages, the highest ranking members of the Collegio, the steering committee of the Senate.

10. Both names are omitted in *BD*.

11. He means of course Cremona, not Venice.

12. Jacques de Chabannes; the town is now Lapalisse.

13. *ad illum*: to Maximilian; the pronoun references are unclear in *BD* as well.

14. In *BD*, "the nobility and members of the papal court."

15. Lit., the Five for steering the Senate; in Venetian parlance, *savi di terraferma*.

16. See 21–22 above.

17. Molin's speech has been recast from Bembo's original by the censors, softening the language, omitting whole sentences, and making the speech to be addressed to the senators throughout instead of being partly addressed to the doge; the revision of the Italian extends as well to ordinary matters of language. See Teza, pp. 89–90.

18. *(res) publica*, playing upon the etymology of the term *Respublica* for Venice.

19. Here the censors omitted the following from Bembo's original (as in D): "and now he mocks and makes fun of us for this, knowing that nothing at all remains of strength in the Republic, nothing of the spirit and vigor of our ancestors in any citizen; he hears of nothing dealt with and managed with dignity, nothing honorable and magnanimous; he sees nothing take place that accords with the majesty of this Republic, of these buildings, of this empire, so well instituted, so durable, so free." See n. 17 above.

20. Here again the censors omitted the following: "Then you will tell me that it was not you alone that lost the empire, but many magistrates and many of the senators, who resolved to give it voluntarily to the enemy, some of whom were preparing to take it, while some only wished to. This is all very well and rightly said, if you had only forbidden it to be done, so far as you could. But you will not dare to give Venice these excuses you have given us; and you are ashamed, I reckon, to have spoken in the Senate in such a timid and servile fashion."

21. Lit., all the gods; Lipsius criticized not only Bembo's usual pseudo-classical plural, but his rare extension of the term to the saints; see vol. 1, p. xx.

22. *patres conscripti*, the classical term, rarely used here; see above, n. 13 to Book 1, n. 10 to Book 7, and 6.22.

23. See 48 above.

24. Equating to 1403, though in fact Padua surrendered to Venice on 22 November 1405.

Bibliography

EDITIONS

Historiae Venetae libri XII. Venice: Sons of Aldus Manutius, 1551.

Rerum Venetarum historiae libri XII. Paris: Michael Vascosanus, 1551.

Quaecunque usquam prodierunt opera, in unum corpus collecta et ad postremam autoris recognitionem diligentissime elaborata, vol. 1. Basel: M. Isingrin, 1556.

Quaecunque usquam prodierunt opera, in unum corpus collecta, et nunc demum ab C. Augustino Curione, cum optimis exemplaribus collata, et diligentissime castigata, vol. 1. Basel: Thomas Guarinus, 1567.

Omnia quaecunque usquam prodierunt opera: in unum corpus collecta cum optimis exemplaribus collata, et diligentissime castigata, vol. 1. Strasbourg: Lazarus Zetzner, 1609–52.

Historiae venetae libri XII. Editio novissima, cum optimis exemplaribus collata, accuratissime castigata, atque indice copiosissimo adaucta. Leiden: P. Vander Aa, 1722. In J. G. Graevius, *Thesaurus antiquitatum et historiarum Italiae*, vol. 5, pt. 1.

Opere del Cardinale Pietro Bembo, ora per la prima volta tutte in un corpo unite, vol. 1. Venice: Francesco Hertzhauser, 1729.

ITALIAN TRANSLATIONS

Della historia vinitiana di M. Pietro Bembo cardinale volgarmente scritta libri XII. Venice: Gualtero Scotto, 1552.

Della historia vinitiana di Pietro Bembo cardinale volgarmente scritta libri XII; Aggiuntavi di nuovo la tavola delle cose piu notabili, coi nomi di tutti i principi, patriarchi, cardinali vinitiani fino al serenissimo Luigi Mocenigo, per M. Alemanio Fino. Venice: Giordano Ziletti, 1570. The text is a reissue of the previous edition.

Istorie veneziane latinamente scritte da Pietro cardinale Bembo. In vol. 2 of *Degli istorici delle cose veneziane, i quali hanno scritto per pubblico decreto.* [Edited by Apostolo Zeno.] 10 vols. Venice: Lovisa, 1718–22.

The edition of Venice, 1729, as in the previous section.

Pietro Bembo, *Istoria Veneziana*. Venice: A. Savioli, 1747.

Della istoria viniziana di M. Pietro Bembo, cardinale, da lui volgarizzata, libri dodici, ora par la prima volta secondo l'originale pubblicati, ed. Jacopo Morelli. Venice: A. Zatta, 1790.

Pietro Bembo, *Opere*, vols. 3–4. Milan: Società tipografica dei classici italiani, 1809. (Edizione dei classici italiani, 57–58.)

MODERN STUDIES

Cochrane, Eric. *Historians and Historiography in the Italian Renaissance*. Chicago, 1981.

Cozzi, Gaetano. "Cultura politica e religione nella 'pubblica storiografia' veneziana del '500." *Bolletino dell'Istituto di storia della società e dello Stato Veneziano* 5–6 (1963–64): 215–96.

Dionisotti, Carlo. "Bembo, Pietro." *Dizionario biografico degli italiani* 8 (1966): 133–151.

———. *Scritti sul Bembo*, ed. Claudio Vela. Turin, 2002.

Elwert, W. Theodore, "Pietro Bembo e la vita letteraria del suo tempo." In *La civiltà veneziana del '500*, pp. 127–176. Florence, 1958.

Gilbert, Felix. "Biondo, Sabellico, and the Beginnings of Venetian Official Historiography." In *Florilegium Historiale: Essays presented to Wallace K. Ferguson*, pp. 275–93. Toronto, 1971.

Lagomaggiore, Carlo. *L'Istoria Viniziana di M. Pietro Bembo*. Estratto dal *Nuovo archivio veneto* 7–9 (1904–1907). Venice, 1905.

Monfasani, John. "The Ciceronian Controversy." *Cambridge History of Literary Criticism*, vol. 3 (1999): 355–401, esp. 397–99.

Pertusi, Agostino, ed. *La storiografia veneziana fino al secolo XVI: Aspetti e problemi*. Florence, 1970.

Santoro, Mario. *Pietro Bembo*. Naples, 1937.

Teza, E. "Correzioni alla Istoria veneziana di Pietro Bembo proposte dal Consiglio dei Dieci nel 1548." *Annali delle università toscane* 18 (1888): 75–93.

Index

Publication of this volume has been made possible by

The Myron and Sheila Gilmore Publication Fund at I Tatti
The Robert Lehman Endowment Fund
The Jean-François Malle Scholarly Programs and Publications Fund
The Andrew W. Mellon Scholarly Publications Fund
The Craig and Barbara Smyth Fund
for Scholarly Programs and Publications
The Lila Wallace–Reader's Digest Endowment Fund
The Malcolm Wiener Fund for Scholarly Programs and Publications